"It's hard to imagine a more comprehensive approach to innovation than that provided by this book, and the lessons and examples are up-to-the-minute fresh. If you are interested in learning about – and then practicing – innovation in business, you have come to the right place."

Thomas H. Davenport, Distinguished Professor of IT and Management, Babson College, Visiting Professor, Oxford University Saïd Business School, Senior Advisor, Deloitte Analytics and AI Practice, Digital Fellow, MIT Initiative on the Digital Economy

"This book is a great introduction to innovation that is unique in its approach with numerous case studies and examples representing leading global corporations. It integrates some of the important topics such as design thinking, lean start-up, and sustainability which I think are very relevant to the topic of Innovation. Student activities at the end of each chapter leveraging attached cases will reinforce learning of the concepts, tools, and frameworks discussed. Well researched and timely publication written by an experienced author, and I am sure students and practitioners will find it very useful."

Pierre Azoulay, Professor, Technological Innovation, Entrepreneurship, and Strategic Management, MIT Sloan School of Management, USA

"This Innovation textbook by Vijay Pandiarajan approaches innovation in a systematic way by explaining concepts and frameworks thoroughly with real-world examples and case studies. I particularly enjoyed its ability to address innovation trends in many industry verticals and discuss lean and design thinking, and sustainability imperatives. This book will certainly benefit undergraduate and graduate students as well as innovation practitioners from the industry."

Feng Zhu, Professor of Business Administration, Technology and Operations, Harvard Business School, USA

"It's exciting to see Vijay launch his book [Business Innovation: A Case Study Approach] for both students and innovation practitioners. The storytelling approach to formally introduce Innovation with frameworks to address the key idea of 'how to advance innovation' is powerful. This can be a one-stop source for those who want to get formally introduced to and practice innovation processes."

Martin J. Curran, Executive Vice President, Corning Innovation Officer, USA

Business Innovation

This book takes a holistic approach to enterprise and innovation opportunities and challenges by addressing the key questions surrounding innovation – what, why, where, and how. It provides an understanding of innovation models and why they are important in the business context, and considers sources of innovation and ways to apply business frameworks using real-world examples of innovation-led businesses.

After providing a solid background to the key concepts related to innovation models, the book looks at why innovation takes place and where the sources of innovation lie, from corporate research to crowdsourced and government-funded initiatives. Innovation models across manufacturing, services, and government are explored, and the impact of design thinking and lean enterprise principles on innovation and sustainability-driven imperatives is measured. Real-life, global case studies are integrated throughout to demonstrate how the concepts can be applied to practice, supported by a new five-dimensional holistic framework for innovation. The questions at the end of each chapter and the concluding remarks reinforce learning and aid critical thinking.

Offering a truly comprehensive and global approach, Business Innovation should be core or recommended reading for advanced undergraduate, postgraduate, MBA and Executive Education students studying Innovation Management, Strategic Management and Entrepreneurship. Supporting materials include PowerPoint slides, test bank questions, and worksheets to practice frameworks.

Vijay Pandiarajan is a faculty member of the Technology & Operations department at the Ross School of Business, The University of Michigan, Ann Arbor, USA. He focuses on teaching and researching Innovation and Technology. Before joining the Ross School faculty, he held leadership positions at various global companies, including at Accenture, Verizon, and Whirlpool Corporation. His educational highlights include a Sloan Fellows MBA degree from the Massachusetts Institute of Technology (MIT) Sloan School of Management, Cambridge, USA, with a focus on Technology and Innovation; a PhD in Industrial Engineering from the West Virginia University, Morgantown, USA; a Master's degree in Aircraft Production Technology from the Indian Institute of Technology, Madras, India; and a bachelor's degree with Honors in Mechanical Engineering from the University of Madras, India. He built Jaguar fighter planes at Hindustan Aeronautics Ltd, collaborating with British Aerospace, Safran (previously Turbomeca), and Rolls-Royce before pursuing his doctoral studies.

Business Innovation
A Case Study Approach

Vijay Pandiarajan

LONDON AND NEW YORK

First published 2022
by Routledge
2 Park Square, Milton Park, Abingdon, Oxon OX14 4RN

and by Routledge
605 Third Avenue, New York, NY 10158

Routledge is an imprint of the Taylor & Francis Group, an informa business

© 2022 Vijay Pandiarajan

The right of Vijay Pandiarajan to be identified as author of this work
has been asserted in accordance with sections 77 and 78 of the Copyright,
Designs and Patents Act 1988.

All rights reserved. No part of this book may be reprinted or reproduced or utilised
in any form or by any electronic, mechanical, or other means, now known or
hereafter invented, including photocopying and recording, or in any information
storage or retrieval system, without permission in writing from the publishers.

Trademark notice: Product or corporate names may be trademarks or registered trademarks,
and are used only for identification and explanation without intent to infringe.

British Library Cataloguing-in-Publication Data
A catalogue record for this book is available from the British Library

Library of Congress Cataloging-in-Publication Data
A catalog record has been requested for this book

ISBN: 978-1-032-04167-4 (hbk)
ISBN: 978-1-032-04187-2 (pbk)
ISBN: 978-1-003-19083-7 (ebk)

DOI: 10.4324/9781003190837

Typeset in Sabon
by Newgen Publishing UK

Dedicated to my beloved parents who sacrificed everything in their lives for our growth.

Mr. A.R. Pandiarajan, BA
&
Mrs. P. Nagarathinam

Contents

List of figures	xv
List of table	xvi
List of exhibits	xvii
Preface	xix
Acknowledgments	xxi

PART I
"What" – Introduction to innovation   1

1 Innovation – General background   3
    1.1 Introduction 3
    1.2 Invention vs innovation 4
    1.3 Historical perspectives of innovation 4
    1.4 Is innovation limited to products? 5
    1.5 Innovation in service 6
    1.6 Concluding remarks 7
    1.7 References 7

2 Models of innovation   9
    2.1 Introduction 9
    2.2 Cosmetic/survival innovation 9
    2.3 Leap forward innovation 10
    2.4 Disruptive innovation 11
        2.4.1 Low-end disruptive innovation 11
        2.4.2 Nascent market disruptive innovation 13
    2.5 Seismic innovation 15
    2.6 Innovation – What has changed now? 16
    2.7 Concluding remarks 17
    2.8 References 18

3 Challenges embracing innovation   19
    3.1 Introduction 19
    3.2 Triangular dilemma 20
    3.3 Market innovation challenges 21

x *Contents*

       3.3.1 Sticky customers 21
       3.3.2 Predictable M&A 21
       3.3.3 Stable supply chain 22
   3.4 *Organizational innovation challenges* 23
       3.4.1 Lack of coordinated innovation strategy 23
       3.4.2 Lack of diversity 24
       3.4.3 Compartmentalization 25
       3.4.4 Risk-averse non-experimental culture 26
       3.4.5 Misaligned incentive 27
       3.4.6 Micromanagement 27
       3.4.7 Span of control 28
       3.4.8 Lack of sense of urgency 28
   3.5 *Stakeholder innovation challenges* 31
       3.5.1 Investor community 31
       3.5.2 Government 32
       3.5.3 Local ecosystem 33
       3.5.4 Employees 34
   3.6 *Concluding remarks* 34
   3.7 *References* 35

PART II
"Why" – Innovation imperatives   37

4 Innovation: A key to business success   39
   4.1 *Introduction* 39
   4.2 *New economic paradigm* 39
   4.3 *Consumers are changing* 40
   4.4 *Competitive landscape changes* 40
   4.5 *Shorter product life spans* 41
   4.6 *Globalization vs localization* 42
   4.7 *Digital tsunami* 42
   4.8 *Technology shaping the business core* 43
   4.9 *Dynamic capabilities* 43
   4.10 *Concluding remarks* 44
   4.11 *References* 45

PART III
"Where" – Sources of innovation   47

5 Sources of innovation   49
   5.1 *Introduction* 49
   5.2 *Corporate research and development* 49
   5.3 *Organizational processes and ecosystems – Integrated value chain* 51
   5.4 *Corporate values and culture* 52
   5.5 *Partnership and open innovation* 53
   5.6 *Strategic resources and talent architecture* 55
   5.7 *Operating model (governance, KPI, structure, accountability, etc.)* 55
   5.8 *Concluding remarks* 56
   5.9 *References* 57

Contents   xi

PART IV
"How" – Approach to advance innovation   59

6 Framework-based innovation approach   61
  6.1 Introduction 61
  6.2 Innovation in action 61
  6.3 Factors impacting innovation 63
    6.3.1 Exogeneous factors 63
    6.3.2 Endogenous factors 63
  6.4 TRIAL© holistic framework for innovation 64
    6.4.1 TRIAL© – Framework innovation dimensions 66
    6.4.2 VASTEFA© leadership framework 76
  6.5 Concluding remarks 82
  6.6 References 83

PART V
Innovations in industry verticals   85

7 Innovations in manufacturing   87
  7.1 Introduction 87
  7.2 Pharmaceuticals 89
  7.3 Heavy equipment 93
  7.4 Automotive 95
  7.5 Semiconductor 98
  7.6 Concluding remarks 100
  7.7 References 101

8 Innovations in the service industry   103
  8.1 Introduction 103
  8.2 Service trend 103
  8.3 Healthcare 104
  8.4 Retail 106
  8.5 Hospitality 107
  8.6 Education 110
  8.7 Wellness 112
  8.8 Banking 113
  8.9 Transportation 115
  8.10 Concluding remarks 118
  8.11 References 119

9 Innovation in government   121
  9.1 Introduction 121
  9.2 Modalities of public service – Mass vs personalized 121
    9.2.1 Personalized on-demand service 121
    9.2.2 Navigation assistance for the disabled 122
    9.2.3 Blockchain-enabled voting 123
    9.2.4 Automated toll collection 124

xii *Contents*

9.3 *Citizen-government redefined boundaries* 126
9.4 *Digital thread and real-time alerts* 127
9.5 *Smart cities* 127
9.6 *Concluding remarks* 128
9.7 *References* 128

PART VI
Economics of innovation 131

10 Measuring innovation 133
10.1 *Introduction* 133
10.2 *Traditional KPIs* 135
10.3 *Innovation risk vs reward – A balanced approach* 137
10.4 *How to value innovation – Organic vs M&A scenarios* 138
10.5 *Concluding remarks* 141
10.6 *References* 142

PART VII
Special topics on innovation 143

11 Design thinking 145
11.1 *Introduction* 145
11.2 *Design thinking for innovation – Why now?* 146
11.3 *Design thinking approach* 147
    11.3.1 Empathize with/listen to customers 147
    11.3.2 Define/understand customer problem 148
    11.3.3 Generate ideas/solutions 149
    11.3.4 Prototype solutions fast 149
    11.3.5 Validate and test solutions 150
11.4 *Success stories – Where design thinking advanced innovation* 151
    11.4.1 Airbnb 151
    11.4.2 Ericsson 153
    11.4.3 Burberry 155
    11.4.4 Bank of America – Keep the Change Program 156
11.5 *Concluding remarks* 157
11.6 *References* 157

12 Lean enterprise and innovation 159
12.1 *Introduction* 159
12.2 *Lean and innovation – Are they mutually exclusive?* 160
12.3 *How lean accelerates innovation* 161
12.4 *Success Stories – Where lean thinking advanced innovation* 165
    12.4.1 Pixar Animation Studios 165
    12.4.2 Dropbox 167
    12.4.3 Zappos 168
    12.4.4 General Electric (GE) 168
12.5 *Concluding remarks* 170
12.6 *References* 171

Contents xiii

13 Sustainability-focused innovation 173

13.1 *Introduction* 173
13.2 *Evolving market orientation toward sustainability – Gen Z* 176
13.3 *Sustainability – A new secular growth driver* 177
13.4 *Success stories – Sustainability-focused innovation* 178
    13.4.1 The Procter & Gamble Company (P&G) 178
    13.4.2 Patagonia 178
    13.4.3 Braskem (Brazil) 179
    13.4.4 Colorifix (UK) 182
13.5 *Concluding remarks* 183
13.6 *References* 184

PART VIII
Case studies 187

Case 1: Amgen – Biosimilar Innovations – by Kavya Sivan 189

Case 2: FedEx – Innovation Through Sustained Adaptability – by Alaina Gregory 195

Case 3: Reliance Jio – From 4G to Digital Innovation – by Hursh Motwani 204

Case 4: Stryker Case Study – Design Thinking Response to COVID-19 – by Kyle Geiger 214

Case 5: The Whirlpool Corporation in 2020: Whirlpool – A History of Sustained Innovation from Within – by Malik Abbasi 225

Case 6: Apple's Swift – A Programming Language Innovation for the Future – by Maxwell Cornellier 232

Case 7: Microsoft – The Age of Nadella – by Serena Wang and Minnie Sun 240

Case 8: The Procter & Gamble Company – A Unique Innovation Approach – by Minnie Sun and Serena Wang 247

Case 9: Timberland – Sustainable Innovation – by Drew Arnson 253

Case 10: Zara-Inditex – Fast Fashion Done Right – by Rocco Pelà 260

xiv *Contents*

Case 11: Patagonia – Leader of a Sustainable Business –
by Suzanna Yik   267

Case 12: Amazon – Head in the Cloud: Transformation
Through Leadership's Lens – by William McCrone   275

Case 13: Ericsson's Innovation Through M&A –
by Derek Kuo   282

Case 14: Samsung's New Age Innovation Using Organization
and Culture – by Derek Kuo   288

Case 15: Sun Pharmaceutical Industries – Innovation Through
Specialty Acquisition Strategy, Technology, Leadership, and
Culture – by Katie Kuhlman   294

Case 16: Ecovative Design – Organizing for Innovation in
Sustainable Biomaterials – by Daniel Meeks   305

Glossary   319
Index   321

Figures

2.1	Models of innovation	10
2.2	Disruptive innovation evolution	12
2.3	Major vehicle manufacturers' market share in the US	13
3.1	Triangular dilemma	20
3.2	Google annual revenue	22
3.3	AWS annual revenue	25
3.4	Innovation efficiency	28
3.5	Innovation trajectory – Corporation 1	29
3.6	Innovation trajectory – Corporation 2	30
3.7	Innovation trajectories – Corporation 1 vs Corporation 2	30
4.1	Worldwide cloud market share	44
5.1	Enterprise Innovation Opportunities Model©	50
6.1	Exogeneous factors	63
6.2	Endogenous factors	64
6.3	TRIAL© framework	65
6.4	TRIAL© framework innovation dimensions	67
6.5	Innovation funnel – Internal vs open innovation	69
6.6	Team inquisitive and imaginative culture vs innovation effectiveness	71
6.7	VASTEFA© leadership framework for innovation	76
6.8	VASTEFA© leadership spider chart	76
6.9	Collective genius framework for innovation teams	80
7.1	Manufacturing – Percentage of GDP	88
8.1	Service – Percentage of GDP	104
8.2	Annual passengers – All flights to and from the US	116
9.1	A toll gantry installed on Illinois Highway, USA	125
10.1	Consumer surplus in demand and supply curve	135
10.2	Net Promoter score	136
10.3	Decision tree for uncertain innovation scenario	140
11.1	Design thinking approach	148
11.2	Design thinking considerations	150
11.3	Interactions between the Enterprise Innovation Opportunities Model© and design thinking	152
11.4	Design thinking approach at Ericsson	154
12.1	Six Sigma distribution	160
12.2	Lean startup framework	162
12.3	Design thinking interactions on lean startup	165

Table

13.1   United Nations sustainable development – 17 goals   180

Exhibits

1.1	Annual growth trend	190
2.1	FedEx financial performance	200
2.2	The pyramid of organizational innovation	201
3.1	Comparative analysis of India's top five telecommunications service providers	205
3.2	Leadership style of Mr. Mukesh Ambani as depicted by his inspirational quotes	207
3.3	Reliance Jio's SWOT analysis	209
4.1	Design thinking: Stryker's Emergency Relief Bed	218
4.2	Stryker's statement of earnings	220
4.3	Stryker's net sales by product Line	221
5.1	Whirlpool net sales	226
5.2	Whirlpool R&D spending	228
5.3	Whirlpool's international market sales growth	229
7.1	Microsoft's 2016–2020 financial performance	244
11.1	1% for the Planet Initiative	268
11.2	Supply chain transparency in innovation adoption categories	271
11.3	Patagonia's electricity usage around the world	271
12.1	AWS culture	277
12.2	Amazon's annual net income	279
12.3	VASTEFA© leadership framework application	280
14.1	Samsung's business units structure	289
15.1	Specialty products added to Sun Pharma portfolio after 2015	301
15.2	Financial impact of specialty Innovations – 2010, 2015, and 2020	301
15.3	Specialty innovations-related financials trend – 2010, 2015, and 2020	302
15.4	2017 Global market share of pharmaceutical companies	302
16.1	Ecovative cofounders Gavin McIntyre (CCO) and Eben Bayer (CEO)	306
16.2	The Mushroom® protective packaging production process, from prototype tooling development to growth and drying to prepare for shipment	308
16.3	Finished Mushroom® protective packaging parts being prepared for drying after growth	309
16.4	Comparison of pure mycelium panel production at lab scale (left) and at pilot production scale (right)	309

xviii *List of exhibits*

16.5 Sliced pure mycelium panels before post processing into MyBacon™ product (left) and MyBacon™ strips after cooking (right) 312
16.6 Design thinking at work to solve key product development questions 314
16.7 Application of the TRIAL© framework to business operations and organization at Ecovative Design 315
16.8 Applying the Enterprise Innovation Opportunities Model© to Ecovative as an innovation-driven organization 316

Preface

When I was formally exposed to the topic of business innovation at the Massachusetts Institute of Technology (MIT) during my time as a Sloan Fellow, it was truly an eye-opener for me to understand innovation the right way. Although I was consulting for over 20 years involved in major innovation-driven business transformation and advising some of the world-renowned global corporations, MIT experience helped me to critically reflect on what the industry is faced with in terms of opportunities and challenges. I found it ironic that the industry considers innovation as the panacea for all their problems and expect a magical cure right away without a comprehensive foundation. Unfortunately, innovation is a process and takes a disciplined organizational approach to realize and sustain success. Innovation must be approached very thoughtfully and holistically with careful planning and orchestration of enterprise activities, and resource commitment, with an experiment-based innovation culture and enduring leadership. Innovation requires a business-context-specific recipe comprised of many ingredients for the final product to be successful.

Students and practitioners of innovation find a plethora of books and reference materials in the marketplace, but unfortunately many books do not integrate many concepts. For example, topics such as design thinking and lean startup are not well integrated into innovation discussion or offered as a standalone topic, which does not help the learners to connect the dots in the innovation space. This book addresses such gaps and approaches innovation from a holistic perspective and reinforces the learning through 16 corporate cases presented in Part VIII. We take the "What," "Why,", "Where," and "How," story-telling approach and present a practical TRIAL© innovation and VASTEFA© leadership frameworks, which are at the heart of the innovation journey. These frameworks were piloted in our semester-long innovation class at the Ross School of Business at the MBA level and found to have enormous success.

We take the discussion further by examining innovations in key industry verticals, and economic considerations. We address design thinking, lean startup, and sustainability topics as an integral part of innovation and show how they generate value at leading corporations.

This book is ideal for either a full or a half semester innovation class both at the graduate and undergraduate business or engineering students, as well as practitioners. The attached 16 cases and focused examples are special aspects of this book and represent current innovation efforts at premier corporations. The cases are presented with the goal of providing real-world relevance of the innovation concepts and frameworks explained. The readers will immensely benefit from this book, particularly when they practice action-based learning in groups by analyzing and answering key questions presented at the end of each chapter as well as in the cases themselves. The additional test bank of questions and practice worksheets to apply the innovation frameworks and Design Thinking approach are provided online part of Digital Learning Resources which make this book a comprehensive resource to master innovation management.

Acknowledgments

I would like to thank my professors Dr. Pierre Azoulay at Sloan School of Management, MIT, Dr. Erik Brynjolfsson at Stanford (previously at Sloan School of Management, MIT) and Dr. Sinan Aral, at Sloan School of Management, MIT, who taught innovation, digital and data science during my Sloan Fellows program at MIT and inspired me to write this book. They have been my constant source of energy to add to the scholarship on the topics that I enjoy learning about.

I want to thank my PhD advisor Dr. Bhaskaran Gopalakrishnan at the West Virginia University, who believed in me and provided me the opportunity to pursue my doctoral studies. The experience I gained under his mentorship is invaluable and unforgettable, and I am always thankful to him.

I also thank professors and my colleagues, Dr. Roman Kapuscinski, Dr. Damian Beil, and Dr. M.S. Krishnan at the Ross School of Business, The University of Michigan, who gave me an opportunity to teach and write this book to educate students not only at the Ross School of Business, but also around the world. I am also thankful to my colleague Dr. Ravi Anupindi at the Ross School of Business for his constant motivation to go the extra mile in whatever I do.

Finally, I thank my loving wife and partner Punitha Vijayakumar and beautiful daughters, Nithya and Priya, who encouraged and supported me to pursue the time-consuming book project and constantly checked on my progress to meet the tight deadline. I am very grateful to them for their countless sacrifice when I was away, head down, and focused on this project.

Part I

"What" – Introduction to innovation

Chapter 1	Innovation – General background	3
Chapter 2	Models of innovation	9
Chapter 3	Challenges embracing innovation	19

1 Innovation – General background

1.1 Introduction

The term *innovation* has been around for nearly a century; however, it is widely recognized to be derived from its predecessor term *invention*. Invention is still a popular term and is used in many contexts but is quite different from innovation.

Merriam-Webster defines innovation as "1: A new idea, method, or device: NOVELTY 2: The introduction of something new."

Oxford Learner's Dictionary defines innovation as "1. innovation (in something) the introduction of new things, ideas, or ways of doing something. 2. innovation (in something) a new idea, way of doing something, etc. that has been introduced or discovered."

Although there is some minor difference in the way the term innovation is defined, there is a general agreement in terms of the newness. For practical purposes, we define innovation as "application or use of newness or invention in a practical or business context to impact the society while generating significant value." Often, innovation utilizes or leverages multiple inventions or innovations [1–4] that exist in different functional or technical domains that are either bundled or combined or integrated to make an impact on the scope and scale of the value realized. The value could be either personal or business and can be either quantified (tangible) or felt (in tangible), or both. At the end of the day, innovation is all about generating value either as a product, service, or process, for which there is a customer who is willing to pay. If there is no perceived value and no one is ready to pay for it, it is hard to justify it as an innovation. It could very well be an invention, and perhaps need some additional work to solve a problem for a use-case scenario so that such inventions demonstrate value for a potential customer. Invention is static without possible application, whereas innovation is taking the invention and applying it to solve a problem, which is action-based in nature.

> For practical purposes, we define innovation as "application or use of newness or invention in a practical or business context to impact the society while generating significant value."

DOI: 10.4324/9781003190837-2

1.2 Invention vs innovation

It is interesting to note that Austrian economist Joseph Schumpeter in 1939 was perhaps the first person who tried to differentiate invention from innovation by stating the following: "Invention is an act of intellectual creativity undertaken without any thought to economic impact, whereas innovation happens when organizations apply inventions to their business to realize economic benefits [5]."

To differentiate invention from innovation, let us look at an example. André-Marie Ampère, a French physicist, from the 19th century (January 20, 1775–June 10, 1836), founded the science of electrodynamics, now known as electromagnetism. Michael Faraday, an English scientist from the 19th century (September 22, 1791–August 25, 1867), built on the above work and further contributed to the study of electromagnetism, particularly the principles underlying electromagnetic induction. Understanding and theorizing of electromagnetism and electromagnetic induction after a significant number of experiments resulted in invention, of course, with no real-use case or application well thought through at that time. Presumably, there was no innovation per se in the minds of André-Marie Ampère or Michael Faraday when they explored and theorized electromagnetism and induction. However, now use of electromagnetism in our commonly used electric motors and power generators is considered an innovation, leverages and integrates inventions from other disciplines such as material science, manufacturing methods, thermal science, control engineering, and power network management.

Another interesting example is the World Wide Web (WWW) invention that everyone can relate to. Berners-Lee first attended Oxford and then worked at the European Organization for Nuclear Research (CERN). Later, around 1989, he began working on an internal technology platform called "Internet" at the US government, which was used by multiple US government agencies such as the Internal Revenue Service, Department of Agriculture, Department of Defense, etc. for over 30 years. His main contribution was in developing a computer program to allow data sharing across intra-government agencies seamlessly with proper access control, which was an issue at that time. Berners-Lee recognized significant value if converted to an open and democratic platform for all and decided to make the program free for everyone to use. The public release of the programming code suddenly took off and resulted in what we know now as the WWW invention [6]. Since then, the WWW has grown in many different directions and it is being leveraged by many businesses, government agencies, communities, academia, and private individuals to support their individual needs. Many businesses such as Google, Amazon, Airbnb, Uber, Facebook, Apple, Microsoft, Netflix, Tesla, Uber, to name a few, have built their business models based on the WWW being at the core. The WWW usage and business dependency on it have become very pervasive and it is experiencing an exponential growth. It can now legitimately be called an innovation, although the value that one receives and the risks associated with it may differ significantly from each other.

1.3 Historical perspectives of innovation

Canadian historian Benoît Godin, who has done extensive research into the origins of the word innovation, states that the term "novation" initially appeared in the 13th century in law journals to refer to contracts with the meaning of "newness." In the

17th century, the term innovator was used to signify a "change agent," which could have someone's ears cut off with lifetime imprisonment as many religious institutions considered use of such words disrespectful and perhaps could instigate mutiny [7, 8].

Given its unpopular and punishing characterization, the word innovation had to wait until the beginning of 19th century to find a new appeal in society. Recognizing the importance of science and technology spearheaded by the second industrial revolution, various resourceful government agencies in countries such as the US, UK, Japan, and some of the European nations, sponsored and provided research grants to foster inventions and facilitated the deployment or commercialization of such inventions through what is called "innovation efforts" to benefit society in general.

Godin observes that innovation has been considered a structured process for more than three decades since the beginning of 1950. The process involved following three waterfall steps: Step 1: Theoretical research, i.e., invention, in labs; Step 2: Development of applications of that research; and Step 3: Leveraging the development of the application to seek economic outcome (value) through commercialization of the invention as usable products or services. Innovation was assumed to have a predictable research outcome tightly coupled to real-world applications and problems, which appealed to corporations and government agencies alike as value became the key driver. James Thompson, who in 1956 founded *Administrative Science Quarterly*, an interdisciplinary journal publishing theoretical and empirical work that advances the study of organizational behavior and theory, published an article that examines the relationship between conditions in bureaucratic structure and conditions identified by psychologists for creativity. Interestingly, contrary to the then-prevailing faith in the structured process for innovation, he concluded that the focus of productivity and organization control found in the bureaucratic structure is not consistent with the needs of innovative behaviors. He suggests that to foster innovation and its output, one needs to have a looser organizational structure, open communication without fear of reprimands, job rotation, increased group processes such as teamwork, continuous restructuring and team realignment, balanced incentives, and changes to conventional management practices [9]. This observation has become the cornerstone of many areas of organizational design and enterprise culture research in the subsequent decades and the findings are being adapted by many industry leaders to advance innovation. The discipline of design thinking and lean startups for innovation, which will be discussed in later chapters, have benefited significantly from James Thompson's work.

1.4 Is innovation limited to products?

Innovation is often hypothesized to be product focused, which is not true. Innovation is not limited to products alone. There is process innovation and business model innovation as well.

The Organization for Economic Co-operation and Development (OECD)/Eurostat Oslo Manual, frequently cited for a common language or understanding of innovation as used for business analysis and planning, identifies innovation as follows:

> **Product innovation** refers to "a new or improved good or service that differs significantly from the firm's previous goods or services and that has been introduced on the market. This includes significant improvements to one or

6 *"What" – Introduction to innovation*

more characteristics or performance specifications, such as quality, technical specifications, user friendliness or usability [10]."

Business process innovation refers to "a new or improved business process for one or more business functions that differs significantly from the firm's previous business processes and that has been brought into use in the firm." This includes the various functions within a firm, such as the production of goods or services, distribution and logistics, marketing and sales, information and communication systems, and administration and management [10].

For example, traditionally manually intensive warehouse inventory processes can be automated leveraging sophisticated radio-frequency identification (RFID) scanners and related computer applications. The inventory process efficiency gains in these RFID-enabled processes are significant. Instead of counting inventories manually by single unit or box at a time, a large incoming shipment sitting on a master pallet, which may contain multiple individual pallets and/or boxes, can be bulk received and put away with relative ease into the warehouse bins or staging units just by scanning the master pallet RFID tag in an RFID tunnel. The labor savings are substantial and, in addition to efficiency gains, the process accuracy is far superior to the error-prone manual methods.

Innovation also could involve a **business model** itself in terms of new cost structure, pricing models including subscription plans, customer acquisition techniques, product and service delivery methods, post-sale warranty/support framework, market selection, etc. Business model innovation could leverage existing products or service innovations to deliver value to customers. Business model innovations are mushrooming in many industry verticals. For example, in the hospitality industry, Airbnb's business model leverages self-serving on-demand technology platform innovations to seamlessly connect the rental property owners and the paying guests, cutting out the expensive reservation agents. Similarly, Uber Transportation Network Company's business model thrives on leveraging intuitive mobile applications, cloud infrastructure, and sophisticated machine learning algorithms to connect car owners/drivers and passengers to facilitate customer rides at affordable cost.

Neither Airbnb nor Uber owns significant rental property or taxies but can compete with asset-rich dinosaurs such as Hilton and Yellow Cabs, respectively. The asset-light business models are built on dynamic commission-based revenue streams that leverage partnerships and special arrangements with the property or taxi owners. These new emerging business models not only break entry barriers for new entrants, but also allow traditional consumers to become non-traditional business owners in the form of an independent gig economy workforce who leverage their personal property, either apartment or personal cars, for a flexible work-life balance.

1.5 Innovation in service

The industries that make up the service sector include, but are not limited to, food, travel and tourism, information and communication technology, multimedia and entertainment, software services, and banking, including fintech. The innovations in the service sector have been significant, especially during the second half of the 20th century [11]. In the US, between 1919 and 2019, the gross domestic product from

Innovation – General background 7

the service sector increased from being less than 50% to more than 85%, primarily because of knowledge sharing and exponential growth in computer and related technology, internet, and mobile phones [11]. In the European Union, the service sector alone accounts for more than two-thirds of the total employment and the gross economic value, which is extremely significant [12]. The service sector innovations are made possible either through product or process or business model, or a combination of these. In the subsequent chapters, this topic will be discussed in detail.

1.6 Concluding remarks

Innovation is about problem-solving, and having a customer to recognize the delivered value and who is willing to pay for the product or service is paramount. If there is no value realized, it will be hard to justify what is delivered is an innovation. Innovation can be product, process, service, or business model specific, or a combination of them. Typically, innovation leverages multiple other innovations or inventions, and the focus is always on value.

Student activities

1. Select Whirlpool and Stryker cases from Part VIII.
2. Review the details and identify the problems solved or the opportunities addressed.
3. Categorize the types of innovations, product, or process, etc., discussed in the case.
4. Rationalize why you have categorized the innovation type the way you have in the previous step.

1.7 References

1. Joe Tidd and John Bessant, "Managing Innovation," Sixth Edition, Wiley Publishers, 2018.
2. Karsten Loehr, "The Science of Innovation," De Gruyter Oldenbourg, 2016.
3. Keith Goffin and Rick Mitchell, "Innovation Management," Third Edition, Red Globe Press, 2017.
4. Allan Afuah, "Business Model Innovation," Taylor & Francis, 2019.
5. Vernon W. Ruttan, Nov 1959, "Usher and Schumpeter on Invention, Innovation, and Technological Change," The Quarterly Journal of Economics, 73 (4), pp. 596–606, Published By: Oxford University Press.
6. www.internethalloffame.org/inductees/tim-berners-lee.
7. Benoît Godin, "Innovation Contested: The Idea of Innovation Over the Centuries," ISSN/ISBN 9780415727204, 2020. B. Godin (2020), "The Idea of Technological Innovation. A Brief Alternative History," Edward Elgar.
8. Emma Green, 2013, "Innovation: The History of a Buzzword – In the 17th century, innovators didn't get accolades. They got their ears cut off," The Atlantic, June 20, www.theatlantic.com/business/archive/2013/06/innovation-the-history-of-a-buzzword/277067/
9. Victor A. Thompson, 1965, "Bureaucracy and Innovation." Administrative Science Quarterly, 10, (1), pp.1–20. JSTOR, www.jstor.org/stable/2391646. Accessed 18 June 2021.

8 *"What" – Introduction to innovation*

10. www.oecd.org/sti/inno/innovation-indicators-2019-highlights.pdf
11. https://corporatefinanceinstitute.com/resources/knowledge/economics/service-sector/
12. Antonio Tajani and Johannes Hahn, "The Smart Guide to Service Innovation," European Commission, 2012. (https://s3platform.jrc.ec.europa.eu/documents/20182/84453/Smart_Guide_to_Service_Innovation.pdf/f196b040-32ab-4df9-a59a-842ad4647032)

2 Models of innovation

2.1 Introduction

Clayton Christensen and Michael Raynor, in their seminal book, *Innovators Solution: Creating and Sustaining Successful Growth* [1], discuss the distinctions among different types or models of innovations: Sustainable innovation, radical innovation, disruptive innovation, etc. The research literature abounds with discussions on different innovation types for a range of business contexts; however, they all boil down to essentially answering two simple questions.

1. Does the innovation involve a complex and sophisticated expertise, techniques, and technologies?
2. How pervasive is the innovation in impacting the customers and market segments with novel business models?

Building on Christensen and Raynor's work, we extend the scope of innovations and describe possible innovation models as represented in Figure 2.1.

2.2 Cosmetic/survival innovation

Cosmetic/survival innovation focuses on improvement to an existing product or process and is typically enabled by new features or functions to satisfy highly demanding and upmarket current customers. This approach allows the commanding of a higher price margin or premium from such customers while making them stick instead of switching to competitors' products. The changes made to existing products and services often are visible to the customers and this is a deliberate effort by the business to draw customers' attention. A bulk of innovations seen in the industry falls in this category [1, 2].

Apple's upgrade of iPhone X to iPhone 11 is a good example of sustainable innovation, where the iPhones belong to the same iPhone family, but iPhone 11 is feature rich. The iPhone 11 has two separate 12mp lenses and next-gen A13 Bionic chip allowing the phone to shoot in night mode, which the customers were demanding ever since Google launched its Pixel 3 phone. The upgraded cameras allow video at 4K resolution with the ability to change the zoom with relative ease. iPhone 11 also boasts better durability, water resistance, battery life, and portrait mode filters [3]. The enhanced features and functions are incremental and leverage similar product architecture with some adjustments to the form factors. One should be able to easily

DOI: 10.4324/9781003190837-3

10 *"What" – Introduction to innovation*

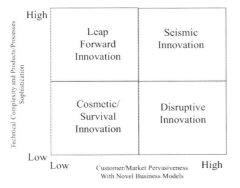

Figure 2.1 Models of innovation.

relate the new iPhone to the previous versions as the evolutionary path is comprehensible and they are built on comparable technologies. Often, such cosmetic/survival innovation is easy to adopt by the existing customer base as they are familiar with the product family and no special training or orientation is expected.

2.3 Leap forward innovation

If the product or process changes are significant and involve complex and sophisticated expertise, techniques, and technologies that are path-breaking and a departure from what is seen at competitors, such innovations are considered leap forward innovations. Such innovations create and use a new body of knowledge and novel ideas, products, or process, a technical or process leapfrog from the existing approaches in the marketplace [4]. It is often difficult to copycat such innovations and provide a superior competitive advantage to the pioneers of the innovators.

Aseptic packaging, an innovation from Tetra Pak, a Swedish firm, perfected a process called flash sterilization to allow refrigerationless handling of perishable commodities such as milk and freshly squeezed juices. This has been a great hit in countries where refrigeration equipment penetration is still a far cry. Even in countries such as the US and those in Western Europe where refrigeration is common, Aseptic packaging finds applications for preserving coffee cream and single-serve juice cartons [5]. The technology in this case is not a simple improvement over prevailing technologies, but very complex, sophisticated, and advanced in nature, allowing enterprises to perhaps sell this innovation to customers at premium pricing. Tetra Pak gained incredible competitive advantage and was able to make a significant market expansion.

Another memorable example of leap forward innovation from the World War II era that gave the Allied forces significant competitive advantage over Germany was high-frequency radio detection and ranging (Radar) technology. The radio waves, at different frequencies (low and high), are used to detect remote objects not seen by the naked eye, and this was first developed as a usable technology by British scientists and engineers in the 1930s. Detection is carried out by transmitting a burst of radio energy and measuring the time it takes to receive it back at the receiver after hitting the object.

The target's direction, height and possibly the approximate location can also be identified. When the war broke out in 1939, Britain had already installed Chain Home (CH) stations along the south and east coast of the country to detect enemy aircraft as far as 80 miles from its border. These stations housed radar systems that were 100 meters high and bulky. This early-warning information alerted British forces to engage enemy forces carefully. However, the Axis forces led by Germany and Japan had also developed their own radar technology around the same time, warranting the Allies a better technology that would give them a superior advantage. This led to the leap forward innovation of the cavity magnetron in 1940 by John T. Randall and Henry A.H. Boot, two researchers of Oliphant's group in Britain, followed by the production of a usable magnetron at the Massachusetts Institute of Technology Radiation Laboratory. The innovation led to the use of more powerful radio waves with a shorter wavelength, allowing more compact and sensitive radar units to be installed on aircraft, ships and land-based military artillery systems. This gave the Allies a much-needed two to three years' technological advantage over the Axis powers, which changed the outcome of the war in favor of the Allies [6, 7, 8].

2.4 Disruptive innovation

There is also another type of innovation whose characteristics are well researched and is labeled as disruptive innovation by Prof. Clayton Christensen [1, 2, 9]. He developed disruptive innovation theory based on the effect of an innovation, typically brought by entrants, to both established firms and other entrants in the marketplace. Disruptive innovation brings products and services to market with a different value proposition compared to existing mainstream products. Initially, Christensen tried to find a correlation between the entrants' disruptive innovation approach and the established firms' ability to grow and sustain in the same market, but over time he and his team were able to develop some causal relationship as well that led to the disruption theory.

Christensen and his team suggested that disruptive innovation could have two different flavors: 1. Low-end disruptive innovation; 2. New market (or Nascent market) disruptive innovation. These are explained below.

2.4.1 Low-end disruptive innovation

Low-end disruptive innovation targets a small, overserved customer base that is dissatisfied with established firms. These customers are served with products and services more than they need and can afford and are quite ready to jump the ship for the right size solution that they can afford. For incumbent established firms, these customers are not profitable and are unattractive. The new entrants recognize the low needs of such customers and their price elasticity and entice them with less sophisticated products and services at an affordable price, which is called disruptive innovation. Slowly and steadily, the entrants expand their footprint and make the established firms flee the low-end market and have them focus exclusively on the profitable high-end market. Given the internal organizational configurations, including how the leadership is incented based on profitability at the established firms, such market refocus does not ring alarm bells in the short run. However, as the entrants continue to make strides by increasing their efforts with higher-performance products and services

12 *"What" – Introduction to innovation*

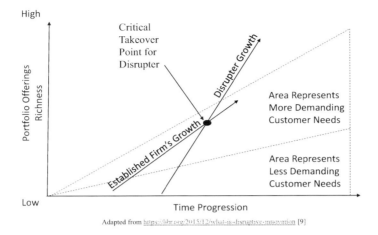

Figure 2.2 Disruptive innovation evolution.

delivered through innovative low-cost business models and are able to entice the high-end profitable market customers, the established firms find themselves running out of time with no options except to move up further and ultimately leave the entire market once and for all [1, 2, 9]. An adapted version of disruptive innovation evolution [9] is presented in Figure 2.2.

There are many examples in various industry verticals of entrants who strategized around disruptive innovation to enter the established low-tier market segments and ultimately prevailed at different upper tiers of the market at the expense of the established firms. The US automotive market is a prime example, where GM, Ford, and Chrysler (Now FCA – Fiat Chrysler Automobiles), the big three original equipment manufacturers (OEMs), dominated the US market for several decades, of course with their own up-and-down performance adapting to macroeconomic cycles. Figure 2.3 illustrates US automotive market disruption by Japanese automakers.

Back in 1960s, the Japanese auto manufacturers started exploring the US market by importing from Japan smaller, reliable, affordable, and highly fuel-efficient cars such as the Toyota Corolla. These cars were disruptive as they did not compete directly with the expensive, bulky, profitable, and luxurious cars from the big three US OEMs. After their initial success, the Japanese slowly moved to the high-end market and offered options such as the Toyota Camry sedan, 4Runner and MR2 sports car, including adding a luxury lineup Lexus in 1989 [11, 12]. Considering the cost challenges and import tariffs, the Japanese took a bolder step in the 1980s to build automobiles in the US instead of importing from Japan. Honda rolled out their first "Japanese-American" locally assembled car at its Marysville, Ohio assembly plant in 1982, followed by Toyota in new Georgetown, Kentucky, Nissan in Smyrna, Tennessee, Mazda in Flat Rock, Michigan, and Toyota with a subcompact car joint-venture with GM in the Fremont San Francisco Bay Area [13]. The disruptive innovation strategy led by Japanese automotive companies allowed them to earn the trust of a sizable US market and over time they have become a fixture of this important market for their longer-term growth and profitability aspirations. Defying the disruption theory,

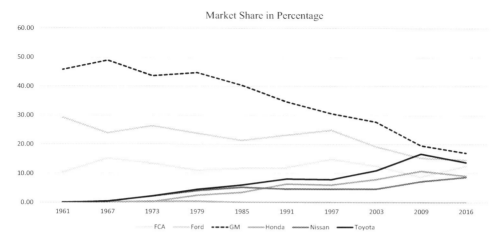

Figure 2.3 Major vehicle manufacturers' market share in the US [10].

however, it did not completely drive the big three US OEMs out of business, although we witnessed oil and financial crises during 1973–74 and 2007–09, respectively, which forced these OEMs to reconfigure themselves, giving them a new life. Over the past four decades, the big three OEMs recognized the new competitive landscape and navigated the challenges through structural transformation, outsourcing, lean processes, and relentless product and quality innovations, including in the emerging segments such as the electric vehicle (EV). They are now content with their reduced market share and lower profitability. The survival of big three US OEMs, and perhaps revival in the case of GM after its bankruptcy in 2009, including their pursuit with the EV are considered an anomaly to Clayton's disruption theory and warrants further investigation in the context of disruption models.

2.4.2 Nascent market disruptive innovation

There is also another type of disruptive innovation that does not tap into the established companies' market. The focus is nascent or new market with a customer base that has not been served by the established firms [1, 9]. This presents a virgin scenario where the disruptive innovator does not have to worry about any established industry benchmark such as potential price points, customer preferences, validated addressable market, etc. In this nascent turf, where there are no established competitors, enticing prospective customers involves educating first the prospective customers on the product and service offerings before acquiring them as customers. Perhaps it may involve trial offers, test drives, generous refund policies, showroom demonstrations, and an extended warranty period to instill confidence in the marketplace. We consider them a green field market segment, as there is no established competition playbook. In the green field market, the disruptor has a lot of leeway to structure the product and service offerings to suit the unique characteristics of the prospective customers. There could be many reasons for the existence of such nascent scenarios, including lack of access for prospective consumers to certain existing

14 *"What" – Introduction to innovation*

capabilities or use cases. Perhaps established firms consciously have ignored this prospective market segment assuming that there is either no demand or the profitability potential is not attractive, or there is a presumed lack of technical feasibility or perceived entry barriers [1], such as lack of utility infrastructure. Lack of standardized public EV chargers if the product offering is EV-related is a good example. Nascent disruptive innovation examples include Amazon Web Services (AWS), a cloud-based on-demand computing and infrastructure provisioning and iPad, a new computer-use category from Apple [14].

In the case of AWS, when the cloud computing services were introduced to customers in August 2006, there was no such comparable service in the marketplace to offer computing, memory, operating system, application development environment, and network capacity over the internet. Many established technology corporations, including IBM, SAP, Oracle, Microsoft, Google, TCS, Infosys, and Accenture, were focusing on on-premises data center-outsourced services for their customers that did not leverage web-enabled computing resource provisioning. There was no concept of public cloud-based resource allocation or multitenant modality for sharing common computer infrastructure over the web. Customers, regardless of their size and scope, were investing a significant amount of their own capital to establish their on-premises data centers, which were fast becoming obsolete, given Moore's law, while requiring a huge army of internal technical staff to support them even if this was outsourced for service management. Both the technology service providers and their corporate clients were ignoring the possibilities of harnessing a completely new internet-based shared computing resource delivery framework for significant cost advantage to the customers. The new business model, web-enabled computing resource provisioning, envisaged using the internet or WWW as the vehicle to offer on-demand computing resource allocation using a common pool of computing power, memory, operating systems, application development environment, and network capacity with relative ease. Amazon quickly simulated the technical and economic feasibility of the new delivery model given its firm belief in its potential to disrupt the market. Amazon took its surplus internal infrastructure resources to the marketplace to be offered as an on-demand web-based provisioning service. Amazon, in the new market not serviced by any of the established firms, did not have any competition to begin with and by default became the monopolistic player. It had the flexibility to structure its offerings, including trial options, pricing bundles, delivery protocol, data security framework, etc., to suit the evolving market dynamics. The nascent customers were extremely skeptical about data security and privacy when they evaluated AWS for the first time, but with some education and trial period experiments, slowly started committing their less critical business computing needs to AWS. This included the non-production environment, such as application development and testing, often called sandbox, which later gained the trust and confidence of the customers to further expand their AWS service utilization for mission critical production needs as well. The established technology firms such as Microsoft or Google did not see AWS as a viable business model during the early days and did not bother to explore the cloud nascent market. Jeff Bezos, Amazon founder and CEO, stated once that, "AWS had little over six years runway without any competition to establish itself as the leader in cloud computing, that is hard to come by typically [15]." The success of AWS's nascent market disruptive innovation is astounding and now the competition is heating up.

> "In 1965, Gordon Moore made a prediction that would set the pace for our modern digital revolution. From careful observation of an emerging trend, Moore extrapolated that computing would dramatically increase in power, and decrease in relative cost, at an exponential pace. The insight, known as Moore's law, became the golden rule for the electronics industry, and a springboard for innovation."
>
> www.intel.com/content/www/us/en/silicon-innovations/
> moores-law-technology.html

In 2010, Apple launched iPad, which was a brand-new category that many established computer manufacturers including mobile phone manufacturers did not quite comprehend in terms of use cases for prospective customers. Although some tablet PCs existed prior to the launch of iPad, the latter was marketed as a consumer device that would fill the gap between smartphones and laptop computers. Apple had the blueprint for iPad even before the iPhone was introduced in 2006, but delayed iPad's market launch for a reason that only a few could understand. It became clearer later through many of Apple founder Steve Job's interviews that product innovation alone does not guarantee results and must be synchronized with a suitable go-to market strategy. In the case of iPad, the learning curve for the prospective customers would have been steeper but for its architecture built on the principles of the ecosystem-based iPhone iOS operating system, enabling a multi-touch, easy to navigate, soft user interface without the need for a hard keyboard. The education imparted through iPhone helped the iPad customers [16] to speed up adoption. Additionally, Apple retail stores served as a hands-on place to learn Apple's new products. Apple so far has sold more than 350 million iPads through six different versions or upgrades [17]. iPad innovation is a classic nascent market disruption with characteristics where a new product category was established with almost no competition that ultimately expanded from pure consumer use to include commercial applications as well. Some of the evolving commercial applications of iPads include airline onboard entertainments systems, inventory tracking and reporting at warehouses, and table-mounted customer ordering, payment, and entertainment systems in restaurants.

The ecosystem-focused iOS operating system approach enabled Apple to orchestrate a successfully coordinated effort of multiple products that were positioned as incremental and nascent market innovation. iPhone's product innovation leveraged AT&T carrier subsidies and exclusivity, which showcased augmented distribution channel innovation, while iPad's disruptive innovation augmented the success of iPhone's install base [16]. Nascent disruptive innovation can certainly leverage existing infrastructure, customer channels, and other established internal and external strategic resources, so long as there is a well-conceived strategy and coordination across business units within an organization.

2.5 Seismic innovation

Seismic innovation is the ultimate harmony of both customer/market pervasiveness with novel business models and technical complexity and products/processes sophistication. It is extremely difficult to achieve this level of innovation maturity, which requires extraordinary ecosystem orchestration, organizational alignment, leverage

16 *"What" – Introduction to innovation*

of strategic resources, enterprise endurance, and seamless cross-team coordination. Often, enterprises wonder how to get there – should we ramp up first on the dimension customer/market pervasiveness with novel business models and then expand technical complexity and products/processes sophistication dimension or the other way around? Or should we make simultaneous progress on both dimensions? It is very subjective and often depends on the internal maturity of products and processes, strategic intentions of the enterprise, the macro/microeconomic situations of the market being pursued, culture, and financial health of the organization. For example, if the product being developed for a market that requires sophistication in products/process offerings while requiring newness in business model given the uniqueness in customer characteristics, price elasticity, competitive landscape, and regulatory regimen, the enterprise may choose to take an innovation trajectory that swiftly ramps up toward the seismic innovation quadrant. For example, Tesla's approach to capitalize on local government financing and incentives to build 2B$ Shanghai Gigafactory in 2019 leveraging local resources to manufacture EV for the China market with possible export to Europe and Japan fits the seismic innovation model. Why? Because it involves newness in business model that leverages local financing to build a factory to not only produce EVs for the local market, but also to export to Europe with a cost-effective approach. This involves sophisticated and highly automated manufacturing know-how to scale up production in record time of less than one year with Model 3 and Model Y passenger cars that are installed with market-leading data-driven technology, including near-autonomous driving capability. Although there are more than 480 EV makers who had registered in China by March 2021, Tesla plays the role of a catfish that can stir things up, setting a high bar for EV competition with its sophisticated data-driven technology and brand power.

Another great example of seismic innovation is Rocket Lab, headquartered in Huntington Beach, California. Khosla Ventures and Bessemer Venture Partners privately funded this high-tech startup recognizing the value of its innovative business model in delivering value to its customers that is expected to grow exponentially. Electron, a rocket approximately 56 feet long, carries micro satellites weighing a total of 500 pounds. These satellites are used by their clients to monitor weather, vegetation, and mineral resources, as well to support scientific research. Because they are affordable, it caters to the needs of poor countries, students, scientists, researchers, and entrepreneurs. The company is perfecting its manufacturing processes to speed up their rocket production, including leveraging 3-D printing technologies and to drive down the cost. Rocket Lab also helps their clients with configuring and building satellites with their pre-built modular components. The business model is creative, which allows on-demand services for nontraditional customers who would like to explore the space at an affordable cost and with convenience. It is akin to making a commercial flight reservation to deploy a satellite [18].

2.6 Innovation – What has changed now?

You may wonder why the innovation topic is getting more attention now than ever before. Regardless of whether it is a corporate board meeting, retail bank customer service, food delivery, grocery store checkout, work from home, and online student exams, the innovation theme is at the front and center. There are many reasons for it. Technology has become more interwoven with businesses' processes as enablers, drivers of value, and primary interface with both internal and external ecosystems. The affordable broad bandwidth internet access in conjunction with personal and professional mobile computing catapulted by digital innovations and cloud-based technology infrastructure have created a highly connected world allowing everyone to become immersed in the digital world. The appetite for real-time data and seamless user experience is simply unstoppable. Information production and consumption is simply overwhelming, characterized by big data with its 5Vs – velocity, variety, veracity, volume, and value. Both businesses and consumers are in catch-22 situation when it comes to satisfying each other. Competition is in hyperdrive and the foundation is shifting without any reference. What is good today is not guaranteed to be good tomorrow. For businesses, there is a constant necessity to reinvent themselves – people, product, process, service offerings, business models, etc., to be relevant. Iconic brands such as British Home Stores, electronics retailers Maplin (UK), international accessories chain Tie Rack, goods retailer Poundworld, Barratts Shoes, Kodak, Sears, Ascena Retail Group (which owned Ann Taylor, LOFT, Lane Bryant, Lou & Grey, and Justice), and Neiman Marcus Group are just a few that are either dead or a step closer to it as they could not withstand the deluge of innovation at their competitors [19]. One cannot turn a blind eye to innovation necessities and that is the reality.

2.7 Concluding remarks

Innovation models could vary – cosmetic/survival innovation, leap forward, seismic or disruptive – depending on the business priorities, business and market needs, and competitive situation. It is important that businesses understand the type of innovation that they pursue so that they can prioritize and coordinate internal resources and activities accordingly. The payoff horizons, resource expertise, customer engagement, and investments vary substantially based on the innovation models. Having a thorough understanding of the innovation models helps plan and manage expectations and execute the strategy decisively. Also, when a new business enters the market with a desire to compete on cosmetic/survival innovation, studies suggest that more than likely the incumbents will succeed [1, 9]and by adjusting their strategy they drive away the new entrants. Incumbents may turn a blind eye if the entrant is disruptive, which is low-end and not profitable. These observations are critical, and businesses must be prudent when they decide on an offering to compete in a market. If the strategy is a low-end disruptive offering, to succeed they need to focus on cost structures and target the minimum expectation of the overserved customers.

There are businesses that are quick to action without adequate upfront analysis but commit to an innovation pursuit and soon find themselves in a situation without any option but to abandon halfway through after spending scarce resources. Frequent failed innovation initiatives will cause chaos and organizational inefficiency, possibly draining resources and accelerating employee attrition. However, with proper upfront due diligence and coordination, businesses can chart a successful course.

18   *"What" – Introduction to innovation*

> ### Student activities
>
> 1. Select the Ericsson case from Part VIII.
> 2. Review the details and identify innovations pursued through mergers and acquisitions (M&A).
>   Do you think the type of innovation they pursued is leap forward? If so, why? If not, what is it and why?
> 3. Also answer the questions listed at the end of the case.

2.8 References

1. Clayton M. Christensen and Michael Raynor, "Innovators Solution: Creating and Sustaining Successful Growth."
2. Clayton M. Christensen, "The Innovator's Dilemma: When New Technologies Cause Great Firms to Fail," Harvard Business Review Press, 2016.
3. www.forbes.com/sites/anthonykarcz/2019/09/11/is-it-worth-trading-in-an-iphone-8-plus-for-an-iphone-11/#5f2a2d256b4b
4. Christian Hopp, David Antons, Jermain Kaminski, and Torsten Oliver Salge, April 9, 2018, "What 40 Years of Research Reveals About the Difference Between Disruptive and Radical Innovation," Harvard Business Review.
5. James Utterback, "Mastering the Dynamics of Innovation," Harvard Business School Press.
6. www.iwm.org.uk/history/how-radar-changed-the-second-world-war
7. https://ieeexplore.ieee.org/document/6735528?reload=true
8. M. H. F. Wilkins, "John Turton Randall (23 March 1905–16 June 1984)," Biographical; https://royalsocietypublishing.org/doi/pdf/10.1098/rsbm.1987.0018
9. Clayton Christensen, Michael Raynor, and Rory McDonald, Dec 2015, "What is Disruptive Innovation?" Harvard Business Review.
10. https://knoema.com/infographics/floslle/top-vehicle-manufacturers-in-the-us-market-1961-2016
11. www.philwrighttoyota.com/history-of-toyota.htm
12. www.scientificamerican.com/article/toyota-and-honda-have-the-most-fuel-efficient-cars/
13. www.latimes.com/archives/la-xpm-1988-10-15-fi-3525-story.html#:~:text=It%20has%20happened%20almost%20overnight,off%20its%20Ohio%20assembly%20line.
14. https://appleinsider.com/articles/19/01/27/apple-got-tablets-right-and-created-a-whole-new-market-with-the-ipad
15. Jeff Bezos explains Amazon's Competitive Advantage (2010) –www.youtube.com/watch?v=psPf-tx9OwY
16. www.prescouter.com/2013/06/steve-jobs-forget-the-product-start-with-the-go-to-market-strategy/
17. www.statista.com/statistics/269915/global-apple-ipad-sales-since-q3-2010/
18. www.rocketlabusa.com/
19. https://crm.org/articles/fujifilm-found-a-way-to-innovate-and-survive-digital-why-didnt-kodak

3 Challenges embracing innovation

3.1 Introduction

Over the past three decades, innovation has become the 'go-to' solution for problems in many organizations. We recently ran into a tier 2 automotive supplier who was trying to integrate an electronic module system into an evolving OEM platform design of their customer. As the final assembly they were trying to integrate into was not finalized, as a supplier they quickly recognized the longer they waited, the more risks they would run into planning for their upstream supply chain as they depended on many other suppliers for materials and components. The leadership team challenged the electronic module system design team for innovation and to come up with a flexible assembly design that would still fit into the 'yet to be finalized' final assembly design within certain acceptable form factor engineering guidelines. Of course, certain aspects of the design features, such as ventilation and vibration related to the functionality, were not negotiable. This required a thorough analysis of possible alternative scenarios for the final OEM platform and design of the electronic module system with flexible fit options without compromising the functionality-driven specifications. The design team iteratively worked with the OEM partner for possible design options and in the end came up with a universal design that would accommodate a few variations on the final design OEM assembly. This out-of-the-box critical thinking combined with detailed analysis and customer discovery allowed all the parties to be successful. This is a good example of what can be innovated under uncertain situations. With the right focus and attitude, organizations can be creative and develop innovative solutions for the task on hand.

It is often easier said than done. Some organizations, such as Google, Samsung, Verizon, Facebook, and Apple, pride themselves as perennial innovators and foster the necessary supportive culture at various levels in their organizations. These are technology-based corporations with unprecedented growth, and they continuously leverage innovations in their ecosystems to their success. The financial moat of these big corporations provides an inherent advantage for innovation either through organic means or through mergers and acquisitions (M&A) by gobbling up complementary innovators. Nonlinear thinking is highly encouraged in their corporate culture and failure is often considered an asset unlike some traditional organizations where failure is treated with stigma or career-ending events. On the other end of the spectrum there are startups that tend to be very innovative, although often cash-strapped. In startups, unlike established firms, it is not necessarily how much resource they have that drives

DOI: 10.4324/9781003190837-4

innovation, rather the survival instincts and audacity to think out of the box under stress shape their innovative behavior.

There are, however, several other traditional organizations, big and small alike, struggling with the idea of innovation and tending to take linear steps and miss out on many innovation opportunities. If a product or business service has been a success and has a decent customer base, these organizations do not want to rock the boat and unwittingly become complacent. They simply do not want to take on risky bets and perhaps burden constrained resources. Unfortunately, some companies experience sudden extinction or are forced to become irrelevant if an existing competitor gets additional product scope and channel uptick through M&A leverage or by radically redesigning their current service offerings. Being risk averse and failing to anticipate and visualize what may be brewing on the horizon in the marketplace will haunt such less innovative organizations for years to come. Nokia and Blackberry are classic examples that lost their relevance in the mobile phone industry, ceding the turf to relatively a newcomer, Apple iPhone, in 2007. Apple revolutionized the mobile phone industry by shifting the focus to software applications and encouraging an application-driven ecosystem based on its popular iOS operating system that significantly enhanced the utility value of its phone. What Apple did was not an invention, but an improvisation or innovation, which leveraged multiple inventions or advancements in many different fields, such as the semiconductor, material science, software architecture and coding, man-machine interfaces, cloud infrastructure, data science, distributed computing, etc., to scale customer value that its competitors could not simply replicate soon enough.

3.2 Triangular dilemma

Through our consulting engagements at many Fortune 500 corporations, including some privately held small/medium business enterprises, we had the opportunity to witness firsthand how certain organizations fail to innovate. The challenges these organizations experience manifest in different forms based on their unique internal setup and how they are positioned in the marketplace. From a macro perspective, we can categorize their challenges into three groups to form the three vertices of a triangle as shown in Figure 3.1, which requires constant adjustments, recalibration, and alignment.

Figure 3.1 Triangular dilemma.

3.3 Market innovation challenges

3.3.1 Sticky customers

Enterprises that have complacent and less demanding customers have a real problem with innovation. Unless the customers' needs and their expectations change, the businesses tend to maintain the status quo and will be reluctant to innovate. This is further accentuated by lack of competition or other available alternatives for the customers in the marketplace. Being a monopoly or a duopoly in a saturated market with a steady stream of revenue and earnings does not incentivize or motivate innovation within the organization.

A great example is the suppliers of 14-inch drive technology to mainframe computer manufacturers such as IBM, Amdahl, and Hitachi in the 1950s, 1960s and 1970s. These mainframe manufacturers and their captive mega customers such as banks had a cozy relationship and were pleased with the mainframe architecture and 14-inch drive. For the manufacturers, their technology was a cash cow and for the customer there was no need for change management within the organization, although it was not very efficient. This led to siloed thinking, and they did not challenge each other. The manufacturers, however, were blindsided and did not recognize the evolution of computer architecture changes in the marketplace resulting in the introduction of the minicomputer by new entrants and the related need for a flexible 8-inch tape drive serving a slightly different market segment.

Another classic example is the internal combustion engine (ICE)-based automotive vehicle. This technology has been around for over a century now. German inventor Karl Benz patented his Benz Patent-Motorwagen in 1886 [1] leading to the birth of modern cars, which became accessible to the masses through the 1908 Model T, from the Ford Motor Company [2]. Since then, the ICE has been perfected with other enhancements such as comfort, safety, and utility of the automotive vehicles. But the traditional ICE-based automotive companies have an extremely hard time innovating and shifting to environmentally friendly vehicles such as electric powered, partly because of their current customers, who are either unwilling or less demanding for a new breed of technology that is not ICE-based such as solar, hydrogen, or battery operated. Companies such as Tesla that do not have the legacy burden of the traditional customer orientation or disposition, as seen with Ford and GM customers, are able to leapfrog on the innovation front with new electric and data-driven technology and able to cultivate a cult-like following among an environmentally conscious customer base.

3.3.2 Predictable M&A

In a fragmented market, if the unforeseen M&A results in strengthening a competitor from product portfolio and channel scope perspectives, then businesses will be on their toes and constantly anticipate the unthinkable and be ready for an uncertain future through innovation. However, if a market has only a few players, and it is easier to predict the M&A activities, the businesses tend to take shelter in their accomplishments and become complacent, committing subpar resources and low priority for the innovation agenda. The innovation priority is further diminished during

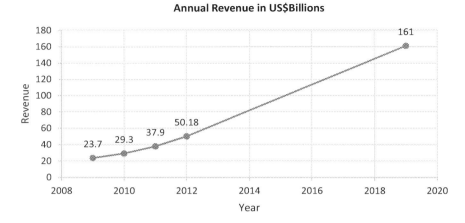

Figure 3.2 Google annual revenue.

economic downturns when the cash flow is tight and other operational priorities take precedence.

A great example is Google's acquisition of DoubleClick for $3.1B in March 2008 [3], a period of economic downturn, and rolling out of the popular DoubleClick Ad exchange the next year. The new system simplified and improved how advertisers put display ads on websites, allowing advertisers more control over who sees their ads. This caught Yahoo, Google's competitor, by surprise, which used to have the display ad dominance for quite some time by controlling the banners and colorful ads that consumers would see on the internet. Yahoo's complacence in not predicting significant M&A of its main competitor, Google, resulted in them losing their dominance in the ad search business and finally getting itself sold to Verizon for $4.48B in 2017 [4], a fraction of what it was worth at one time. Google's added technological innovation propelled its revenue growth from $23.7B in 2009 to $29.3B in 2010, $37.9B in 2011, $50.18B in 2012, and $161B in 2019 [5], as illustrated in Figure 3.2. In 2019, more than 70% of its total revenue was derived from advertising [6], which came at the expense of Yahoo and other search advertisement competitors.

3.3.3 Stable supply chain

For many organizations, the supply chain focuses on producing and delivering products to customers in a timely manner within the set cost parameters and service levels. If the supply sources are stable and predictable with consistency, there is a lack of incentive for the businesses to innovate. Innovation is further disincentivized if there is no competition in the marketplace or the incremental gains do not have material impact.

A good example is traditional community-based grocery chains such as Kroger, Safeway, etc., which have been around for many decades. These chains have an extensive footprint in less urban areas. Although they experimented with many technologies and process improvements such as self-scanning/checkout, RFID, dynamic pricing, etc., not much was realized in terms of transforming customer experience and consistent margin improvements. Though incremental automation and software application deployment drove overall back-office efficiency gains, processes such as customer checkout, in-store inventory management, etc., continue to involve significant human dependency. This industry is notoriously known to suffer from razor-thin profit margins. The grocery supply chain is perhaps stable and is locally or regionally managed with a predefined supply chain network and distribution centers. If there is no produce or supplies for a few days, the local customers will understand it and can wait until the produce or the supplies are replenished at the store. If there is unexpected foot traffic on any given day and there is a long line before checking out, their customers may not care much and will continue to be patient. They will not switch overnight to a competitor or quit shopping altogether at these locations. There is no sense of urgency for these stores to innovate the operational model dramatically and seek alternative methods to improve customer experience.

However, upward trend of urbanization brings a new breed of customers who either want groceries to be delivered to them or cannot afford to stand in long lines before they check out. For these customers, time is scarce, and they value shopping convenience. Their predisposed comfort level with consumer technologies such as mobile phone, frictionless mobile payments, and online shopping applications significantly amplify their expectations when they shop at local grocery stores. The new breed of customers' preferences and behaviors keep changing given the rapid innovations in the consumer technologies and, unfortunately, the traditional grocers are not quite ready to handle this challenge. However, disruptors such as Amazon bring a new mindset to this industry with highly automated and cashierless store technologies such as Amazon GO Just Walk Out technology [7] that leverages innovations from computer vision, deep learning algorithms, artificial intelligence (AI), sensor fusion, real-time data analytics, etc. To meet the demands of the new generation of shoppers, these disrupters do not take comfort in the stable supply chain. They are obsessed with customer experience and do not hesitate to disrupt the status quo. They constantly innovate their business processes and evolve their business models. The interesting fact is that these disruptors are ready to share such innovations with other competitors, only to challenge themselves along the way for more such innovations. Amazon GO Just Walk Out technology is now available for other retailers to benefit from on a license basis.

It is simply a paradigm shift for many and is serving as a catalyst for the whole industry to make strides on the innovation journey.

3.4 Organizational innovation challenges

3.4.1 Lack of coordinated innovation strategy

Oftentimes, businesses claim that they have an innovation strategy that is managed centrally such as central marketing at the headquarters or at the decentralized level such as country specific manufacturing. There is nothing wrong with this approach so long as everyone within the organization is aligned and activities are coordinated, leveraging synergy across the enterprise without burdensome bureaucracy or duplication of efforts. This is vital for the organization's success as resources are harnessed efficiently and effectively. However, oftentimes, what we experience is islands of

24 "What" – Introduction to innovation

innovation activities within the organization that have poor visibility across the enterprise with lost opportunities for synergy from development, testing, cost, market timeliness, and utility value perspectives.

Corporations promote regional innovation in the name of regional autonomy as they are closer to their local customers but fail to cross-pollinate expertise and leverage local or regional innovations across the organization. For example, at one of the largest home appliances manufacturing companies based out of the US, regional business units in EMEA (Europe, Middle East, and Africa), South America, and Asia/Oceania, were given significant latitude in deciding technology and business capability independent of corporate position. This led to innovating solutions with a myopic view in isolation, often reinventing what already existed in other business units, draining the enterprise resources and resulting in lower overall corporate margins. This caused ineffective go-to market strategies as there are no lessons learned from the previous experience. Although the regional autonomy aspirations were generally viewed favorably, the fragmented approach without corporate-wide coordination led to overall inefficiencies in innovation making no real progress. Overall, the organization was struggling with innovation challenges as coordination and synergy across business units was suboptimal and failed to deliver value in a timely manner within budgetary constraints.

However, there are organizations that recognize these challenges and address them effectively. An example is AWS's introduction in August 2006. Initially, it started as an internal infrastructure build at many geographical locations with web-enabled computing, memory, and network capacity provisioning to meet the regional and time-zone dependent needs, but over time the internal technical resources supply overwhelmingly exceeded the internal demand during the off-season cycle, which happened to be non-holiday periods. The idea of the necessity for steady and even exploitation of infrastructure was floated within the organization to justify its technology investments [8]. Quickly the opportunity to monetize through lease or offer the heavily invested infrastructure over the web as a service to external customers was conceived with minimal or no disruption to Amazon's own e-commerce business needs. Significant internal coordination and related innovation activities on a global basis allowed Amazon to make AWS a viable business reality, which is now more than $35B business on an annualized basis with over 37% annual growth rate, contributing to more than $9B 2019 operating income. Without extensive transparency and internal innovation coordination, it would not have been possible for Amazon to realize such a huge market opportunity and stand up a successful business unit. The AWS success is astounding, as illustrated in Figure 3.3, and now the competition is heating up.

3.4.2 Lack of diversity

Organizations often struggle with augmenting innovation capabilities through diversity and there are many confounding explanations. Although some take pride in promoting diversity in organizations, they do not quite follow through after the initial onboarding of diverse resources.

Innovation is not black magic, and it entails a concerted effort. Parachuting diversity at workplaces does not guarantee the desired outcome. Diversity at the workplace must be approached with a clear purpose and not used as a tool of convenience.

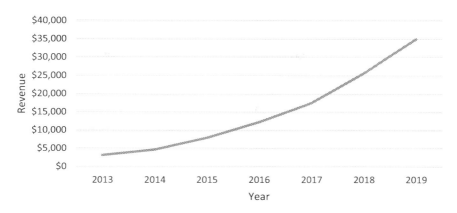

Figure 3.3 AWS annual revenue.

Although there are several statistics that reveal how well diverse organizations outperform their peers that do not practice diversity, some companies lack internal diversity policies and the audacity not to experiment this compelling proposition. To be innovative, multiple perspectives and idea generation are critical. Diversity on dimensions such as culture, ethnicity, gender, geography, language, experience, age, and skills, to name a few, bring such plurality and richness in ideas and perspectives. However, to make the chemistry work among such diverse talents, patience, commitment, orchestration, empowerment, sense of purpose, common vision, and team concept are absolutely required. A homogenous workforce, though it may have a semblance of compatibility and may deliver tactical innovation results, in the long run, due to lack of diversity in thoughts and experience, will invariably run into challenges that may inhibit its ability to think out of the box with a rich mix of timely developed solution options for the problem or opportunity on hand.

A great example is Pixar, the most creative and successful innovation company that kicked off a renaissance in digitally animated film. Steve Jobs, founder of Apple, Inc. acquired the computer graphics division of Lucas Film, Ltd in 1986 for $5M, renamed it as Pixar, and developed it over 20 years with additional investments to become the most enviable computer graphics animation company. Pixar was later acquired by Disney in 2006 for $7.4B, making Steve Jobs the largest shareholder with more than 7% of Disney ownership. Steve Jobs once said it took eight to ten years to assemble and foster a diverse yet cohesive team with the right chemistry before Pixar could release blockbuster digital animation movies such as *Toy Story*, *Monsters Inc.*, *The Lion King*, and *Finding Nemo* [9]. There was no shortcut or silver bullet to Pixar's innovation success and, undoubtedly, diversity of talents and resources played a critical role in its great success, which subsequently helped transform the entire movie industry.

3.4.3 Compartmentalization

Many organizations suffer from what is called islands of activities that are detrimental to fostering collaboration. For example, in a typical setup, organizations

26 *"What" – Introduction to innovation*

are internally grouped based on their core functional focus, such as marketing, finance, human resource, manufacturing, procurement, supply chain, IT, research and development (R&D), etc., for internal reasons, but often cross-team collaboration is less than optimal for enterprise-wide initiatives. This is primarily due to misalignment in priorities that the individual departments are driving and how they are measured and incented on their performance. There is another major component that is often overlooked, which is the internal leadership politics, creating never-ending friction between functional groups. The teams are further hampered by the inadequacies of technology or integrated business architecture to share vital business information such as inflight innovation initiatives and lessons learned from completed projects.

We observed such frictions at one of the largest Fortune 100 corporations where deliberate attempts by some group vice-presidents (VP) to derail other group VPs' initiatives. They often practiced either delaying tactics in providing vital information and/or committing subpar resources from their group for innovation projects driven by other functional groups. They did not treat enterprise priority the same as their own internal priority and indulged in perpetual cross-team finger-pointing, contributing to delayed suboptimal corporate innovation outcomes. The irony was that, although the group VPs made a firm commitment to drive enterprise initiatives before their common boss, a senior VP, their individual actions and guidance to their own teams were quite contradictory. In the end, some of the group VPs were let go when a new CEO took the helm, after carefully studying the dysfunctional situation through interviewing lower-level staff and evaluating some of the failed innovation initiatives.

3.4.4 Risk-averse non-experimental culture

Many organizations have built a corporate culture that is risk averse and often find themselves as laggards on the innovation front. Innovation thrives in an organization where the environment is safe to experiment with different ideas for the given problem or opportunity and not become bogged down with a constant threat of backlash or retribution. Of course, there is nothing wrong with having an evaluation process, success criteria, timeline, project prioritization, etc., supporting innovation efforts, but it is critical that innovators are not penalized if their efforts do not result in immediate benefits. Also, the corporate environment should be transparent and conducive for employees to share their ideas without the fear of losing ownership or intellectual property rights. Being an employer, the corporation owns the innovation of its employees generated using workplace resources, including the time spent at the workplace for innovation, but the contributors should be duly recognized, and the rewards may be shared proportionately. The environment should also be agile in its approach to allow faster experiments so that options or ideas for a problem or opportunity can be tested, lessons learned from failures, and a viable innovative solution can be developed. For startups, by default, the native culture is supportive of experiment-based innovation; however, it is seldom the case in a well-established organization. The culture that has been nurtured over time to be risk averse is hard to change overnight and is congruent to a big ship that is very difficult to turn around quickly.

3.4.5 Misaligned incentive

Incentives are essential for innovation and, after all, no one works for free. However, we notice at times that innovative and curious employees leave their lucrative corporate jobs with reputable corporations, seeking alternative employers or opportunities. The motivation may sound incomprehensible on the surface of it, but a little bit of research will make it obvious that somewhere something ticked off such good productive and innovative employees.

Often the root cause for such an exodus is misaligned incentives. Employers must develop a transparent, consistent and employee-driven approach in rewarding either an employee or a team that contributed to the innovation outcome. Innovations are often the result of team efforts, and singling out an individual or a team in a rush without proper due diligence for recognition or rewards will precipitate employee revolt. Aggravating possible discontent among employees is the political rivalries between functional heads and their tendencies to favor their own team members when the credit for innovation belongs elsewhere within the organization.

While consulting at a major pharmaceutical corporation, we experienced one such situation where a few highly valuable and contributing technical team members handed in their resignation at the same time soon after a few other individuals were promoted as a recognition for their role in a successful new technical product launch. Unfortunately, that assessment was called into question. These events happened so quickly that the post-product deployment planning and support suffered significantly without true key contributors to field customer issues. This reminded the leadership of the downside of misaligned incentives and rushing to judgment without considering facts.

3.4.6 Micromanagement

Innovators by default prefer to be left alone, but that is not the case often in organizations. Innovation typically is a team effort, but the individuals within the team naturally enjoy freedom with a certain degree of reporting requirements within a span of control. Google once setup Google X, where moonshot projects were experimented. Interestingly, this group had an arm's length relationship with the parent corporation Google, and Google X was not directly responsible for advancing and managing Google's core products or services daily. The model was very strategic and, by design, protected the engineers and scientists at Google X from micromanaging their tasks.

In a conventional organization, it is rather difficult to let employees operate on a longer leash. It requires a lot of trust, self-motivation, drive, and strategic purpose. Corporations that are innovation leaders continuously experiment with different organizational models and management styles to motivate and foster innovation. In general, innovation flourishes with less management, particularly when the pursued opportunity is abstract, yet very ambitious, such as moonshot projects at Google X. Not many organizations are good at managing innovators and, through an iterative approach, this can be developed and calibrated to the given unique situation. The management also must shift its operating model's focus from "I" to "T" philosophy, meaning that while recognizing "individual" talents, larger emphasis has

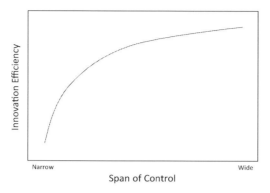

Figure 3.4 Innovation efficiency.

to be given to the "team" approach, as often innovation thrives in establishing and fostering the right chemistry among individuals who have diverse expertise and personalities [10].

3.4.7 Span of control

Span of control and innovation efficiency have a direct relationship as illustrated in Figure 3.4. A narrow span of control has fewer people reporting to one manager and typically results in more levels of reporting in the organization. This leads to a deep hierarchical organization with more bureaucracy and delayed decisions, resulting in more friction for innovation. On the other hand, innovation leaders tend to have a flat hierarchy, also called a wide span, with more people reporting to one manager, encouraging increased peer level collaboration among the staff. A deep organizational hierarchy promotes politics, bureaucracy, mistrust, fear, insecurity, favoritism, delays, and micromanagement. For innovation to flourish, employees should be given more latitude and be empowered so that they can make quick decisions on their own, accelerating the innovation process. Google X was known to have a flat hierarchy, like many other innovation leaders, such as Pixar, Disney, and Starbucks, at least in some of their functional areas, to allow employees to collaborate freely with their peers and learn from their iterations and mistakes. We do not want to impede innovation progress with unnecessary organizational layers and approvals, which only contributes to innovation inefficiency. Startups are by nature flat in their structure, which supports enhanced collaboration and innovation while allowing team members to take on multiple responsibilities, inject fresh perspectives, and make independent yet coordinated decisions.

3.4.8 Lack of sense of urgency

Many organizations suffer from lethargic leadership that is risk averse and does not have the entrepreneurship mindset. To put it bluntly, they do not operate with an "owner's mindset," a trait that is absolutely required for corporations that strive to be the leader in the industry in which they operate. Amazon and Starbucks are great examples of where the leadership at each of their business units operate with an ownership mindset that constantly assesses their competitiveness with a relentless appetite for product and service offering innovations to stay ahead of the pack, much like the front runners in a marathon race. When corporations do not fear the unknown, they will be surpassed overnight by the competition, and there are numerous examples discussed in the previous sections. Corporations must be very thoughtful and strategic as they innovate as resources to innovate are scarce, both within and external to the corporations. Often there are certain windows of opportunity that present well and are conducive to advance innovation. Continuous competitive assessment and adjustments to the internal innovation effort is vital to stay ahead of competition. As indicated in Figures 3.5, 3.6, and 3.7, Corporation 1 and Corporation 2 have multiple products in the innovation and commercialization pipeline, but they have slightly different trajectories or slopes for growth. These growths depict how effective they are in their innovation as reflected by market share and revenue growth. There will be an inflection point where the competition will surpass the current leader, often through innovative products and services, which will redefine the competitive landscape. The growth trajectories can also be considered as an angle of attack, a term often used in the aircraft industry. If the innovation angle of attack of a corporation is better than the competitor, it is fair to assume that their marketplace performance is materially better as well, relative to the competitor. Corporate leaders must anticipate these trends and respond proactively with a sense of urgency. As depicted in the diagrams, there is a window of opportunity represented by the area between the growth or angle of attack curves. This, however, is diminishing for Corporation 1, or the current industry leader, as one approaches the inflection point. This is mirrored by the severity curve of the competitor's innovation threat. Apple iPhone surpassing Nokia and Samsung phones, Google's search ad surpassing Yahoo's search ad are great examples of these phenomenon.

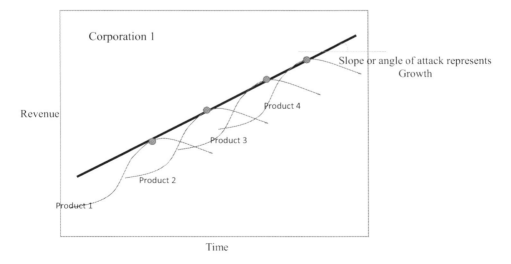

Figure 3.5 Innovation trajectory – Corporation 1.

30 *"What" – Introduction to innovation*

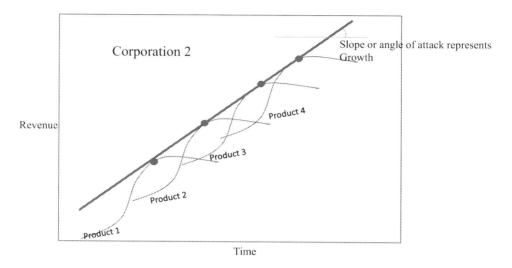

Figure 3.6 Innovation trajectory – Corporation 2.

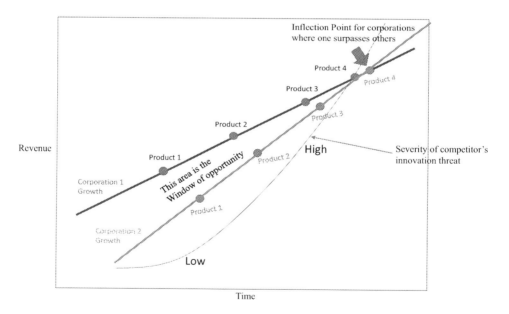

Figure 3.7 Innovation trajectories – Corporation 1 vs Corporation 2.

> If the innovation angle of attack of a corporation is better than the competitor, it is fair to assume that their marketplace performance is materially better as well, relative to the competitor.

Corporations must avoid a sense of complacency and not simply indulge in bureaucratic processes to torpedo incoming ideas with no clear vision or roadmap for experimentation. The innovation window narrows down when the competition heats up and when they realize they are closer to the inflection point, they are pretty much in crisis mode. The actions taken during this crisis mode are simply band-aid solutions and will not result in innovative products or solutions that can cut into consumer surplus. A great example is how the dinosaurs of the ICE-based OEMs in the auto industry responded to the threat posed by companies such as Tesla. We hear so many deals and collaborations made by these OEMs, including their effort to gobble up small and upcoming electric- or hydrogen-based automotive manufacturers that have no prior history or footprint in the automotive space. It clearly demonstrates their desperate attempts to get ahead in the Tesla-dictated warfare and, so far and as expected, these OEMs are struggling to show real success and are still a few years away from delivering electrified data-driven semi-autonomous cars.

> Consumer surplus is an economic measurement of benefits realized by consumer. A consumer surplus occurs when the price that consumers really pay for a product or service is less than the price they are willing to pay. Consumers will pay for innovation from their surplus, but not for band-aid solutions.

3.5 Stakeholder innovation challenges

Stakeholders represent different segments of society and are central to corporate innovation. This select group of stakeholders influence how conservative or aggressive the corporation is in innovating new products or services or new business models. We highlight some of the innovation challenges related to this critical group of stakeholders.

3.5.1 Investor community

Depending on where the corporation is operating and how they are legally set up, the investor expectations may vary, which has a direct impact on how much risk the corporation is willing to take as it embarks upon innovation initiatives. For example, many publicly traded corporations in the US are evaluated on short-term metrics, by quarter, and investors typically tend to have less patience and demand top- and bottom-line performance benchmarks met consistently on a shorter horizon. This may compromise the needed investment, which requires a longer time horizon to address innovation challenges. Eventually the corporation may suffer from lack of new products and services, be unwilling to experiment with new business models, or fail to expand into new market opportunities. On the other hand, some of the pre-initial public offering (IPO) corporations or privately held corporations may have more leeway to experiment and market new products and services as their investor community is patient on the timeline to realize the expected performance so long as the progress is encouraging and moving along the roadmap for perhaps a successful IPO debut. There are many examples, such as Uber, Lyft, Avedro, BioNTech, Spotify Technology SA, Zoom, Pinterest, and Shopify, which took their time to grow the

32 "What" – Introduction to innovation

business or user base over many years through relentless innovation before their IPO debut.

Established publicly traded corporations such as Kodak and Nokia did not have the luxury of staying persistent on the innovation front and retaining their market dominance. Lack of timely digital photography innovation and continued reliance on analog or paper films made one of the best-known global corporations, Kodak, irrelevant overnight when the digital revolution took on between 1996 and 2000. It lost grounds to Canon, Nikon, Sony, Fuji, and many other relatively unknown digital camera manufacturers. Investor pressure to meet short-term goals prevented Kodak from investing in the future through digital innovation and subsequent commercialization. It was complacent with its cash cow product lines from the previous generations and just did not pivot to the new reality in a timely manner. Although Kodak eventually tried to catch up with digital camera products, it had already lost its market leadership position and first mover advantage in digital photography and became less attractive to its supposedly loyal customer base. The rest is history. As consultants at Kodak during those periods, we witnessed its struggle firsthand and appreciated how difficult it was for an iconic corporation to lose its premier market position.

Nokia, another popular global brand for mobile communications, from Finland, with a 49.4% global market share [11] in 2007 through their hardware innovation, became complacent and turned a blind eye to what could be done with software innovation. When Steve Jobs introduced the iPhone in 2007, the mobile communication game already had changed its focus from hardware to software. The new paradigm allowed users additional capabilities through software applications on the phone, with advanced cameras, games such as Angry Bird, Global Positioning System (GPS), productivity tools such as Evernote, Simplenote, Wunderlist and Dropkick, [12] etc., in addition to simply communicating with others as a phone. Nokia's operating system, Symbian, is much to blame for losing Nokia's competitiveness as it was not a match for Apple's potent and flexible iOS operating system. The rest is history, and Nokia, once valued at $300B, was bought by Microsoft for a meager $7.2B in 2014, only to be soon sold to others and partly written off. It is a big corporate tragedy, widely attributed to lack of timely innovation [13, 14] and commercialization, being complacent, driven by short-term goals precipitated by investor expectations.

At the other end of the spectrum, Uber, Spotify, and Airbnb are great examples of where the private equity and venture capital investors from different funding series demonstrated their patience and provided the necessary resources for the corporations to innovate and grow to be ready for IPO. These corporations are worth tens of billions of dollars now and can grow aggressively in terms of user adoption and market penetration.

3.5.2 Government

Governments play a key role in either encouraging or discouraging innovation through funding or regulation. In terms of funding, often governments from many geographies prioritize their strategic technological or societal needs and encourage innovations at universities or corporations. Premier funding agencies in the US include the National Science Foundation, National Aeronautics and Space Agency (NASA), Defense Advanced Research Project Agency, Environmental Protection Agency (EPA), and National Institutes of Health. NASA, for example, provided over $12B to Space X, a privately held corporation run by the serial entrepreneur Elon Musk, to build and run Falcon rockets and Dragon capsules to carry cargo and astronauts to space stations. Space X has been extremely successful [15] and, as of March 2020, its Falcon 9 family of reusable rockets has flown 84 successful missions with fewer failed launches. The overall cost-effectiveness of these rockets has been very attractive to NASA and the Department of Defense, and Space X's breakthrough innovation would not have been possible without government support. Similarly, the US government, through its Operation Warp Speed program [16, 17], granted Pfizer $1.95B and AstraZeneca $1.2B to develop COVID-19 vaccines at an accelerated pace.

On the other hand, a certain relaxation of standards and compliance requirements by governments have the potential to discourage innovation at corporations. For example, the President Trump administration relaxed [18] automobile fuel efficiency guidelines by reducing the 5% annual increase to 1.5% a year through model year 2026. This seriously undermined the environmental consequences of automobile pollution and discouraged the automotive sector from innovating aggressively to reduce emissions. Unfortunately, the automotive sector is the largest source of climate-warming greenhouse gas emissions in the US. With the new US administration in 2021, the rules may change, putting the corporations in a constant dilemma about how to navigate the innovation challenges driven by unpredictable government priorities and policies. These uncertainties are one of the major reasons why the traditional automotive OEMs, such as Ford, GM, Chrysler, etc., are unable to make a swift switch to electrification of their newer models as there has been no real incentive to aggressively pursue longer-range battery innovation that is affordable for mass consumption.

3.5.3 Local ecosystem

For innovation efforts, the local ecosystem is another key stakeholder, which has a direct impact on the outcome. Porter's [19] diamond model also reinforces the importance of the local community or market in terms of factor conditions and related supporting industries for innovation.

For example, in the US we have Silicon Valley in California, a 25-mile stretch that is part of the Santa Clara Valley, south of San Francisco Bay and locked between San Francisco and San José. This valley has been at the forefront of technological innovation, producing economic output that is much more than the collective contribution of many other industrialized nations [20]. This area is characterized by the active participation of leading venture capital firms (e.g. Andreessen Horowitz, Sequoia Capital, Benchmark, Accel, Index Ventures) with their mentoring and networking capacity; industry and top research university (e.g. Stanford, UC Berkeley) partnerships; electronics and software-focused efforts with applications in computing, cyberspace, security, defense, communications, instrumentation, and space; strong inter-firm collaborations; non-enforceable non-compete agreements for employees; and spin-offs on steroids. The local ecosystem is so fertile for innovation pursuits from technical, financial, and marketing perspectives [21]. There are many other cities that try to emulate Silicon Valley's success, such as Bangalore in southern India, Zhongguancun in the northwestern part of Beijing, and the eastern end of the M4 corridor in the UK, but their success has been mixed and not as effective.

Many me-too cities that embark on the journey of becoming the next Silicon Valley, often struggle to show results as the path is arduous, time-consuming, and requires a

34 *"What" – Introduction to innovation*

lot of coordination and longer-term commitment from various stakeholders, including local government agencies. It takes, perhaps, several decades before the seeds of such efforts yield results. Often, temporary failures or any delays in achieving innovation success are viewed as intractable setbacks by certain stakeholders, who either abandon the journey immediately or make frequent detours that encourage the rest of the ecosystem players to seek opportunities elsewhere. A good example for such lack of innovation resilience is local governments taking a shorter-term view for incentives such as time-limited tax concessions or subsidies in offering industrial lands to attract new businesses instead of committing to a longer-term effort and promoting supporting business-friendly policies. This is further precipitated by any changes in the local governments or their governance philosophies.

3.5.4 Employees

Employees are crucial to innovation success. However, having curious minds with the audacity to think out of the box requires a well-thought-out organizational model and an environment with less supervision. The traditional organizations are accustomed to an in-house R&D team approach for innovation, which in the traditional sense is designed to either drive incremental improvements to existing products or services in the near term, or a bureaucratic process-driven longer-term research effort that may not guarantee a commercially viable product. Sustaining employees' motivation for a longer-term innovation pursuit in a culture that is not consistent with the freelance-driven mindset of the new breed of employees is guaranteed to fail, which is tantamount to force-fitting a square peg in a round hole. In addition to assembling the right talents to advance innovation, organizations need to understand and address employees' priorities, both personal and professional, and support them with the right work environment, including organization architecture, incentives, training, work engagement models, location, and productivity tools, etc. Successful startups establish the right culture and environment for their employees to thrive and often cross-train them to hedge against employee attrition. It is easier said than done and often large organizations struggle to change their course and they run into the chicken and egg dilemma with onboarding of talented employees and establishing the right work environment.

It is common that talented employees have unique expectations when it comes to where and who they want to work for. They are influenced by their demography and personal situations as well. One size does not fit all, hence it is paramount to understand what an individual employee needs and to customize the employment offerings that align with their expectations. For example, providing a subsidized daycare facility for employees' young children may not excite someone who is either a single or does not have kids so would therefore not benefit from such amenities.

3.6 Concluding remarks

Although businesses and customers benefit from innovation opportunities, there are numerous challenges to overcome. The triangular dilemma seen by businesses from market, organizational, and stakeholder are not uncommon, but the approach to deal with them in the context of globalization, digital penetration, mushrooming startup

Challenges embracing innovation 35

culture, ever-demanding consumer preferences, and connected customers requires a fundamental shift in how businesses are led and managed.

Boundaries are becoming blurred between customers and competitors. New entrants muscle their way into any industry segment regardless of their pedigree through M&A and technology is taking center stage. Technology giant Apple foraying into automotive; startup SpaceX conquering space, which was traditionally the stronghold of NASA in the US; online retailer Amazon pushing its boundaries far beyond retail and into health care and webservices; Airbnb, another startup, challenging the status quo in the hospitality segment and going head to head with incumbents such as Hinton and Marriott; these are just a few observations that force us to revisit our orthodoxies and reframe our approach to lead and innovate our businesses.

The good news is that if the businesses adapt to the new reality and put in place the right tools, processes, culture, and leadership to innovate, and evolve their businesses, success can be assured. We will discuss our TRIAL© [22] innovation and VASTEFA© [23] leadership frameworks in subsequent chapters.

Student activities

1. Select the FedEx and Reliance cases from Part VIII.
2. Review the details and list the problems or issues they try to address.
3. Discuss the organizational approach, leadership style, and the tools/technology they used. Leverage any updated online resources to supplement the information provided in the cases.
4. Also answer the questions listed at the end of the cases.

References

1. https://en.wikipedia.org/wiki/Carl_Benz
2. www.history.com/topics/inventions/model-t
3. https://money.cnn.com/2009/09/18/technology/google_display_ads/index.htm?postversion=200909181
4. www.cnbc.com/2017/06/13/verizon-completes-yahoo-acquisition-marissa-mayer-resigns.html
5. www.statista.com/statistics/266206/googles-annual-global-revenue/
6. www.statista.com/statistics/266249/advertising-revenue-of-google/
7. www.amazon.com/b?ie=UTF8&node=16008589011
8. www.marketwatch.com/story/how-amazon-created-aws-and-changed-technology-forever-2019-12-03
9. https://en.wikipedia.org/wiki/Pixar
10. Thomas J. Graham (Ed). "Innovation the Cleveland Clinic Way: Powering Transformation by Putting Ideas to Work." Chapter 4. McGraw-Hill, 2018.
11. www.bbc.com/news/technology-23947212
12. https://thenextweb.com/apps/2010/12/29/10-best-productivity-apps-of-2010/
13. www.newyorker.com/business/currency/where-nokia-went-wrong
14. www.helsinkitimes.fi/business/16809-whatever-happened-to-nokia-the-rise-and-decline-of-a-giant.html

36   *"What" – Introduction to innovation*

15. en.wikipedia.org/wiki/SpaceX
16. www.sciencemag.org/news/2020/05/doubts-greet-12-billion-bet-united-states-corona-virus-vaccine-october
17. www.nytimes.com/2020/07/22/us/politics/pfizer-coronavirus-vaccine.html
18. www.npr.org/2020/03/31/824431240/trump-administration-weakens-auto-emissions-rolling-back-key-climate-policy
19. www.isc.hbs.edu/competitiveness-economic-development/frameworks-and-key-concepts/pages/the-diamond-model.aspx
20. https://interestingengineering.com/the-origin-story-of-silicon-valleyand-why-we-shouldnt-try-to-recreate-it
21. Timothy J. Sturgeon, "How Silicon Valley Came To Be," in "Understanding Silicon Valley: Anatomy of an Entrepreneurial Region." Martin Kenney, (Ed.), Stanford University Press, 2000.
22. Vijay Pandiarajan, "TRIAL© Innovation Framework," WMBA Win 2021 Class Slides, Ross School of Business, The University of Michigan, 2021.
23. Vijay Pandiarajan, "VASTEFA© Leadership Framework,' WMBA Win 2021 Class Slides, Ross School of Business, The University of Michigan, 2021.

Part II
"Why" – Innovation imperatives

Chapter 4 Innovation: A key to business success 39

4 Innovation
A key to business success

4.1 Introduction

Businesses are at a crossroads and are forced to continuously assess whether the orthodoxies that brought them success in the previous era are still true and sustainable. Businesses are witnessing, on the one hand, some of their established peers either declaring bankruptcies at an accelerated pace or losing their relevance, and, on the other hand, some peers attempting to reinvent their businesses at breakneck speed to hold off competition from disrupters who epitomize innovation at the core of everything they do. The reality is that tides are rising in the sea of industry and to lead and survive one must rise above the tide to gain control over the situation. Continuous innovation in product, process, organizational architecture, and business models to engage and excite ever-changing customer expectations is the new normal. The status quo is simply not going to make it.

4.2 New economic paradigm

The world population has more than doubled in the last six decades from 3 to 7.8 billion from 1960 to 2020 and is expected to reach a whopping 9.9 billion by 2050, an increase of 25% [1]. Innovations in basic science and health care have steadily increased life expectancy. The global middle class is on the rise with an exponential demand for newer products with rich personal experiences. Technology innovations, particularly in the digital space, in the past few decades have made huge strides in connecting the global societies, raising consumer expectations [2] and are unstoppable. However, the social, economic, and environmental challenges are taking center stage – the rising inequality between the world's rich and poor, uneven debt crises, trade deficits between nations, power struggles among many nations, and relentless and unabated depletion of natural resources and environmental pollution at the expense of ecological balance. The situation is simply daunting and appears insurmountable. The good news is that there is a growing awareness among societies of these challenges, and digital innovations such as social media can amplify such concerns and priorities for the common good of everyone. For businesses to be successful and relevant, they need to recognize the new reality of the world and must reinvent themselves constantly to meet the ever-changing expectations and concerns of their customers, including the societal and personal values they uphold.

DOI: 10.4324/9781003190837-6

4.3 Consumers are changing

We live in a completely different world compared to the one we inherited a few decades ago. The new-age customers, for example, millennials (born between 1981 and 1997) and Gen Z (born between 1997 and 2012), are more experience-focused than product-focused and tend to exhibit less loyalty to a particular company. Deloitte's study [3] attributes this to evolving changes to the environment they live in. Burdened by economic pressures, including education, healthcare, and lifestyle choices, they seek purchasing options and usage flexibility in the marketplace to meet their personal needs. Given the technology revolution that we witness, an abundance of options is presented to them that did not exist before. For example, constrained by car ownership challenges in the urban cities, the new-age customers use ride-hailing services such as Lyft, Uber, or Didi, which are inexpensive and convenient. Similarly, they leverage Airbnb for short-term stays, perhaps for a small group social outing, instead of seeking expensive full-service traditional hotels. The well-accepted practice of the ownership model is taking a back seat to the new and evolving utility or subscription model – "pay as you use." The bottom line is that consumers are changing, their demands are evolving, and the businesses are taking notice of those changes.

4.4 Competitive landscape changes

In the last few decades, the competitive landscape has transformed significantly, [4] influenced by rapid globalization, the increased role of technology at the core of products and services, a knowledge-based economy, and exponential growth in the adoption of high-bandwidth internet access. Taking a chapter from Porter's Five Forces framework [5], the number and power of a company's rivals, new entrants, suppliers, customers, and alternative products have become uncertain. The market does not offer stability for incumbent businesses, and technology innovations have diminished entry barriers for new competition or alternative products in less capital-intensive markets.

The organizational boundaries are becoming blurred as the term "coopetition" (compete as well as cooperate) is taking a new meaning for businesses to survive and thrive [6]. No one company can claim to capture value from the entire value chain, now morphed into ecosystems. Product and service bundles and platforms are the new reality, and organizations continuously rearchitect their business models to stay relevant to their customers. Interdependency between businesses could be healthy if they are built on the foundation of mutual trust. For example, Apple, as it allows its software partners to develop and deploy mobile applications through its App Store for the end users to consume, takes 30% standard commission from in-app purchases of digital goods [7]. Similar models exist for other ecosystems as well. The value capture mutually benefits all the parties. However, for example, in the process of selling products on Amazon's e-commerce platform, many third-party vendors are often surprised to see Amazon' own products competing with them soon after their products are brought to the platform [8].

Protecting one's own intellectual property has become a challenge with these less demarcated business boundaries. Also, there is an emerging trend where the new entrants or startups get swallowed, often by established firms if they have the financial muscle power. Facebook acquiring WhatsApp and Instagram is a great example that

Innovation – A key to business success 41

benefited Facebook, but significantly diminished a healthy competition in the social media vertical [9]. In the healthcare industry, for example, hospitals that compete for patients, share patient health records with their competitors through an integrated electronic medical record framework consistent with the Health Insurance Portability and Accountability Act (HIPAA) standards, allowing for speedy and a continuity of patient care. This is a healthy coopetition where competition exists while cooperation is promoted, and where there is a common interest; that is, patient care. The businesses are at an inflection point to innovate with a sense of urgency to respond to this transformative competitive landscape change.

> "The Health Insurance Portability and Accountability Act of 1996 (HIPAA) is a federal law that required the creation of national standards to protect sensitive patient health information from being disclosed without the patient's consent or knowledge. The US Department of Health and Human Services issued the HIPAA Privacy Rule to implement the requirements of HIPAA. The HIPAA Security Rule protects a subset of information covered by the Privacy Rule."
>
> www.cdc.gov/phlp/publications/topic/hipaa.html

4.5 Shorter product life spans

As society grapples with social, economic, and environmental challenges while trying to enrich one's quality of life, personal growth, and financial freedom, newer opportunities for better products, services, and business models are recognized. This provides impetus for innovations in many facets of value creation in the market space. This quickly has a cascading effect on many industry verticals as the innovations in one industry vertical have the potential to disrupt products and services in other verticals, and the impacted businesses are forced to respond or incorporate such innovations. This creates a virtuous cycle of reinforcements, a symbiotic phenomenon, which encourages innovation in all related industries.

As speed to market is critical to gain first mover advantage, many corporations use agile methodologies to develop quickly minimum viable products (MVP) to gain customer confidence before optimizing and scaling them up. This in turn reduces the overall time taken for new products to reach the market from the incubator idea. Consumers, provided with many options available at the same time, are willing to try alternative products and services, unlike in the past. No one product or company can claim to be at the top of the consumer preference list for ever. The outcome of this phenomenon is shorter life span for products as the marketplace is crowded with me-too products.

This is further accentuated by digital marketing as the new-age consumers spend more time on social media platforms such as Facebook, Instagram, YouTube, WeChat, Tencent Weibo, and Snapchat, allowing such product and service options to be presented to them by marketers. No one needs to visit a shopping mall to learn about new products, and vendors do not need to have a physical store front to share product information with a customer. The market has no entry or consumption barriers, which was simply unheard of a decade ago. Given the hypercompetition and overall market uncertainties, both on the supply and demand front, the pressure is simply mounting

42 *"Why" – Innovation imperatives*

on existing businesses to constantly innovate and keep their products and services fresh and updated.

4.6 Globalization vs localization

Corporations, small and large, find themselves at the intersection of global commerce, facilitated by technology innovations. Merchants, regardless of their size, are now promoting and selling their products on popular global platforms such as Amazon, Shopify, Etsy, BigCommerce, Magento, WooCommerce, Alibaba, Tencent, eBay, etc. The businesses that traditionally focused on local market opportunities are unchained and are free to scale up at a pace they could never dream of in the past. The traditional value chain functions such as planning, manufacturing, supply chain logistics, order management, and finance, are made easy with digital orchestration and distribution leveraging support services from global ecosystems. For example, small flower producers in Mexico or Chile can connect with global customers in the US, Canada, and China without having to worry about some of the local logistics to deliver the products to the customers. An estimated $900M worth of fish, from tilapia to tuna, first caught in the US, are sent to China for processing and then imported back into the US companies to sell to consumers in the US [10].

Although the value chain appears to be very complex, it is made simple and coordinated by the participating agents leveraging digital assets. The newfound, yet growing commercial opportunities are incenting corporations to invest in innovation related to product, process, and business models to reach beyond their traditional markets, and the status quo is not withstanding this emerging trend. If the businesses do not respond to this trend and do not participate in the new global business framework, they may struggle to get ahead or may even be out of existence sooner rather than later.

4.7 Digital tsunami

Since the advent of the digital economy at the beginning of the 21st century, driven by the deluge of digital innovations such as the high-speed internet and accentuated by mobile computing, micro services, big data, cloud infrastructure, AI, and machine learning, the world has changed forever. We are experiencing a mushroom impact of the digital innovations on all segments of our global economy. Businesses across the globe consider this new realm a digital tsunami and are intrigued; many are desperate to participate. Customers are connected and are empowered with their voices heard, thanks to the social media platforms. Their product reviews are far more sought after and relevant for new customers than the producers' description of products. Product comparisons are made in real time with relative ease from home, sometimes by pajama shoppers, and often user experience is weighed higher in many of the purchasing decisions.

Producers, to some extent, have become bystanders after launching their products as the install base (customers who have their products) is in the driver seat to promote or drive out their products. However, global corporations such as Apple, Estée Lauder, Nike, and Starbucks, are leading the charge by regaining control over their offerings through innovations and immersing themselves in the trenches of where customers operate. Excessive customer obsession in their agile business model with the ability to orchestrate a business strategy that incorporates cross-industry digital trends to connect and coexist with their customers are benefiting them.

As scary as it looks, the digital tsunami certainly provides an immense opportunity for businesses to broaden their horizon and understand their customers better than before, to craft and deliver solutions that can delight their customers and maintain a loyal following.

4.8 Technology shaping the business core

Technology is at the front and center of what businesses do today and there is no denial. However, there are many businesses that continue to keep technology departments as a service arm and not an integral part of their business. Often, technology groups are at the receiving end rather than being at the initial stage of crafting business strategy. This grossly undermines how technology can influence a business strategy and possibly diminishes the value proposition. At the least, there ought to be a seat at the strategy table for technologists.

There are some exceptions, where the product itself is a technology product. For example, infotainment in an automotive company obviously involves a technical platform and technology is an integral part of strategy development. However, developing a strategy for example to provide same-day delivery to customers of an existing product may involve a technology team at the tail end of business team discussions, just for technology enablement during implementation. This perhaps has the potential to ignore some of the cost-effective business scenarios. In the above example, the strategists may elect to use an existing central warehouse to ship out products, which may involve more resources while being expensive, and perhaps with shipping delays as the customer geography is far off from the warehouse.

In our own personal experience at a major telecom corporation, for same-day delivery strategy development, first of its kind in the telecom industry in North America, our corporate business team was open and inclusive from the get-go, allowing the technology team to influence the business strategy. The tech team demonstrated the same-day delivery feasibility to use local retail stores as a micro warehouse, numbering more than 2,500 stores, instead of a centralized warehouse, based on online customer order ZIP codes. This proved to be effective and inexpensive, allowing simple adjustments to the e-commerce portal and local point of sale system (POS) system, with an added training for store personnel on web order processing, including pick, pack, and ship, while preserving brand consistency in the quality of customer shipments. This is a great example of how technologists can shape a business strategy as technology opens new possibilities for doing business.

4.9 Dynamic capabilities

The literature is overwhelmed with the scholarship on the dynamic capabilities topic, and it has always been the cornerstone of success for many organizations. Kathleen Eisenhardt and Jeffrey Martin define dynamic capabilities as "The firm's processes that use resources – specifically the processes to integrate, reconfigure, gain, and release resources – to match and even create market change. Dynamic capabilities thus are the organizational and strategic routines by which firms achieve new resource configurations as markets emerge, collide, split, evolve, and die [11]." From

44 *"Why" – Innovation imperatives*

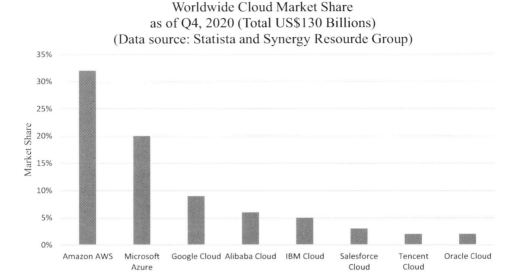

Figure 4.1 Worldwide cloud market share [12].

an innovation standpoint, just traditional organizational resources alone (human resources, materials, production machinery, manufacturing factories, etc.), cannot guarantee an effective innovation outcome. It is more than organizational resources and must include dynamic capabilities or the internal processes as well. The dynamic capabilities ought to be carefully planned, nurtured, implemented, and continuously calibrated to harness the value of organizational resources in the pursuit of innovation – whether products or process or business models.

As the name implies, dynamic capabilities must be agile and market sensitive. Organizational dynamic capabilities must align and adjust proactively to market dynamics so that time-sensitive innovation initiatives can be orchestrated to gain competitive advantage. Culture plays a critical role as well and augments dynamic capabilities. Innovation is a team effort and orchestrating a culture that fosters innovation by challenging and supporting creativity in the organizational context is a prerequisite to success.

AWS is a great example of how Amazon was able to leverage its dynamic capabilities to tap into the potential cloud market, which was considered impractical in 2006 by its competitors, including Microsoft, Google, and IBM. As illustrated in Figure 4.1, AWS is still leading this nascent market with a market share of more than 32% because of its first mover advantage and literally monopolized the market for the first six years without any competition.

4.10 Concluding remarks

Businesses have experienced mixed success during the first quarter of 21st century. It started off with remnants of the dot-com bubble, followed by a financial crisis between 2007 and 2008, and most recently the COVID-19 global pandemic. Major bankruptcies and industry consolidations exposed many businesses to their vulnerabilities, and they reinforced the need to be agile, resilient, and innovative. As many failed businesses made it to the list of underachievers, there are good number of businesses that have demonstrated their innovative prowess, resilience, and success with a growth never seen before. Amazon, Whirlpool, Alibaba, Microsoft, Nike, Walmart, Home Depot, Apple, Alphabet, Tencent, Taiwan Semiconductor Manufacturing Co. (TSMC), Toyota, and Samsung are just a few that are recognized as innovation leaders for their audacity to constantly reinvent themselves to be relevant to their customers through their innovative products, processes, and service possibilities.

In our research, we observe that the above successful companies understand the impact of innovation on their market performance and have carefully architected their internal dynamic capabilities, culture, and leadership models while leveraging technology to its fullest potential at every facet of their organization. They are not introverts but are extroverts. They actively collaborate with both their customers and partners and do not miss a beat of their ecosystem. This allows them to calibrate and innovate their offerings proactively so that they are only disrupted by themselves rather than by competitors or entrants.

Student activities

1. Select Microsoft and Apple cases from Part VIII.
2. Review the details and list the problems or issues they try to address.
3. Discuss the organizational approach and the tools/technology they used.
4. Also answer the questions listed at the end of the case.

4.11 References

1. www.prb.org/2020-world-population-data-sheet/
2. https://sustainabledevelopment.un.org/content/documents/617BhutanReport_WEB_F.pdf
3. www2.deloitte.com/us/en/insights/industry/retail-distribution/the-consumer-is-changing.html
4. Abby Ghobadian, Nicholas O'Regan, Howard Viney, and David Gallear, "Creating Value in the New Competitive Landscape," in "Strategy and Performance," Palgrave Macmillan, London, 2004, https://doi.org/10.1057/9780230523135_1
5. www.isc.hbs.edu/strategy/business-strategy/Pages/the-five-forces.aspx
6. https://hbr.org/2021/01/the-rules-of-co-opetition
7. www.theverge.com/21445923/platform-fees-apps-games-business-marketplace-apple-google
8. www.cnbc.com/2020/04/23/wsj-amazon-uses-data-from-third-party-sellers-to-develop-its-own-products.html
9. https://screenrant.com/facebook-whatsapp-purchase-date-cost/
10. www.wsj.com/articles/u-s-seafood-industry-vulnerable-to-tariffs-aimed-at-china-1533812400
11. Kathleen M. Eisenhardt and Jeffrey A. Martin, "Dynamic Capabilities: What Are They?" Strategic Management Journal Strat. Mgmt. J., 21: pp. 1105–1121 (2000).
12. www.statista.com/chart/18819/worldwide-market-share-of-leading-cloud-infrastructure-service-providers/

Part III
"Where" – Sources of innovation

Chapter 5 Sources of innovation   49

5 Sources of innovation

5.1 Introduction

As discussed before, the term innovation has been popular the past few decades and many businesses consider this as a panacea to solve all their problems. There are new organizational roles such as chief innovation officer being created at many organizations. Unfortunately, without an innovation strategy and disciplined approach, the full potential of what innovation can offer is difficult to materialize and sustain. Having the desire to achieve innovation results is not enough and it is critical to answer questions on "where" and "how" before committing resources and initiating innovation projects. In our research we find that innovation initiatives fail for lack of a comprehensive understanding of the task and a well-crafted upfront strategy. In this chapter, we analyze the question "where" in the form of sources of innovation to establish an opportunity set for businesses to navigate and prioritize innovation initiatives. The next chapter is dedicated to the larger question of "how" to achieve innovation.

We propose The Enterprise Innovation Opportunities Model© [1]as presented in in Figure 5.1 to capture possible innovation sources within the extended enterprise ecosystem and discuss a few highlights from this model in subsequent sections. These sources themselves may be an opportunity to innovate to advance the organizational innovation agenda in the form of product, process and business model.

5.2 Corporate research and development

In a traditional business setting, the corporate R&D group takes the lead role to initiate and manage innovation. Of course, there are different R&D models, fully centralized or partially decentralized to leverage resource concentration at distributed locations. Longer-term strategic initiatives involving the development of a new product line or new platform for next-generation products typically leverage centralized models. Internal corporate funding models allocate budgets, and efforts are coordinated centrally for such longer-term projects. Regional business units may lead some of the operational or tactical innovation projects, which may involve corporate resources and expertise.

It is also customary for business units to support corporate R&D efforts, such as in Siemens [2], where the business unit is a direct beneficiary of the results. However, corporate R&D is gaining increasing notoriety for its inefficiency. For example, big life sciences companies such as Pfizer, Bristol-Myers Squibb, GlaxoSmithKline, and

DOI: 10.4324/9781003190837-8

50 "Where" – Sources of innovation

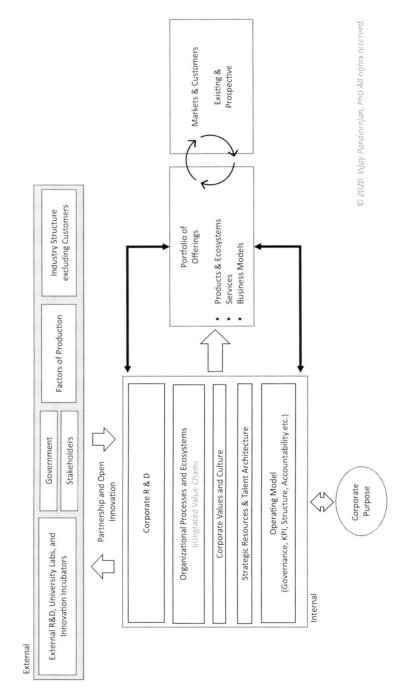

Figure 5.1 Enterprise Innovation Opportunities Model© [1].

AstraZeneca [3] that historically depended on corporate R&D, are hamstrung by bureaucracy with a layered management structure and legacy HR processes that stifle the innovation outcome [4], particularly when they are challenged by upstart entrepreneurial biotech firms.

The key for success at central R&D is to de-layer the organization, empower, employees and promote entrepreneurial culture, develop satellite facilities across its global footprint that are closer to the market and customers, and foster company-wide collaboration through agile processes. The McKinsey survey on R&D, which received input from more than 1,000 executives, echoed that sentiment of cross-collaboration for efficient innovation outcomes and to bridge the gap between recognizing market priorities and what is being done internally [5]. Corporate R&D is still vital for strategic innovation pursuits and can be reconfigured and repurposed with significant economies of scale across many distributed business units. Resources can be optimized by eliminating pockets of reinvention through knowledge sharing and seamless coordination. With the right culture, incentive systems, metrics, and an integrated digital platform such as internal social media, corporate-wide collaboration can reestablish strongly the role of corporate R&D [6]. They could serve as test beds for regional innovation initiatives as well to make sure that entire ecosystem resources and expertise are leveraged to mitigate knowledge gaps within the enterprise.

5.3 Organizational processes and ecosystems – Integrated value chain

For product innovations, corporate R&D is the right place to start with, although there could be opportunities in other areas within the enterprise. However, for enterprise process innovations, the natural landing place is the ecosystem or the integrated value chain functional domains where the organizational processes are managed and executed. Garvin defines organizational processes as collections of tasks and activities that together transform inputs into outputs [7].

Whether it is human resource management, forecasting, sales and operations planning, manufacturing, procurement, warehouse management, inventory management, plant maintenance, quality management, or sales/marketing, the underlying processes to develop and deliver the company offerings to its customers are a great source of innovations, particularly when there are shrinking resources and advancement in technology. After all, they constitute the dynamic capabilities the organization needs to compete in the marketplace. The innovations in the process domain could have significant potential for cost savings, increased sales, agile response to customers, and improved customer experience.

Enterprise processes allow and connecting with customers directly. Any reduction in customer friction as they navigate transacting with the business will create a satisfied and loyal customer base. For example, in the mobile application-enabled business transaction framework, businesses replace the legacy practice of requiring cash or other credit cards during the checkout process with frictionless sale by pre-storing the payment methods or enabling mobile scan. Amazon Go and ride-hailing services such as Uber or Lyft use such automated checkout techniques, which are considered process innovations. Technology enablers have the potential to integrate fragmented processes across the organizational landscape and optimize them for coordinated operational performance using a centralized common data source.

52 "Where" – Sources of innovation

The ecosystems embody both internal and external value chain functions. While internal value chain functions have better visibility, control, and are easier to drive innovations, external value chain functions generally tend to present challenges as there are more uncontrollable variables one needs to worry about such as industry standards and external partner constraints.

Regardless, the ecosystems present never-ending opportunities to innovate and realize improved organizational performance and customer experience.

5.4 Corporate values and culture

Corporate values and culture are not simply a set of banners and slogans along with many other dust-collecting wall posters for organizations to show pride. If correctly conceived and internalized through innovation, they are powerful instruments for employees and partners to have a collective identity, a feeling of having connected with the organization's mission and empowerment, a sense of pride, and help drive a certain organizational behavior, to work in unison to achieve organizational goals.

Corporate values are highly debated and analyzed both in academia and industry, but they are essentially organizational philosophies, beliefs, and principles [8] that serve as a guard rail as the organization engages in delivering value to its customers while competing in the marketplace and conforming to the expectation of its stakeholders.

Corporate culture is again one of the organizational management topics well researched and documented, but with various interpretations and prescriptions. Merriam-Webster defines culture as "the set of shared attitudes, values, goals, and practices that characterizes an institution or organization." The definition is simple, yet it is one of the most difficult topics for organizations to develop, manage, and adjust to in the environment they operate.

Patrick Lencioni, in his extensive industry engagement [9], finds that there is a disconnect between what is branded as values and what is really practiced. Poorly conceived and practiced corporate values statements have the potential to create dispirited, distrustful, and disloyal employees and undermine business credibility at all levels, both within and outside. This is antithetical to innovation aspirations and requires a serious introspection.

Lencioni suggests four imperatives as organizations define and develop values: 1. Understand the different types of values: core, aspirational, permission-to-play, and accidental; 2. Be aggressively authentic; 3. Own the process; and 4. Weave core values into everything.

The top four corporations of the 50 most innovative companies, Alphabet, Amazon, Microsoft, and Samsung, in the BCG's analysis in 2020 [10] all have one thing in common – a genuine and sincere embodiment of core values in their organizational culture and day-to-day practice with an obsession for customer delight through innovation. Does it mean they found the right recipe for innovation success? Not necessarily, but they are on the right trajectory, which may require some course correction along the way with a dynamic closed feedback loop with all the stakeholders.

Innovation leaders are actively transforming and innovating their corporate culture to support entrepreneurship-based innovation. They are rushing to Silicon Valley to learn what is under the hood at many of the entrepreneurship firms that thrive on innovating new products, business capabilities, and business models. Procter

Sources of innovation 53

& Gamble (P&G), known for its innovation prowess, is no exception as it had to reinvent itself again. In 2016, it took some of its senior leaders on a tour to Silicon Valley to understand first-hand lean startup and the entrepreneurial ecosystem from the source. When they returned, they initiated a program called GrowthWorks – a new way of problem-solving to meet customer demands. The idea was how to innovate with metered funding, accelerate innovation through MVP while engaging customers in a closed loop, approach innovation with a problem mindset instead of solution mindset, and foster an entrepreneurial culture where small yet cohesive teams with mixed skills work toward a faster outcome while taking on risky bets without the fear of losing their jobs [11]. Consulting firms such as Bionic helped corporations to adopt lean innovation principles using proprietary methods that unleashes organizations that suffer from internal frictions.

Approaching innovation with an entrepreneurship mindset and developing a culture and operating model that is conducive, corporations of all sizes can rediscover their innovation mojo and spawn innovation once again [12].

5.5 Partnership and open innovation

It is simply insane for anyone to think that organizations can manage innovations all by themselves and do not need any partners or external input. There used to be a corporate firewall not long ago to keep corporate innovation pursuits within the organization's four walls and this was limited to badged employees only. Xerox and Kodak just two examples of organizations that truly believed in closed innovations, like many organizations after World War II, and they succeeded for quite some time. However, things started to change, given that we now live in the connected world and knowledge sharing has become an imperative for both personal and business purposes.

Particularly after witnessing the technology innovations spearheaded by IBM, Apple, Microsoft, Google, Netflix, etc. at warp speed, a whole new set of characteristics has come to define the innovation environment (tech and non-tech alike) – entrepreneurial mindset, fail-fast discovery, spontaneous association, nonlinear collaboration, risk taking, and customer obsession. Traditional organizational models do not even come close to these prerequisites – traditional models are inflexible, riddled with layered bureaucracy, title and power-hungry leadership, asymmetrical reward systems, risk-averse portfolio management, snail-paced liner discovery, and misaligned market focus. In the new trend of jump-starting innovation, more organizations are looking beyond their corporate boundaries and planting seeds for an extended ecosystem, which allows outside partners and innovators to collaborate with them for mutual benefits. After Prof. Henry Chesbrough introduced Open Innovation to the world in 2006, corporations have been racing to add the missing puzzle in their quest to innovate new products, business processes, and business models [13].

There are numerous examples that illustrate the profound impact of open innovation on a business.

LEGO® created an open innovation platform called LEGO® Ideas in 2008 and has generated several popular LEGO® sets, including Central Perk, Big Bang Theory, and Adventure Time [14, 15]. These were successful in capturing trends and prevailing culture from a different customer demography, which otherwise would not have been addressed by LEGO®'s internal staff.

54   *"Where" – Sources of innovation*

Samsung is another well-respected innovation leader that leverages external partnership and open innovation to augment internal product initiatives. Samsung, well known for their hardware prowess, is foraying into the software arena for a more immersive customer experience. It has organized innovation opportunities identification and execution under the arm Samsung NEXT within Samsung Electronics. Recognizing the need of the hour, Samsung NEXT, unlike Samsung Electronics, is built on the theme of entrepreneurship and has assembled an impressive executive team, comprising founders, investors, engineers, designers, strategists, and product managers [16]. Samsung NEXT is approaching innovation through four distinct focus areas: NEXT Product, Ventures, Mergers & Acquisitions, and Partnerships. The new model allows investing in external early-stage startups, acquiring promising complementary growth plays, and leveraging design development synergy through external partnership. This new approach allows Samsung to deliberately challenge the ingrained bureaucratic culture at the parent electronics division with a "garage mindset" of entrepreneurs from the extended ecosystem.

Partnership with government could be another source of innovation. Government's role is typically seen in enacting policy guidelines that foster innovation for national priorities, providing expertise and support structure, including measured funding [17, 18]. In the US, for example, "Nearly a third of US patents rely directly on US government-funded research," says Dennis A. Yao, Professor of Business Administration at Harvard Business School. The government funding has increased fivefold in the last half a century, from less than $20B to more than $100B a year, and it has plateaued now. On the other hand, corporate R&D funding for innovation has been steadily rising, accounting for more than 69% of all R&D spending, while the US government hovers around 22.5%, according to the Congressional Research Service. One of the ways to measure how the government funding fuels innovation is by analyzing the number of patents filed with agencies such as the US Patent and Trademark Office, which now allows patent filers' acknowledgments in its database. Defense Advanced Research Project Agency, National Science Foundation, NASA, or the National Institutes of Health, Department of Defense's Small Business Innovation Research and Small Business Technology Transfer initiatives are just a few that are often acknowledged for having funded the patents filed by academic institutions, private citizens, and private and publicly traded corporations.

In the space exploration vertical, the US government prioritized government/private partnership and invested more than $7.2B on 67 space companies between 2000 and 2018 with a sole purpose of fostering innovation to bring the cost down for future space exploration. These companies also received technical expertise from NASA, which was acknowledged by SpaceX's CEO Elon Musk when his company launched its first Dragon cargo capsule to the International Space Station in 2012. SpaceX had a budget of $1B during its first decade of operation, and NASA chipped in almost half of that according to the Space Angels report [19, 20]. The interesting development is that once these entrepreneurs get seed money from the government and make progress on their innovation, they can attract significant private capital from other sources, including venture capital firms. SpaceX is now valued at $74B [21] and the US Government played a significant role in its innovation success.

Another prime example for government-funded innovation is how the COVID-19 pandemic caused the US and German governments to fund and accelerate the vaccine discovery at R&Ds such as Moderna and BioNTech. Moderna received over $2.5B from the US government part of the Warp Speed program and BioNTech received $445M from the German government [22, 23].

5.6 Strategic resources and talent architecture

Resource-based theory suggests that strategic resources are the ones that competitors cannot readily acquire. Typically, strategic resources are rare, extremely valuable, difficult to imitate, and cannot be substituted [24]. To gain competitive advantage on the innovation front, businesses must own strategic resources. This could be intellectual property rights, special processes or techniques, access to rare raw materials, talent pool, etc.

For innovation, the strategic talent pool is the one that is creative, shares organizational vision and values, and is committed to succeed. It could be subject matter experts, architects, designers, problem solvers, or effective story tellers. The strategic talent pool may sound replicable, but if we insert context or the competitive domain, they may be unique, which is a competitive advantage. We have seen such individuals across many industry landscapes during our consulting engagements and, interestingly, their senior leadership recognizes them and makes sure they are inserted where necessary to drive critical innovation outcomes. They are not the same as HIPPO (the Highest Paid Person's Opinion), but are driven, results-focused, and team players.

To sustain innovation success, such resources need to be managed carefully and hence the strategic talent architecture is crucial. Often, organizations are content with onboarding key talent that could become strategic resource over time but fail to nurture their personal and professional aspirations. Given the hypercompetition for talents, there is a huge risk of losing them to a competitor if their individual needs are not met. It could be as simple as having their voices heard, having the right reporting structure, providing necessary training opportunities to develop their professional skills, organizational succession planning with the right roadmap, establishing complementary talents to drive innovation results, etc. This essentially leads to planning and executing the right talent architecture that is adaptive to the situation on the ground, both within and outside, to make sure that strategic resource is engaged and productive. They are a great source of innovation if approached carefully as they have the potential to spot opportunities and develop ideas or solutions either as an individual or a team, and cascade them within a larger organizational setting. It is imperative that organizations recognize such resources as they embark on the innovation journey.

5.7 Operating model (governance, KPI, structure, accountability, etc.)

It is not uncommon to get different answers from business leaders to a simple question: What is an operating model? Often leaders are focused on their specific assigned areas and it is difficult for them to see the enterprise in its entirety. Per Deloitte, the operating model represents how value is created by an organization and by whom [25]. We would further add that it should include for whom the value is created and how the value is captured. This assumes what the value is, which is typically a solution to either an internal or external customer problem in the form of a product, a process, or a service. Successful businesses develop high-level business strategies, and execute them flawlessly. These strategies could be for five-year or ten-year horizons and may vary depending on the context. The key for business success is how to execute the business strategy, which entails developing an operating model that consists of the organizational structure, performance measures, governance, and the accountability matrix to drive results and be compliant with local laws and industry standards.

As the marketplace changes, the operating model must adapt as well for the business to be relevant to its customers. Enron Corp, Pacific Gas & Electric Company, MCI, Lehman Brothers Holdings Inc., Washington Mutual Inc., SemGroup, L.P, Circuit City Stores Inc. [26, 27, 28], etc. declared bankruptcies as their operating models were not sensitive to marketplace changes and failed to adapt. Enron Corp had ethical issues as well, with questionable governance and lack of transparency of their accounting methods. In essence, these businesses were not sustainable because of poor operating models and were shunned by their customers and stakeholders alike. This reinforces the need for continuous calibration of the operating models for organizations to survive and thrive in the marketplace, taking continuous feedback from their stakeholders. It is not just product innovations that make an organization successful, but also the innovations within the operating model that are crucial for end-to-end business operations, both within and outside. Organizations need to balance product, process, and business model innovations with operating model innovation to be successful. An operating model is another source of innovation for organizations to consider.

5.8 Concluding remarks

As businesses set out to initiate and manage innovation, they must carefully consider the sources of innovation opportunities as depicted in the Enterprise Innovation Opportunities Model©. Given the limited resources to pursue any initiative, a prioritized approach will benefit the businesses. As suggested earlier, innovation is not a standalone activity and, within the context of extended enterprise, active coordination across multiple initiatives is a prerequisite to deliver value at speed and scale. The synergy helps to mitigate reinventing the wheel through knowledge sharing and minimizes the overall risk. Interestingly, in our research we find that innovation leaders significantly benefit from exploiting multiple sources of innovation simultaneously. SpaceX, for example, is involved in internal R&D-based innovation pursuits for affordable rocket launch while partnering with NASA, a US Government agency, learns from their extensive aerospace experience, and leverages their source of capital. In addition to intra-enterprise engagement, successful innovation companies have deliberately sought out young external ecosystem partners to bring a much-needed entrepreneurship and startup mindset to strengthen their internal innovation culture.

Student activities

1. Select P&G cases from Part VIII.
2. Review the details and list the problems or issues they try to address.
3. Discuss the source of innovation opportunity they pursued. Try to map it to the Enterprise Innovation Opportunities Model©. Use Case 16: Ecovative Design as a model where such mapping is illustrated.
4. Also answer the questions listed at the end of the case.

5.9 References

1. Vijay Pandiarajan, 2021, "The TRIAL© Framework Enterprise Innovation Opportunities Model©," WMBA 21Wint 2021 class notes, Ross School of Business, The University of Michigan.
2. Karim Lakhani, "Open Innovation at Siemens," (HBP – 9-613-100, March 2015).
3. https://en.wikipedia.org/wiki/Pharmaceutical_industry_in_the_United_Kingdom
4. Ken Banta and Jeff Karp, "Rescuing Scientific Innovation from Corporate Bureaucracy," Harvard Business Review, May 2020.
5. https://sloanreview.mit.edu/article/organizing-rd-for-the-future/
6. www.mckinsey.com/business-functions/strategy-and-corporate-finance/our-insights/building-an-r-and-d-strategy-for-modern-times
7. David A. Garvin, "The Processes of Organization and Management," MIT Sloan Management Review, July 15, 1998.
8. https://blog.smarp.com/the-importance-of-company-values
9. Patrick M. Lencioni, "Make Your Values Mean Something," Harvard Business Review, Jul 1, 2002.
10. www.forbes.com/sites/louiscolumbus/2020/06/28/the-most-innovative-companies-of-2020-according-to-bcg/?sh=495204532af3
11. Emily Truelove, Linda Hill, and Emily Tedards, "Kathy Fish at Procter & Gamble: Navigating Industry Disruption by Disrupting from Within," HBP, 9-421-012, July 10, 2020.
12. Eric Ries, "The Lean Startup: How Today's Entrepreneurs Use Continuous Innovation to Create Radically Successful Businesses," Currency, Illustrated edition, September 13, 2011.
13. Henry Chesbrough, "Open Innovation: The New Imperative for Creating and Profiting from Technology," Harvard Business Review Press; First Trade Paper edition (September 1, 2006).
14. www.onova.io/innovation-insights/four-examples-of-open-innovation
15. www.lego.com/en-us
16. www.samsungnext.com/leadership
17. www.innovations.harvard.edu/role-government-technology-innovation-insights-government-policy-energy-sector
18. https://hbswk.hbs.edu/item/government-funded-research-is-increasingly-funding-corporate-innovation
19. https://sbir.nasa.gov/content/publications
20. www.theverge.com/2019/6/18/18683455/nasa-space-angels-contracts-government-investment-spacex-air-force
21. www.cnbc.com/2021/02/16/elon-musks-spacex-raised-850-million-at-419point99-a-share.html
22. www.usatoday.com/story/news/factcheck/2020/11/24/fact-check-donations-research-grants-helped-fund-moderna-vaccine/6398486002/
23. www.bloomberg.com/news/articles/2020-11-09/pfizer-vaccine-s-funding-came-from-berlin-not-washington
24. https://open.lib.umn.edu/strategicmanagement/chapter/4-2-resource-based-theory/
25. www2.deloitte.com/content/dam/insights/us/articles/5078_architecting-an-operating-model/DI_architecting-an-operating-model.pdf
26. www.mondaq.com/unitedstates/insolvencybankruptcy/75260/the-year-in-bankruptcy-2008--part-2
27. http://content.time.com/time/specials/packages/article/0,28804,1841334_1841431_1902021,00.html
28. https://busmuseum.org/wp-content/uploads/2018/07/BMNews-100108.pdf

Part IV

"How" – Approach to advance innovation

Chapter 6 Framework-based innovation approach   61

6 Framework-based innovation approach

6.1 Introduction

In the previous chapters, we reviewed innovation to answer the questions "what," "why" and "where." In this chapter, we address the most important question of "how", and students are introduced to the five-dimensional TRIAL© holistic innovation framework to advance innovation in a business context. Their understanding is further strengthened through a set of case studies of successful global corporations, such as Timberland, Samsung, Sun Pharmaceuticals, and Amazon, where the students can apply and practice the holistic framework either in individual or group settings. They will further learn how to manage and sustain innovation once initial groundwork is established.

The literature is inundated with several approaches to deal with the innovation issues discussed in the previous sections. For many organizations, often the challenge is where to start the innovation journey and how to persist when the organization is constantly adjusting and responding to its external environment, particularly to the changes to competitive contours, technological advancements, stakeholder dynamics, access to a qualified talent pool, customer expectations and the global macroeconomic landscape.

After an extensive study spanning a decade or more, we have come to believe that innovation is essentially a process that begins with TRIAL© or experiments comprising a set of coordinated activities to either improve an existing product, process, or service or to develop a new offering. The innovation could also simply be a business model focus, leveraging existing resources and infrastructure with some adaptation. Certainly, innovation is not a eureka moment and it takes time to realize as there are many iterations and stakeholder engagements, at least in the context of a business.

6.2 Innovation in action

For product innovation, Tesla is a great example for how an idea or concept is developed over a period through experiments or TRIAL©. Tesla's ability to develop its all-electric data-driven vehicles with great success did not happen overnight. It started off with a Roadster model prototype in 2006 by the founders Eberhard and Tarpenning after securing $30M investments from Elon Musk in 2004, and struggled to commercialize this model given the huge price tag of $100,000. Cash-strapped, Tesla received further investments in 2009 to the tune of $50m from Daimler AG in exchange for a 10% stake in the company [1], a $465M loan from the Department of Energy, $50M investment

© 2022 Vijay Pandiarajan   DOI: 10.4324/9781003190837-10

62   *"How" – Approach to advance innovation*

from Toyota in 2010 [2], and $226M through IPO in 2010. Through sustained experimental effort on battery technology, electric power transmission, dynamic suspension design, data-driven vehicle control, and other safety features, Tesla evolved its product offerings such as Model X, Model S, Model 3, Model Y, etc., to meet mass consumer expectations with different price points and charging ranges [3, 4].

For business model innovation, Apple, Uber, and Lyft are great examples. Apple charges premium for its iPhone products (on an average, these phones are priced at $600+) while exploiting distribution channel innovation, having the wireless carriers such as Verizon and AT&T to subsidize, either partially or completely, the products for end consumers to purchase with service contracts. This was a revolutionary idea, which was a non-starter for its competitors before [5]. This business model innovation proved the skeptics wrong as they second-guessed Apple's ability to sell its products at premium. The superiority of Apple products and its premium status convinced the carriers of the demand for Apple products, and they chose to subsidize the products while being creative in structuring the service contract to offset possible loss.

Uber and Lyft, ride-hailing companies, practically do not own any physical assets in terms of passenger vehicles or taxis on their balance sheet. However, their innovative business models are built on integrated technologies such as mobile platform, GPS, online payment system, and ride-sharing applications with a sophisticated machine-learning algorithm to manage dynamic demand and supply for given service levels. They eliminate customer friction points in transactions, and leverage third-party, driver-owned automobile assets to offer seamless experience and compelling business value to their consumers.

Uber's success did not happen overnight, as its founders Travis Kalanick and Garrett Camp conceived their ride-hailing idea when they could not get a ride on a cold winter evening in Paris during 2008. They soon developed and perfected a mobile application that would let people tap a button and get a ride immediately [6]. Lyft, on the other hand, started in 2007 by Logan Green and later joined by John Zimmer, in the name of Zimride, inspired by crowdsourced carpool networks in Zimbabwe, offered a long-distance ride-sharing service between college campuses [7] before evolving into Lyft, a short-haul ride-sharing company leveraging a mobile application-based passenger ride request. It took the founders more than a decade, multiple rounds of millions of dollars of investment from Coatue, Alibaba, Andreessen Horowitz, Rakuten Inc., Carl Icahn, Didi Chuxing, and GM before going public in a 2019 IPO for $2.34B, and involved series of TRIAL©s to perfect its business models and service offerings to realize what we come to experience as Lyft.

Managers and business leaders who have responsibility to spearhead the innovation agenda in organizations need a simple yet comprehensive approach to both the creation of innovation mandates and in bringing them to fruition. TRIAL©, by nature, does not guarantee innovation results and, unlike physics or mathematical science where Force (F) = Mass (M) x Acceleration (A) or 1 + 2 = 3, one must be ready to embrace unexpected outcomes or failures along the way before the anticipated success is realized. Uncertainty is an inherent characteristic of innovation. However, persistent embrace of a disciplined organizational approach during the innovation journey could mitigate risks, and a positive outcome is feasible.

In researching and analyzing many successful as well as less successful organizations across multiple industry verticals for innovation efforts, we recognize some themes and patterns emerging, which guide us to develop a framework for a disciplined approach to decode the mystery and improve the odds of innovation success. There are reasons why certain organizations such as Google, Apple, Tesla, Amazon, Lego, Netflix, P&G, etc. are perennial innovators and capitalize on the innovation outcomes whereas others such as JC Penney, Harley-Davidson, Caterpillar, Nokia, IBM, Kodak, Sears, Hitachi, Toshiba, and Kohl's either flounder or lag the innovation leaders. This chapter proposes an innovative framework called TRIAL© to bring a structure and a comprehensive approach to enhance the efficiency of the innovation journey to achieve the targeted success.

6.3 Factors impacting innovation

Speaking of innovation challenges based on our discussion in the previous chapters, we can conveniently group them into two sets of factors: Exogenous and endogenous.

6.3.1 Exogeneous factors

Exogeneous factors as depicted in Figure 6.1 are difficult to control, being external to the organization and often its influence on these factors is partially uncertain. Such factors could include customers, competition, external supply chain, investors, government policies, and other ecosystem players.

6.3.2 Endogenous factors

In contrast, endogenous factors as depicted in Figure 6.2 are the ones within the direct control and influence of the organization. This typically includes employee diversity, workforce engagement models, leadership models, open innovation models, reward

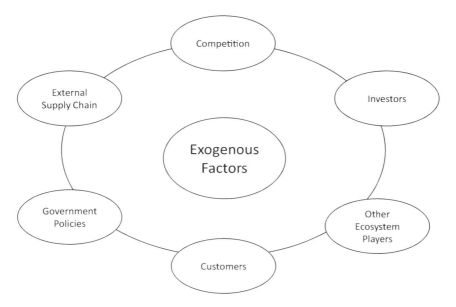

Figure 6.1 Exogeneous factors.

64 *"How" – Approach to advance innovation*

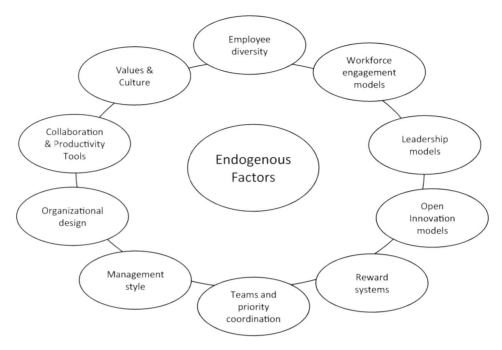

Figure 6.2 Endogenous factors.

systems, teams and priority coordination, management style, organizational design, collaboration and productivity tools, and values and culture.

As the old saying goes, a bird in the hand is worth two in the bush; since the exogenous factors are difficult to manage or control by the organization, we will only review the endogenous factors that the businesses can control for the TRIAL© [8] framework discussion to show how we can steer the innovation journey to success with examples.

6.4 TRIAL© holistic framework for innovation

The innovation process is typically driven by a bunch of repetitive activities, dependent or independent, either to develop a new product or process, improvising an already-existing product or process, deploying a new business model, or tweaking an existing business model. The key observation here is that the innovation process is iterative, nonlinear, and experimental-based, with or without external partnership, often with continuous outcome evaluation against preset metrics using a closed loop process, leading us to use the term TRIAL© for the framework [8] itself. We will explain the TRIAL© innovation framework in detail in the following paragraphs.

An example of exploring and innovating a new product is the new lithium-ion battery technology developed by Tesla by partnering with physicists from Canada's Dalhousie University [9]. Tesla recently filed a patent in the name of "Dioxazolones and nitrile sulfites as electrolyte additives for lithium-ion batteries" [10]. This innovation, once commercialized, is expected to offer more than a million-mile yield (miles) during the battery's life. The longevity of a battery is typically measured in terms of the number of discharge cycles, and one full discharge cycle is 100% of a battery's single charge amount (range). For Tesla Model S, it is claimed that a full single charge (one cycle) supports a range of approximately 370 miles. With a typical 100kWh lithium-ion battery found in a Tesla Model S, the maximum discharge cycle expected is 1,000–2,000 over the battery's lifetime, which on an average is approximately equivalent to 370 x 1,500 = 555,000 miles over 11–15 years of vehicle life. With the innovation of million-mile battery life, Tesla will be on a trajectory to capture a major automotive market share as its competitors are struggling to catch up with Tesla's current range of 220–370 miles battery offerings. Tesla set a high bar for itself and coordinated its organizational activities to achieve that hefty goal. It was an intense effort, which was iterative or TRIAL© process that included many interim milestones with some setbacks along the way, but in the end the innovation outcome is expected to be a success.

TRIAL© innovation framework, presented in Figure 6.3, represents disciplined and coordinated organizational effort on multiple dimensions that can contribute to a sustainable innovation outcome. This framework maps various organizational efforts depicted as endogenous factors in the vertical axis to TRIAL© dimensions on the horizonal axis.

The endogenous factors represent a generic business context and the weight or influence of these individual factors specific to a given TRIAL© dimension may vary depending on the business context and their unique configuration. The "X" notation indicates general relevance, and the intensity of the factor itself is denoted by multiple "Xs." For example, "Values & Culture" is relevant for all TRIAL© dimensions, except for "Technology & Tools." However, "Values & Culture" is more pronounced

Endogenous Factors	T	R	I	A	L
	Technology & Tools	Resources & Resilience	Inquisitive & Imaginative Culture	Achievement & Adaptability	Leadership & Latitude
Collaboration & Productivity Tools	XXX	X		X	X
Employee diversity		X	X	X	X
Workforce engagement models	X	X	X	X	X
Open Innovation models	XX	X	X	X	X
Reward systems		X	X	XXX	XX
Teams and priority coordination	X	XX	X	X	X
Values and Culture		X	XXX	XX	XXXX
Organizational design		X	X	X	X
Management style		XX	X	X	XXX
Leadership Models	X	X	XX	XX	XXXXX

Figure 6.3 TRIAL© framework.

"How" – Approach to advance innovation

for dimensions "Inquisitive & Imaginative Culture" ("XXX") and "Leadership & Latitude" ("XXXX") than other dimensions, "Resources & Resilience" ("X") and "Achievement & Adaptability" ("XX"). As the innovation journey is attempted, businesses may use this framework to assess and increase their maturity of the endogenous factors in their context relative to various TRIAL© dimensions. To bring a systematic approach to innovation, it is suggested that they follow the steps below:

1. Map all the endogenous factors to TRIAL© dimensions.
2. Assess the maturity of each of the endogenous factors and it is likely that all are required to support the TRIAL©-based innovation. Carefully exclude any mapping if it is not required – for example, Culture & Values is hard to map to Technology & Tools.
3. For your context, assess the intensity levels of these endogenous factors on the TRIAL© dimensions and represent them with "X" or "XX" or "XXX", etc. For example, "Management Style" is applicable to all the TRIAL© dimensions except "Technology & Tools," but its influence intensity is high on the "Resources & Resilience" and "Leadership & Latitude" dimensions, and hence more focus is needed to make sure management style is consistent with fostering innovation.
4. Prioritize the endogenous factors that need more efforts relative to baseline to satisfy TRIAL© dimensions.
5. Coordinate and balance such efforts before the innovation journey is initiated. For example, if "Leadership & Latitude" is more pronounced, it is important to have the right leadership in place that satisfies other expectations as well. Having the right leader certainly helps set the tone for the organization in its pursuit of successful innovation.

    Imagine Amazon without its leader Jeff Bezos or Tesla without Elon Musk. Many endogenous factors can be shaped and nurtured if the leadership is right and committed.
6. Repeat the process during the innovation journey and recalibrate and adjust the efforts as needed.

Note: Please access Digital Learning Resources provided with this book for TRIAL© framework worksheets that discuss with example the approach-as-is mapping with maturity levels, assessing intensity levels, prioritizing, and clustering TRIAL© dimensions for specific actions.

6.4.1 TRIAL© – Framework innovation dimensions

Innovation is not just about setting a goal and driving efforts to realize it. It requires well-coordinated and balanced planning to make sure certain critical prerequisites are in place before the innovation journey begins. To understand the prerequisites, we propose TRIAL© framework dimensions as illustrated in Figure 6.4, which are discussed below.

6.4.1.1 T – Technology & Tools

For innovation, technology and tools are central. Regardless of the industry vertical or the type of innovation initiatives, technology and tools have become the foundation for people to collaborate, share ideas, discuss solution options, and present critiques.

Figure 6.4 TRIAL© framework innovation dimensions.

- T Technology & Tools
- R Resources & Resilience
- I Inquisitive & Imaginative Culture
- A Achievement & Adaptability
- L Leadership & Latitude

Often, the human resources, both employees and contractors, in global organizations are dispersed across many geographies, particularly when the work-from-home model is widely adapted as in the response to the COVID-19 pandemic. It is becoming an acceptable norm to allow office workers, with some exception, to avail themselves of remote working possibilities and the emphasis is more on getting connected rather than being physically co-located. Having the right set of technology and tools to support and enable employee collaboration as well as remote access to corporate resources is critical for the innovation journey.

Technology and tools are equally indispensable when organizations orchestrate collaboration with external entities as they expand their organizational boundaries. Engaging vendors for product co-development, complying with government agencies for reporting, managing customer orders to glean customer perspectives, and integrating third-party logistics providers such as FedEx, UPS, USPS, and DHL, etc. are just a few examples of where technology and tools are much pronounced. Workforce collaboration and distributed teams are on steroids and the market trends driving them are many:

- Technology: Continuous connectivity, virtualization, social media, and augmented reality
- Business: Globalization, agility, hypercompetition, transparency, and risk mitigation
- Content: Video, blogs, Wiki, forums, internal social media, and spontaneous association
- Mobility: Bring your own device, work anywhere and on-demand, synchronous content, microservices, and application ecosystem

When organizations embark on innovation, it is paramount to address the technology and tools needs at the very beginning of the initiative. Business solutions and their architecture themselves often require technology components, not as a mere catalyst, but being part of solutions. Without due recognition of the role of technology and tools in the solution exploration, the solution options are rather limited. After all, our 21st century economy is technology-driven and everything revolves around technology. For example, in one of the Fortune 100 organizations that provides landline and wireless communication services and sells mobile phones and their accessories to its customers, we were exploring options to support same-day delivery of cell phones and related accessories to customers. Some of its customers, who had some unexpected phone

68 "How" – Approach to advance innovation

incidents such as broken phone or water damage, wanted replacement phones immediately. Some of these customers had certain medical conditions and functional phones could be lifesavers. Our internal technology group had its initial conversations with business counterparts, who requested same-day delivery need to support customer need. Soon, our technology group learned that the business had some predispositions on the technology landscape and its capabilities and had some incorrect assumptions. They were of the view that the existing technology simply could not support same-day delivery needs without extensive modifications or new enterprise software systems. Instead, they went ahead and pretty much framed the delivery solution options around business process changes with centralized warehouse planning and additional manpower. The solution options considered were expensive and complex, prone to human error, with no transparency across the supply chain. When we proposed technology-based solutions with simple changes to the existing order management system that leverages customer order-specific ZIP codes for nearby retail stores to be used as a micro distribution center by rerouting e-commerce orders for fulfillment, they simply could not believe it. After a few experiments and through active involvement of the business and training the retail store employees on how to process customer orders for pick, pack, and ship tasks, the business was ecstatic at the possibilities of technology. This innovation, although not leapforward or breakthrough in nature, did create the possibility to support a new business model; that is, same-day delivery, opening a new channel for both revenue generation and enhancing customer experience. As an industry-first service, we piloted them at several key markets to delight our customers.

The lessons learned here are bringing in technology discussion early, when innovation opportunity is explored. As a business leader, to support innovation, applying the TRIAL© framework begins with technology review. This has the potential to perhaps short-circuit a prolonged unproductive options analysis, often resulting in abandoned innovation effort because of delays and expensive alternatives that organizations cannot afford. Delayed innovation results in lost market opportunity and customer churn.

At McDonald's, the global fast food company, its partners are testing blockchain technology to increase traceability of meat from farm to table, which has significant implications for food safety and quality. During COVID-19, when social distancing was mandated, McDonald's further explored methods to leverage automation and robotics to assist its human workforce and improve their productivity and safety [11]. This illustrates yet another example of where technology-based innovations are critical to run the business effectively.

6.4.1.2 R - Resources & Resilience

At the heart of innovation are the creative or smart resources and their resilience. As innovation is a process, the path to success requires an audacity to not give up. Iterative experiments, alternatives evaluation, and learning from mistakes while redoubling the effort to achieve the desired outcome are valued as key success factors at storied innovators such as Starbucks, Apple, P&G, Facebook, Samsung, and Google. These characteristics embody resilience of an organization that is committed to succeed through innovation.

Innovation initiatives in organizations could either be a new program with a vision or goal, or an extension of existing programs with an ongoing goal or a mandate.

Regardless, identifying, onboarding, and nurturing key resources that would become part of the programs require a sustained effort and continuous evaluation of the program goals and objectives. It is rather easy to spot the resources for innovation efforts based on their academic qualifications, previous accomplishments, or demonstrable skills or training. However, if one were to limit the recruiting efforts to simply matching what is stated as hard skills, such as designing products or programming in certain computer languages such as JavaScript, Python, Java, or Swift, and not exploring one's other soft skills, including resilience, communication, social, and ability to persevere, or "grit", the recruiting effort is only partially complete, and it cannot guarantee innovation results.

Organizations are increasingly recognizing their recruiting gaps and have included techniques to assess communication and social skills. However, skills assessment related to resilience and ability to persevere are still lacking and often there are inadequate methods. This has been recognized but is hardly addressed because organizations refuse to give up old orthodoxies in their human resource practice. They are less convinced of the possibility that candidates' past failure experiences may benefit their organization in being innovative. For example, some old school businesses continue to incorrectly believe that failure to succeed is baggage and often during the hiring process they actively seek any missteps taken by the candidates in their current or previous jobs. This is often held against them instead of considering such failure to achieve certain results an opportunity to get better in future innovation efforts. Success by failure is not an oxymoron [12] and can truly benefit the innovation aspirations. Babies do not walk from day one. They crawl and walk, of course after falling many times. If the recruits have fallen before, We can be certain that they are well prepared to take on new challenges and opportunities with more confidence.

"I have not failed; I've just found ten thousand ways that won't work."
- Thomas Edison

It is also interesting see more than ever that organizations are reaching out to external sources in the form open innovation contest [13] as opposed to completely relying in internal resources, also called internal innovation, to complement internal resources. The differences are illustrated in Figure 6.5. In open innovation contest,

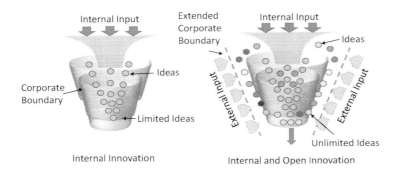

Figure 6.5 Innovation funnel – Internal vs open innovation.

70 *"How" – Approach to advance innovation*

these organizations establish reward systems to motivate and generate new ideas while providing clear guidelines on the contest rules and the expected outcomes for such rewards. This encourages diverse resources that are determined and resilient to achieve the stated innovation goals within the stated timeline. The number of ideas generated from the open innovation model is typically much higher than from internal innovation, which is limited. Open innovation, if designed carefully with a reward and evaluation system, can entice more participants from outside of corporate boundaries and has the potential to get some quality ideas as well.

For example, Netflix ran an open innovation competition from 2006 through 2009 [14] for the best collaborative filtering algorithm to support their DVD-rental and video-streaming service. The goal of the open competition was to predict accurately user ratings for film recommendations based on previous ratings by masking competitive information about customers by using an anonymized dataset. Although Netflix had its own matching algorithm, Cinematch, and it was reasonably effective, they were not completely satisfied and wanted to improve the algorithm's accuracy by more than 10%. The contest was open to the public with some exceptions. On September 21, 2009, the grand prize $1,000,000 was awarded to the BellKor's Pragmatic Chaos team, which bested Netflix's own algorithm for predicting ratings by 10.06%.[15]. BellKor's Pragmatic Chaos consisted of two Austrian researchers from Commendo Research & Consulting GmbH, Andreas Töscher and Michael Jahrer (originally team BigChaos); two researchers from AT&T Labs, Robert Bell, and Chris Volinsky; Yehuda Koren from Yahoo! (originally team BellKor); and two researchers from Pragmatic Theory, Martin Piotte and Martin Chabbert [16]. More than 20,000 teams had registered for the competition from over 150 countries, while 2,000 teams had submitted around 13,000 prediction sets [17]. The resources involved in this competition were profound and diverse in their expertise and very resilient to achieve the set goal. The competitors were so focused on solving the issue on hand that a few of them decided to collaborate as one team. The synergy and commitment were on display throughout the entire contest period that spread over multiple years.

To innovate and sustain the success, it is critical that organizations focus on the resource and resilience aspects along with other dimensions of the TRIAL© framework. Regardless of the resourcing strategy, internal vs external, resilience needs must be addressed to achieve the desired results.

6.4.1.3 *I – Inquisitive & Imaginative Culture*

Smart resources are essential for innovation efforts, but they do not guarantee innovation results. Organizations are good at assembling smart resources, thinking that their technical expertise will magically translate into an innovation outcome, which is a not the case. Resources also need to possess inquisitive and imaginative skills or else they are simply followers and cannot make progress on an innovation agenda. Curious minds typically visualize the outcome by exploring alternative paths to solve problems and generally do not give up until the goal is achieved. Innovation does not take a linear path to generate solutions for the given problem or opportunity, and entails thinking out of the box and applying nonlinear methods or perspectives. Unless the resources are inquisitive and take the initiative to analyze the problems and explore solution options on their own, time and effort will not be spent effectively to achieve the desired outcome. In other words, innovation requires some degree of independent

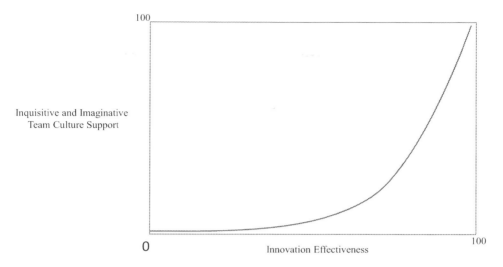

Figure 6.6 Team inquisitive and imaginative culture vs innovation effectiveness.

effort that is fueled by an inquisitive and imaginative culture. Of course, this can rise to a new level if the teams exhibit a collective inquisitiveness and imagination as illustrated by Figure 6.6, where there is a correlation between innovation effectiveness and team inquisitive and imaginative culture based on our industry research.

When the Google X program was set up at Google to explore moonshot projects [18], curiosity and imagination were much needed to handle problems that mirrored science fiction's, with orders of magnitude impact on society. The resources both at the individual and team level were called upon to meet such challenges of extraordinary scope and scale. Some of these innovative projects that demanded a high degree of inquisitive and imaginative culture are discussed below.

Self-driving technology-based vehicles – This was completely a new idea and Google X embarked on this to reshape the mobility industry given the advancements in data science, sensors, machine learning, AI, GPS, and advanced real-time computing. The applications for the self-driving vehicles are huge, and the impact could be orders of magnitude. The project required a completely different mindset and imagination by anticipating and visualizing real-time navigation and collision scenarios under a wide spectrum of traffic conditions and weather situations. Just automotive and information technology expertise would not cut it to make this idea work. Google recognized this well and established a team culture to foster inquisitive and imaginative skills from the get-go.

Google did not just hire people with just automotive and information technology skills, but totally committed to nurture an innovative culture by providing the team members with the freedom to experiment and express ideas, a flexible work schedule, supporting infrastructure, and opportunities to leverage the best resources both from within and outside of Google. The result was amazing, with more than 20 million autonomous vehicle miles [19] and roughly 300 years of collective human driving [20]. Now the team is spun off as a separate entity, Waymo, part of Alphabet, and available to public in cities such as Phoenix, Chandler, Gilbert, Mesa, and Tempe.

72 *"How" – Approach to advance innovation*

Makani energy kites – This is an effort to harness untapped wind energy. Makani Power was acquired by Google in 2013, building on its prior investment to the tune of $15M. The energy kites, the core product of Makani Power, were very sophisticated and modeled after propeller-based airplanes. They can generate up to 600 kilowatts of energy to support more than 300 homes. There are various models of these tethered kites, which are attached to a ground power Grid station. As the kites' fly, the propellers on the kites are spun by the wind, which generates power in the sky and is transmitted to the ground station [20]. This required significant curiosity and imagination for engineers to build and perfect a working model. Google X was so committed to these ambitious projects, given its strategic impact on society, and the Google X culture was instrumental.

Disney/Pixar, a perineal innovation leader [21], also practices an inquisitive and imaginative culture. Disney/Pixar's successful production of *Star Wars*, *Toy Story*, *A Bugs Life*, *The Incredibles*, *Finding Nemo*, and *Monsters, Inc.* were by no means an accident. The most recent successful launching of Disney+, competing head on with streaming content industry leader Netflix, was a carefully orchestrated effort spanning many years, assembling and fostering highly creative and imaginative teams complemented by skilled technology resources that delivered much-anticipated innovation results.

6.4.1.4 A – Achievement & Adaptability

Another important element of the TRIAL© framework is achievement and adaptability. The need to internalize the innovation "expectations" as "outcomes" are often overlooked in corporations. The innovation outcomes are typically stated as objectives or goals for projects and are posted on the wall, perhaps with every team member's signature, but soon to be forgotten as it gets treated just like any other poster to pass by. Unless the expected outcomes are internalized by the team and the individuals, it will be hard to achieve the expectation. In innovation programs, the team must prioritize "achieving" the goal as opposed to having a goal and simply experiment with ideas, "hoping" to realize the goal at some point. Merriam-Webster defines achieve as "to carry out successfully," to "accomplish." It makes such a huge difference if the focus is to achieve instead of simply stating the goal. As innovation involves iterative processes and continuous improvements, it is hard to manage that task with standard project management techniques and tools. Establishing a definitive timeline toward the target state works well for repeatable outcomes such as implementing known enterprise software systems such as SAP, Oracle, or Microsoft Dynamics in a new environment or organization; however, it is totally different if we are trying to innovate, let us say, 400-mile-range batteries. The latter involves a significant amount of coordinated, sometimes unstructured and unplanned experiments, and by internalizing the goal to achieve the end state generates "internal drive" within the team or the individuals committed to the task. Interestingly, if the focus is to "achieve" with an internal drive, the team may not need a project manager and other overheads, and one should expect boundless energy, motivation, and focus from the team members to deliver on the goals. It is equally imperative to lay out the big picture for the team to achieve the goal, otherwise if someone is working in a silo and does not have a sense for the overall vision or impactful outcome for the project, they will hardly be able to relate to the bigger impact of the innovation initiative with their own output, which is limited in quality and scope.

Focusing on achievement is the single most motivational factor for a satisfied employee as per the six-year motivation research study at Texas Instruments, back in 1950 [22] and is still true in the new millennium. The Texas Instruments study interviewed different employee groups, such as scientists and engineers, from an population of more than 17,000 employees for their satisfaction and delivery output at work, and the study concluded that feeling of achievement is the greatest factor along with a few other ones such as recognition, advancement, responsibility, competent supervision, nature of work, and company policy and administration.

A great example for how achievement takes center stage in motivating a workforce to realize what otherwise would be simply a dream is the SpaceX program. Given the complexity of the task on hand, literally rocket launch, SpaceX, founded in 2002 in Hawthorne, California, has assembled a highly skilled and diverse team over a period of two decades. The skills include jet propulsion, rocket engines, control systems, fluid dynamics, aerodynamics, avionics, astronomy, geopositioned tracking, sophisticated computer programming, materials science, electrical systems, thermodynamics, sensory systems ranging from smart digital transducers to sophisticated tracking laser range finders, optical systems, finance, human resources, contract, and marketing management, etc. [23]. As diverse and specialized as the skills and individual's interests are, the task to get the teams to work together and accomplish the bigger mission was a herculean one. In this environment, however, one may feel good at completing a specific task in a narrowly assigned area, such as designing the outer case for a stage 1 booster rocket, but the real feeling of "achievement" in terms of feeling ecstatic is realized when the SpaceX's Falcon 9 rocket is successfully launched, and the stage 1 booster rockets are brilliantly retrieved [24, 25]. SpaceX has been able to prioritize 'achievement' for employee motivation and its perennial innovation success is a great story to emulate.

In our experience, we have seen, time and again, many major enterprise programs either drag their feet to deliver certain innovations or capabilities on a preset timeline or simply reduce the scope to declare victory. This perhaps maybe construed as partial achievement and it results in enormous cost to the end consumers as the promised deliverables or products may lack required functions or features, diminishing the value proposition. The primary reason for these underperformances is not committing to the idea of "achievement" at the team level to internalize the goals for a home run, instead being content with task-level management. Many organizations design employee financial incentives such as annual bonus, etc. tied to organizational performance, but it does not necessarily have the same impactful outcome and motivate employees on a collective basis as an internalized achievement-based approach. So, what must organizations do? They must induce a feeling of achievement, both at the individual and team level, by relating the employee responsibilities and contributions to the big picture innovation mission such as in SpaceX. A sense of higher-level purpose is what is required to achieve the impact, where the whole is greater than the sum of its parts, as postulated by philosopher Aristotle. The achievement-based model lays emphasis on the TEAM, an acronym for "together everyone achieves more."

The other critical component in this context is that teams must be adaptable to the new reality of achievement-based team dynamics. As the bigger picture or the grand innovation mission is embedded in individual roles while executing the assigned micro-level tasks, the employee may be called upon to trade expertise or skills within or across teams for the benefit of a higher innovation outcome and the impact. In the traditional organizational model, division of responsibility and expertise-driven roles

74 *"How" – Approach to advance innovation*

do not match up well with multitasking, cross-training, and a team-based approach, and such collaboration proposals are frowned upon and met with criticism. The new model promoting innovation success emphasizes synergy and sometimes requires sacrifice at all levels to achieve the bigger reward. This will require adaptive skills on the part of team members, and they should readily mesh well with the larger team, despite the skills and personality differences.

At Pixar, a synergistic innovation culture encouraged people to help each other produce the best output. There existed a brains trust to promote peers, giving feedback to each other. An individual or a team could discuss openly their work-in-progress of an idea or an innovation with other teams or experts for a few hours and get raw feedback with no sugar-coating as the intention was to make the idea work the best for Pixar, the bigger purpose. There was no ego, and nobody pulled any punches to be polite. Pixar thrived with this team dynamic as teams came to trust each other and respect one another. The individuals and teams recognized the value of getting the fix for the innovation problem from their colleagues prior to hitting the theaters and receiving such feedback from the audience, which would be too late. Pixar encouraged open communication within and across teams, at all levels, which was based on trust to resolve issues and scrapped the need to go through time-consuming and bureaucracy-ridden proper channels and permissions. The film directors took the feedback and adapted it as soon as possible to realize a positive outcome for the projects they were working on. Adaptability was at the core of Pixar's success.

Postmortem review sessions at Pixar further strengthened the team dynamics as opportunities for future improvements were vigorous and open without the fear of backlash as everyone focused on the bigger purpose, which was organizational achievement [26].

6.4.1.5 *L – Leadership & Latitude*

At the core of innovation programs is the leadership component. In surveying several corporations with different degrees of success, it is commonly seen that a musical chair approach is practiced for leadership that inherently imposes breakpoints and detours that frequently confuse the innovation team. Leaders are chosen in many established organizations based on their previous accomplishments, either within or outside of their corporations, and a higher percentage of such chosen ones do not transfer readily their previous success to the new roles or opportunities. Corporations' lack of innovation experience compounded by culture clash with newly installed leaders are commonly seen as the recipe for more frequent leadership change.

Regardless of the organization's predisposition related to innovation challenge, the right innovation leaders could help transform the status quo. There are great examples of such successful innovation leaders in the corporate world who defied the traditional orthodoxies. For example, Jack Welch took over the mantle of GE in 1981 as a CEO soon after Ronald Reagan assumed US presidency. Welch's predecessor, Reginald H. Jones, ran GE well, with over \$1.5B annual profit and \$26B revenue, considered tenth-largest corporation at that time. However, during that time, there was a tectonic shift happening in GE's manufacturing as led by Japan and other East Asian countries, who were able to produce quality consumer products such as televisions, cassette players, toasters, etc. at a much lower cost than GE. The previous leadership simply could not recognize the needed strategic shift in GE's business model. But Jack Welch, through his strategic insights and leadership innovation, sensed the urgency to innovate GE's business model by rebalancing its product portfolio, smaller US manufacturing footprint, and global expansion. He challenged less profitable manufacturing activities in the US to demonstrate cost efficiencies and incorporate Six Sigma quality culture at the core. He expanded GE's portfolio to include investments, banking, etc., which at that time were extremely profitable.

In over 20 years of Jack Welch's tenure as a CEO, GE grew from $26B revenue to a $130B global conglomerate, while GE's market cap witnessed a meteoric rise from $14B to $410B, which no other enterprise could boast. How did this happen? Well, Jack Welch took an innovative leadership style for GE, pivoting to entrepreneurial corporate culture, parting ways with Alfred Sloan's model of bureaucracy-based approach with middle managers and strategic planning departments, which was popular in the years before. Welch subscribed to Darwinian corporate culture based on the belief that natural selection, where "readiness to respond" was by far the most powerful factor in determining who the winner is, which required continuous innovation in the enterprise context. As a leader, Jack Welch believed that GE should control its own destiny, and not others. He was fine with less perfect but quick answers instead of consensus-driven delayed answers, and emphasized dynamic organizational capabilities to adapt quickly to market landscape changes. In his autobiography, Welch mentioned that his goal was to create "a company filled with self-confident entrepreneurs who would face reality every day." Fortune recognized him as "Manager of the Century," and for the third consecutive year, *Financial Times* recognized GE as "the World's Most Respected Company." Although GE had a phenomenal run for a quarter century until he left in 2001, some of Jack Welch's decisions to expand into banking, etc. became a liability during the 2008–10 economic crisis [27].

Another great innovation leadership example is Steve Jobs and his ability to think out of the box, either in challenging IBM personal computers with an intuitive customer-friendly iMac personal computer design, or Sony's bulky Walkman with a less than three inches of lighter and elegant user-friendly iPod music platform with searchable, indexable, and downloadable features, or Blackberry's and Nokia's smartphones with an iOS ecosystem-driven software application focused iPhone with a touchscreen. He created a whole new product category with an innovative iPad that enabled software applications ranging from kids using them to play video games to warehouse employees using them to manage inventories.

So, what is the difference here that made Steve Jobs an exceptional innovation leader? Was he born with innovation skills? The answer is no. But Jobs developed the skills to visualize and anticipate what the customers would need or be helped by with product solutions and spotting the talents that could help him realize that vision. So, how did it work and was it that simple? It took several years of persistent efforts to get things done and it was not easy. The innovation leader's task is analogous to moving a mountain to see the other side, which is not readily seen by others.

As discussed, leadership is a critical element for the innovation pursuit as it sets the tone for all other efforts in the organization. To bring additional focus, we propose a sub-framework, VASTEFA© leadership framework [28] within the TRIAL© framework, which is discussed in the following section in detail.

6.4.2 VASTEFA© leadership framework

The innovation leader's task is very difficult, having to manage the expectations of various stakeholders, including the employees, while the innovative solution is developed iteratively. It requires certain special skills, and many can be acquired and perfected over time. A framework, VASTEFA© [28], as illustrated in Figure 6.7, is proposed that captures the essential leadership skills to consider before a leader is committed to the innovation pursuit. Interestingly many of these skills can be imparted through focused training and must be part of the succession planning process when future leaders are identified and groomed within an organization.

The skills depicted in the VASTEFA© leadership framework [28] for innovation may have different levels of maturity in organizations and can be presented as in Figure 6.8., the VASTEFA© leadership spider chart. But, after some reflection and self-assessment, the innovation leaders can strive toward maturing and balancing them over time with a priority that is suitable to the specific organizational need.

The components of the framework are discussed in detail below.

Vision - Truly believing in the vision and persuading the team and the investors on this belief,

Action - Being in the trenches and showing in action through persistent efforts,

Support - Securing seamless support, both financial and strategic resources to the team,

Team - Putting together teams with complementary skills, developing the right chemistry and engagement culture that can collectively deliver,

Experiment - Being patient, persistent, and have the courage to allow experiments and learn from failures,

Feedback - Constantly seeking feedback from the end consumers and peers of the evolving innovation,

Adaptability - Building the dynamic capability for the organization to adapt to the changing needs of the marketplace.

Figure 6.7 VASTEFA© leadership framework [28] for innovation.

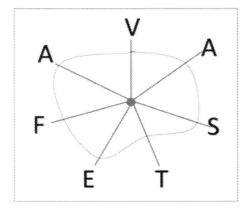

Figure 6.8 VASTEFA© leadership [28] spider chart.

© 2022 Vijay Pandiarajan

6.4.2.1 Vision

"Vision is the art of seeing what is invisible to others." - Jonathan Swift [29]

An important trait of a successful leader is having the vision and inspiring his/her organization to achieve that vision.

The key is to visualize the target solution and develop an action plan to realize it. Rallying the troops to not only follow but have them lead and contribute to their respective functions with a self-drive is paramount to get to the finish line. This requires strong communication skill with the ability to translate the vision in terms of a comprehensible description for other experts to map it to their specific technical areas. For example, the vision of Elon Musk when he founded SpaceX in 2001 was to deploy rockets that are cost-effective and competitive. But NASA has been around for many decades, so perhaps they had that vision as well, as each launch costs them hundreds of millions of dollars. So, what did Elon Musk do differently in realizing his vision? He analyzed the challenge and architected a high-level solution that involved retrieval of stage 1 booster rockets after each launch, which could reduce the deployment costs significantly. He put together a diverse team that had complementary skills and secured enough venture capital funds to experiment with his ideas. Through multiple iterations, tests, failures, feedback, and improvements, SpaceX was finally now able to deploy rockets with the ability to retrieve booster rockets, reducing dramatically the deployment costs. He was able to communicate and inspire his team on his vision, and they ended up believing and owning his vision. With persistent effort and self-drive, the team was able to carry forward on the most difficult task, moving the mountain. The rest is history.

6.4.2.2 Action

"Vision without action is just a dream, action without vision just passes the time, and vision with action can change the world." - Nelson Mandela

One of the skills that many successful innovation leaders persistently demonstrate is their ability to spend time with their teams in the trenches and be part of the action. Many startups have flat organizational structures and often have a co-located workplace. This allows the leaders and other employees to see eye to eye, learn from each other, and act together. As the innovation environment is collaborative and involves teams, being together and acting together establishes trust and mutual respect among team members and motivates everyone on a common purpose. Successful leaders do not have excuses to isolate themselves and as a habit they work together in teams to drive innovation success collectively. Elon Musk at Tesla does not have a corner office, nor does Mark Zuckerberg at Facebook. Their organizations are riding the innovation frontiers, and their organizational output is a testament to the effectiveness of the leadership tactics.

6.4.2.3 Support

Innovation does not happen in a vacuum and needs key resources such as subject matter experts, programmers, analysts, infrastructure, tools, data access, testers, and

78   *"How" – Approach to advance innovation*

program managers. As many of them are hard to find and often expensive given the competitive landscape, securing adequate funding is vital. Many startups, though, struggle to secure funds, there are established processes to raise the necessary capital in the form of series/round A, B, C, D, etc., based on solution potential and growth metrics – customer penetration, usage statistics, etc. However, established corporations typically have annual allocation or budgeting, and multiyear continuous funding for longer-term innovation initiatives is faced with challenges, compounded by uncertainties in the business environment, strategic priorities, and leadership change. In our interactions with many corporations we witnessed critical resources either being multitasked across many programs or partially committed during the innovation journey. Political dimensions add further complexity to funding uncertainties, and the net result is project delays or subpar innovation performance. Several studies including PWC have found statistical significance in the funding impacts on the quality of innovation [30, 31, 32].

So, how do we deal with it? Depending on the innovation initiatives, it will be helpful if complete transparency is established from the beginning and top leadership such as the corporate board is aligned on some of the strategic innovation initiatives. The senior leadership needs to be apprised on the criticality of the programs, including the strategic imperative for the organization. Organizational support for the innovation journey in terms of resources and priority is paramount and can be accomplished through endurable mechanisms to allow innovation pursuits, so long as there is a promise and purpose.

Organizations go through a lot of uncertainty that could impact the continuity of innovation programs – sponsorship change or unplanned existing product recall withdrawing key resources from innovation projects to name just two. Innovation leaders should possess special skills, including marketing their programs to their stakeholders, and secure their seamless support regardless of tactical roadblocks. They should be able to persuade them on the innovation vision, strategic imperatives, and the approach to realize it. It is not easy for innovation leaders to master such skills overnight but they can steadily develop them over time. One does not need to be a genius but must be a master of providing a compelling value proposition of the idea. Startup leaders Elon Musk from Tesla, Travis Kalanick and Garrett Camp from Uber, Tobias Lütke from Shopify, and Brian Chesky, Joe Gebbia and Nathan Blecharczyk from Airbnb are great examples for their skills in persuading their stakeholders and securing financial support for their innovation teams despite all the odds stacked against them when they were growing their businesses.

6.4.2.4 Team

> "Talent wins games, but teamwork and intelligence win championships." - Michael Jordan

Teams are fundamental to the innovation journey. Forming a team is a two-step process. The first step is assessing the program needs and recruiting top talent for such requirements. It could be starting from scratch or filling any talent gaps. Given the competitive landscape and talent war, high performers are in demand, which requires a lot of selling of the program, and inspirational leadership. The talent could be scouted internally or externally, or a mix of both. High achievers do not want to work for mediocre leaders and be part of underachieving teams; hence, innovation leaders must take recruiting skills seriously and fortify themselves with a strong team to attract and recruit high achievers. There is a belief that if you give a small idea to a high-performing team, they will expand the idea and deliver big. On the other hand, if you give a great idea to a mediocre team, they will poorly execute on the opportunity and deliver far less to everyone's dismay.

The second step is to make sure that the team dynamic is developed with the right engagement culture that respects each other, leverage the complementary skills, persevere together with mutual trust, and work toward the common vision. It is becoming more evident that innovation success hinges on the effective performance of the team rather than on a few individuals [33]. Prof. Linda Hill, Harvard Business School, conducted an extensive innovation research on innovation leadership and proposes a collective genius framework to enhance the performance of the innovation team. An adapted version of the framework is presented in Figure 6.9.

She argues that innovation demands the creation of community with a sense of common purpose and that has the "willingness" to do the hard work, which is framed under innovation culture, and the "ability" to do the hard work under capabilities, which completes the innovation journey. In essence, the innovation leaders should create: 1. The right culture that fosters a sense of purpose, shared values, and rules of engagement; and 2. Capabilities that promote creative abrasion, agility, and resolution [33].

The culture and capabilities are the two pillars that the leaders must stay focused on as they build innovation teams. There is a continuous interplay between these two pillars to make progress on the innovation. At no time should abrasive and provoking ideas criticism be personal or disrespectful to team members, and healthy engagement rules should lay the foundation for trusted collaboration. On a personal level it should be inconsequential but should advance and converge innovation resolution. For speedy resolution, to toss out ideas that lack promise while allowing prioritization of interesting ideas, transparent process and accountability ought to be established to earn the trust and respect of the team. After all, ideas are tied to individuals or groups, and decisions on "go or no-go" are a sensitive matter and objective, yet an expeditious approach is central to sustain team engagement and enduring success. The innovation leadership must recognize this fundamental prerequisite before betting big on innovation initiatives.

It is extremely hard for a traditional leader to pivot to the collective genius framework, but this framework reflects how some of the most successful corporations, such as Disney/Pixar, IBM, Google, eBay, HCL, Volkswagen, Pentagram, Pfizer, etc., are able lead on the innovation front with the culture and capabilities depicted.

6.4.2.5 Experiment

"Experimentation keeps new ideas rising to the surface." - Joseph Orr

"Failure is an option here. If things are not failing, you are not innovating." - Elon Musk [34, 35]

The innovation leader does not take a linear path to achieve end results. She recognizes the value of iteration and a nonlinear path to experiment with various options before choosing the optimum innovation solution. This is a paradigm shift for traditional leaders who treat experiment as a science project with no commercial implications. The right innovation leader should not have any qualms about experiments, rather

80 *"How" – Approach to advance innovation*

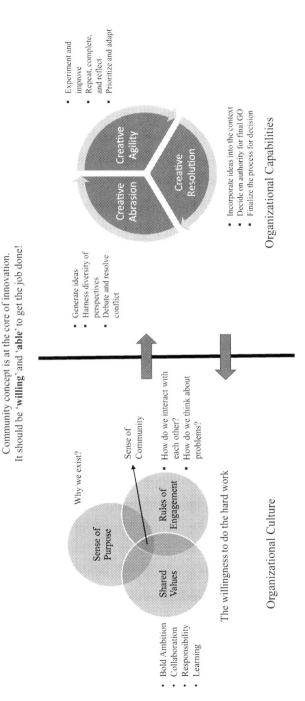

Figure 6.9 Collective genius framework for innovation teams.

Adapted from Prof. Linda Hill, Harvard Business School [33]. Reprinted with permission of Harvard Business Publishing from "Collective Genius: The Art and Practice of Leading Innovation" by Linda A. Hill, Greg Brandeau, Emily Truelove, and Kent Lineback. Copyright 2014 by Linda A. Hill, Greg Brandeau, Emily Truelove, and Kent Lineback; all rights reserved."

she should encourage the team to fail fast to learn from the infeasible solutions before perfecting the solution. Given the iterative and experimental nature of innovation, the leaders face a challenge in estimating the timeline for success as they are often under the gun to produce results.

A great example is the recent COVID-19 vaccine mandate for the some of the major pharmaceutical companies to produce effective vaccines within six to ten months duration, which was unheard of in the history before. Depending on the problem addressed or solution developed, such challenges can be mitigated by supplementing the physical experiments with digital simulation techniques to evaluate solutions. Innovation leaders should be patient while the experiments are run and allow the teams to complete their process. Experiments offer insights into what works and what does not work and have the potential to avoid possible embarrassment in the marketplace if blindsided by deficiencies or incompleteness of the solution. It is worth the time and effort to pressure test possible solutions thoroughly and validate the hypotheses before scaling up the solution.

6.4.2.6 Feedback

> "I think it's very important to have a feedback loop, where you're constantly thinking about what you've done and how you could be doing it better." - Elon Musk, Tesla, and SpaceX [34]

Traditional leaders may have apprehension about seeking feedback on interim solutions for obvious reasons, such as relaying a poor perception of the solution, possible backlash in continuing the project, time delays, and distrust. The feedback could be from various quarters, including customers and other project leads, who may not have any direct expertise on the problem being solved. The key idea in soliciting feedback is to get various perspectives and address the deficiencies before the innovation is commercialized and released to the actual customer. Product recall is an expensive proposition, and no one wants to be holding the bag as new innovations are launched.

Elon Musk at Tesla actively seeks customer feedback through social media platforms (he has more than 57 million followers on Twitter) and tries to address them as much as possible. One such feedback was a criticism on the quality of the car body frames. He considered the feedback seriously and implemented an innovative solution on the newly launched Tesla Model Y. This SUV has a single large cast rear subframe, eliminating the need for assembly of many subcomponents, making it easier to manufacture while improving stiffness and crashworthiness, and the reducing the misfits in assembling individual components. It was learned that the innovation entailed an advanced manufacturing method [35].

6.4.2.7 Adaptability

> "It is not the strongest of the species that survives, nor the most intelligent that survives. It is the one that is most adaptable to change." - Charles Darwin [36]

Great leaders are fearless to adapt and this is a prerequisite for innovation success. The Principles of War, an accepted tool to assist US warfighters, believes in the value of the axiom "no plan survives first contact with the enemy. But the ability to take the

82 *"How" – Approach to advance innovation*

commander's intent and plans and then adapt them to the current situation and environment to accomplish the mission is one of the traits of U.S. military fighting men and women and is arguably a trademark of American culture." [37]. This fits extremely well in the business context as the competitive landscape and consumer preferences keep changing. What is considered good today may not be good tomorrow. Hence, keeping an eye on the changes in the operating environment and adapting the innovation solutions are central to the leadership success. Adaptive leaders display their skills through their mental ability, attitude, and physical characteristics [37]

Successful leaders allow reasonable latitude to their teams as they embark on delivering on the innovation agenda. This implies allowing a longer leash on the teams and not micromanaging the innovation tasks. Many organizations make a conscious decision to separate critical innovation groups from their parent organization, allowing necessary flexibility for the teams to function, not impeded by any bureaucracy. Google X, a separate entity from Google to drive moonshot projects in the earlier days of Google, is a classic example of providing the much-needed latitude for innovation. This implies giving them a free hand to run the project as they feel comfortable in terms of onboarding and managing the resources, the ability to take risks, and prioritizing the deliverables.

6.5 Concluding remarks

We observe that the innovation journey has many uncertainties, and the task could be daunting for many businesses. Some struggle with the right approach to begin the journey. If they approach it as another conventional project and just focus on requirements, resources, timeline, and results, they will be disappointed, may drain organizational resources, and frustrate many. Innovation is a double-edged sword, as it promises business value, but also requires necessary investment with the willingness for a disciplined team-based approach. Organizational repositioning with a capacity that is conducive to fostering innovation requires methodical introspection and gaps assessment. The TRIAL© framework and VASTEFA© leadership framework are our proposals to help lay the foundation before innovation initiatives are kicked off. Using these frameworks, businesses can self-assess their maturity levels on different dimensions and position their organization for innovation success. There is no short cut to taking a methodical and measured approach to innovation. Once the innovation pursuit is in motion, businesses need to recalibrate and adjust their organizational capacity in terms of endogenous factors for market fit as the environment, both within and outside, changes constantly.

Student activities

Activity 1:

1. Select Timberland, Zara-Inditex, Samsung, and Sun Pharmaceuticals cases from Part VIII.
2. Review the details and list the problems or opportunities they try to address.
3. Discuss the approach to innovate through the lens of the TRIAL© framework. As you do, incorporate current information from their corporate websites and relate to our framework.
4. Also answer the questions listed at the end of the case.

Framework-based innovation approach 83

> **Activity 2:**
> 1. Select the Amazon case from Part VIII.
> 2. Review the details and list the problems or opportunities they try to address.
> 3. Discuss the leadership approach to innovate through the lens of the VASTEFA© leadership framework.
> 4. List potential challenges for the new leader at Amazon and recommend possible solutions or detours that may be appropriate for the future.

6.6 References

1. www.cnbc.com/2019/02/07/daimler-ceo-tesla-mercedes-talking-about-working-together-again.html
2. www.industryweek.com/finance/article/22018589/toyota-sells-stake-in-tesla
3. www.thestreet.com/technology/history-of-tesla-15088992
4. www.businessinsider.com/tesla-history-timeline-2020-biggest-milestones-and-moments-2020-4#the-dual-motor-model-s-also-served-up-insane-mode-a-0-60-mph-time-in-the-model-s-p85d-of-32-seconds-9
5. www.businessinsider.com/apples-iphone-carrier-subsidies-2014-4
6. www.uber.com/newsroom/history/
7. www.cnn.com/interactive/2019/03/business/lyft-history/index.html
8. Vijay Pandiarajan, "TRIAL© Innovation Framework," WMBA Win 2021 Class Slides, Ross School of Business, The University of Michigan, 2021.
9. www.forbes.com/sites/arielcohen/2020/12/30/teslas-new-lithium-ion-patent-brings-company-closer-to-promised-1-million-mile-battery/#221e60a233e3
10. https://electrek.co/2019/12/26/tesla-patents-battery-chemistry-cheaper/
11. www.cnn.com/2020/07/17/perspectives/coronavirus-meat-shortages-mcdonalds/index.html
12. Jeff Stibel, "Why I Hire People Who Fail," Harvard Business Review, December 09, 2011.
13. Andrew King and Karim R. Lakhani, 2013, "Using Open Innovation to Identify the Best Ideas," Sloan Management Review, 55(1), pp. 41–48.
14. https://en.wikipedia.org/wiki/Netflix_Prize
15. "The Netflix Prize," archived from the original on 2009-09-24, retrieved September 7, 2012.
16. "Netflix Awards $1 Million Netflix Prize and Announces Second $1 Million Challenge," archived from the original on September 25, 2009, retrieved September 24, 2009.
17. James Bennett, and Stan Lanning, (August 12, 2007) , "The Netflix Prize," (PDF) , proceedings of KDD Cup and Workshop 2007.
18. www.entrepreneur.com/article/326836
19. https://waymo.com/safety/
20. www.theverge.com/2019/12/9/21000085/waymo-fully-driverless-car-self-driving-ride-hail-service-phoenix-arizona
21. https://thewaltdisneycompany.com/disney-ranks-high-among-fast-companys-most-innovative-companies/
22. Scott Myers, "Who Are Your Motivated Workers," Harvard Business Review, Jan 1964.
23. www.quora.com/What-skills-are-needed-to-be-an-electrical-engineer-at-SpaceX
24. www.spacex.com/
25. www.truscore.com/resources/leadership-style-of-elon-musk/
26. Ed Catmull, "How Pixar Fosters Collective Creativity," Harvard Business Review, Sept 2008.

84 *"How" – Approach to advance innovation*

27. www.nytimes.com/2020/03/02/business/jack-welch-died.html
28. Vijay Pandiarajan, "VASTEFA© Leadership Framework,' WMBA Win 2021 Class Slides, Ross School of Business, The University of Michigan, 2021.
29. https://quotescover.com/jonathan-swift-quote-about-vision
30. PricewaterhouseCoopers (2003), Building Better Performance: An Empirical Assessment of the Learning and Other Impacts of Schools Capital Investment: DFES Research Report 407, March 2003.
31. PricewaterhouseCoopers (2007), Building Schools for the Future: Technical Report: Appendix E: Literature Review: www.teachernet.gov.uk/management/resourcesfinanceandbuilding/bsf/
32. PricewaterhouseCoopers (2010), Evaluation of Building Schools for the Future (BSF): 3rd Annual Report: Final Report February 2010: www.teachernet.gov.uk/management/resourcesfinanceandbuilding/bsf/
33. Linda A. Hill, Greg Branden, Emily Truelove and Kent Lineback, "Collective Genius: The Art and Practice of Leading Innovation," Harvard Business Review Press, 2015.
34. www.t-three.com/soak/insights/4-things-elon-musk-can-teach-us-about-effective-leadership
35. https://insideevs.com/news/398022/cast-parts-model-y-specialists/
36. https://quoteinvestigator.com/2014/05/04/adapt/
37. https://apps.dtic.mil/dtic/tr/fulltext/u2/a415124.pdf

Part V

Innovations in industry verticals

Chapter 7	Innovations in manufacturing	87
Chapter 8	Innovations in the service industry	103
Chapter 9	Innovation in government	121

7 Innovations in manufacturing

7.1 Introduction

Before we present the innovation models in manufacturing, it is important that we reflect on the industry revolution over the past three centuries. Britannica defines [1] industrial revolution as the process of change from an agrarian and handicraft economy to one dominated by industry and machine manufacturing. The origins of such revolution were seen at the beginning of the 18th century in Great Britain and slowly became widespread over rest of the world. There are four distinct phases in the industrial revolutions – first, second, third, and the fourth [2].

The first industrial revolution, recognized for steam-powered machinery and efficient manufacturing, was primarily seen in Britain during the period 1760 to 1830 [3]. It slowly spread to Belgium, Germany, and France. Some of these technologies found use in coal and iron mines, textile mills, and steel manufacturing, and soon expanded their footprint into erstwhile Soviet Union and China. As India was colonized by the British, it became a natural landing place for machinery and manufacturing techniques as well.

The second industrial revolution was recognized during late 19th and early 20th centuries, characterized by automatic operations with the use of electricity and perhaps early versions of computing machines. Highly automated and moving assembly lines to produce automobiles such as Ford's Model T is a good example of this revolution. At the beginning of 19th century, building on many innovations from before, new types of energy were needed to power factories as the industrial pace and output increased. This led to generating electricity using various conventional sources of energy such as coal, oil, natural gas, etc., which powered machinery. The industry experienced large-scale mechanization in the early to mid-19th century before embracing automatic operation in the second half of the 20th century [4, 5]. Although Edison formed Electric Illuminating company in New York in 1882 and powered parts of Manhattan, it took another 30 years before it found widespread adoption in rest of the US. Electricity was central to the second industrial revolution.

The third industrial revolution, witnessed in the second half of the 20th century, embodied the widespread use of electronics, telecommunications, and mainframe, mini and personal computers. These innovations allowed space exploration, nuclear research, biotechnology, and material science. The major innovations from this era include programmable logic controllers and industrial robots, which took the industry by storm. The manufacturing industries started adapting flexible automation with dexterous robotics and advanced control systems.

DOI: 10.4324/9781003190837-12

88 *Innovations in industry verticals*

The fourth industrial revolution is the one we live in, ushered by the digital revolution that is characterized by the convergence of high-speed internet, cloud computing, AI, machine learning, big data analytics, edge computing, augmented reality, mixed reality, virtual reality, digital twins, autonomous vehicles, mobile computing, internet of things (IoT), and cognitive computing. The pace of impact of this revolution has surpassed all other previous industrial revolutions and is gaining more popularity and adoption. In some parts of the world, including Asia and Europe, it is also known as Industry 4.0. The evolving 5G mobile connectivity that allows machine to machine real-time interaction makes autonomous factories a real possibility, with a potential to displace the industry labor force from their traditional shopfloor role to non-imitable cognitive roles. This revolution transcends industry verticals, and no industry is impervious to the digital tsunami. A United Nations study suggests that digital technologies have advanced more rapidly than any innovation in human history, making inroads into both developed and less developed nations in just two decades [6]. It is hoped that, at some point in the future, this revolution will establish a level playing field for all countries to prosper.

Manufacturing, which has progressively leveraged these industrial revolutions, is a critical industry vertical for many countries. However, growth and size of the manufacturing sector varies among countries and Figure 7.1 illustrates manufacturing as a percentage of GDP in select countries.

We review the industry evolution through innovations in some of the major industry verticals: Pharmaceuticals, heavy equipment, automotive and semiconductor in the following sections.

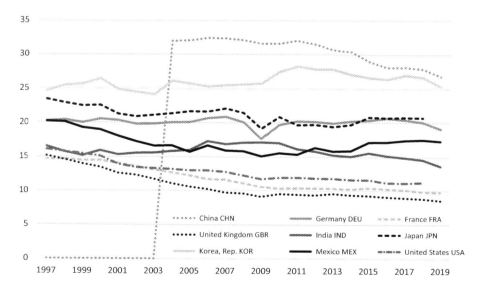

Figure 7.1 Manufacturing – Percentage of GDP.
Source: https://data.worldbank.org/.
https://data.worldbank.org/indicator/NV.IND.MANF.ZS?locations=US-CN-DE-IN-JP

7.2 Pharmaceuticals

Pharmaceuticals has been a pivotal industry for society over the past century, with a constant quest for drug discovery to meet evolving therapeutic human needs. Although life expectancy has steadily increased over this period [7], primarily because of improvements in sanitation, hygiene, housing, and education, the drug innovations in the pharmaceuticals industry played a very significant role as well. For much of the past century, the industry was reactive to the human crises, whether it was through epidemics such as cholera, malaria, or plague, or diseases such as tuberculosis, or chronic ailments such as asthma [8]. The new drugs discovery is a result of molecule formulations leveraging the advancements in active ingredients. Dr. Alexander Fleming in 1928 pioneered such a groundbreaking discovery with penicillin, an antibiotic to treat bacterial infections, which revolutionized the industry, leading to the development and mass use of many different antibiotics such as quinolone derivatives and anti-HIV drugs. Other advancements such as chemotherapy, pain medication, and anti-inflammatory drugs followed suit.

Drug innovation in the form of discovery is a complex, expensive, and time-consuming process, which requires a vast number of resources from many functional domains. The pharma researchers are confronted with changing science – more complex diseases where the science is difficult and failure risks higher. This is compounded by increasing regulatory requirements, excessive testing against comparator (investigational or marketed) drugs, clinical trial recruitment and retention challenges, larger and diverse clinical trials, and the needs of chronic and degenerative diseases [9]. It is also reported that after spending three years on drug discovery with a meager 12% odds of entering advanced clinical phases, it takes over ten years to penetrate the targeted commercial markets [9]. According to a recent study by the Tufts Center for the Study of Drug Development and published in the *Journal of Health Economics*, the average cost to develop a drug has increased from $802M to $2.6B, an increase of 145%, adjusted for inflation [10]. The traditional method of counting entirely on internal R&D for new innovative drugs discovery is becoming increasingly less attractive and untenable.

Corporations such as Roche Holding AG, Pfizer, and Novartis, Bristol-Myers Squibb, Merck, and many others are breaking the old drug discovery paradigms by looking outside of their corporate boundaries and establishing partnerships with startups and other external biotech firms. They inject seed capital where there is a promising pipeline for a possible commercial licensing opportunity upon drugs approval. The industry is leveraging cutting-edge databases, sophisticated warp-speed data analytics software, including innovations in AI, machine learning, deep learning, and powerful collaboration tools to aid faster and less expensive drug discoveries. The pharma researchers are benefiting from the democratization of technology in general as advanced by Google, Facebook (now called Meta), Amazon, Microsoft, and NVIDIA. The knock-on effect of the technology innovations that the pharma industry is experiencing is real and the value proposition is compelling.

For example, Roche Holding AG a major life science company with a market capitalization of $283.85B, has embraced AI in its drug discovery. In 2018, Roche acquired machine learning company Flatiron Health Inc., which is focused on accelerating cancer research and improving patient care. Roche is also partnering with

90 Innovations in industry verticals

Owkin and IBM Watson, leaders in machine learning technologies to support its drug development. For clinical trials, Roche is partnering with Sensyne Health, a clinical AI company, headquartered in the UK.

Pfizer, another large life science company with a market capitalization of $187B, has been partnering with IBM Watson Health since 2016 to internalize machine learning technologies in drug discovery. In 2018, Pfizer partnered with an AI pure play, Atomwise, and became a member of the Machine Learning for Pharmaceutical Discovery and Synthesis Consortium (MLPDS), which is actively supported by MIT researchers and technologies.

Novartis, another major life science company with a market capital of $197.43B, has heavily invested in AI and machine learning and collaborates with IBM, Intel, MLPDS, and Microsoft. It is also working closely with QuantumBlack, an advanced analytics firm headquartered in the UK, which was acquired in 2015 by McKinsey & Company, a leading strategy and management consulting powerhouse.

The following technology innovations are a few examples that drive great success in the pharmaceutical companies.

> *High-performance specialized hardware*: To process and run large sets of complex data and run machine learning algorithms, businesses require high-performance computing platforms. Google's Tensor Processing Unit and NVIDIA's DGX-1 provide the pharma industry with the much-needed powerful hardware platform.
>
> *Scalable cloud infrastructure*: Regardless of the size of the corporation, access to scalable cloud-based infrastructure is becoming a reality. Google Cloud, Microsoft Azure, and AWS are a few that can provision computing resources over the internet at a fraction of an ownership computing model, allowing the users to build and execute drug discovery AI-based analytics software solutions. For example, Bigfinite, a startup that raised over $8.5M in 2017, leveraged AWS to develop such multiple AI solutions supporting US-based Federal Drug Administration (FDA) compliant drug discovery tasks [11].
>
> *Standardized open-source and tools*: Machine learning is complex and expensive and uses various technical frameworks that make it hard to embrace by non-tech pharma researchers. However, there is good news. Open-source, yet standardized frameworks for machine learning-based development, such as Google's TensorFlow, Microsoft's Cognitive Toolkit, Amazon's MXNet, Meta's Torch, etc., are gaining more traction and adoption because of their simplicity and affordability, with user-friendly studio-style development tools. Azure ML Studio and Cortex AI studio are becoming the standard for experiment and support iterative drug discovery.
>
> *Big data*: To support drug discovery, historically the pharma companies relied on internal data sets collected through experiments. This is inadequate given the nature of the problems that the researchers must deal with. Now there is an incredible opportunity for scientists to access data outside of their corporate systems, which exists both in public domains and in a much larger ecosystem of partners, academic institutions, and scientific laboratories. These data sets are growing and are very useful to train machine learning algorithms. Some of the pharma-specific data sets include general datasets, image tasks, genome datasets, hospital datasets, and cancer datasets. There

are also chemical databases that include the ChEMBL database (1.8 million molecules with known bioactivities, over 12,000 targets, etc.), ZINC15 databases (over 100 million purchasable drug-like molecules for virtual screening), and REAL databases (over 680 million synthetically accessible drug-like compounds, all synthetic routes being validated in thousands of lab experiments) [11].

Never have pharma researchers had the luxury of such access to and affordability of vast and diverse data sets supported by both AI and machine learning tools that have come to refine and accelerate the drug discovery process. A great example is how Pfizer, Moderna, Johnson & Johnson, and AstraZeneca were able to develop COVID-19 vaccines within six to eight months, including conducting clinical trials, defying legacy corporate constraints [12].

> *Collaborative data-sharing platforms*: Data sharing is not an option for pharmaceutical companies, but it is a necessity for drug discovery. To make strides, collaboration with peer researchers is vital. Some of the pharma projects require 1,000 times more data than even the richest individual pharma company could collect or afford on its own [13]. To train machine learning models on drug discovery, the larger the data sets, the better the outcome will be. Pharmaceutical companies and researchers immensely benefit by sharing their trial data, which is typically big data comprising both structured and unstructured information. Obviously, there are challenges in terms of competitive reasoning not to share proprietary information, but there are certain phases of research that lend themselves well for sharing to advance the common good of the industry in general. For rich real-time data sharing and enterprise collaboration activities which involve intense computer model simulation, NVIDIA Omniverse™ is a great platform innovation that is available on a subscription basis.

Technology platforms such as Vivli, a non-profit organization, is Microsoft's Azure cloud-based environment that allows open searches of clinical trial data, with more than 1.5 million participants representing little over 100 countries [14]. Notable collaborators include Biogen, Duke University, Johns Hopkins University, Pfizer, and Aegerion Pharmaceuticals [15]. This platform access is free but requires citation of the data source when used and provides secure connectivity to multiple related data platforms.

Transcelerate is another biopharmaceutical data-sharing platform with a mission to allow collaboration among the global biopharmaceutical R&D community to foster the development and delivery of high-quality new medicines [16]. tranSMART is another open-source platform supporting public-private partnership for informatics-based analysis and data-sharing supporting clinical and translational research. Corporations such as Johnson & Johnson, AstraZeneca, and Pfizer, and academic institutions such as the University of Michigan, Harvard University, and Carnegie Mellon University are actively involved in the tranSMART platform [17].

The pharmaceutical manufacturing process consists of many distinct operations, such as blending, granulation, milling, coating, tablet forming, filling, packaging, etc. [18]. It is a combination of batch and continuous or flow process techniques. Batch level traceability is a fundamental requirement in this industry for quality assurance and containment reasons in the case of recall. With the evolving and coordinated

92 *Innovations in industry verticals*

regulatory regimens from the US, UK, Europe, and Asian nations, the industry is required to embrace standardized and repeatable manufacturing processes, automation, and quality control methods for consistent and reliable products. The regulatory agencies now require the manufacturers to submit Chemistry, Manufacturing and Controls, and Common Technical Documents that capture comprehensive raw materials data, manufacturing process parameters, and quality assurance data. Good manufacturing practices are at the heart of all this industry's manufacturing facilities. Manufacturing technology and process innovations from other industries, including automotive and chemical, were transplanted, customized, and optimized to support its unique needs.

On the chemical data analysis and instrumentation front, to speed up the process, innovations such as high-performance liquid chromatography, gas chromatography, nuclear magnetic resonance, and X-ray diffraction find immense use.

The pharma industry is also investing heavily in innovations on biologics and biosimilars. Biologic drugs contain derivatives from human, animal, or microorganisms by using biotechnology [19]. Interestingly, this is an advanced therapy to treat psoriasis, diabetes, Crohn's disease, osteoporosis, ulcerative colitis, rheumatoid arthritis, and other autoimmune diseases. Biologic is a $386.7B market and is growing [20]. Innovations involving novel targets, modifying agents, and manufacturing systems catapult the growth of these products. Once the patent on biologic expires, it is expected that biosimilar drugs will hit the market.

This industry is also experiencing many innovations in the form of new delivery platforms and concepts. Digitalized medication and smart pills, and 3D and 4D printing are gaining more adoption.

Digitalized medication and smart Pills are becoming popular. The world's first FDA-approved pill, called Abilify MyCite, from Proteus Digital Health, for the treatment of schizophrenia or bipolar disorder, a technology for viable "medication adherence", is a reality. The pill uses a sensor to digitally track whether patients have ingested their medication. Proteus was founded in 2001 with notable investors such as Oracle Corporation, Novartis, and The Carlyle Group and is growing.

This medication adherence technology is being explored for critical type 2 diabetes and drug abuse epidemic situations. Proteus reports that medication non-adherence costs the US over $290B annually as patients, if medications are not taken as prescribed, end up in critical conditions in hospitals. There is also another product, a swallowable IntelliCap® single-use capsule that contains a microprocessor-controlled drug delivery system. This allows programming the chip to suit any delivery patient need [21].

3D printing has been around for a few decades, but 4D is an evolving area that spurs curiosity from across the medical community. 3D printing leverages a stereolithography process where ultraviolet light is used to cure a material layer by layer during the printing process. It is a rapid and accurate manufacturing method of customized fabrication of soft structures. It uses unique materials that have a self-deformation property and are adopted by scientists for research purpose [22, 23, 24]. 4D printing is like 3D printing; however, it adds a fourth dimension of transformation as a function of time and some parameters. This allows the printed product to react with its environment, such as temperature/humidity, etc., and change its form as per the requirements. Some of the fascinating bio applications include smart stent, organ printing, and skin graft [25].

7.3 Heavy equipment

The heavy equipment, also called construction equipment, industry involves heavy vehicles that are designed for moving earthwork. The market is projected to reach $186.42B by the end of 2026 from its 2018 levels of $128.46B, with a brisk compound annual growth rate (CAGR) of 4.8% [26]. Typical examples of heavy equipment include Bulldozer, Tower Crane, Excavator, Backhoe, Loader, and Dump Truck [27]. This industry, like others, has evolved significantly over the past few centuries through relentless innovations. In the US, rapid urbanization during the second industrial revolution led to the need for heavy machinery to support efficient and large-scale agricultural activity.

Benjamin Leroy Holt, an American, invented a combine harvester in 1886 and a steam engine tractor in 1890. They served agricultural purposes well. John Froelich followed through on these innovations and built a gasoline-powered tractor. These early inventions set the stage for future inventions in the following century. After the first bulldozer built in 1920 was successfully used to move earth, many new construction projects started using them. Soon after World War II, baby boomers led the reverse migration, from urban areas to suburban areas, creating huge demands for heavy equipment supporting new structures, commercial and residential.

The demand for innovation to design and build high-capacity multi-functional heavy equipment, from cable-operated controls to hydraulic systems, skyrocketed in 1956 when the US Senate and House approved a conference report on the Federal-Aid Highway Act (also known as the National Interstate and Defense Highways Act), which was signed into law by the President Dwight D. Eisenhower [28]. The innovation journey continued in the 1970s as manufacturers refocused their attention to crew safety and added rollover protection structure, canopies, handholds, and guards.

The coal mining industry in the US, after the 1973 oil embargo, provided another boost to the demand cycles for heavy equipment. This lasted for over a decade, but soon the demand slipped, resulting in industry consolidation, leaving just a few players such as Caterpillar and John Deere in the US, sending the competitors, International Harvester, Caterpillar, Euclid, and Allis Chalmers, to dust [27, 29, 30].

In the 1990s, when the first-wave Tier 1 environmental laws were legislated to regulate diesel engine emissions, further innovations came along for cleaner engines, which constituted a major portion of earth-moving equipment. Tier 2 and Tier 3 environmental laws, much stricter, took hold between 2000 and 2010, and the manufacturers had to innovate again to comply with the new laws. Also, when the consumer trend shifted from ownership to rental, new rental companies sprang up that prioritized affordability, durability, and reliability, to which the equipment manufacturers had to adjust.

The industry is growing again, and there are several international brand names gaining significant market share that include US-based Caterpillar and John Deere, Japan-based Hitachi and Komatsu, Sweden-based Volvo, China-based Sany Heavy Industry Co., XCMG Group, and Zoomlion, South Korea-based Doosan Infracore, Germany-based Liebherr Group, and India-based Mahindra Construction Equipment.

The heavy equipment industry is at an inflection point and, as the equipment is commoditized, the focus of manufacturers shifts to irresistible customer service to distinguish themselves from the pack. The supply chains are globalized and service parts planning and availability has become a high priority. Given the digital transformation penetrating all the industries alike, the heavy equipment industry is no exception and is seeing the benefits as well. To improve the overall equipment uptime, system reliability, real-time equipment monitoring, system performance, fuel efficiency, and crew safety in hazardous and remote project locations, digital innovations such as telematics, electromobility, autonomous machinery, big data analytics, AI, machine learning, IoT, GPS, and digital twins are integrated into the heavy equipment system.

For example, one of the major US-based equipment manufacturers has recently embarked on an innovation project that integrated telemetry data from disjointed business units to provide a differentiated and seamless unified data-based service to its customers using the IoT and data science. The project used Microsoft Azure cloud-based infrastructure and its IoT services for its newly developed enterprise-wide telemetry platform. This platform collects and analyzes telemetry data in real-time from remotely operating equipment and products from the field sites. The unified data warehouse and analytics platform located centrally feeds many enterprise applications for near-real-time equipment maintenance planning and allows immediate response to changed conditions of the connected equipment at the field locations. The system integration was enabled through an application programming interface (API) layer that serves as a gateway for other regional systems as well [31].

Another interesting example where digital innovation is at play is Japan-based Kawasaki Heavy Industries Ltd, with an annual revenue of $14.5B. Kawasaki has six companies and 95 subsidiaries, with more than 36,000 employees deployed in six continents. Given the industry's shift from *products to service focus* as a differentiating factor and that competition is stiff, with significant structural changes happening in the industry, Kawasaki was at crossroads to make the right business decision. Given its successful past, it did not want to compromise its growth goal and set out an ambitious annual growth target of 5%, with a cumulative growth target of 70% by 2030. This is an ambitious goal for the industry. But the challenge was how to achieve this impossible goal when there was so much uncertainty in the industry [32]. Kawasaki developed a two-pronged innovation strategy – product and service innovation, and business model innovation to address this challenge. The enabler to support this strategy was to use advanced IT technology across its value chain and offer subscription-based business services for maintenance.

To capture market needs based on real-time customer sentiments, Kawasaki started leveraging customer feedback from social media and integrating it with the engineering group that could rapidly fine tune product development. To support predictive maintenance of field equipment at customer sites, IoT-enabled sensors with cloud infrastructure were leveraged to collect real-time data that laid the foundation for a subscription-based customer service business. As they had several internal systems such as customer relationship management, product data management, enterprise resource planning, and manufacturing execution systems, which were operating as disjointed systems with process and data structure difference, Kawasaki decided to deploy Aras, an integrated product lifecycle management platform, delivered as a service to its business units so that they all could function seamlessly with interchangeable data sets. Aras is based on the Microsoft .NET Framework and SQL Server, which is widely used by many corporations, including Airbus, GM, Sandia National Labs, INSITU-Boeing company, and Fuji Film [33].

7.4 Automotive

The automotive industry has a rich tradition of innovation since its humble beginning in 1775 when James Watt developed a dependable steam engine. It took more than 75 years until the 1850s to be retrofitted for personal automobile use. Between 1859 and 1876, automobiles made the shift from steam powered to gas- or petrol-based internal combustion four-cycle engines, largely due to the innovation work of Benz Patent-Motorwagen, Nikolaus Otto, George Brayton, Gottlieb Daimler, and Wilhelm Maybach. Moving away from manually cranking the engine to start, electric starting was pioneered by H.J. Dowsing in 1896 and Cadillac commercialized it around 1912 [34, 35]. This was followed by a competing innovation by Rudolf Christian Karl Diesel, who in1897 built a 25-horsepower, four-stroke, single vertical cylinder compression engine [36]. Diesel engines provided higher thermal efficiency with simpler design and led to greater market adoption.

As automotive vehicles suffered from skid-related accidents, Karl Wessel and Dunlop Maxaret worked on the problem and developed anti-skid systems. From its basic design, Chrysler improved it to include a computerized, three-channel, four-sensor-based anti-lock braking system and installed it on its 1971 Imperial model. As manual gear shift for speed adjustments was challenging for some drivers, engineers from Brazil, José Braz Araripe and Fernando Lely Lemos, improvised the compressed air-based automatic transmission design by Canadian Alfred Horner Munro, and used hydraulics for automatic transmission that was very efficient.

Other automotive innovations, such as airbags, power steering, GPS integration, catalytic converter, three-point seat belts, stability control systems, smart key ignition, cruise control, collision avoidance systems, infotainment, etc., leveraged innovations from other fields, including semiconductor, software, chemical, material science, and sensors, which tend to get better every day and are in common use. Many of the innovations are necessitated by government regulations inspired by consumer safety, social norms, and environmental movements.

The United Nations predicts that 68% of the world's population will live in urban areas by 2050 [37], causing tremendous traffic congestion, environmental problems, and parking issues. This is forcing the legacy automotive OEMs to reevaluate their business strategy, defying the traditional ownership model that led them to their growth thus far. Inspired by technology businesses such as Spotify, Netflix, Amazon Prime, SalesForec.com., and Microsoft that have successfully embraced subscription models making their services affordable to consumers, OEMs are exploring the new consumer trend with some versions of subscription-based mobility solutions that are rooted in electrified data-driven platform architecture. The solutions may include autonomous driving, battery-powered locomotion design, robot taxis, ride-sharing, over-the-air software update, connected office and living room, etc. Although there are quite a lot of uncertainties and technical and regulatory hurdles, subscription models tend to promote sharing of resources, significantly expanding the overall utilization of a given automobile. Take for example the commercial grade treadmill and other fitness equipment in commercial fitness centers that cost a fortune to the fitness center owners, but they provide a reliable and durable service during the equipment life, maximizing the owner's profitability and user experience. As OEMs prepare to embrace the new subscription normal, their automobiles need to be reliable and

96 *Innovations in industry verticals*

durable like commercial grade fitness equipment for higher and continuous utilization, unlike single-owner cars that sit idle in a garage for most of the time. The subscription model for automobiles will create whole new ecosystem of service businesses, including system monitoring, traffic dispatch, service and maintenance, insurance, battery swap, etc., that will cater to the needs of high-intensity asset usage scenarios where data will become the differentiator for competition between OEMs. The automobile itself may become a commodity and the success of the mobility solution would largely depend on seamless orchestration of the various activities within the connected ecosystem.

Apple, a highly innovative corporation, is foraying into the automotive market with its own mobility solution as it perfects its battery and autonomous driving technologies. This is expected to send a seismic shock through the industry and will challenge the traditional OEMs, including EV market leader Tesla, to innovate their business model with technologies and service design that hinges upon an ecosystem and network-based approach rather than just focusing on an individual vehicle. Peter Rawlinson, the CEO of Lucid, another high-end electric car manufacturer, used to work for Tesla, and commented that vertically integrated manufacturing provides strategic control over key resources to sustain competitive edge [38]. Tesla is proving the point by producing its own battery cells at a pilot plant in Fremont, California in addition to getting battery cells from Panasonic, Samsung, LG and CATL through a longer-term partnership with prices and supply commitments locked in. Tesla makes the battery packs in Reno, Nevada, co-anchored by Panasonic, who makes cells.

Automotive companies are high capital intensive with low free cash flow and are very vulnerable to business cycles and recession every 10–15 years, unlike pharmaceuticals or high-tech companies. Their margins are historically low and do not enjoy secular growth. Secular growth is typically the outcome of fundamental changes, including consumer preferences, which happens within a sector or industry, creating a spurt in new customer demand. To survive and compete on a sustainable basis, automotive companies must constantly reinvent themselves and innovations are paramount.

One of the ways some of the legacy OEM players and the upstarts can innovate their business models is to leverage external contract manufacturers. EV pure plays Tesla, Rivian, Chinese EV players such as Nio, XPeng, and Li Auto, and Lucid stand to benefit as they embark on scaling up production. Economies of scale are important to be competitive, particularly when battery technology is expensive. Although Tesla has been building its own giga factories to produce automobiles and batteries, it may change course, given the sense of urgency, to lead the pack on a sustainable basis. It may either leverage third-party manufacturers or establish partnership with an established legacy OEM for volume production to sustain first mover advantage that it enjoys currently.

Apple, which is actively exploring mobility solutions, may very well harness third-party contractors, including Taiwan-based Foxconn, which helped produce its iPhones for a very long time. There is a precedence in other industries as well to harness third-party contractors for volume production. For example, pharma companies such as Pfizer have been leveraging contract manufacturing organizations for quite some time to cut costs, allow speed to market, and focus on the product design; that is, drug discovery. Catalent Inc. and Lonza Group AG are part of 200+ networked contract manufacturing organizations that help Pfizer in manufacturing its established medicines [39].

On the automobile design front, particularly long-range battery technologies, data-driven autonomous vehicle architecture, and electricity powered drive train, traditional OEMs are catching up to the market leader Tesla. Their approach is mixed, with internal development and external partnership. Ford, for example, has announced plans to invest $29B toward electric and autonomous vehicles through 2025. GM, its archrival, is spending $27B by the end of 2025 with an aspiration to launch 30 EVs globally. Volkswagen (VW), a European OEM, has pledged an investment of $86B toward electric and autonomous vehicles [40, 41].

The investment race is on fire. These companies are also partnering with external companies to shore up their EV ambitions. For example, GM is working with LG Energy Solution to develop and mass produce its own battery cells, which is cost-effective and supports the second generation Ultium pack. This unique technology uses nickel cobalt manganese aluminum chemistry, reducing the expensive cobalt content by more than 70%. If successful, this innovation will pave the way for mass consumerization of EVs [41], which is central to drive positive cashflow.

VW is partnering with the Northvolt facility in Skellefteå, Sweden and has placed a battery cell order for $14B, while developing a new unified battery cell at its own Salzgitter site in Germany. By the end of 2030, VW expects to have a total of six cell factories to secure uninterrupted supply of batteries for all its production, while bringing the kilowatt hour cost to around $119.19, making electric mobility affordable [42]. VW is also exploring a new unified prismatic battery, an alternative to the pouch-style battery that it has been working on partnering with Korean firms LG Energy Solution and SK Innovation, and the race to perfect the battery technology at an affordable price is becoming interesting [43].

Cruise, a self-driving startup car maker, privately owned by GM and Honda, is partnering with Microsoft Corp to support autonomous vehicle technology architecture, which is valued at $30B [44]. GM, given that it is a legacy OEM, transplants technology from technology behemoth Microsoft Corp in its effort to leapfrog into the autonomous space, which is commendable. But GM must change its culture, mindset, and leadership style this time as it embarks on learning and internalizing new technology. Its earlier partnership with Toyota in 1984 through the New United Motor Manufacturing Incorporated plant in exchange for technology, Toyota Production System, to produce Chevy Nova and learn how to improve quality across its North American plants, did not go as well as planned before succumbing to recession and declaring bankruptcy, costing shareholders more than $50B [45, 46].

Ford, on the other hand, so far has depended heavily on external partners to supply its battery cells and is now seriously considering producing batteries internally to control its destiny [47]. Ford has invested little over $500M in Rivian, a Michigan- based EV startup founded in 2009 that just went public giving Ford more than 12% ownership in Rivian. The original plan to leverage Rivian's skateboard platform for Ford's EV development, however, is abandoned. Rivian has other investors as well, including Amazon, T. Rowe Price, and BlackRock Inc., and is planning to roll out all-electric pickup trucks – the R1T, and the companion R1S SUV. Ford's recent launch of EVs Mustang Mach-E SUV and proposed Lightning truck F-150 is gaining a lot of interest in the marketplace.

98   *Innovations in industry verticals*

Although partnership is at play in the EV automotive, as mentioned before, there is a tendency to vertically integrate the supply chain, and this comes with a huge cost at the beginning. Such integration is vulnerable to cost inefficiencies over time, muddled with chaos and delays unless there is a strong patent portfolio that provides sustainable competitive advantage.

7.5 Semiconductor

The term semiconducting was first used by Alessandro Volta in 1782, but it was not until 1833 that Michael Faraday observed a semiconductor effect when electrical resistance of silver sulfide decreased with temperature. Karl Braun researched it further to observe a diode effect where current flows freely in only one direction between a metal point and a lead sulfide. In 1901, Jagadis Chandra Bose patented "cat whiskers," the first semiconductor device to detect radio waves [48, 49].

Semiconductors are made from pure elements such as silicon or germanium, or compounds such as gallium arsenide, and through a doping process different levels of impurities are added to impact the relative conductivity of the material [50]. These materials have lower resistance to the flow of electrical current in one direction, say copper, than in another, say plastic, giving them the name semiconductor. The discovery of semiconductor materials has paved the way for many devices to be invented and commercialized. Regardless of the context, business or personal, electronic devices that use semiconductors are seen everywhere. Smartphones, laptops, televisions, radio equipment, home security cameras, kitchen appliances, automobile infotainment, etc., are ubiquitous and have become the fixture of how we define ourselves and our lifestyles, at the least in the developing and developed world. The sophistication and performance of the semiconductor has been doubling every two years while costs are trending downward, thanks to Moore's observation, which has defined the industry for over 50 years [51].

The semiconductor production typically follows a series of steps: 1. Design and digital simulation using sophisticated equipment; 2. Raw materials selection, including sand and other pure and compound materials; 3. Ingot production, where the sand is purified, melted, and formed into a cylinder, also called ingots; 4. Blank wafer, using high-tech machines, where the above cylinders are cut into thin slices and polished; 5. Finished wafer – printing electrical circuit designs, called chips; 6. Cut wafer – finished semiconductors, as many as several thousand per wafer, are further cut into individual semiconductors called dies; 7. Packaged chip – the dies are packaged together, called finished semiconductors that are ready for use; and 8. Inserting them into electronic devices such as a motherboard in a laptop [50].

The innovations in the semiconductor industry, although challenged by the physical limitations of our ability to compress many circuits more than ever we did, show there is still room to grow. Companies such as Advanced Micro Devices), NVIDIA, Apple, Qualcomm, Samsung, IBM, etc., are pushing the processing threshold and coming up with highly dense microcircuit designs that are measured using a scale "nm", which stands for nanometer, one billionth of a meter, also expressed as 0.000000001 or 10–9 meters. In semiconductor chip design, "nm" refers to the length of a transistor gate – the smaller the gate the more processing power that can be packed into a given area. Some of the above companies have already achieved and perfected 5 nm architecture design and the semiconductor foundries such as TSMC and Global Foundries are responding to manufacture them, which is an extremely challenging task. IBM just announced that it has made a breakthrough in development of the world's first chip with 2 nm technology, which is impressive [52].

It is interesting to note that not satisfied with the nm density metric approach to measure the semiconductor performance, some scientists from MIT, Stanford, University of California/Berkeley, and Taiwan-based chip manufacturer TSMC are proposing a new "density metric" approach designed to be a more holistic gauge, which is called LMC density metric [53]. LMC, stands for the density of logic (D_L), the density of main memory (D_M), and the density of the interconnects linking them (D_C). This leads semiconductor development into 3D chip architecture as opposed to the current 2D design, with immense potential to increase chip processing capacity [54].

Another exciting area of innovation related to computing in general is seen in quantum computing. Quantum computing harnesses quantum mechanics phenomena to solve complex problems that traditional computers, including super computers, cannot solve in a timely manner.

Quantum computers are the size of a household fridge and like how bits are used in a conventional computer, a quantum computer uses quantum bits or qubits (CUE-bits) to store information in quantum form. IBM has pioneered the development of quantum computers and is still evolving. IBM allows public access to such computers using its cloud infrastructure for free. These computers are programmed using open-source Qiskit designed in Python. It involves two steps to use these special computers. First, create vast multidimensional spaces to represent large and unique problems. Second, use specialized quantum wave interference algorithms to solve problems in this space and translate them back into human comprehensible form [55]. It will take decades before these innovations find widespread adoption given some of the technical challenges, including processing consistency, which need to be addressed first for mass consumption.

Some other exciting semiconductor innovations are on the horizon as the human need is exponentially growing by the day. As space exploration is getting exciting, advanced gravitational wave detectors are being innovated to operate under extreme conditions of temperature and/or radiation, which existing semiconductor device models find challenging. For patients with glaucoma disease, which may lead to blindness, elevated intraocular pressure (IOP) needs to be monitored precisely and controlled in real-time. Existing IOP monitoring techniques and semiconductor systems have limitations. A Samsung/Caltech team have published an innovation that allows precision monitoring of IOP in real-time, using a miniaturized (500-µm diameter, 200-µm thick) optomechanical nanophotonic sensor implant. This is very significant and may benefit a large segment of the affected population [56].

The automotive industry is increasingly using large amounts of semiconductor chips in the form of microcontrollers. They manage what is called advanced driver-assistance systems, fuel management, rollover safety systems, powertrain, climate systems, infotainment, and climate control systems. They run complex computer programs that require efficient nonvolatile memory. Collectively they make up system on chip, which needs to deliver reliable and high performance under demanding conditions, with no to low power consumption. In a recent International Electron Devices Meeting, one of the teams demonstrated an ultra-dense (cell size = 0.019µm2) embedded phase-change memory technology for automotive system on chips that meets the stringent

100 *Innovations in industry verticals*

AEC-Q100 Grade 0 standard for automotive reliability, which has the potential to take the industry by storm as data processing is becoming intense in real-time for autonomous cars [56, 57].

Samsung engineers recently demonstrated first of its kind single chip lidar beam scanner innovation, which uses light waves, unlike radar, which uses radio waves. Single chip lidar is very fast and supports real-time complex data processing for highly demanding applications such as autonomous vehicle navigation, including real-time collision avoidance, high-speed industrial robotics, and mixed/augmented-reality applications. The lidars available today are bulky, expensive, and use traditional mechanical beam scanners with motors and rotating mirrors. The single chip lidar will lead to low-cost, compact lidar systems with no separate light source and flexible installation options [56, 57].

7.6 Concluding remarks

Manufacturing industries have evolved over the past few centuries and relentless innovation has been the key driver. However, this industry's growth over the past ten years or so has been remarkable, largely influenced by the digital innovations from the technology sector. As a matter of fact, the manufacturing industry is enjoying a symbiotic relationship with the technology sector as they both mutually benefit and reinforce each other.

Industry 4.0 and 5G are getting increased attention in many board strategy meetings. Industries are rushing to become digitally connected and orchestrate autonomous factory functions replacing the traditional workforce with "bots," a short form for "robots," to increase productivity and minimize costs. The electronic workforce, driven by computer programs, can execute tasks without human guidance, raising concerns at many governmental agencies for fear of increased unemployment and possibly lost payroll tax revenues for them. The apprehension is real, and it is a matter of time before massive adoption of "bots" become a new normal. This will force the traditional workforce to elevate their skill sets so that they will become producers of programs and technology instead of being the consumer of technology as they are today. Obviously, there are several social and ethical questions to be answered as not everyone is quite ready to switch their roles and become a technologist.

Regardless of the type of manufacturing company, they must be ready to adapt to the digital trend. The pace of digital penetration is unprecedented and manufacturing companies do not want to be left behind. Interestingly, the manufacturing landscape is becoming very exciting as there is a convergence of many innovations to deliver value to the customers.

Student activities

1. Select the Amgen Pharmaceuticals and Whirlpool cases from Part VIII.
2. Review the details and list the problems or opportunities they try to address.
3. Discuss the innovation approach and its relevance to Industry 4.0
4. Also answer the questions listed at the end of the case.

7.7 References

1. www.britannica.com/event/Industrial-Revolution
2. https://ied.eu/project-updates/the-4-industrial-revolutions/
3. www.economist.com/leaders/2012/04/21/the-third-industrial-revolution
4. https://sciencing.com/sources-energy-1800s-8126819.html
5. www.nationalgeographic.org/article/industrial-revolution-and-technology/
6. www.un.org/en/un75/impact-digital-technologies
7. www.nature.com/scitable/content/life-expectancy-around-the-world-has-increased-19786/
8. https://manufacturingchemist.com/news/article_page/The_evolution_of_the_pharma_industry_From_reactive_to_disruptive/157976
9. "Biopharmaceutical Research and Development: The Process Behind New Medicines," http://phrma-docs.phrma.org/sites/default/files/pdf/rd_brochure_022307.pdf
10. www.policymed.com/2014/12/a-tough-road-cost-to-develop-one-new-drug-is-26-billion-approval-rate-for-drugs-entering-clinical-de.html
11. www.biopharmatrend.com/post/76-democratizing-artificial-intelligence-in-pharmaceutical-research/
12. www.healthline.com/health-news/how-much-will-it-cost-to-get-a-covid-19-vaccine#Heres-what-the-government-has-spent-so-far
13. Kat McGowan, 2017, "Sharing is daring," Stanford Social Innovation Review, 15, pp. 13–14, http://libproxy.bus.umich.edu/login?url=https://www-proquest-com.libproxy.bus.umich.e du/magazines/sharing-is-daring/docview/1931647727/se-2?accountid=34476
14. Flora Southey, (2018, July 23), PhRMA-backed data sharing platform looks to engage with CROS,SPONSORS. Retrieved February 27, 2021, from www.outsourcing-pharma.com/Article/2018/07/23/PhRMA-backed-data-sharing-platform-looks-to-engage-with-CROs-sponsors
15. Vivli platform process at a glance. Retrieved February 24, 2021. https://vivli.org/about/data-request-review-process/
16. www.transceleratebiopharmainc.com/our-mission/collaborative-model/
17. https://pubmed.ncbi.nlm.nih.gov/24303286/
18. https://bulkinside.com/pharmaceutical-processing/
19. www.medicinenet.com/biologics_biologic_drug_class/article.htm
20. https://drug-dev.com/technological-breakthroughs-aiding-the-biologics-market/
21. www.nanalyze.com/2018/01/9-examples-digital-medication-smart-pills/
22. Mohd Javaid, Lalit Kumar, Vineet Kumar, and Abid Haleem, 2015, "Product Design and Development Using Polyjet Rapid Prototyping Technology," Contr Theor Inf, 5(3), pp. 12–19.
23. Guofeng Hu, Alireaz Damanpack, Mahdi Bodaghi, and Wei-Hsin Liao, 2017, "Increasing Dimension of Structures by 4D Printing Shape Memory Polymers Via Fused Deposition Modeling," Smart Mater Struct, 26(12), pp. 1–38.
24. Zhen Ding, Chao Yuan, Xirui Peng, Tiejun Wang, H. Jerry Qi, Martin L. Dunn, 2017, "Direct 4D Printing Via Active Composite Materials," Sci Adv, 3, pp..1–6.
25. Mohd Javaid, Abid Haleem, 2019, "4D Printing Applications in Medical Field: A Brief Review," Clinical Epidemiology and Global Health, 7(3), pp. 317–321, ISSN 2213-3984.
26. www.globenewswire.com/news-release/2020/06/18/2049895/0/en/Construction-Equipment-Market-to-reach-USD-186-42-Billion-by-2026-Major-Companies-are-Focusing-on-M-As-for-Establishing-a-Wider-Consumer-Base-says-Fortune-Business-Insights.html
27. www.customtruck.com/blog/history-of-the-heavy-equipment-industry/
28. www.senate.gov/artandhistory/history/minute/Federal_Highway_Act.htm
29. www.deere.com/en/loaders/backhoes/
30. www.caterpillar.com/

102 Innovations in industry verticals

31. www.cognizant.com/case-studies/heavy-equipment-iot-platform
32. www.smartindustry.com/articles/2020/case-study-how-kawasaki-heavy-industries-digitally-transformed-its-business/
33. www.aras.com/en
34. https://interestingengineering.com/20-greatest-innovations-and-inventions-of-automobile-engineering-from-the-first-engine-to-today
35. https://en.wikipedia.org/wiki/Benz_Patent-Motorwagen
36. www.britannica.com/biography/Rudolf-Diesel
37. www.un.org/development/desa/en/news/population/2018-revision-of-world-urbanization-prospects.html
38. www.cnbc.com/2021/03/02/tesla-vs-lucid-heres-how-the-ev-rivals-are-and-arent-alike.html
39. www.cnbc.com/2020/05/08/pfizer-to-outsource-some-drug-production-focus-on-corona-virus-vaccine.html
40. www.motortrend.com/news/ford-ev-investment-2025/
41. www.gm.com/electric-vehicles.html
42. www.cnbc.com/2021/03/15/vw-to-ramp-up-battery-production-with-six-gigafactories-in-europe-.html
43. https://finance.yahoo.com/news/power-play-volkswagen-abruptly-pulls-065929726.html
44. www.reuters.com/article/us-gm-microsoft-autonomous/cruise-gm-partner-with-microsoft-to-ramp-up-self-driving-vehicles-idINKBN29O1MO
45. https://hbr.org/2009/09/nummi-what-toyota-learned
46. www.npr.org/templates/story/story.php?storyId=125229157
47. www.govtech.com/transportation/Ford-Explores-Making-Its-Own-Electric-Vehicle-Battery-Cells.html
48. www.thoughtco.com/what-is-a-semiconductor-1991409
49. Argonne National Laboratory, "NEWTON – Ask a Scientist," Internet Archive, February 27, 2015.
50. www.semiconductors.org/semiconductors-101/what-is-a-semiconductor/
51. www.intel.com/content/www/us/en/silicon-innovations/moores-law-technology.html
52. https://newsroom.ibm.com/2021-05-06-IBM-Unveils-Worlds-First-2-Nanometer-Chip-Technology,-Opening-a-New-Frontier-for-Semiconductors
53. www.hpcwire.com/2020/06/01/10nm-7nm-5nm-should-the-chip-nanometer-metric-be-replaced/
54. https://spectrum.ieee.org/semiconductors/devices/a-better-way-to-measure-progress-in-semiconductors
55. www.ibm.com/quantum-computing/what-is-quantum-computing/
56. www.designnews.com/electronics/15-semiconductor-electronic-innovations-2021/gallery?slide=4
57. https://ieee-iedm.org/

8 Innovations in the service industry

8.1 Introduction

Merriam-Webster defines service as "the work performed by one that serves." Although it tends to humanize the process, service is no longer solely human-centric. Of course, an individual or a group is receiving certain service, but the provider of a service can no longer be assumed to be a human being. This does not mean that the service cannot be individualized. There is a widespread belief that the service sector in the economy is people-intensive and rest of the economy is capital-intensive. Given the influx of technology innovations in many facets of the economy, such a traditional belief is no longer true. Service components exist regardless of the industry sector, whether manufacturing or construction. For example, although we consider Hewlett-Packard as a computer manufacturing company, it has significant service components, including sales and marketing, customer service for post-sales support, etc. Similarly, Ford is an automotive manufacturing company with substantial service activities, including sales and marketing, customer financing and lease payments, post-sales service support, and dealership network management. Factors such as consistency, speed, productivity, and cost-effectiveness that tend to define, for example, the manufacturing industry are now dictating the service industry as well. To bring focus to our service industry discussion, we consider healthcare, retail, hospitality, education, wellness, banking, and transportation as a few examples, along with many others that make up the service industry.

In 1972, Harvard professor Theodore Levitt in his article on "Production-Line Approach to Service" beautifully discusses the possibilities of applying some of the manufacturing or automation concepts, techniques, and technologies to drive efficiency in the service business [1, 2, 3]. It was remarkable because that was the time when mainframe computers were just making inroads into corporate banking and payroll functions, and desktops, laptops, mobile phones and iPads had not yet been conceived. Here we are in the first quarter of the 21st century experiencing the tremendous impact of the fourth industrial digital technologies and innovations, blurring the boundaries of industry sectors and allowing incredible possibilities for individualized customer service at scale.

8.2 Service trend

The service sector has been growing significantly over several decades and no country is an exception. As world bank data in Figure 8.1 illustrates, service as a percentage of

DOI: 10.4324/9781003190837-13

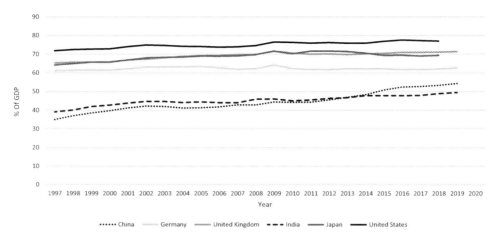

Figure 8.1 Service – Percentage of GDP.
Source: https://data.worldbank.org.

GDP in such countries as the US, UK, Japan, China, and India is already at 76.5%, 70%, 68.9%, 53.9%, and 47.8%, respectively. Given the overall prosperity and improving quality of life in the developed and developing countries over several decades, the population can now afford more services in addition to the physical products they consume for personal needs. Whether it is education, housing, tourism, banking, food services, telecommunication, healthcare, and fitness services, the increasing service demand triggers a matching response from the industry that has begun to leverage technology innovations to feed the appetite.

Personalized shipments from Amazon, Alibaba, and Harry & David food company, customized vacation package for our dream destinations from travel agencies, food, or grocery delivery by UberEats, Grubhub, Postmates, Instacart, and DoorDash, personal yoga trainer on Zoom on weekends, concierge medical services during office breaks, etc., are just a few that we have started cultivating as a routine that used to be either luxury or beyond comprehension just a few decades ago. This trend is a virtuous cycle and lifts the service industry overall. We discuss the trend and the innovations seen in a few of the service sectors in the following sections.

8.3 Healthcare

Healthcare is one of the greatest beneficiaries of technology innovation. The traditional human-intensive, time-consuming, and error-prone value chain, particularly at the doctor's office and hospitals where services are delivered to the patients, are getting a significant face lift through the application of technology such as secure cloud-hosted electronic medical records (EMR), revenue cycle management, and video-enabled telemedicine [4]. There are many innovations used to diagnose patient medical conditions using magnetic resonance imaging (MRI), computed tomography (CT), and ultrasound imaging (sonography) with great success [5]. Surgeons and patients are increasingly provided with cost-effective robot-assisted precision surgeries, particularly for situations such as coronary artery bypass, gall bladder removal, hip replacement, hysterectomy, kidney stone removal, kidney transplant, and cancer tissue removal from delicate parts of the body such as blood vessels and body organs [6]. There are also significant advancements seen in the genomics scientific field for personalized medicine. Genomics, the study of genes, makes it possible to predict, diagnose, and treat diseases effectively. A human genome is made up of 23 chromosome pairs with a total of more than 3 billion DNA base pairs. DNA sequencing, gene editing using technologies such as CRISPR (Clustered, Regularly Interspaced, Short Palindromic Repeats), Big Data, and AI hold significant promise to find cures for the most difficult medical challenges including cancer.

Electronic medical records (EMR): From small physician offices to large hospital systems, there is a growing trend to adapt EMR application systems, for example in countries such as the US, where the government mandated the HIPAA of 1996 to protect sensitive patient health information from being disclosed without the patient's consent [7]. EMR systems such as Epic Systems, Allscripts, eClinicalWorks, athenahealth, and NextGen Healthcare allow compliance with such requirements using simple to use application systems that integrate and automate mundane office functions. They include patient scheduling, patient follow up with text alerting/ reminders, capturing and sharing patient demography, insurance information, voice-activated physician's diagnostic and treatment notes, and medical imaging and lab results. These systems also transfer prescriptions to networked pharmacies and diagnostic test centers. Many EMR systems that are integrated with patient portals allow patient/doctor communications in a secure and confidential manner. Many such EMR systems have extensions that allow revenue cycle management functions that typically include the electronic submission of insurance claims, posting insurance payments, generating patient statements for outstanding patient balances, and forecasting revenue. EMR-enabled processes are integrated end-to-end, reducing manual entries and related errors, and providing a high degree of operational efficiency and transparency to authorized users to manage the medical facilities.

As physical paperwork is reduced and replaced by digital methods, this allows the conducting of sophisticated data-driven analytics to understand the overall performance of the medical practice. Furthermore, it enables the maintenance of close connection with patients in real-time to make sure the prescribed treatment plans are effective and to possibly intervene proactively if there are issues. The issue could be as simple as adjusting the dosage of the medication or switching over to alternative ones that have lesser side-effects based on patient feedback.

In China, there has been a Ministry of Health five-year mandate to digitize hospital records and embrace EMR systems, initiated in 2011, and the success has been noticeable. China has more than 18,700 general hospitals and it was a huge task [8]. In India, however, EMR adoption is low for various reasons. Big hospital chains such as Fortis and Apollo have such systems in some of their hospitals, but overall there are significant barriers to implementing EMR [9]. India has 43,486 private hospitals, with 1.18 million beds, while there are 25,778 public hospitals with 713,986 beds. The private hospital infrastructure accounts for nearly 62% of all of India's health infrastructure, and lack of standards makes it hard to embrace EMR [10]. The insurance reimbursement concept is still evolving in India, and most of the hospital expenses are paid through cash

106 Innovations in industry verticals

payments upfront by the patients and their families, reducing the need to digitize the patient treatment history and submitting them to insurance carriers for reimbursement. Lack of an integrated EMR system makes sharing of patient's history across hospitals and physicians extremely difficult. There are significant opportunities to improve the overall healthcare efficiency in India, reduce the healthcare cost burden to patients by minimizing expensive duplicate procedures such as X-rays, ultrasonography, MRI, angiography, positron emission tomography, radioisotope scanning, and CT.

Telemedicine: The other important technology innovation that has gained more adoption, particularly during the COVID-19 pandemic when physical doctor's office visits were restricted, is telemedicine. Many EMR systems have a built-in telemedicine capability to allow patients to remotely have a video chat with their physicians using their mobile phones or a personal computer. Of course, there are limitations to what medical services can be rendered over telemedicine, with possible disparity in the reimbursable insurance payments. We believe that even after the pandemic, the use of telemedicine will continue, perhaps increase, particularly for the older population as well as the remotely located rural population that experience logistical challenges in making physical visits to the doctor's office. In developing countries, access to healthcare facilities can be greatly improved through telemedicine, which has the potential to reduce long waiting times at the hospital and dependence on transportation. As broadband internet and smartphone access may be a barrier in some developing and underdeveloped countries, they may explore community kiosk options and set up tele-visit technologies for patients to avail.

8.4 Retail

The word retail represents selling of goods and services to end consumers for a profit. Its origin can be traced all the way back to the 8th century (January 1, 701–December 31, 800) on ancient Agora in Athens, Greece. Agora was also known as a marketplace or a place for people to assemble [11]. The broader definition of retail encompasses traveling street merchants often seen in places such as Indian cities, mom-and-pop stores often seen on street corners, larger standalone department stores, sprawling shopping malls sheltering numerous shops, and online e-commerce platforms [12].

In the evolution of retail stores in the US, departmental stores such as Macy's (1858), Bloomingdales (1861), and Sears (1886) played a vital role in enabling and adopting many new innovations. That included the first bell-ringing cash registry to record sales, invented by James Ritty in 1883. The cash registry was widely used across the world and can still be seen in many shops. The arrival of minicomputers/ PCs and software applications led to the development of POS that integrated with modern cash registry and provided enhanced functionality for store merchants to manage their end-to-end retail operations. This included inventory management, daily store reports, automated back-end stock replenishment order generation, etc.

With credit card and other mobile payment integration, retail is adopting banking industry and fintech innovations to allow frictionless customer experience during the checkout process. With the advent of high bandwidth anytime anywhere internet access and affordable smartphone devices, consumers are increasingly searching online to learn about and purchase products and services, leading to retail's seismic structural change for an omnichannel presence.

Consumers, given their diverse work-life balance, tend to leverage multiple (omni) channels to interact with retail businesses; for example, searching product details online using a mobile phone on a tram while commuting to work, creating a shopping cart on a desktop computer at home, physically inspecting the product at a local brick-and-mortar store, completing the shopping cart, and making payments for door delivery on a desktop at home, and possibly returning the product at a different brick-and-mortar store in a nearby town. If the retail merchant is to be successful in responding to customer preferences through disparate channels and provide a seamless customer experience while still making money, they must implement omnichannel technology innovations at their retail and online stores and make sure the customer trails are tracked, managed, and followed through. Although the task seems daunting, many retail merchants are successfully navigating through a complex maze of customer journeys, leveraging big data, AI, and machine learning innovations.

For the customer-facing functions, there are significant advances at the physical retail stores as well to enrich customer experience, which includes auto checkout with simple barcode scanning, or mobile application-based flash checkout, such as Amazon Go.

On the back-end of the retail stores, highly integrated enterprise systems such as SAP, Oracle, or Microsoft Dynamics, fed by front-end POS systems, allow automatic real-time merchandise replenishment management, including triggering signals to the supply chain when certain inventory thresholds are hit. For the warehouse and inventory management functions, in addition to semi-automated barcode scanning, a non-contact RFID technology is used to transfer RFID-tagged shipment data to drive efficiency while reducing labor.

As social media sites such as Facebook, Instagram, YouTube, Pinterest, Twitter, Reddit, WeChat, Snapchat, WhatsApp, TikTok, Vimeo, Viber, etc. have become the home for many customers, these sites are targeted by the retailers and manufactures alike to drive traffic to their own storefront – online and on-site. As a byproduct, digital marketing is taking off and the retailer industry is pouring in money in billions. The global total retail sales in 2020 was $23.3T dollars, of which $18.5T was from brick-and-mortar stores and $4T from online platforms [13]. Digital innovation has literally taken the retail industry by storm and there is no let up on the pace and penetration.

8.5 Hospitality

Within the service industry, a subset of services such as lodging, restaurants, theme parks, transportation, cruise, tourism, and event planning is generally considered hospitality services. As the disposable income of people in both the developed and developing nations is on the rise, given the overall upward trend of the middle classes, the hospitality industry is gaining significant momentum, resulting in the creation of numerous job opportunities. Convenience, entertainment, relaxation, adventure, and social outings are some of the themes this industry is focused on and is leveraging some of the digital innovations from other industries to provide seamless and integrated services to its customers.

The industry has two fronts to manage: Firstly, customer- and partner-facing; and secondly, its back-end internal operations. On the customer-facing and partner-facing sales, marketing, payments processing, promotions, partnerships management, customer loyalty, and customer complaints are a few of the functions that leverage innovations, particularly digital innovations, from many industry verticals. At the back-end, depending on the specific subsector, property or asset maintenance,

108 *Innovations in industry verticals*

day-to-day operations, staff management, and financials management are some of the value chain functions that are supported by several technologies and industry best practices.

Let us look at a few examples. In the case of theme parks, Disney is a popular one where one could experience the convergence of many technologies, right from making online reservations to being guided to specific on-site entertainment. The past Chairman & CEO of Disney, CEO Bob Iger, is quoted as saying, "Technology is lifting the limits of creativity and transforming the possibilities for entertainment and leisure." At Disney, the use of digital technologies has been used to transform customer experience, enhance operational efficiency, personalize connected products, and enhance interactivity across channels such as theme parks, studio entertainment, interactive media platforms, and physical stores [14, 15]. One of the cool experiences that visitors have at Disney is the magic band that they wear on their wrist. This is a colorful all-in-one device that seamlessly connects one to all the vacation choices, such as resort reservation, dining reservation, theme park tickets, and magic photo memory maker, etc. One can use this band to enter the parks, access your Disney resort hotel room, and shop at Disney stores [16]. Additionally, it enables Fast Pass+ access to all the experiences that one has selected online, not having to wait in long queues. It provides a lot of convenience to the visitors, who do not have to carry a purse or wallet to move around within the Disney property.

Disney Studios released a Movies Anywhere application that lets consumers buy and watch films across different devices and to digitally self-curate a collection of movies, including DVDs that they purchased previously [17]. Disney's video game unit released a video game allowing players to choose and personalize characters from its popular Disney and Pixar collection to meet their individual game adventure needs. Disney's customer obsession and its ability to exploit digital transformation are simply magical.

Another great example for numerous technology innovation adoptions is in the cruise line industry. This industry has steadily grown over the past few decades with $37B annual revenue serving more than 30 million passengers. River, sea, and ocean cruises are some of the options provided to customers with several new travel destinations every year and a wide array of personalized cruise products, services, and experiences. The cruise industry is becoming a mainstream leisure option in many parts of the world, particularly in the US, Canada, Europe, the Mediterranean, Australia and New Zealand, the Arctic, and the Antarctic geographies [18]. The results of an Florida-Caribbean Cruise Association (FCCA) survey indicate that 88% of people surveyed find cruises more relaxing and 82% find cruises less hassle than land-based vacations [19].

The industry is rapidly adopting innovations from many other industries while adjusting to changing demographics – families with children, young adult couples, and singles who have significantly different needs and budgets. The modern cruise vessels are becoming very sophisticated with luxury amenities and high-tech entertainment and have an average capacity of 550 passengers per vessel. Some of the well-recognized brands include Carnival Corporation, Royal Caribbean Cruises, and Norwegian Cruise Line. The commonly seen entertainment services include casino gambling, massage therapies, swimming lessons, concerts, youth programs, spa treatments, and shore excursions. From two-to-three-day mini cruises to two-to-three-week trips, voyages are bundled with many customized options that cater to the needs of diverse customers.

Innovations in the service industry   109

Some of the innovations that delight customers in these cruise lines include virtual check-in, geo-location, augmented reality, chatbots, wearables [20], virtual views, technology-based entertainment, tricked-out top decks, and the Magic Carpet [20]. Let us review a few of them.

Virtual check-ins – Imagine the nightmare experience if thousands of passengers must use human-assisted check-in and embarking on vessels within a few hours. To make the process frictionless and enjoyable, Royal Caribbean is leveraging facial recognition technology. Once the passengers upload their passport and a selfie onto their website at home, upon arrival at the cruise ship, they can board immediately after a simple security check, bypassing any queues. Royal Caribbean claims that it has reduced the boarding time from 90 to 10 minutes [19].

Geo-location – Some of the cruise ships are huge. For example, *Symphony of the Seas* from Royal Caribbean, is an 18-deck cruise ship measuring longer than a nuclear-powered aircraft carrier – that is 1,188 ft long, has 18 decks, 22 restaurants, 24 pools, 2,759 cabins, and a park with over 20,000 tropical plants. It has a capacity of 6,680 passengers, with a crew of 2,200 [21]. It will be very difficult for passengers to navigate, but mapping technology using location intelligence makes it painless. MSC Cruises' Mobile for Me app, once loaded on a phone, can provide turn-by-turn directions to assigned cabin to restaurant to concert, etc. HERE location intelligence technology provides real-time flow and concentration of people in different parts of the ship, such as concert hall, restaurants, and pool tec, allowing the management to deploy staff appropriately [19].

Augmented reality – For example, *Celebrity Edge*'s cruise application provides its guests a guided tour of the boats' key features as they walk around without human assistance. Using HERE Places technology, passengers are able to experience virtual shore excursions and immerse themselves in the destinations before buying the actual package. This try-before-you-buy is essential, as FCCA's study suggests that 68% of cruisers consider destination as the most important factor influencing their holiday choice and sampling the experience motivates them to make their purchasing decision [19].

Wearables – Similar to Disney's wrist band, MSC Cruises' bracelet and Carnival and Princess Cruises' Ocean Medallion stores personal information such as food allergy and credit card, etc. to enjoy more than 130 smart onboard services. It allows parents to keep track of their children as well, so long as they wear bracelets and parents have access to their mobile phones [19].

Virtual views – Booking an inside cabin without ocean view is a less expensive alternative for budget-conscious consumers. How about feeding them live footage of the ocean view if they have a balcony cabin? – Virtual Balcony. Royal Caribbean offers exactly that experience using a large high-definition LED screen with a real-time video feed of the ocean from digital cameras mounted on the bridge, stern, and sides. Disney Cruise Line had offered similar services before in the form of porthole windows showing ocean footage with Disney characters, making them a memorable magical experience.

Historically, high bandwidth connectivity has been an issue at sea. However, there are several private enterprises such as Global Eagle (US), Intelsat SA (Luxembourg), Eutelsat (France), Telesat (Canada), Arqiva (UK), AsiaSat (China), Swarm (US), and Telenor Satellite (Norway) [22], which deploy low-orbit satellites that will improve

110 *Innovations in industry verticals*

high-speed internet connectivity at an affordable price. This will significantly increase the demand for the cruise industry as people do not have to sacrifice their addiction to high bandwidth streaming services such as Netflix, etc. while at the sea.

These cruise lines are transforming into smart floating cities by leveraging technology innovations and are in direct competition with land leisure services. The consumer has plenty of choice now when it comes to choosing their vacation plan, which is good.

8.6 Education

The word educate means "to train by formal instruction and supervised practice especially in a skill, trade, or profession," per the Merriam-Webster dictionary. Etymologically, education is derived from the Latin word ēducātiō ("A breeding, a bringing up, a rearing"). Education is a process and began during the prehistory period, between the use of the first stone tools by hominins 3.3 million years ago and the invention of writing systems [23].

More generally speaking, education is all about facilitating learning, or the acquisition of knowledge, skills, values, morals, beliefs, and habits. It started off with oral instruction, storytelling and observing – one person to another. As cultures expanded the knowledge – art, medicine, agriculture, hunting, community living, etc., gradually formal education started to develop when one to many, and many to many "passing of knowledge" became a necessity. In Europe, Plato, around 400 BCE, founded the Academy of Athens. In 330 BCE, the city of Alexandria in Egypt followed suit and became the intellectual cradle of Ancient Greece. In China, Confucius (551–479 BCE), was a philosopher whose approach to governance, learning, and society is still having a major influence on educational systems in the Far East nations such as China, Japan, and Korea. Nalanda Academy, a Buddhist monastery in India, was recognized as a reputable center of learning during the 4th century as it contributed to the emergence of a powerful India and attracted several scholars from Tibet, China, Korea, and Central Asia [24].

Here we are in the 21st century, where the need for education has only accelerated and has not slowed down. Population has grown millions of times since prehistoric days and societal needs are exponentially growing. Human beings are on a constant quest for better quality of life, resources to support their lifestyles, and methods to safeguard themselves from unpredictable diseases and natural calamities. Formal mass education has become a necessity for survival and defines our modern society, although many underdeveloped countries are struggling to catch up.

To support such massive demands placed on the education systems, constant reinventing of our existing structure, process, and tools for learning is essential. Innovation is a prerequisite to sustain educational success. It is no surprise that innovations are on the rise and permeating the educational systems across early childhood (age 3 to 8), primary (age 8 to 15), secondary (age 15 to 19), tertiary (undergraduate and postgraduate higher education), and vocational (trade or craft) spectrum. Given the diverse needs of students, in-person as well as remote learning, technology innovations are significantly impactful in reshaping our educational systems on all facets – school selections, student and teacher recruitments, course content generations, content consumption, course evaluations, and student engagements. Increasingly, teachers are leveraging technologies to enable innovative pedagogical methods to make learning effective, particularly where skills development is a major focus.

Higher education in many countries is challenged today more than ever before. The educational system is called on to serve a diverse spectrum of students – highly gifted to hard working to less than motivated students, to nontraditional students who are over of 25 years of age [25]. The wider spectrum of universities – private-elite, private liberal arts, public, community, and for-profit – offer a lot of options for students to choose from, but they are not cheap. There is always a question of value, and students recognize it more than ever. For students, seeking a better education comes at enormous cost, and affordability is largely influenced by family income as well. Without family support, it is quite possible for a student in the US to rack up a few hundred thousand dollars' debt before graduation. There is no guarantee that the degree will serve the student well to repay the debt. University tuitions are on the rise, but the earning potential for many students upon graduation is on the decline. This compels the university system to drive efficiency, reduce costs, and make the program affordable to students by extending some form of scholarship. The competency imparted to students has to be aligned with market needs to realize the full potential of a university degree. The industry is valuing soft skills as well as technical skills. To train students on soft skills such as teamwork, communication, leadership, etc., historically required a physical presence within four walls, but is increasingly being emulated by online immersive tools and the impact is felt.

As the world is changing fast, including government priorities, increased stakeholders' expectations, shrinking budget, surging nontraditional student population, rising faculty and staff expenses, emerging for-profit and online competitors, and growing global faculty and student mobility, the educational systems need to adapt and constantly innovate to satisfy many different stakeholders at the same time [25].

The innovation focus areas within the education sector that warrant discussion are: 1. Access to quality educational contents that were historically limited to privileged social class; and 2. Educational experience and convenience for both students and the teachers.

Access to quality educational contents: Unlike the past, innovations related to democratizing the educational materials are on the rise. Massive Open Online Courses (MOOCs) providers such as edX, Coursera, Udacity, Khan Academy, iversity, Kadenze, Udemy, Canvas Network, and Cognitive Class, offer affordable remote learning opportunities to students all over the world with simple access to contents and certificates programs over the internet [26, 27]. Both regular and professional students significantly benefit from this. Many MOOCs are either free or may charge a small fee but have an impressive collection of universities and businesses represented. For example, edX has more than 160 universities and corporate partners, including MIT, Harvard, UC Berkeley, the University of Texas system, University of British Columbia, Brown University, Caltech, Columbia University, University of Pennsylvania, New York University, the University of Chicago, University of Oxford, Peking University, IIT Bombay, Australian National University, Google, IBM, and Microsoft. edX offers more than 2,800 courses on subjects such as humanities, mathematics, and computer science, with 34 million learners worldwide, representing all seven continents, and 100 million enrollments across its courses [28]. The edX platform makes it easier for students to consume the contents and practice them as well through engaging video lectures, data visualizations and interactive elements, quizzes, open response assessments, and virtual environments. Other platforms provide similar offerings and the competition between them is heating up. The good news is that students have a

112 *Innovations in industry verticals*

choice now to pick courses from the menu of options that could either supplement their learning modality if they are registered with a traditional in-person school system or customize their certificate or diploma directly from one of the MOOCs.

Educational experience: The in-person learning modality within the four walls of university systems is getting a boost from the induction of modern technology tools. Traditionally the learning took place through teacher to students or one to many teaching models. The whiteboard was central for the teacher to display their mastery of knowledge and for students to copy from. Note taking was key and students reproduced what was written on the board into their personal notebook. There was literally less interaction or collaboration, and listening to the teacher was rewarded. This style of teaching is transforming in many schools, particularly in business schools, where interactions and collaborations are emphasized to enrich the overall learning experience. Studies have shown that collaborations and multi-mode engagements promote learning and help processing of new concepts and theories with relative ease. In-room simulation tools, including virtual and augmented reality tools, are finding significance in providing immersive experience to the students.

For example, ClassVR is a virtual and augmented reality system for classroom learning. It offers an engaging, immersive experience for students and makes learning a fun activity for all ages. The immersive experience dramatically increases students' ability to retain what was learned and sparks curiosity to explore further [29]. The system includes standalone virtual reality headsets and a real-time classroom delivery platform, ClassVR Portal, with classroom controls for teachers to manage contents.

Not all the students are excited about giving a written response for a teacher or other students' questions. To foster discussion and engagement, tools such as FlipGrid allow students to share ideas and opinions in a fun and hands-on way with a short video-log, as video submissions are often more enticing to students [30]. It is common now to share video clips from platforms such as YouTube in class to provide either some background information on a new topic or to reinforce how some ideas are being practiced in certain environments. What if the students and teachers can annotate the video in real-time with their comments and share with everyone in the class to foster collective learning and understanding of the topic? Tools such as VideoAnt transform the monotony of simply listening to videos into an engaging and contributing activity while having fun. There are also tools such as Padlet for creative collaboration using a range of different mixed media sources. When the classes are in session, students can share videos, images, or personal comments on a virtual corkboard, while allowing other students to comment on others' contributions or start their own strand [30].

Tools such as Zoom, Microsoft Teams, etc. allow remote video-based real-time lecturing and small team activities, possibly emulating the classroom environment. During the COVID-19 pandemic, these tools have become very popular and provided an option to continue learning when social distancing and school lockdown were enforced in many countries.

8.7 Wellness

The Global Wellness Institute defines wellness as the active pursuit of activities, choices, and lifestyles that lead to a state of holistic health. It has many dimensions, including physical, mental, emotional, spiritual, social, and environmental. Wellness has its roots in ancient civilizations from India, China, Greece, and Rome, and has become

Innovations in the service industry   113

a vibrant growth industry in the past four decades across the globe. The approach typically takes natural means, including natural supplements, aerobics, meditation, yoga, outdoor and indoor sport activities, dance, etc., to achieve the health goals as opposed to relying solely on modern medicine and medical procedures. It is estimated that the industry was $4.5T in 2017 representing roughly 5.3% of global economic output [31].

It is interesting to note that wellness is diametrically opposite to the illness paradigm and the operating environments are much different. For example, illness is reactive and episodic, and is focused on getting better with a treatment plan designed by trained clinicians who are often labeled specialists. They represent clinical specialties such as neurology, dermatology, obstetrics and gynecology, pediatrics, ophthalmology, psychiatry, urology, allergy and immunology, and oncology, and by design are siloed and internally focused. Family medicine and internal medicine disciplines try to coordinate the treatment plans. On the other hand, wellness is proactive and is focused on improving and maintaining physical, mental, and spiritual health, approaching it holistically to prevent diseases by giving control to the individuals, who can structure a customized and integrated plan that fits their lifestyle and personal goals with help from the wellness trainers or coaches.

The landscape of the wellness industry is very fragmented. Both the consumers and the value providers are either individuals or small groups who leverage innovations in the digital technology space for their success. Communication, collaboration, visualization, and performance monitoring are some of the functions enabled by the digital technologies to drive seamless customer experience [32].

For example, yoga is a form of exercise that originated from India thousands of years ago to achieve physical and mental well-being by focusing on body strength, flexibility, and breathing. Yoga training classes are popular, particularly among the younger population, and are offered in many health clubs, community centers, private leisure centers, etc. During the pandemic, yoga went virtual, using tools such as Zoom. There are apparel companies that have come up with embedded smart technologies, taking their businesses to the next level. Nadi X is one such apparel technology that listens to body movements using vibrational feedback and guides the customers with gentle pulses around the hips, knees, arms, and ankles through their yoga flow. The Nadi X mobile app allows customizing the yoga plan as well [33].

Peloton is an emerging fitness product and service company that specializes in designing and manufacturing treadmills, bikes, apparels, etc. and bundles them with virtual instructors on a subscription basis. It provides special mobile applications as well, with a simple to use interface allowing users to customize the fitness program to suits one's mood, goals, music taste, experience level, and workout schedule. Digital tools are exploited to provide an immersive experience for some of their workouts, including embedding chosen outdoor terrain outdoor activities [34].

8.8 Banking

Banking is a term that embodies credit and lending transactions facilitated by banks. The modern banking processes can be traced back to the 14th century in the prosperous cities of Renaissance Italy where banking was practiced. With the growth of consumer and business needs, particularly in the context of a globally connected world with trade, speed, flexibility, reliability, and accuracy have become critical parameters

114   *Innovations in industry verticals*

to determine the efficacy of banking transaction. With cross-industry technology innovations, including high-performance computing, cloud infrastructure, digital and distributed financial ledgers, sophisticated user access controls with hardened digital security protocols, and mobile computing, enabled by both global and regional standards, banking operations have become efficient. Banking is traditionally known to have both customers facing front-end functions as well as back-office operations.

With the growing appetite for user-friendly digital tools and convenience from the consumer and small business community, this industry is becoming more disrupted than ever before. Fintech, a short form for financial technology, is a revolution that seeks to automate financial services, both consumption and delivery, by empowering the users in the ecosystem. Fintech uses specialized software programs including AI and machine learning-enabled algorithms that can be run on mobile phones and back-end cloud servers [35]. Some of the products and services they offer include payment processing, online and mobile banking, online and peer-to-peer (P2P) lending, person-to-person payments, and other financial services. Companies such as PayPal, Square, Goldman Sachs, Green Dot, MercadoLibre, and Ant Group [36] are some well-recognized ones in the fintech landscape. Many of them are startups or a separate entity within the larger corporation and defy the orthodoxies that existed in the big banking systems for centuries. There are more than 26 unicorns (ones valued at over $1B) in fintech, and the list is growing.

The fintech industry is getting a lot of capital from venture capital firms as well as from established corporations. Goldman Sachs, a global brand, is transforming aggressively from an investment bank and wealth manager to a full-featured technology-enabled consumer bank and has released the Marcus savings and personal loan platform. The goal is to reduce the physical footprint and run consumer banking with high efficiency. It entered the credit card business through an exclusive arrangement for Apple's credit card [36].

PayPal, another well-known name in online payment processing, owns Venmo, a person-to-person payment platform. Its growth is astounding and has attracted a lot of new entrants with a significant addressable market. Venmo has more than 361 million loyal global customers and it is a matter of time before its customer base crosses a billion.

Square, a competitor to PayPal, focuses more on merchants. It grew by first enabling merchants to accept credit cards using their mobile phones with a simple plugged-in card reader and then expanding to a large-scale financial ecosystem with sophisticated POS capabilities. Its Square small business capital lending platform is gaining a lot of traction. Its Cash App, a consumer financial service offering introduced in 2013, is very popular and is growing more than 100% every year. Square is also enabling its merchants to have omnichannel presence with its Square Online Store platform, which has picked up more adoption during the COVID-19 pandemic.

Fintech is on fire with a lot of innovation, and traditional banking and financial establishments are on notice. The following are some of the trends in this industry [35].

- Cybersecurity – Technology to make online transactions safe by reducing possible crimes
- Blockchain technology – A digital ledger that is distributed and that is immutable with a community of blockchain miners for validation eliminating traditional labor-intensive audit functions

Innovations in the service industry 115

- Cryptocurrency and digital cash – Digital currency applications built on blockchain foundation
- Smart contracts – Leverage blockchain to make value contracts that get executed based on preset events occurring
- Insurtech – To disrupt the insurance industry with technology
- Regtech – Leverage technology to assist financial service firms comply with local laws such as anti-money laundering and know your customer protocols
- Robo-advisors – Use sophisticated AI and machine learning algorithms to reduce investment advice rendered to customers without sacrificing quality

8.9 Transportation

Transportation has been one of the most visible and relatable industries to adopt innovations from many other industry verticals. Human needs have transformed the style and approach to transportation over human history on the planet. Transportation is defined as the movement of goods, people, and anything else from one place to another, accomplished using various means. Humans first traveled on foot, and as their community living concept developed and survival needs expanded, they started traveling to far-off places in search of food, water, and livable weather conditions. From 4000 BCE to 3000 BCE, animals such as horses, donkeys or mules, oxen, camels, and even smaller animals such as goats or large dogs were used for transportation, including farming. The backbone concept for surface transportation, the wheel, was first invented and made of wood in Iraq in 3500 BCE to drag heavy objects on land. This was followed by water-based transportation exploration around 3100 BCE, using floatable canoes that were created by digging cavities into a burnt slab of wood. Egyptians further enhanced the propulsion of these canoes using wind energy, which led to the development of sailing boats. Romans are credited with the idea of building roads in Europe to move chariots and military weapons from 1700 BCE to 500 BCE [37]. The chariots were heavy vehicles with solid wheels, with wooden carriages covered by animal skins.

As the industrial revolutions took off during the 18th century, steam-powered mechanizations to electricity-based automation to computer-controlled motorization to cyber-machine convergence resulted in the development of many types of transportation, such as trains, motor cars, trucks, airplanes, and trams, for faster, efficient, and mass movement of people and goods. No doubt the innovations in the transportation sector greatly influence how our lifestyles are shaped, community activities are organized, educational systems are coordinated, corporations collaborate, cross-border trade is conducted, wars are waged between countries, shipping lanes are harnessed, and economy is managed. Transportation is no longer about just moving from one place to another, but has a focus on experience that decides the choice of the modality. We will discuss a few methods of transportation and their innovation trends.

Air Travel: Since the Wright brothers invented a powered aircraft in 1903 [38] that was controllable for a sustained flight, the aircraft design and use case scenarios have expanded from manual controls with single passenger to fly-by-wire systems that are semi-automatic, computer-regulated aircraft flight control systems with an advanced electronic interface carrying hundreds of passengers traveling across continents, to military aircraft for precision warfare missions traveling at a speed two to three times that of sound.

116 *Innovations in industry verticals*

The aircraft industry has experienced unprecedented innovation in terms of engineering that provided superior aerodynamic structural design, computer-integrated hydro-mechanical control systems, advanced power systems in the form of jet engines for aircraft propulsion as well as to support the entire cabin power needs, sophisticated navigation systems including automatic direction finder, inertial navigation, precision compasses, radar navigation, VHF omnidirectional range and global navigation satellite system, and instrument landing systems. Passenger safety has played a key role in the continuous quest for innovating a highly dependable and safe aircraft performance.

The industry has experienced fluctuating demands, with some major downward pressure during the 9/11 crisis and the COVID-19 pandemic. Also, the need for bigger planes such as Boeing 747-400 with a capacity of 605 passengers and Airbus A380-800 with a capacity of 853 passengers has waned over time given the huge operating costs. Relatively smaller and fuel-efficient planes such as Boeing 777-300ER with a capacity of 550 passengers and Airbus A330-300 with a passenger capacity of 440 are becoming popular [39]. The overall pair passenger trend to and from the US is shown in Figure 8.2 and, except for a few sharp bumps, the demand is steady with some minor uptick.

Added to safety and cost considerations, passenger comfort also has become a priority. For example, pressurizing the cabins at 8,000 ft above sea level is common for long-haul planes given the aircraft weight and material considerations, but it reduces the oxygen saturation level by 4%, which is okay for many people, but not ideal. High altitude or acute mountain syndrome such as dizziness, headache, muscle aches, and nausea could be a concern if the cabin is pressurized to 8,000 ft above sea level. But a new study published in the *New England Journal of Medicine* suggests that pressurizing the cabins to 6,000 ft may be a better thing to improve passenger comfort, which will be similar to sea level. Aircraft such as the Boeing 787 are leading the innovation by using composites rather than aluminum, which allows Boeing to pressurize to 6,000 feet providing maximum comfort to passengers [40].

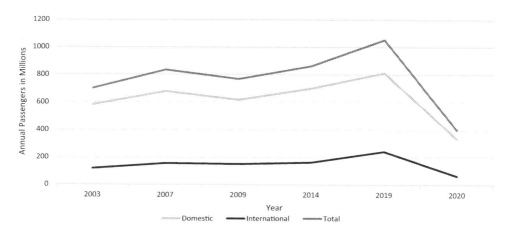

Figure 8.2 Annual passengers – All flights to and from the US [41].
Source: www.bts.gov/newsroom/passengers-all-2020-us-based-flights-down-62-2019.

Aircraft noise is another area of concern, primarily contributed to by the jet engines. Airbus 380, Airbus 350, and Boeing 787 are some of the well-known aircraft that are powered by some of the most innovative, yet quieter engines from GE, Engine Alliance, a joint venture between General Electric and Pratt & Whitney, and Rolls-Royce Trent 900 to achieve maximum passenger comfort [42, 43, 44].

There are several other innovations to improve the passengers' comfort levels, particularly on trans-continental flights where jet lag and the long travel time is a drag on passengers. Replacing the boring fluorescent lights with mood lighting helps ease the travel discomfort. Mood lighting helps with managing jet lag while relaxing the passengers. With controlled and pleasing color options during boarding, inflight, and disembarking, passengers can experience comfortable travel throughout the entire journey, overcoming the stress and sleeplessness often felt with traditional infight arrangements. Aircraft companies conduct extensive human psychological studies as they design the interior of aircraft.

Also, many modern aircraft are fitted with onboard digital entertainment and increasingly manufacturers are exploring offering virtual windows, leveraging digital technologies. Emirates Airlines already offers virtual windows for its first-class middle seat passengers. No matter where one sits in the future, every passenger may be able to look through a window, real or virtual. Passenger experience is a priority for many airlines to be competitive and the aircraft manufacturers are involving interior designers to design the airplane cabins to maximize the passenger comfort.

Ride-hailing service: Hitchhike and lift are some terms that have been around for a very long time to get a free ride from a passing vehicle. Now the process has taken a new commercial tone with a business model innovation and is considered as the ride-hailing service, which is growing fast. The global ride-hailing market in 2020 was estimated at $113B and is expected to reach $230B in 2026 with a CAGR of 8.75% [45]. Digital innovations are spurring new business models of companies such as Uber, WingZ, Lyft, Didi, etc., which effectively exploit third-party-owned automobiles to generate revenue for their corporations.

It is an on-demand service that connects willing and idle independent automobile drivers with passengers who need transportation. Both riders and drivers are required to download a mobile application to their phone with GPS-integrated tools so that ride requests can be sent in real-time to which willing drivers respond to offer a transportation service for a dynamically determined fee by the ride-hailing company. The company takes a cut, typically 20–30%, and uses the pre-registered credit card to charge the rider for the service and electronically deposits the driver compensation to the driver's pre-authorized bank accounts.

Industry observers point to some benefits of this model, including reducing drunk driving, traffic congestion, and pollution [46, 47]. The adoption of this new service model is largely seen in urban areas, and a survey finds that only 15% of adults in the US have used this service and a little over 33% were unaware of the offerings. Less than 3% surveyed indicated that they used this service at least once a week.

Another research finds that total vehicle miles traveled increases because of the growth in ride-hailing options. A 2018 study by the former Deputy Commissioner of Traffic and Planning at the New York City Department of Transportation, Bruce Schaller, suggests that using 2017 data, ride-hailing services contributed to an annual increase of more than 5.7 billion miles traveled across the nine largest metros in the

118 *Innovations in industry verticals*

US [48]. The convenience offered by these services induces additional demand and people prefer to take a ride rather than taking a walk or cycling to a place, adding to vehicle miles traveled. University of Colorado researchers also find that for every 100 miles traveled by passengers using ride-hailing services, there are another 70 miles, called deadheading and commuting, traveled by the drivers to pick up the passengers from their pickup locations [49]. The claims made by previous studies on pollution reduction may be contradicted by the overall vehicle miles traveled increase.

This industry heavily uses big data analytics, AI, machine learning, neural networks, and GPS-based navigation for efficient logistics planning that reduces overall pick-up time and deadheading and commuting, and determining surge pricing considering dynamic supply and demand scenarios. The major focus of these corporations is to increase the overall revenue, profitability, and ridership achieved by maximizing the number of passengers served per travel mile, reducing the operating cost, minimizing passenger waiting time, and enhancing the overall rider and driver experience. Lately, passenger safety has drawn a lot of attention and the ride-hailing companies are scrambling to device techniques, tools, and processes to make sure safety goals are achieved.

The industry is known to conduct experiments with different products or services and does not hesitate to bring most viable products (MVP) in an incremental manner to different markets. Uber, for example, is the epitome of the tech industry phrase "move fast and break things." Uber launched its flagship product called Express Pool, etc. through iterative experiments and collecting field data from various markets before the service model was optimized [50].

Depending on the markets and countries they serve, these companies exploit loopholes in the local employment laws by avoiding employee taxes and benefits to maintain a lower cost structure. Some markets such as California in the US and London in the UK resist such employee exploitation and require these companies to consider drivers as regular employees instead of treating them as independent workers (gig workers). Employees, not contractors, qualify for holiday pay, sick pay, and healthcare benefits. This will also reduce the drivers' overall tax obligations as the companies will now be responsible for employer taxes, not the contractors [51, 52].

The next wave of innovation in this industry is to adopt robot taxis as the autonomous vehicle technology is perfected and the necessary ecosystem such as insurance, automated charging and battery swapping, fleet maintenance service, is developed. This will obviously involve huge upfront investments for these companies, but over time it has the potential to reduce the operating costs and perhaps will enhance passenger safety. With robot taxis, the ride-hailing companies do not have to worry about conventional classification of labor, etc. as there are no drivers, but the companies may be imposed some form of workforce or social replacement tax in some states or countries.

8.10 Concluding remarks

The service sector is experiencing a healthy demand and, interestingly, it is embedded in many other sectors as well in addition to being a sector by itself. This sector takes advantage of their closeness to customers who are continuously connected with them digitally. With the right organizational positioning and innovation capacity, service sector innovation leaders can respond proactively to customers' preferences and expectations and delight them. Amazon, Alibaba, Starbucks, Malaysia's Maybank,

Innovations in the service industry 119

ANZ Taiwan bank, Singapore Primary and Secondary Education System [53], and Singapore Airlines are a few examples that are so obsessed with customer experience and have the right orientation and innovation capacity to innovate and grow. Their effort is not an isolated innovation initiative within their organization, but a well-orchestrated enterprise-wide relentless pursuit. TRIAL© innovation and VASTEFA© leadership frameworks find greater relevance and application at these corporations.

Student activities

1. Select the Zara and Apple cases from Part VIII.
2. Review the details and list the problems or opportunities they tried to address.
3. Discuss their approach to innovate through the lens of the TRIAL© framework.
4. Also answer the questions listed at the end of the cases.
5. Research their corporations using online resources, including annual reports and develop a fit-gap analysis by applying the VASTEFA© leadership framework. Use the attached Amazon case as a reference for VASTEFA© leadership framework mapping.

8.11 References

1. Theodore Levitt, September 1972, "Production-Line Approach to Service," Harvard Business Review, https://hbr.org/1972/09/production-line-approach-to-service
2. https://hbr.org/2006/10/what-business-are-you-in-classic-advice-from-theodore-levitt
3. https://hbr.org/1976/09/the-industrialization-of-service
4. Robert F. Higgins, Diana Maichin, Sep 16, 2013 "A Note on Healthcare IT and Applications to the Healthcare Industry," Harvard Business Review, (Revised: Oct 6, 2016) https://hbsp.harvard.edu/product/814033-PDF-ENG?Ntt=healthcare+service+industry+technology+innovations&itemFindingMethod=Search
5. www.fda.gov/
6. www.uclahealth.org/robotic-surgery/what-is-robotic-surgery
7. www.hhs.gov/hipaa/index.html
8. www.researchgate.net/publication/337293396_Electronic_Health_Records_Adoption_in_China's_Hospitals_A_Narrative_Review
9. www.greenbook.org/marketing-research/emr-market-india-growth-challenges-40073
10. www.institutmontaigne.org/en/blog/private-healthcare-india-boons-and-banes
11. www.alaturka.info/en/culture/definitions/2357-agora-2
12. www.bigcommerce.com/blog/retail/#what-is-retail
13. www.statista.com/topics/5922/retail-market-worldwide/
14. https://capgemini.com/consulting/wp-content/uploads/sites/30/2017/07/disney_0.pdf
15. Wall Street Journal, July 2014, "Disney's Iger on the Future of Leisure: Technology Built on Storytelling."
16. https://disneyworld.disney.go.com/faq/bands-cards/understanding-magic-band/
17. TechCrunch, February 2014, "Disney Launches Disney Movies Anywhere, An iTunes-Integrated App Where Fans Can Build Their Movie Library."
18. www.statista.com/topics/1004/cruise-industry/#dossierSummary__chapter1
19. https://360.here.com/cruise-ship-technology

120 *Innovations in industry verticals*

20. www.cruisecritic.com/articles.cfm?ID=1697
21. www.cnn.com/travel/article/worlds-biggest-cruise-ships/index.html
22. https://en.wikipedia.org/wiki/List_of_communication_satellite_companies
23. https://en.wikipedia.org/wiki/Prehistory
24. https://en.wikipedia.org/wiki/Nalanda
25. Dustin Swanger, June 2016, "Innovation in Higher Education," www.fmcc.edu/about/files/2016/06/Innovation-in-Higher-Education.pdf
26. www.mooc.org/
27. https://online.purdue.edu/blog/education/how-has-technology-changed-education
28. www.edx.org/schools-partners
29. www.classvr.com/
30. www.teachthought.com/technology/12-tech-tools-for-student-to-student-digital-collaboration/
31. https://globalwellnessinstitute.org/what-is-wellness/
32. https://globalwellnessinstitute.org/initiatives/digital-wellness-initiative/digital-wellness-trends/
33. http://total-yoga.org/technology-weaved-yoga/
34. www.onepeloton.com/
35. www.investopedia.com/terms/f/fintech.asp
36. www.fool.com/investing/stock-market/market-sectors/financials/fintech-stocks/
37. www.lelandwest.com/planes-trains-automobiles-the-history-of-transportation.cfm
38. www.wright-brothers.org/Information_Desk/Just_the_Facts/Airplanes/Wright_Airplanes.htm
39. https://simpleflying.com/airbus-a330-vs-boeing-777/
40. https://abcnews.go.com/Health/Healthday/story?id=4507808&page=1
41. www.bts.gov/newsroom/passengers-all-2020-us-based-flights-down-62-2019
42. www.Airbus.com
43. www.Boeing.com
44. https://captainjetson.com/aviation/8-new-airline-passenger-comfort-features-and-inventions/
45. www.mordorintelligence.com/industry-reports/ride-hailing-market
46. Adam Conner-Simons, January 4, 2017, "How Ride-Sharing Can Improve Traffic, Save Money, and Help the Environment," MIT News, http://news.mit.edu/2016/how-ride-sharing-can-improve-traffic-save-money-and-help-environment-0104
47. Andrew J. Hawkins, Oct 4, 2017, "Does Uber Lead to Less Drunk Driving? It's Complicated," The Verge, www.theverge.com/2017/10/4/16418782/uber-drunk-driving-crashes-study-cities
48. Sebastian Gancarczyk, September 26, 2019, "Ride-Hailing Part 2: Its Effect on Vehicle Miles Traveled," www.iaai.com/Articles/ride-hailing-part-2-its-effect-on-vehicle-miles-traveled
49. Alejandro Henao, and Wesley E. Marshall, 2019, "The Impact of Ride-Hailing on Vehicle Miles Traveled," Transportation, 46, pp. 2173–2194. https://doi.org/10.1007/s11116-018-9923-2
50. Chiara Farronato, Alan Maccormack, and Sarah Mehta," Aug 11, 2020, "Innovation at Uber – The Launch of Express POOL," Harvard Business Review, 9-619-003.
51. www.wired.com/story/uber-lyfts-gig-work-law-expand-california/
52. www.natlawreview.com/article/uk-supreme-court-confirms-uber-drivers-have-worker-rights
53. https://ncee.org/country/singapore/

9 Innovation in government

9.1 Introduction

> "Data and technology can fundamentally change the way government operates."
> - Stephen Goldsmith

Merriam-Webster defines government as the "body of persons that constitutes the governing authority of a political unit or organization such as the officials comprising the governing body of a political unit and constituting the organization as an active agency or the executive branch of the government and is being responsible for the direction and supervision of public affairs." Governments' responsibilities include setting up public policies, establishing rules, tax management, planning and executing public infrastructure, including roads, township utilities, such as water, gas, electricity, health systems, educational systems, community facilities, and emergency service management. If it is a central or federal government, the responsibilities may have a broader scope, such as external affairs, national security and military, national social security, education, and health system, etc. For discussion purposes in this book, we focus on local or municipal governments only.

Governments in partnership with public and private enterprises focus on delivering public service and strive to enhance citizens' experiences through innovation. The OECD states that such innovations involve overcoming old bureaucratic structures and modes of thinking and embracing new technologies and ideas. Although innovations have the potential to bring efficiency and impact citizens' experience, it is not straightforward. Overcoming bureaucracy, siloed thinking, outdated procedures and tools, inadequate funding and trained staff, lack of citizens' trust in governments, opaque systems, subpar innovation culture, and favoritism are common impediments for successful innovation programs. Despite the obstacles, there are significant advancements in many local governments across many geographies.

9.2 Modalities of public service – Mass vs personalized

9.2.1 Personalized on-demand service

Public service that has been built on a mass consumption model is being replaced by an individualized on-demand service model. For example, in countries such as India there would be, in fact there still are, a long line of citizens to pay their utility bills, which come under government services. Electricity and water supply in many parts

DOI: 10.4324/9781003190837-14

of the world are still controlled by local governments and monthly bill payments are accepted at select government- run offices. Likewise, to pay personal property taxes, citizens must go to government-run municipal offices. This is a huge inconvenience for people who work during the day as well as for parents who support young children's needs at home. Also, senior citizens find these outdated procedures very challenging as they cannot stand under the burning sun for an extended time in some of the tropical Asian countries such as India, Sri Lanka, Thailand, Vietnam, and Indonesia. Many government agencies now offer web-based on-demand payment options, personalized with user-specific secure login credentials. Users can set up payment schedules and link them to invoices and their bank accounts or personal credit cards. This allows a lot of freedom for citizens as they can now manage bill payments even when they travel and are out of town.

In many developing countries, it is customary to supply low-earning citizens with subsidized essential items such as rice, wheat, sugar, cooking gas cylinders, etc. through local government supply depots. Citizens must physically visit these depots and often wait in long lines enduring an excessive time commitment and physical and mental stress. This inefficient antiquated service model is changing fast, and some governments are planning to door-deliver such supplies if the citizens set up online accounts and schedule the drop-off times when they are home and which are convenient to them. Mobile applications, broadband internet access, and convenient online account management are driving service efficiency in some of these countries and a lot more needs to happen.

In many countries, property deed transfer and title search for no encumbrance verification requires citizens to physically visit local government offices and wait for hours to get it done. This is another service managed by government agencies in many countries. Depending on the urgency of the situation, some citizens attempt to take a short-cut approach, cutting through the lines by offering additional tips to the service personnel, breeding corrupt practices. This is changing in many places as online title search is becoming more mainstream. However, deed transfer still requires on-site visits and privatizing these services may leverage enhanced technology use, reducing the overall waiting time and improving citizens' experience. In the US, many private title companies coordinate such services remotely with the citizens before the scheduled title transfer event, which is also called the closing date, which happens at a physical location. The experience is seamless and many developing countries can adapt.

Some governments are embracing user-centric application design principles from the tech industry to innovate government services offered through digital stores. Big data analytics and machine learning-based voice-activated digital assistants seem to be the trend to provide a frictionless personalized service to citizens.

9.2.2 Navigation assistance for the disabled

Big cities are known for the hustle and bustle of urban life where disabled people are left out from many of the city activities that make these cities great. The visually impaired population is at a major disadvantage in navigating these busy cities. World Health Organization estimates that at least 2.2 billion people are either blind or visually impaired and many of these cases were preventable [1]. Governments have a role to play in integrating such a disadvantaged population into the mainstream activities of the cities. Poland is experimenting with enabling physically handicapped citizens, particularly visually impaired, with smartphones to navigate their city on their own to participate in the city's activities. The City of Warsaw launched "Virtual Warsaw," a virtual smart city, deploying hundreds of Bluetooth beacons that communicate directly with GPS-enabled applications that can be downloaded and installed on one's smartphone, providing real-time guidance to city locations. This promotes inclusiveness and accessibility for those who would otherwise be ignored [2].

9.2.3 Blockchain-enabled voting

In representative democracies, the voting process is the core pillar of success, and its integrity and reliability are paramount to lend credibility to elected governments and their representatives. Lately, there has been intense discussion and speculation around the voting process regardless of whether it is paper ballot or electronic voting machines. Although government and private partnerships tried to assure the quality and integrity of the process in many countries such as the US and India, the two largest democracies with more than 350 million and 1.35 billion people living in these countries, respectively, some segments of the population are still skeptical and challenge the election outcome. In the US in 2000 there were numerous repeated cases of counting of ballots cast manually in the state of Florida, which proved crucial in deciding the outcome of the national presidential election, which was finally settled by the Supreme Court. This uncertainty was repeated in the most recent US presidential election of 2020 as well in some states and shows no signs of improvement.

To address these concerns, interestingly, alternative voting process innovations are being explored by some local governments that leverage next generation technologies such as blockchains. This avoids delays in receiving and counting mail-in ballots as well as having to wait in long lines before one can cast one's vote. It is more personalized in the sense that one can vote when it is convenient within an allowed time window spanning multiple days as opposed to using a more mass voting model with strict time-limited in-person requirements.

West Virginia in the US, for example, was piloting a program to allow its military workers to vote remotely via a blockchain-enabled platform from foreign countries. The state also offered the opportunity for its overseas workers to cast their vote via the blockchain network that distributed and stored their votes in 16 different geographically distributed ledgers, making it difficult for hackers to tamper with. In 2017, the popular Rock and Roll Hall of Fame used Votem's blockchain voting system to register 1.8 million votes to select Hall of Fame inductees. This blockchain-based voting process proved that it was effective and secure at a scale that can be leveraged for future political voting scenarios as well. Votem uses a secure token that enables voters to easily vote online from their mobile devices, assuring verifiability, accessibility, security, and transparency [3]. Votes cast and tracked through a blockchain provide for an easier and secure way of counting votes and at lower cost, which could be significantly reassuring to developing nations where their existing voting infrastructure is far from optimal. Also, allowing only authorized election officials to selectively verify the voter credentials and choices made if needed, provides additional confidence in the entire process.

Another blockchain-based voting experiment took place in Colombia in 2016 when expatriates could not vote officially. Colombia is one of the countries in the

124 *Innovations in industry verticals*

world that has more citizens living abroad, estimated at around six million [4, 5]. A non-profit Democracy Earth Foundation set up Plebiscito Digital, a blockchain-enabled voting process to allow expatriates to approve the peace agreement between the Colombian government and the largest rebel group, the Revolutionary Armed Forces of Colombia, known as the FARC. It was very innovative, as not only did the organizers asked for "Yes" or "No" for the peace deal, but each voter could vote on sub-themes of the proposed peace treaty and indicate the relative importance of each one. Democracy Earth Foundation was able to identify the deal breaker in the peace treaty, pointing to the overwhelming "No" among the participants to one particular statement of the treaty that asked, "Do you agree with the political participation of the FARC and opening up democracy?" [5]

Blockchains are immutable decentralized ledgers that capture any transaction, including a voting decision by the voter, and is shared with a peer computer network for validation using a mining process driven by high-performance computer resources while protecting the original identities of the transaction parties, including voters. Although this seems to be a long process with massive technology use, there are cost-effective methods to implement a blockchain-based voting process. At the core of the blockchain process is a private key cryptography, peer-to-peer network, and blockchain program. The private key cryptography secures identities and hash functions to make the blockchain immutable. P2P machines on the network help maintain the consistency of the distributed ledger and the blockchain program gives the blockchain its protocol based on the context. Every voting transaction, including the voter identities and their voting choices, are captured in the digital block, which is equivalent of a digital store. A cryptographic hash (sometimes called "digest") is a kind of "signature" for a text or a data file. Secure Hash Algorithm (SHA)-256 generates an almost-unique 256-bit (32-byte) signature for a text. For example, the hashing function that is used by the Bitcoin blockchain is the SHA-256 hashing algorithm. A cryptographic hash function is a very complicated formula that takes any string of input, such as voter information and choices, and turns it into a unique 64-digit string of output such as:

636A7PD9CAFE34N7CDE6C1270E17F7730MN62GA7511A57F700D415F0D 3E1USK68C

If any information changes, including voter choice, the output will be totally different. Blocks also include a random number called Nonce (e.g., P#$@12), added to the transaction data and the signature of the previous block to generate the signature of the given block. Only hashes (signatures) that meet certain requirements are accepted on the blockchain for a given protocol, and this is called the mining process. Miners try to find as many random nonces as quickly as possible until they find the one that together with rest of the block information results in a signature that confirms to a protocol such as certain number of leading zeros. In the SHA-256 protocol, a block will only be accepted in the blockchain if its digital signature starts with a seven-consecutive number of zeros [6].

9.2.4 *Automated toll collection*

In many countries, manual toll booths on highways are common, manned by toll collectors. These result in long traffic delays and environmental pollution. In cities such as New York or Chicago, there could very well be hundreds of cars on the highway, resembling a parking lot, waiting to pay tolls and causing significant inconvenience to passengers, including employee productivity loss at workplaces because of delays and possibly loss of lives when emergency vehicles such as ambulances are blocked in the traffic jam, preventing them reaching hospitals. Many of these toll roads are managed by the governments and in some instances by private organizations.

Technology innovation is slowly finding its way to streamline the toll collection process and alleviate the friction that consumers experience using the manual methods. Some of the overarching goals of these innovations include ease of traffic flow, toll vehicle identification accuracy, appropriate customer charges, user-friendly transactions, timely and correct bank deposits, and fraud or scam avoidance [7]. There are differences in the type of innovations deployed to suit the given situation. For example, 91 Express Lanes in California, next to Los Angeles, a ten-mile stretch established in the median of an existing free highway, SR-91, carries more than 300,000 vehicles a day. This uses a multilane automatic vehicle identification (AVI) system leveraging dedicated short-range communications (DSRC), one-way or two-way short-range to medium-range wireless communication channels specifically designed for automotive use. AVIs are mounted on the gantry above the highway as shown in Figure 9.1. Each customer is given a transponder and required to fix it to the vehicle windshield so that when the vehicle crosses that AVI reader, the transponder communicates the customer and vehicle information to the AVI that updates a

Figure 9.1 A toll gantry installed on Illinois Highway, USA.
(Photo taken by the author Dr. Vijay Pandiarajan, 2021).

126 *Innovations in industry verticals*

back-end computer application, allowing automatic charges to be applied to the customer account. This is further enhanced by taking pictures of the vehicle registration plates using a sophisticated high-speed camera for further validation and enforcing rules on violators.

Setting up AVI requires gantries and maintenance catwalks, which is not suitable for long stretches of highway, particularly with many cross sections. For example, in Germany, when the highway authorities had to design an automated toll collection for 7,458 miles of highway that had more than 5,200 sections, the AVI reader was not practical given how expensive the gantries were, for both installation and maintenance. This was further complicated by the fact that these highways were used by customers from 36 countries and speaking more than 23 languages. There were other concerns as well related to electronic-data security and the need to abide by international laws and decrees regarding data protection and privacy. To address these issues, the engineers had to innovate outside of the DSRC solution and eventually architected an innovative solution that leveraged the GPS system. The solution requires vehicles to be equipped with a GPS antenna, which can be easily located, and it recognizes that it is at a toll section. The GPS system sends the vehicle information to the nearby toll invoicing center, which it can do in real-time using mobile phone technology. With prior account setup, the payment processing of the customer is subsequently triggered automatically [7]. These innovations make the government services more efficient and effective with frictionless transactions.

9.3 Citizen-government redefined boundaries

Historically, governments assumed the role of service provider and the citizens the service receiver role, which was linear and unidirectional. Governments operated behind closed doors and were not transparent. This relationship is now shifting to bidirectional given the asymmetric advantage that citizens may have in some areas where the government agencies either lack skills or funding. By allowing more citizens to participate in governance, an open government model, the policy decisions can be pragmatically impacted for a more cohesive society. However, this new business model innovation requires government employees, particularly civil servants, to understand and appreciate an inclusive culture where they coexist with citizens and develop solutions to address citizens' needs. Citizens are after all the customers the governments serve and that realization sometimes is hard to find in many situations.

Brazil is leading the way through active citizen engagement in educating and training government employees. The City of São Paulo has developed a platform called Agents of Open Government to foster peer-to-peer learning involving private citizens, government employees, civil society groups, and communities. Knowledge is power, and skilled and able private citizens are given resources to develop training courses [8, 9]. São Paulo's 150,000 civil servants became the beneficiaries of citizen-led training. In November 2015, 24 citizen-led courses were developed and offered not only to civil servants but also to social activists and the general population. The courses were structured around four main topics: Open and collaborative technology; transparency and open data; networked communication; and mapping and collaborative management. The effort is transforming the skill base of the government in São Paulo, which is influencing their ability to make collaborative and data-driven public

Innovation in government 127

policy decisions leveraging innovation in the fourth industrial era information technology digital assets.

9.4 Digital thread and real-time alerts

Natural disasters often occur with no warning and cause significant human and property loss. Flooding, earthquake, storms, or hurricanes are just a few that some communities and local governments handle with little to moderate success. In Indonesia, the Jakarta metropolitan area, also called the Greater Jakarta, is the most populous metropolitan area that experienced flooding frequently. To provide early warning alerts to citizens to move to higher ground before a flood hits them, PetaBencana. id., a web-based tool, has been created. This tool shows citizens and government emergency response personnel a real-time flood map and the progression of flooding. This tool receives a real-time feed from strategically located hydraulic sensors and citizens' social media posts from platforms such as Facebook, Twitter, Instagram, etc. Big data analytics and AI-based predictive algorithms are some of the advanced digital innovations behind this online tool that drive the digital flood map. This innovation has been very helpful to mass mobilize residents with relative ease in the event of flooding and manage the scarce emergency rescue resources [10].

In the US, there is an AMBER Alert Web Portal Consortium, a public/private partnership and Code Amber that is deployed as an integrated state-by-state alert system that links law enforcement and citizens with a goal to rescue kidnapped children. Code Amber, an integrated real-time alert, delivers its XML-based news feed to major media, government, and wireless telephone service websites in every state and province in North America. The organization delivers more than 1,200,000 web-based messages per day that communicate critical information about child abductions to the public. The detailed data includes physical descriptions and pictures of the victims, and alerts are delivered to personal cell phones, emails, pagers, and other communication devices once the AMBER Alert is declared. It uses mapping technology and is effective and focused in sending alerts to regions that are closer to where the actual kidnapping occurred for quick action by the law enforcement agencies. Corporate sponsors subsidize this service, which is provided practically free to state governments and the public [11].

9.5 Smart cities

Smart cities are another great growth opportunity where governments are partnering with technology innovators to architect cities of the future. Essentially it is an idea based on the connectedness of people and the environment leveraging information and communication technologies to foster sustainability imperatives and address the growing urbanization challenges. Intelligent networks, big data, Wi-Fi and Bluetooth technologies, cloud infrastructure, smartphones, smart sensors, and IoT are just a few innovations that enable smart cities. Citizens simply pair their devices with a city's smart physical infrastructure and effortlessly consume needed services by the touch of a button or voice-activated framework. If orchestrated well, it will allow citizens to be productive in their personal and professional lives, allowing them to lead a healthy stress-free normal life. It is expected to reduce traffic congestion, improve air quality, ease noise pollution, optimize energy consumption, and cut crime. Singapore, Dubai,

128   *Innovations in industry verticals*

Oslo, Copenhagen, Boston, Amsterdam, New York, Bengaluru, Chennai, and London are just a few from a long list of cities that are already on the move to become smart, and public-private partnership is on impressive display in these initiatives [12,13, 14].

9.6 Concluding remarks

Governments have lagged behind private enterprises in terms of innovation for a very long time, burdened by bureaucratic inefficiencies, capital constraints, and risk averse posturing. This, however, is changing fast, influenced by affordable access to technologies, public pressure to be transparent, and increased public-private collaboration. Although governments have led major capital projects for many years that have laid the infrastructure foundation in both developed and less developed countries, that paradigm is shifting, and private enterprises are taking on some responsibilities. Innovation-driven startups such as Alibaba, Tencent, Flipkart, Infosys, Paytm, etc. were able to raise billions of dollars through public and private investments, boosting the economy and employment opportunities, and raising the tax base. They are challenging local governments to innovate and streamline their service processes to get better on the scale of ease of doing business in return for much-needed investment to boost their local economies.

Governments are responding and shifting their attention to streamline their internal and service delivery processes to entice such innovation-driven businesses. Like rising tides lift the boats, surging innovations in the private sector are lifting the innovations in the machinery of governments as well. This pivot has far-reaching consequences within all levels of government – federal, state, municipal, etc. – and they are on a trajectory to improve the lives of their citizens through efficient services and public accountability.

Student activities

1. Select one of your favorite countries where there have been some visible innovations mentioned in government communications.
2. Identify one such innovation initiative and try to characterize it in terms of process, technology, and people.
3. Analyze such characterization through the lens of TRIAL© and VASTEFA© leadership frameworks.
4. Discuss what worked and what did not work and recommend a few action items for the chosen government assuming you are hired as a consultant.

9.7 References

1.   www.who.int/publications/i/item/9789241516570
2.   https://bloombergcities.medium.com/how-partnership-with-the-visually-impaired-helped-virtual-warsaw-380d52a40db1
3.   https://digitalchamber.org/the-future-of-voting-is-blockchain/
4.   https://words.democracy.earth/a-digital-referendum-for-colombias-diaspora-aeef071ec014

5. www.oecd-forum.org/posts/28703-how-blockchain-can-change-voting-the-colombian-peace-plebiscite
6. Vijay Pandiarajan, Lecture Notes, Information Management System, Wint A Session, 2021, Ross School of Business, The University of Michigan.
7. www.ibtta.org/sites/default/files/unrestricted/Estiot_Heurtebis.pdf
8. City of São Paulo: Agents of Open Government: Brazil's largest city is embarking on a massive experiment to have citizens educate its public employees. www.thegovlab.org/static/files/smarterstate/saopaulo.pdf
9. http://saopauloaberta.prefeitura.sp.gov.br/index.php/tudosobretudo/
10. OECD, "Embracing Innovation in Government Global Trends," February 2017, www.oecd.org/gov/innovative-government/embracing-innovation-in-government.pdf
11. www.govtech.com/archive/AMBER-Alert-Web-Portal-to-Integrate.html
12. www.thalesgroup.com/en/markets/digital-identity-and-security/iot/inspired/smart-cities
13. www.thehindu.com/real-estate/the-smart-cities-of-india/article19445207.ece
14. www2.deloitte.com/content/dam/Deloitte/us/Documents/process-and-operations/us-cons-deloitte-smart-city-trends-and-case-studies.pdf

Part VI
Economics of innovation

Chapter 10 Measuring innovation   133

10 Measuring innovation

10.1 Introduction

Innovation is about solving a user problem or satisfying a user need using scarce resources. This is considered "value" in the eyes of the user for which there is compensation provided; however, for innovators a good understanding of the cost to generate such value is necessary and hence economics and measurements are important. Economics, a social science, in the context of innovation is about making sure that such scarce resource commitment returns adequate value when there are alternative opportunities for value generation. In other words, when one is presented with competing choices for deploying scarce resources, the question from an economics standpoint is to logically select the right kind of innovation pursuit that delivers maximum value to the users while generating maximum compensation or reward to the innovators. However, the contexts are not always black and white for innovations; for example, the type of customer needs could vary, either optional vs mandatory or government compliance related. If the safety features in an automobile or aircraft require an emergency innovation response from the OEMs such as Ford or Airbus, the customer price may take a lower priority relative to the need to solve the safety problem immediately. Perhaps the cost to innovate and deliver the safety solution could be much higher than the price charged to the customers, or there may sometimes be no charge at all to customers, while there is significant value realized by the customer.

We discussed earlier that innovation is a process and takes the form of projects to realize it. It is not Archimedes' eureka moment. It takes skilled and creative individuals in the form of a team that represents multiple disciplines or organizations, both internal and external to a corporation or a business. The innovation process could involve resources such as materials, tools, software systems, programing, algorithms, hardware devices, testing equipment, and other documented intellectual property rights. The innovation efforts are often planned and executed through an organized set of activities. Perhaps it goes through iterative experiments, prototypes, and pilots, often met with failure before manifesting as a viable commercial success at scale.

For a given problem or opportunity, one could explore multiple approaches in the form of distinct projects. For example, in the case of electrification of automobiles, there could be three different possibilities:

1. Battery electric vehicle: The vehicle has one energy storage system, a battery that is charged from external power sources such as a home charger or a public charging

DOI: 10.4324/9781003190837-16

134 *Economics of innovation*

station. There is no method or system onboard to generate electricity and this makes it completely dependent on an external power source.

2. Plug-in hybrid-electric vehicle: These vehicles have one energy storage system, a battery, onboard to power the transmission. The battery can be recharged when the vehicle is in use by an auxiliary ICE. But the primary charging happens using an external power source like the pure battery electric vehicle.

3. Hybrid-electric vehicle: These vehicles have multiple energy storage systems that can independently or together provide propulsion power to the vehicle for shorter distances using an onboard electric motor. However, the vehicle is equipped with a traditional ICE, which is the main source of power for the propulsion system and longer distance travel [1].

For the above requirement or user need, we have three different programs or projects, which ought to be managed differently given the nature of supply chain differences, innovation challenges, underlying economics, and total addressable market opportunity set.

Regardless, for the given constrained resources within an organization, the ultimate task is to prioritize such projects and rationalize them based on a set of guiding principles and KPIs. The time horizon perhaps could vary – strategic, tactical, and operational. The organization may ultimately take on any one of the programs or projects based on its unique ability to innovate and execute.

Strategic plan – A strategic plan takes a holistic view of the organization and considers its vision, objectives, and values to competitively position the business in the marketplace. The time horizon is longer-term, could be four to ten years. These plans will involve corporate board members in addition to the executive leadership and could initiate mega projects that are not expected to yield immediate benefits but are foundational and strategic. For example, the Apple electric car project (codenamed "Titan") is an electric car project undergoing R&D by Apple Inc., which is a huge innovation initiative and requires multiyear strategic resource commitment. Such project innovations could be a leap forward in nature.

Tactical plan – The tactical plan, also called milestone plan, defines the tactics the business uses to accomplish the mega goal set out by the strategic plan. The tactics exist in the form of projects that support the overarching strategic project. These tactical projects typically have a duration of a year or less and delineate the strategic plan into actionable smaller baskets with expected outcomes, deadlines, budgets, and resources. The project innovations could be of the cosmetic/survival or leap forward type. An example of these innovation could include developing an air update program to the infotainment system in an EV, leveraging home Wi-Fi.

Operational plan – The operational plan defines the day-to-day management of the business. These plans provide a roadmap to realize the tactical plan outcome within a shorter timeframe. These plans are richer in detail – procedures, policies, engagement rules, resource allocation, measurements methods, incentives, etc. [2]. The operational plans are little projects that could have a duration of weeks or months, resulting in cosmetic/survival innovations that are essentially improvements to existing products or processes, which allow the business to tackle and block the competitors in the marketplace. Examples could include innovating a new pricing plan for existing products or services that either beats out competition or matches a potential entrant. T-Mobile is known for disrupting the wireless communication industry with its continuously evolving pricing plan for new and existing customers, such as no-contract postpaid services and absorbing exiting contract balances from other carriers for new customers who switch to its services. Competitors such as Verizon or AT&T have to dynamically model and innovate matching pricing scenarios to keep their customers from switching. Although any such change may have longer-term implications on the profitability of these companies, a dynamic innovation response is imperative to stay in business.

10.2 Traditional KPIs

"If you can't measure it, you can't improve it."

- Peter Drucker

Measurement holds the key for success of any innovation project. The question for project managers is then how to measure the success of the project. Projects involve investments of resources and efforts with an expected outcome that solves a customer problem, enhances customer experience, or satisfies an unmet demand from a customer.

There are both qualitative and quantitative benefits associated with such outcomes. For example, if the perceived value is higher and the customer is willing to pay more than the equilibrium price on the supply and demand curve, then the innovation can exploit the consumer surplus, as illustrated in Figure 10.1, positively impacting the profitability margins of the product or service that is delivered to the

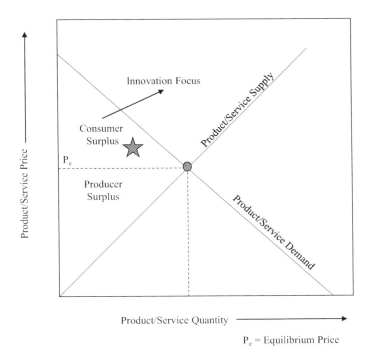

Figure 10.1 Consumer surplus in demand and supply curve.

136 *Economics of innovation*

customer. Apple, for example, commands a huge premium for its products and services as the perceived value is higher than what could be a typical equilibrium price in a competitive smartphone market flooded with products from Samsung, Xiaomi, OPPO, Motorola, Google, LG, Alcatel, Nokia, and others [3]. So, one of the KPIs for an innovation is the price that the innovator can command. The other KPIs could include the market share the product can capture, and how many other auxiliary product or service sales the new product can promote if there is a synergy across a product family. For example, Apple iPhone sale impacts positively the number of application downloads from Apple Store and related subscription revenue for Apple [4]. These KPIs can be measured and quantified, and these are quantitative indicators that the business can monitor to fine tune the innovation to achieve the desired results.

On the other hand, there are also qualitative performance indicators that are hard to quantify precisely. For example, through internal workflow enhancement innovation, employees can now collaborate more and exchange ideas, and their overall morale is increased. It is quite challenging to measure employee morale, which is qualitative in nature. However, one can stretch these morale qualitative results by measuring over a period employee productivity and employee retention rates through reduction in attrition. Observing trends and measuring specific values are possible.

Customer satisfaction, another important indicator, is a tricky one to measure, but can be categorized as qualitative. However, techniques such as Net Promoter Score (NPS) are used to get a read on customer satisfaction by asking the customers to answer the following question on a 0–10 scale: How likely is it that you would recommend a product or service to a friend or colleague or a family member? The customer who responds can be grouped as follows:

- Promoters (score 8–10): Loyal enthusiasts who will recommend the products and services
- Passives (score 5–7): Satisfied but not visible enthusiasts who may switch loyalty to other competing products
- Detractors (score 0–4): Unhappy customers who can damage your brand and impede growth through negative word-of-mouth

NPS calculation [5] can be framed as illustrated in Figure 10.2.

Let us say:

The percentage of Detractors = D and the percentage of Promoters = P

$\Rightarrow$ Net Promoter Score = NPS = P − D

NPS could range from a low of 'minus 100' (all customers are Detractors) to a high of 'positive 100' (all customers are Promoters).

$\{a \ldots\ldots\ldots\ldots b\} \Rightarrow \{NPS \in Z: -100 \leq x \leq +100\}$

'a' and 'b' are the lower and higher values.

Figure 10.2 Net Promoter score.

Measuring innovation 137

Customer-obsessed organizations such as Amazon, Verizon, Apple, P&G, Starbucks, Whirlpool, Samsung, etc. use NPS periodically to gauge their innovation ability to excite and retain their customers with a goal of growing their business. An NPS of 100 is the best scenario but is difficult to achieve.

It is critical that innovations are tied to KPIs and monitored periodically so that the effectiveness of the innovation efforts are calibrated and aligned with customer expectations. After all, innovations do not mean anything if there is no closed loop process with customers whose problems are not solved and if the solution's value is not recognized.

10.3 Innovation risk vs reward – A balanced approach

The innovation process does not guarantee outcomes, but certainly is a steppingstone for what one is eventually attempting to achieve. The entrepreneurship world continuously debates risk vs reward measures, and action is the key for entrepreneurship. If there is no action, there is neither a need to worry about risk nor the reward. Innovation is at the heart of entrepreneurship, whether in a startup or in an established corporate R&D setting, and hence attention to the risk vs reward consideration is essential for success. Risk of failure implies resource waste, opportunity cost, employee attrition, customer dissatisfaction, etc., while reward entails boosting employee morale, delighting customers, gaining market share, improving profitability, and strengthening collateral product/service offerings.

Balancing risk and reward is essential as there is no success without experimenting and testing possibilities. This implies that failure is unavoidable, but the key is to learn from it and apply it to further the innovation journey that culminates in success. With the right innovation management, which is demonstrated through authentic leadership, team diversity, resource commitment, risk tolerance, supportive experimental culture, and a non-punishing reward system, the odds of innovation success can be improved. Innovation leaders such as P&G, Google, Corning, Whirlpool, Microsoft, AMD, Verizon, Tesla, and Apple religiously practice agile and lean development methodology, which values customer engagement throughout the innovation process and MVPs before full-scale product or service rollout.

Innovation risks can also be mitigated significantly if there is a good alignment with the overall business strategy. For example, innovation can be construed a success in a limited setting, perhaps a carefully controlled market, but considered a failure if scaled up for consumption in markets that are not adequately prepared to receive the innovation. It is not necessarily the innovation itself that is to be blamed, but the inadequacy of the ecosystem or support system to deploy a particular innovation could be the cause. For example, when one of the major wireless carriers deployed industry-first same-day delivery for its customers, the innovation team carefully coordinated from the beginning with all other supporting groups, including sales and marketing, operations that managed 2,000+ retail stores and multiple regional warehouses, finance, and customer service. The purpose was to make sure that when the same-day orders were dropped from the e-commerce site to the local retail store for pick, pack, and ship based on the customer order zip code (postal), there was enough inventory at the store, store personnel were trained to ship like a warehouse operator maintaining brand consistency on the packaging, local UPS/FedEx was seamlessly communicated through the system for timely pick-up, and store personnel were informed about

138 *Economics of innovation*

the potential order drop for planning. Although the same-day delivery innovation itself was limited to Oracle-based e-commerce and store POS systems, the logistics processes and the overall supporting ecosystem determined the success of the innovation initiative. As the complexity was challenging in preparing 2,000+ stores for such rapid delivery, the company had to cherry pick select markets (little over seven or eight states) where there was a compelling need and customers could pay for the premium service. It was declared a great success, both financially and logistically. There were significant lessons learned from such select pilot deployments, which helped refine the solution before other markets were explored. Had they not gone through such concerted efforts of coordinating but deployed the solution in all the markets (50 states where the company operated), the innovation would have been considered a failure and unmanageable. Scaling is a critical factor in mitigating risks and managing innovation success.

10.4 How to value innovation – Organic vs M&A scenarios

Organic scenarios: When multiple competing internal (organic) innovation projects are evaluated, it is a standard process to use techniques such as internal rate of return (IRR) or net present value (NPV).

In the case of IRR, each competing project's investments (cash outflow) and expected return (cash inflow) are iteratively discounted at different internal rates to current value (today's value). The discount rate that offers a current value of "zero" after adding all the discounted outflow and inflow is called IRR. The project that has the highest IRR is the most desirable, purely from an economics standpoint. It does not consider compliance, competitive, or other qualitative priorities [6].

In the case of NPV, for a predetermined corporate discount rate, which is typically the rate of return the company expects on their investment for each project, all the cash outflows (investments) and inflows (returns) are discounted to current value and added together [7, 8, 9]. If the net value is positive, we consider the project is worth investing in. To select the project on a comparative basis from a basket of competing projects, the project NPV must satisfy two requirements: 1. Positive; 2. highest among all the projects.

So, the project that is determined to have the highest positive NPV is selected for investment. This, however, does not consider compliance or other qualitative priorities. Here we make a significant assumption that we have a good estimate of the cash inflows and outflows, which are difficult in the real-world scenarios.

There are also project decisions to be made that may involve probabilities and dependencies. This is often the case for innovation projects where there are uncertainties. The following example illustrates one such scenario [10]:

SmartDesign company has a patent for a jet engine component. It can sell the patent for a one-time market value of $400,000. Alternatively, it can take one year to develop a prototype of the patented design with an investment of $100,000 and make it a marketable product to aircraft manufacturers and service providers. The useful life of the component is five years after one year of development.

If SmartDesign decides to develop the prototype, the chances of making a commercially successful one is 80%. If the development fails, the patent itself will lose its value and can only be sold a year from now for just $250,000. In the event the development is successful, SmartDesign has a mutually exclusive choice of:

Measuring innovation 139

1. Sell the prototype to OEMs for $200,000 after the development (end of year 1 from now) with additional annual royalty payments of $300,000 for years 2 to 6. There is no direct marketing effort from SmartDesign company.

(or)

2. SmartDesign can market directly. There is a 65% probability that the product is a great success and can generate cash inflows of $400,000 per annum but there is a 35% probability that it will not be a success and can involve cash outflows of $45,000 per annum. The cash flow figures are for each of years 2 to 6.

SmartDesign uses a weighted average cost of capital of 7% to discount its future cash flows.

Given the innovation options and uncertainty, what is the best course of action?

Year 1 discount factor T1 for a weighted average cost of capital of 7% = 0.935
Annuity factor (T1-T6) = 4.767
Annuity factor (T2 through T6) = 4.767-0.935 = 3.832
If design development fails a year from now:
The NPV = $250,000x0.935-$100,000 = $233,750-$100,000 = $133,750.

Decision steps:

Decision 2 (working backwards):
Decide whether we need to sell the prototype and realize royalties or market directly.

Choice 1: Selling the prototype and realizing royalties for years through 2–6.
The NPV = $200,000x0.935+$300,000x3.832-$100,000 = $187,000+ $1,149,600-$100,000 = $1336,600-$100,000 = $1,236,600

Choice 2: Marketing directly

1. Great success for years 2–6 – The NPV = $400,000x3.832-$100,000 = $1,532,800- $100,000 = $1,432,800
2. Not a success for years 2–6 – The NPV = -$45,000x3.832-$100,000 = - 172,440- $100,000 = -$272,440

The expected NPV of marketing directly = 0.65x$1,432,800+0.35x-$272,440 = $931,320-$95,354 = $835,966.
As selling the prototype and realizing royalties result in an expected NPV of $1,236,600, which is better than marketing directly with an expected NPV of $835,966, the selling of the prototype option is better. Of course, this is based on whether we decide (Decision 1) to develop a commercial prototype.

Decision 1:
Decide whether we need to develop a commercial prototype or sell the patent.
There is an 80% of chance of succeeding in developing a commercial prototype and 20% chance of meeting with failure.

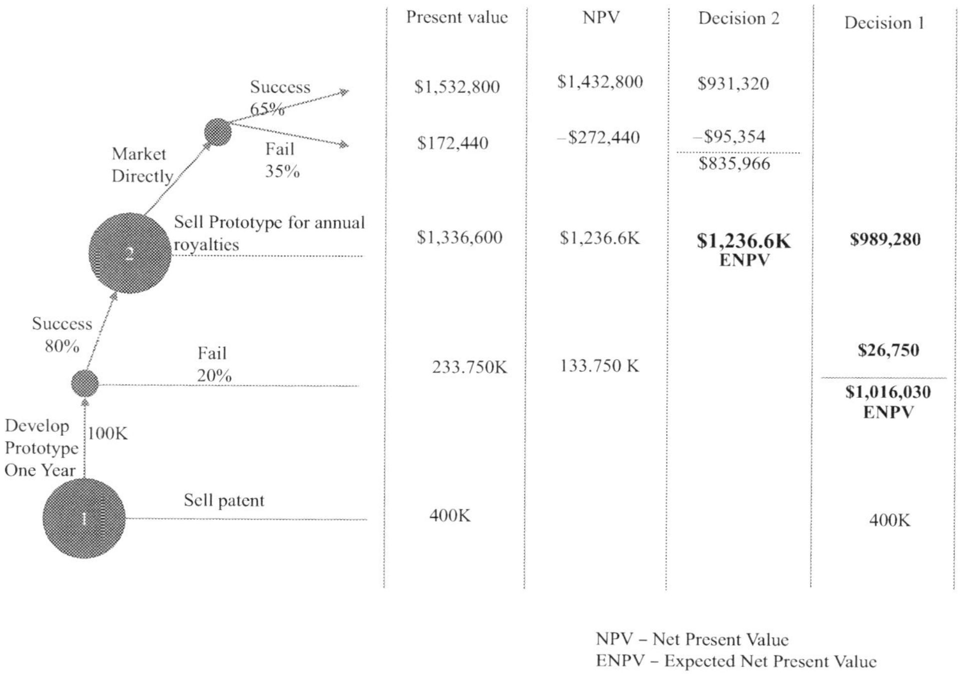

140 *Economics of innovation*

	Present value	NPV	Decision 2	Decision 1
Success 65%	$1,532,800	$1,432,800	$931,320	
Fail 35%	$172,440	−$272,440	−$95,354 / $835,966	
Sell Prototype for annual royalties	$1,336,600	$1,236.6K	**$1,236.6K ENPV**	**$989,280**
Fail 20%	233.750K	133.750 K		**$26,750** / **$1,016,030 ENPV**
Sell patent	400K			400K

NPV – Net Present Value
ENPV – Expected Net Present Value

Figure 10.3 Decision tree for uncertain innovation scenario.

So, the expected NPV of the development decision is = 0.80x$1,236,600+ 0.20x$133,750 = $989,280+ $26,750 = $1,016,030.

So, the development option provides an estimated NPV of $1,016,030, higher (by $616,030) than the non-development option that simply sells the initial patent for $400,000.

Final decision: Therefore, the development option with selling the prototype and realizing royalties is the best approach. Figure 10.3. illustrates the decision tree for this uncertain innovation scenario.

Note:

Annuity factor calculation [11]

The annuity factor for "n" periods at a periodic yield of "r" is calculated as:

Annuity Factor $(n, r) = (1-(1+r)^{-n})/r$

where n = number of periods and r = periodic cost of capital.

An annuity factor can be used to calculate the total present value of a simple fixed annuity.

The annuity factor is the sum of the discount factors for maturities "1" to "n" inclusive when the cost of capital is the same for all relevant maturities.

M&A scenarios: For internal project evaluations, when we do such analysis using either IRR or NPV, we consider them organic as many of the cost drivers related to the project investment emerge from internal efforts where the organization may have better financial visibility as well as controls. However, if there are acquisitions involved based on select innovations that one considers complement the parent organization's internal assets, the evaluation approach could slightly differ. For example, Apple acquires a company every three to four weeks, and the target companies are not necessarily its competitors [12]. To date, Apple's largest acquisition was the $3B purchase of Beats Electronics, the headphone maker, followed by another popular music recognition software company, Shazam, for $400M. Unlike other major technology competitors, Apple's focus is on acquiring technology and talent that complements its already-existing portfolio. The acquired technology has a specific purpose and more than likely they are integrated seamlessly into current products soon after the acquisition.

Another great example is when Apple acquired PrimeSense, an Israeli 3D sensing company. Apple was struggling with facial recognition, and the acquisition allowed them to quickly integrate the 3D sensing technology with its iPhones and implemented what is now known as Apple's FaceID. Likewise, Dark Sky, a weather app acquisition laid the foundation for the basis for iPhone's iOS 14 weather-specific features. Beddit, a sleep tracking product company, is another example of Apple's acquisition that made immediate financial impacts.

So, from the M&A investment standpoint, M&A cashflow both from standalone as well as in an integrated mature product perspective are crucial to truly assess the value potential. While understanding innovation synergy-related cost savings is important, integration costs and technical viability need to be examined as well. Any challenges on these dimensions may significantly escalate the initial outlay and possibly recurring costs associated with maintaining integration. The overall economics in these scenarios get murky if key technical experts onboarded through acquisition exit before their agreed upon period. Other considerations include a strategic need to preempt potential competitors from acquiring such critical technology in the interest of market share. This obviously drives premium associated with any such acquisitions.

10.5 Concluding remarks

Measurements are essential aspects of innovation success as planning and execution require expected outcomes to be defined upfront. This suggests innovation initiative valuation techniques to be considered as competing projects are evaluated for their return potential. Unlike conventional internal projects where there are more certainties and perhaps predictable outcomes, innovation projects are uncertain and often involve probabilities and decision trees. We may still use NPV and IRR methods, but will overlay probabilities and estimate the performance outcome. The innovation projects that have the highest outcome potential will obviously be the choice to pursue. Interestingly, probabilities are often judgmental based on prior experiences. In the case of M&A scenarios, there are other valuation considerations such as integration costs, synergy, competitiveness, and liability to be incorporated before committing to any such transaction. Often the quality of assumptions made in these scenarios impact

142 *Economics of innovation*

the innovation program decisions and hence every attempt must be made to be closer to the reality.

Student activities

1. Review the above SmartDesign company example.
2. Change the initial one-time patent market sale value to $150,000 instead of $400,000.
3. Change the chances of SmartDesign's ability to make a commercially successful prototype to 50% instead of 80%.
4. What is the best course of action for SmartDesign? Develop a decision tree and show your work.

10.6 References

1. McKinsey Quarterly, "Electrifying Cars: How Three Industries Will Evolve," www.mckinsey.com/~/media/McKinsey/Industries/Automotive%20and%20Assembly/Our%20Insights/Electrifying%20cars%20How%20three%20industries%20will%20evolve/Electrifying%20cars%20How%20three%20industries%20will%20evolve.pdf?shouldIndex=false
2. www.cultivateruralleaders.com/cultivate-rural-leaders-blog/2019/11/3/strategic-tactical-and-operational-where-is-your-organization-strong-and-where-does-it-need-work
3. www.counterpointresearch.com/us-market-smartphone-share/
4. https://buildfire.com/app-statistics/
5. www.netpromoter.com/know/
6. https://hbr.org/2016/03/a-refresher-on-internal-rate-of-return
7. www.businessmanagementideas.com/firms/mathematical-analysis-of-investment-project-firm-management/11433
8. https://efinancemanagement.com/investment-decisions/how-is-risk-related-to-net-present-value
9. https://hbr.org/2014/11/a-refresher-on-net-present-value
10. www.accaglobal.com/pk/en/student/exam-support-resources/professional-exams-study-resources/p4/technical-articles/conditional-probability.html
11. https://wiki.treasurers.org/wiki/Annuity_factor
12. www.bbc.com/news/business-56178792

Part VII

Special topics on innovation

Chapter 11	Design thinking	145
Chapter 12	Lean enterprise and innovation	159
Chapter 13	Sustainability-focused innovation	173

11 Design thinking

"Design thinking is a human-centered approach to innovation that draws from the designer's toolkit to integrate the needs of people, the possibilities of technology, and the requirements for business success."

- Tim Brown, Executive Chair of IDEO

11.1 Introduction

Merriam-Webster defines design as "to create, fashion, execute, or construct according to plan" and "to conceive and plan out in the mind." A painter, an artist, a movie director, an animation cartoonist, a fashion designer, or any other designer for that matter, before they design or develop a product or solve a problem, first attempt to understand its purpose, the audience, and visualize the solution. However, the problem itself may be nebulous and lack details and may require an iterative probing approach to conceive and crystallize the problem.

Unless we know the "what," in other words, what is to be addressed or solved, it is meaningless to think about the solution let alone the development of it. After all, innovation is about value generation in the form of solution with an expectation that the customer will pay for the solution. Once we have secured the problem definition, the solution development is the logical next step, which may involve iterative options analysis, testing, and customer validation.

In short, design thinking is a comprehensive approach to understanding the problem as the end user experiences it, not necessarily how they express it, and taking an iterative approach to conceive and develop solution options that result in the best solution, which addresses the customer problem, who may eventually pay for the solution. The focus is about thinking and learning about customer experiences both in the current and future states and designing a robust solution that is best for the defined problem. It is all about problem-solving with humans being at the center. The power of design thinking output in terms of the solution quality and making the customer realize what is not obvious but is very important and valuable to them differentiates design thinking from other product development approaches.

DOI: 10.4324/9781003190837-18

146 *Special topics on innovation*

> Design thinking is a comprehensive approach to understanding the problem as the end user experiences it, not necessarily how they express it, and taking an iterative approach to conceive and develop solution options that result in the best solution, which addresses the customer problem, who may eventually pay for the solution.

Nobel laureate Herbert Simon, in his seminal work *The Sciences of the Artificial*, defines human problem-solving as "the one involves nothing more than varying mixtures of trial and error and selectivity. The selectivity derives from various rules of thumb, or heuristics that suggest which paths should be tried first and which leads are promising." [1, 2, 3]. His problem-solving definition fits the design thinking approach. There are many variations of design thinking approaches, but all of them are invariably built on the core principles of Simon's heuristic search and problem-solving thesis. In the previous sections we discussed the TRIAL© holistic innovation framework, which is a tool the organizations can use to strategize and position them at the macro level to define and advance the innovation agenda. Design thinking, on the other hand, is a solution development approach that thrives at the tactical and operational level where actions are executed engaging end users to understand problems, ideate, prototype, and validate solutions. There is a symbiotic relationship between the TRIAL© holistic innovation framework and design thinking. Organizations can immensely benefit from them if they understand and orchestrate such relationship.

11.2 Design thinking for innovation – Why now?

Until a few decades ago, innovations that took years to develop were acceptable as typical roadmaps for new products, service, or new business initiatives spanning multiple years. Corporate R&D would be the major source of organized innovation efforts and it was hard for new entrants to make inroads given the investment and technological barriers. Organizing talent by new entrants for innovation initiatives was a challenge as well given the incumbents' advantages of well-resourced corporate R&D centers [4]. The innovation culture at these laboratories did not experience a sense of urgency as the customer expectations were rather predictable based on their previous consumption patterns of products and services.

However, in the past two decades or so there has been a tectonic shift in many industries given the rapid technological advancement and unpredictability of consumer preferences. The new generation of consumers, Gen X: born between 1965 and 1979/80 (65.2 million people in the US), Gen Y/ Millennials: born between 1981 and 1996 (72.1 million in the US), and Gen Z: born between 1997 and 2012/15 (nearly 68 million in the US) [5] are increasingly obsessed with technology innovations and have become in some sense addicted and have internalized them in their lifestyles.

This trend has created opportunities for many startups as they have access to not only the same technology innovations, but also highly valued customer preference information with relative ease. Social media platforms are one such example of how to harvest customer preferences that new entrants can benefit from to innovate new products and services. Additionally, as the consumer preferences and expectations constantly change, there is a need for businesses to innovate quickly and go to market at an accelerated pace. Longer lead times for innovations are not an option and Michael E. Porter's five force competitive framework [6] is being challenged as never before.

It is hard for businesses to reach a point of equilibrium as there is always a necessity to be on the edge and innovate. Change is a constant driving force for business survival. Businesses need to be in the trenches of customers as they design their products and services to meet customers' evolving expectations. The product life cycles are shortening and many businesses must innovate faster to keep up their financial growth measures. Innovation leaders such as Apple and Samsung make claims that they generate little over 50% of their overall revenue from products and services introduced in the past five years. It is not a trivial matter and business is simply not as usual. Complacency has no place in the corporate world. No company can afford to sit on its laurels but must be future-focused. The good news is there is a tremendous opportunity for businesses to prosper so long as they empathize and relate to the customers, both within and outside an organization. This is the key aspect of design thinking [7].

11.3 Design thinking approach

Design thinking is a human-centric iterative process to solve customer problems where the customer is the center of the universe. The customer is continuously engaged to understand and define their needs, refine assumptions, generate ideas, prototype quickly, and validate and optimize solution options. There are several flavors of design thinking in the industry but the five-phase process from the Hasso Plattner Institute of Design at Stanford (aka the d.school) is widely practiced [8]. An adapted version of the design thinking approach is presented in Figure 11.1 The key phases of design thinking are:

- Empathize with/listen to customers
- Define/understand customer problem
- generate ideas/solutions
- prototype solutions fast
- validate and test solutions.

11.3.1 Empathize with/listen to customers

"To create meaningful innovations, you need to know your users and care about their lives."
- Hasso Plattner Institute of Design at Stanford (d.school)

Empathize involves listening to customers to understand their needs supplemented with experiencing their problems or issues by being in their trenches. It is also possible that what is spelled out as needs or requirements in the written document is not complete and lacks the emotions and feelings of the customers. Understanding customer journeys entails a 360-degree approach.

There are different techniques one can use to truly understand what the customer needs. For example, storytelling, observing how the customer is performing their task with current process and tools, doing it ourselves taking instruction from customers, conference room discussion, customer-prepared template-based requirement documents, etc. These techniques are not mutually exclusive and together

148 *Special topics on innovation*

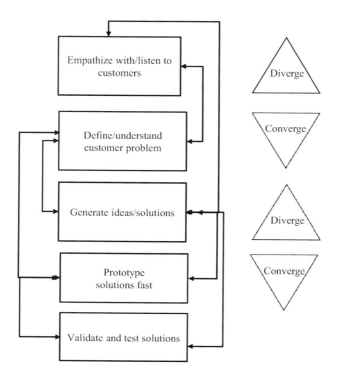

Figure 11.1 Design thinking approach.
Adapted from the Hasso Plattner Institute of Design at Stanford (aka the d.school) [8].

Note: Please access Digital Learning Resources provided with this book for Design Thinking step-by-step worksheets.

they provide a comprehensive view of the needs of the customers. It is interesting to note that this phase is divergent in scope and scale, as typically one starts with fewer requirements that are obvious, but end up with many times those requirements, requiring further analysis, grouping, tossing out redundant and irrelevant needs, and possibly prioritizing those that will be processed in the next phase.

11.3.2 Define/understand customer problem

"Framing the right problem is the only way to create the right solution."
- Hasso Plattner Institute of Design at Stanford (d.school)

Once the problem details are gleaned, the next important phase is to make sure that the problem definition is further crystalized and structured in a form that can drive the subsequent solution development activities. It is not enough just to have the problem definition crystallized, but there ought to be a feedback loop with the customer. To this end, one needs to relay the problem definition back to the customer to make sure they understand it and sign off on the details. If there are still gaps in the understanding, appropriate adjustments can be applied to have a complete alignment with the customer.

Techniques and tools such as pictorial illustrations, storyboards, etc. can be used to supplement standard procedures such as formatted requirements documents. This closed-loop process secures customer confidence and earns their trust as we move forward with solution development phases. This phase results in a well-defined problem statement and details that are convergent in nature relative to the set of requirements received at the beginning of this phase.

11.3.3 Generate ideas/solutions

"It is not about coming up with the 'right' idea, it's about generating the broadest range of possibilities."

- Hasso Plattner Institute of Design at Stanford (d.school)

The ideate phase takes input from the problem definition phase to trigger solution search. There could be many solution possibilities for the defined problem set. Solution ideation is a process that involves intense analysis of the problem set including researching the context, competitor portfolio, and adjacent industries. Existing patent search, comparable use case review, expert interviews, literature search including academic thesis and market reviews, conference room brainstorming, strawman discussion, storyboards, virtual and paper mockups are a few approaches and techniques used frequently. This phase needs to be carefully managed to allow idea generation and judging the emerging ideas should be delayed until the later phase. It is possible to prioritize the ideas pool based on some high-level confidence level, but the actual vetting will happen during prototype.

11.3.4 Prototype solutions fast

"Build to think and test to learn."
- Hasso Plattner Institute of Design at Stanford (d.school)

Prototype is a critical phase that takes the ideas and builds a physical or virtual sample or a model of the final product to further analyze and evaluate the technical and commercial viability of the idea. System designers, system analysts, end users, and integration specialists are just a few stakeholders who significantly influence building prototypes and qualify them for further validation and tests. It could involve coding a solution if it is a software-related product. It may involve simple mockup screens or user interfaces or screen sequences using traditional illustration tools without any real programming code. 3D printing and stereolithography techniques can be leveraged for physical models.

It is common that if an idea does not withstand the evaluation criteria and does not completely address the problem definition, the idea is tossed so that the project resources can be prudently committed on ideas that have the potential to succeed. Selection bias and subjectivity should be avoided by making sure that the evaluation criteria are diligently applied. It is a common practice at leading innovators such as Google and Apple to have a formal evaluation council that consists of a manageable number of unbiased individuals representing key business units and technical groups including the end user community. There could be several feedback loops to the previous phases to adjust and fine-tune the prototypes based on improved understanding of the problem definition and this is completely acceptable. The evaluation council

150 *Special topics on innovation*

could suggest possible improvements and can suggest resubmitting the prototype for re-evaluation.

11.3.5 Validate and test solutions

> "Testing is an opportunity to learn about your solution and your user."
> - Hasso Plattner Institute of Design at Stanford (d.school)

The last phase in design thinking is validating the solutions from the prototype phase. Validation is significantly different from prototype in many respects. In this phase actual customer data and contexts are used and the products are built real to the actual commercial specifications. For software products, actual coding is developed, and programs are built conforming to industry best practices and thoroughly tested. Compliance needs are addressed from safety and industry standards perspectives. For all practical reasons, validation stage innovation should be closer to real commercial products that will be launched as a next step. The goal here is to make sure that the customer experiences the innovation that is in the form of a product or service that genuinely addresses the defined problem and realizes value for which he/she is willing to pay. More than likely, the initial iterations in validation may uncover some gaps from the customer perspective, and with a proper feedback process such gaps can be addressed to develop a fully functional innovation that meets or exceeds customer expectation. It is possible that a few innovations, even after reaching this validation phase, may be tossed out from further considerations if the use cases do not see a good fit.

For design thinking to succeed, there must be a balanced consideration of factors related to human/customer, technology, and economics as indicated in Figure 11.2. As technology and economics are crucial to define problems and develop solutions, they should not be an afterthought as we engage customers to understand their problems. As one empathizes with customers to understand their problem or a business opportunity, technology could assist as a tool to listen as well as being an enabler to quickly generate ideas. Likewise, a sense for economics is key from the beginning as it defines some boundaries for the extent of effort to be committed to pursue the opportunity.

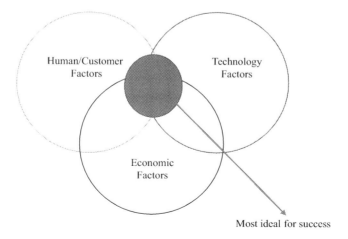

Figure 11.2 Design thinking considerations.

Design thinking cannot be approached in isolation. Organizational resources and capabilities must be leveraged to realize the full potential. This is achieved through establishing a tight relationship between the Enterprise Innovation Opportunities Model© that we discussed previously and the design thinking process. This is illustrated in Figure 11.3. As there could be several unknowns as one explores customer needs, having a broad back-end support from various stakeholders as depicted in the Enterprise Innovation Opportunities Model© helps generate many ideas and solutions. Design thinking process steps, including prototypes and validation, can immensely benefit as well by orchestrating seamless enterprise-wide coordination.

11.4 Success stories – Where design thinking advanced innovation

11.4.1 Airbnb

Airbnb, Inc., founded in 2008 by Brian Chesky in San Francisco, is a disrupter to the traditional hotel chains such as Marriott, Hilton, and Holiday Inn. Airbnb operates an online platform, both mobile application and website, which allows customers to make reservations for homestays or lodging for vacation and tourism. They do not own properties, but as a marketplace operator they connect retail property owners and rental customers and take a modest commission for successful reservations. Airbnb prequalifies the properties and their owners based on their corporate standards from a hygiene and safety standpoint and uses customer and a property owner feedback rating system to promote quality, reliability, and compliance behaviors. At the end of 2011, having experienced more than a million nights booked with 13 international offices and in 182 countries, instead of celebrating Christmas night, the CEO Chesky was trying to understand how Walt Disney used storyboards to focus its team and create their first full-length animation film, *Snow White*. Chesky had doubts about the sustainability of the success and did not want to be victim of his own success, rather he wanted to disrupt his business before others could disrupt Airbnb.

With Rebecca Sinclair, an ex -designer at IDEO, a design thinking pioneer, being the Head of User Experience Research and Design, Chesky charged her with the responsibility to lead a nights-and-weekends initiative, also called Snow White, to help Airbnb with making sure they have perfect product-market fit. Marc Lowell Andreessen, an entrepreneur, co-author of Mosaic, the first widely used web browser and a co-founder of Netscape browser and Silicon Valley venture capital firm Andreessen Horowitz, once commented that "product-market fit is the only thing that matters." This implies that the market wants products only when it matters to them. This requires critical research into what the customer wants, which is design thinking, and that is precisely what Chesky was exploring.

Airbnb once considered the website and the application where customers make reservations as the products. But through the Snow White initiative, taking a page from design thinking and empathizing with customers, it soon recognized that customers consider the entire trip and related experiences as Airbnb's product and not just the website and the application to make reservations. This was an eye-opener for Airbnb to shift its focus toward the overall Airbnb experiences and position it as a lifestyle company. Taking it further, Airbnb created an innovative culture of engaging its internal teams to use a storyboard framework and develop a narrative of customer journeys when they use Airbnb's services and impact all the customer touch points.

152 *Special topics on innovation*

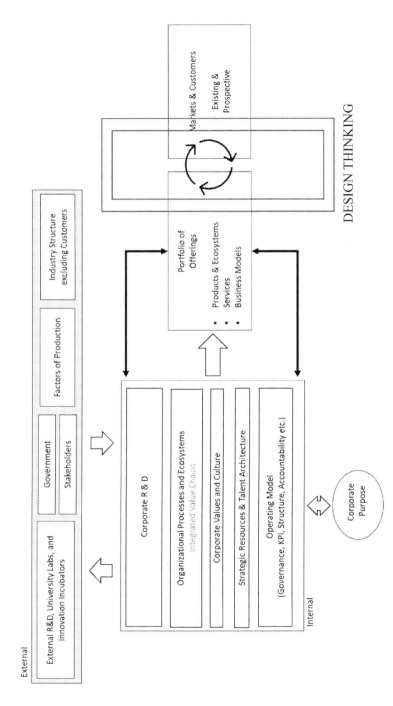

Figure 11.3 Interactions between the Enterprise Innovation Opportunities Model© and design thinking.

Design thinking 153

This was further refined, solutions developed, prototyped, and validated with real customers to enrich their overall experiences. Airbnb has internalized design thinking in their environment to innovate and deliver customer value on a continuous basis [9].

11.4.2 Ericsson

Ericsson is a Swedish multinational networking and telecommunications company headquartered in Stockholm, founded in 1876. It employs more than 99,000 people globally. Some of the products and services marketed by Ericsson support mobile and fixed network operators such as Verizon, Vodafone, and T-Mobile. Ericsson products are widely seen in communications and network infrastructure services and multimedia solutions. Ericsson leads next generation 5G network backbones as well. There is a pressing need for Ericsson to constantly predict the marketplace trend and develop and perfect solutions before the market is ready for it. The consumer may not yet recognize the problem, but Ericsson must infer by observing the market and device solutions. This does not happen magically given the technology challenges and the regulatory processes to be complied with in the telecom industry vertical that varies across international boundaries.

Ericsson uses design thinking to address the challenge. Their four-step process is illustrated in Figure 11.4. and is explained below:

Step 1: Research problems/opportunities

This step uses divergent thinking that involves a creative thought process to develop a sound understanding of the need through open and free-flowing discussions within teams. The outcome of this step is listing of "opportunity spaces" that allow potential solutions to be developed. Instead of approaching the problem identification with predisposed technology solutions, per Joakim Formo, Strategic Design Director at Ericsson ONE, "one needs to approach more broadly at an area or industry level, for example, mobility and the transportation of people and goods. Do not simply look for new transport solutions – transport is just one means for gaining access to goods, places or people." The discussions are facilitated with open-ended questions and materials, such as pictures, which can stimulate the discussion to generate as many perspectives as possible. Typically, such discussions involve a diverse set of people who have backgrounds in the humanities, design, psychology, basic science, gaming, and engineering. Select interviews are part of the research as well. The identified "opportunity spaces" are finally sorted and grouped into categories to help structure the data and specific topics for solution consideration [10].

Step 2: Consolidate

This step takes the unfiltered yet sorted and clustered problem areas from the previous step, and using convergent thinking and a logical review, identifies opportunity areas that offer promise for success. The focus is to visualize future scenarios that are enabled by current and future technologies. Mind maps and detailed sketches are a few tools used to deep dive the scenarios so that a finite number of opportunity areas can be defined for solution development. In the context of the mobility project, the team finally reduced a vast array of opportunity areas into four focused application

154 *Special topics on innovation*

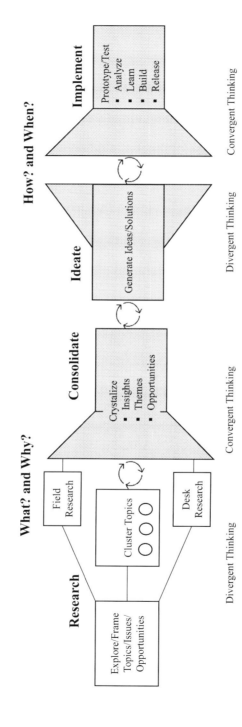

Figure 11.4 Design thinking approach at Ericsson.
Adapted from Ericsson.com - Ericsson ONE's four-step process for predicting future technologies [10].

areas: The physical movement of things and people; digital experiences and services; city planning and infrastructure; and then an abstract layer, which included things such as legal agreements and policies. Per Joakim, the team subsequently tried to apply technologies into each of these application areas to realize value. Care was taken to make sure such areas complement Ericsson's capabilities or it is something it was looking to expand. The final output of this step is well-defined opportunities of specific problems for solution development using technologies [10].

Step 3: Ideate

This step is again divergent thinking that seeks generating as many ideas and solutions as possible for the prioritized problem set. As the ideas are generated, feasibility evaluations are conducted in parallel to make sure that robust ideas are identified, perhaps combined and advanced for prototype efforts. To frame ideas, the teams might start off with user scenario-specific questions such as "how can we make public transport preferable to private transport?" and "what if we have a personalized public transport?" Tools such as detailed sketches and other visual illustrations are powerful in comprehending and analyzing solution options to be able to move forward with prototyping [10].

Step 4: Implement

In this step, again focus is the key and hence convergent thinking is resorted to and based on the inputs from the previous step, prototyping activities are conducted that may involve adding further details to visualization and sketches and perhaps developing physical products. Prototypes are developed in a collaborative way for team members to critique and add value. Prototypes provide a firm grasp on the solution, which can be further developed into a fully functional product. It is a very iterative process, and one might go back to the previous step activities either to reconfirm or integrate ideas to enrich the final recommended solution.

Ericsson firmly believes in storytelling of abstract ideas that is built on previous research, ideas, and discoveries, and allows everyone to understand the purpose of the innovation initiative; that is, Ericsson must think ahead, understand market trend, figure out the most important problem set and apply or develop appropriate technologies to solve the problems. For problem identification, ideas generation, and solution development, customer engagement from the market is key and Ericsson carefully orchestrates all the steps seamlessly in an iterative manner, keeping design thinking constructs as the foundation [10].

11.4.3 Burberry

Burberry is a UK-based luxury fashion house, founded in 1856 by Thomas Burberry in Basingstoke, UK. It designs, manufacturers, and distributes high-end personal fashion products such as leather goods, trench coats, footwear, eyewear, fragrances, and cosmetics, with a 2020 annual revenue of £2.63B. Its global network of stores and e-commerce platforms offer its customers easy access to its products and services. It manufactures its products predominantly at its own facilities in Keighley and Castleford as well as in other parts of Europe, while leveraging some third-party facilities as well. It owns a leather goods center of excellence in Italy and has a global supplier network [11].

156   *Special topics on innovation*

Given how seasonal the fashion industry is, predicting customer preferences is vital for Burberry's success. Angela Arhendts, who served as CEO from 2006 to 2014, recognized digital technology's role in designing customer-centric products with real-time customer inputs through social media collaboration between its brand and the customers [12]. In 2006 the company's growth was a meager 2%, with an annual revenue of £743M, and there was a sense of urgency to right the ship back to growth trajectory. The answer was empathizing with customers using design thinking principles, which used social media to connect with customers and make the designs "exciting and relevant" to the market. Burberry's luxury customers included millennials and they decided to not only actively engage them, but also make them a loyal customer base. How did they do this? A personalized digital marketing strategy allowed Burberry to align its product design to millennials' values – "cool and innovative" – using continuous customer feedback. For example, it used Facebook creatively to connect with its customers one at a time, and by 2011 had more than one million followers, outpacing all other competitors in the luxury space [13].

Customers influenced Burberry's fashion design, which made it far more personal and compelling, resulting in building a loyal base who became advocates for its products. Burberry was not just listening to its customers, but also empowered them to co-create its products, with no external designer expense. This democratization of co-creation benefited everyone and Burberry was back on the growth trajectory with 2014 revenues of more than £2.33B [14].

11.4.4 Bank of America – Keep the Change Program

Bank of America, headquartered in Charlotte, North Carolina, US, was formed after NationsBank's acquired BankAmerica in 1998. It is a holding company and, with global footprint, offers services related to personal and business banking, wealth management, home loans, auto loans, investment management, credit cards, etc. Its 2020 annual revenue was a little over $46.8B with a market capitalization of $355B. In 2004, recognizing the need to understand the customer in designing banking products such as savings account features, etc., it partnered with IDEO, a design firm that has a solid reputation for spearheading human-centered design thinking practices that are ethnography-based in nature.

The banking industry is typically conservative, particularly in embracing out-of-the-box thinking. Partnering with IDEO to experiment in design thinking was a radical departure to the prevailing practices that were heavily dependent on internal corporate R&D. The task given to IDEO was to figure out how to develop an exciting savings account product for people who did not have a savings account. Unfortunately, people who did not have such savings accounts were largely living paycheck to paycheck, but the teams' scope for generating insights were not limited to just this group of people. Taking a design thinking approach to tackle this challenge, the IDEO and Bank of America teams wanted to first empathize with customers to get a better insight into their situations and the challenges related to earning potential, spending behaviors, and savings approach. Instead of making assumptions, they actively interviewed hundreds of people in their homes and at workplaces from different geographies and observed their money-handling practices. Interesting patterns emerged during the study: Back then, prior to online banking, checkbooks were widely used, and people had a tendency to round up the numbers in checkbooks for easy calculation, leaving some buffer for spending.

This observation became the lynchpin for the team to design a savings account product called "Keep the Change Program." Once the customer opens a savings account with a debit card issued for spending, the expenses would be automatically rounded up to the nearest higher number. This extra rounded amount would be automatically posted as a credit to the newly created savings account, matched by Bank of America with some predetermined amount as an additional incentive.

After iteratively developing and testing the product with real customers, it was officially launched at the end of the second quarter of 2005. It became an instant success with more than 12 million customers rushing to open savings accounts, resulting in more than $2B dollar net savings. Given the size of assets held by the bank, in trillions, it was not significant, but it brought a sense of emotional pride in the minds of the bank customers that they could also save and manage their expenses prudently [15].

In summary, design thinking led to empathizing with customers, which is hard sometimes, and brought a service product innovation at Bank of America that impacted millions of customers in an effective way.

11.5 Concluding remarks

Design thinking is a problem-solving approach that brings discipline to engage and listen to customers from problem definition to solution development and testing. It is a paradigm shift from pushing products and solutions to customers to pulling customers into solution development by engaging them and understanding their problems intimately from the beginning. Many corporations are achieving benefits by implementing design thinking and nurturing a sympathizing culture that respects the value of customer engagement. Although there are variations of the design thinking approach being practiced in the industry, fundamentally the basic tenets remain the same – for effective problem-solving, customer engagement is critical.

Student activities

1. Select and Ecovative Design cases Stryker from Part VIII.
2. Review the details and list the problems or opportunities they tried to address.
3. Discuss their design thinking approach to innovate and develop solutions.
4. Also answer the questions listed at the end of the case.
5. Analyze these corporations, leveraging both the case and online resources to understand the interactions between the Enterprise Innovation Opportunities Model© and design thinking approach. State your findings.

11.6 References

1. https://philippevandenbroeck.medium.com/herbert-simon-the-sciences-of-the-artificial-1969-1998-a9f6294f4717
2. Herbert A. Simon, "The Sciences of the Artificial – 3rd Edition," The MIT Press, 3rd edition, October 1, 1996.
3. https://medium.com/bygone-econ-icons/herbert-a-simon-navigating-the-maze-25bc9d5e9 017\ https://www.kasasa.com/articles/generations/gen-x-gen-y-gen-z

158 *Special topics on innovation*

4. www.shrm.org/hr-today/trends-and-forecasting/special-reports-and-expert-views/Pages/Andrew-Smith-Chris-Baer.aspx
5. www.kasasa.com/articles/generations/gen-x-gen-y-gen-z
6. Michael E. Porter, March 1979, "How Competitive Forces Shape Strategy," Harvard Business Review.
7. www.wired.com/insights/2014/04/origins-design-thinking/
8. https://dschool.stanford.edu/resources/getting-started-with-design-thinking
9. www.forbes.com/sites/emilyjoffrion/2018/07/09/the-designer-who-changed-airbnbs-entire-strategy/?sh=3cda91da2c36
10. www.ericsson.com/en/blog/2020/7/technlogy-forecasting-and-design-thinking
11. www.burberryplc.com/en/company/business-model.html
12. www.goodworklabs.com/3-innovative-design-thinking-examples/
13. www.digitalsurgeons.com/thoughts/design-thinking/four-businesses-using-design-thinking-principles-to-drive-results/
14. www.statista.com/statistics/263885/burberrys-worldwide-revenue/
15. www.designbetter.co/design-thinking/empathize

12 Lean enterprise and innovation

12.1 Introduction

Lean has its origins in the practices suggested by Taiichi Ohno (1912–1990) through the Toyota Production System. It focused on reducing waste and eliminating inefficiency and was later relabeled as lean in the US. Some of the central pillars of lean include *jidoka* (quality focus), *kanban* (just-in-time inventory focus), and *muda* (waste avoidance focus). Despite having roots in the manufacturing domain, the approach has become popular across many industry verticals [1]. Lean attempts to avoid steps that do not add value to the final product that the customer is not willing to pay for. There is also another waste avoidance method called Six Sigma, which eliminates waste in the form of reducing variation within the process and is measured by statistical standard deviation that falls on both sides of the mean in a normal distribution curve [2].

The Six Sigma approach uses two important concepts: 1. Customer-defined acceptable lower and upper specification limits to calculate specification spread; and 2. The process spread, ± 3 standard deviation of sample data measured by range, variance, and standard deviation. The details are presented in Figure 12.1.

To measure the acceptability of a product or service that is considered within the quality expectations of the customer, short-term process capability is calculated by computing the ratio of specification spread to the process spread. Higher short-term process capability reflects less process variation, which is desirable to the customer [3]. There are also special situations where the data distribution could be skewed and may have to be handled as special cases. If the sample data is skewed toward the left of the mean, the distribution is considered as having negative skewness, and if the data is skewed toward the right of the mean, the distribution is considered as having positive skewness [4]. The discussion related to skewness is beyond the scope of this chapter.

Six Sigma leverages statistics and a data-driven approach and is based on the normal distribution curve observations of the sample data:

> 68% of data points fall within one standard deviation from the mean,
> 95% of data points fall within two standard deviations from the mean,
> 99.73% of data points fall within three standard deviations from the mean,
> 99.9937% of data points fall within four standard deviations from the mean,
> 99.99994% of data points fall within five standard deviations from the mean, and
> 99.9999998% of data points fall within six standard deviations from the mean.

DOI: 10.4324/9781003190837-19

160 *Special topics on innovation*

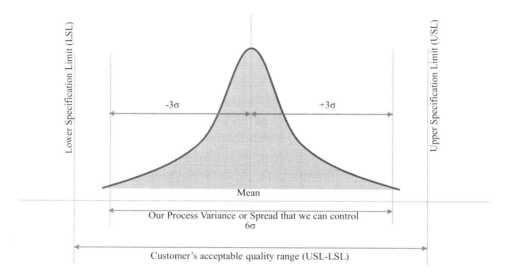

Figure 12.1 Six Sigma distribution.

12.2 Lean and innovation – Are they mutually exclusive?

Both lean and Sig Sigma have come to dominate the product and service industry through a combined discipline called the Lean Six Sigma discipline and have proven to be very successful in delivering quality performance that meets or exceeds customer expectations.

In the context of innovation, it is important to understand the role of lean, and perhaps Six Sigma as well. Innovation is a process and often achieved through trial and error or experiments, although it can be orchestrated with a structure and tools. Faster experiments allow more solution options for review and further refinement and perhaps integration of some of them to produce a solution that best meets the customer demands, who will pay for the innovation, whether it is a product, process, or business model. The iterative nature of such experiments if orchestrated carefully with lean inputs or resources instead of elaborate and expensive approaches, will enable more experiments and options to be executed within the given resource constraints. This will encourage senior executives to foster more innovation initiatives as they become more comfortable with such risk- mitigated experiments that do not drain corporate budgets unlike the legacy practices for innovation. Adding customer engagement during the lean process is the icing on the cake as real-time validation and alignment further enhances the overall innovation process and accelerates the solution convergence. This dovetails well with the design thinking approach that we discussed in the previous chapter.

It is debated rather vigorously whether lean approaches make any sense at all during the innovation process. It is common knowledge that lean not only strives to eliminate waste, but is also anchored on the principles of advancing quality, disseminating knowledge, fostering mutual respect across the organization, delivering solutions faster through efficient methods, and optimizing the interconnected system.

Lean enterprise and innovation   161

But there is a school of thought that subscribes to the idea that innovation is an independent creative process and should not be constrained by other motives, including lean initiatives. Also, there is a belief that lean is about waste elimination, while the innovation process is all about idea generation and there is no recognized waste yet. They are interesting perspectives, but not quite right.

12.3 How lean accelerates innovation

The above arguments about innovation perhaps may make sense in an unlimited resource situation but this is not realistic. Corporations utilize budget frameworks to address multiple issues or innovation opportunities simultaneously, and involve prioritization and resource allocation, including capital, materials, subject matter experts, project managers, etc. Also, there could be a sense of urgency to deliver innovations if there is a pressing issue with current offerings or an intense competition that is either already delivered or on the verge of delivering superior products that will make our products irrelevant. In these situations, corporate innovation efforts must respond to the needs of many stakeholders under more than one constraint and still increase the solution opportunity set. This is only possible if lean approaches are embedded in the innovation efforts. They are not mutually exclusive, rather they complement each other for the overall good of the corporation.

In the context of lean, there has been a widely adopted practice called "lean startup." It is an iterative and accelerated approach for product and process improvement by creating minimal viable products (MVP), while allowing the customers to validate the value along the way. This practice can be seen at many of the successful startups in Silicon Valley as well as at other startups across the globe. Established corporations are jumping on the lean startup bandwagon as well to recalibrate their innovation approach to accelerate speed to market necessities. Often lean startup is associated with entrepreneurship, and it is important to recognize the nexus between innovation and entrepreneurship. The latter is all about a pursuit of an opportunity through innovation to create value to the identified customers or markets, and along the way recognizing and mitigating financial and implementations risks, often in resource-constrained chaotic situations, and eventually building a financially and logistically sustainable business. So, lean startup is all about innovation, creating and capturing value, and building successful business, both new and within an established one.

For example, during the 2008 recession, although P&G had recession-proof portfolios comprising of billion-dollar products in dishwashing, haircare, healthcare, general hygiene, laundry household, and skincare market segments, the need for more breakthrough and disruptive innovations was felt [5]. The acquisition of Gillette for $54B in 2005, the largest ever in the consumer products industry, accelerated the sense of urgency to grow and demonstrate synergy [6]. To regain and sustain market leadership, there was a necessity to build superior innovation capacity that is consistent with young startups such as Facebook, Amazon, Netflix, and Google, which existed at that time. To break from internally focused orthodoxies, P&G took business unit presidents for "innovation tourism" to Silicon Valley and exposed them to lean startup and the entrepreneurial ecosystem [7]. They had the opportunity to meet with some of the best-known practitioners, founders, and thought leaders on entrepreneurship and innovation such as Steve Blank, and gain insights into how some of the startups are on steroids in innovating new products and business models at lightning speed. Upon return, the experience set the stage for implementing a lean startup culture at P&G, first at its fabric care business unit and gradually making inroads into other core businesses. The P&G team quickly recognized that some of their earlier assumptions such as their innovation processes were less certain and had to be reassessed. The innovation tourism helped their leadership understand the effectiveness of the iterative innovation process based on the lean startup framework [7].

Lean startup is a paradigm shift from the linear or waterfall model where the customer is at the receiving end and often would see the final product when all the development efforts are completed. Lean startup, however, is an iterative yet structured approach that engages customers early to test the hypothesis of a business model so that products and service values can reach customers quickly in solving their problems or meeting their unmet demands. Entrepreneurs and innovators alike benefit immensely using the lean startup approach [8].

The lean startup approach can be applied to any software, physical, process and service domains. Blank, Ries, and Osterwalder and Pigneur [8, 9, 10] are the original contributors to the lean startup framework that took the entrepreneurship and established corporations world by storm [11]. The following components are the building blocks of the lean startup framework [5, 8, 9, 10, 12, 13], which is illustrated in Figure 12.2:

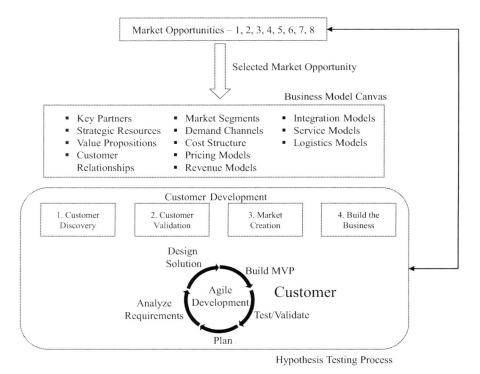

Figure 12.2 Lean startup framework.

Gruber, M., & Tal, S. (2017). Where to play: 3 steps for discovering your most valuable market opportunities. Pearson.

Adapted from Components of Lean Startup Framework [13]

1. Finding and prioritizing market
2. Developing business models
3. Validated Learning
4. Building minimum viable products (MVPs)
5. Persevere or pivot from the current course of action

We will discuss them briefly and how they interact with each other to accelerate developing and delivering customer aligned innovation.

Finding and prioritizing market opportunities

The important starting point for innovation is identifying and prioritizing market opportunities. When we talk about market, it entails customer definition and the qualification of the customer so that value creation and commercial viability can be assessed. Research suggests that more than 70% of the innovators may have to shift to different markets from the previously identified ones and requires a restart that many find challenging given the inflexibility of the support structure to carry out the innovation [14]. If the innovators had considered multiple markets upfront, they may have a better foundation to handle the situation [15]. Tools such as Market Opportunity Navigator, developed through academic research that supports the lean startup framework, can help the innovators to identify the most viable market for their pursuit [12, 13]. The questions addressed here are not just how to play, but also where to play. Figure 12.2 indicates possible markets to be considered as 1, 2, 3, 4, 5, 6, 7, and 8.

Developing business models

Business models are set of hypotheses or assumptions that can be expressed as stories that describe how the enterprise works. Peter Drucker, the management guru, always wanted to make sure some of the following questions are addressed before products and service are innovated and built: "Who is the customer? What does the customer value? How do we make money in this business? What is the underlying economic logic that explains how we can deliver value to customers at an appropriate cost?" [16]. The lean startup framework allows designing the business models that will be further validated. The business model canvas in Figure 12.2 highlights some of the essential components to be addressed such as key partners, strategic resources, value propositions, customer relationships, market segments, demand channels, cost structure, pricing models, revenue models, integration models, service models, and logistics models [17].

Validated learning

From the innovator's perspective, generating a business model is nothing but "leaps of faith" that they must validate by engaging customers and learning from them. The lean startup framework requires such validation in an iterative manner and fine-tunes the original business models that truly reflect the customer problems with the solution that creates and delivers value. Blank, Dorf, and Ries suggest that innovators must use scientific experiments to test their hypothesis and learn from it while refining their business models. They should be open to the idea of establishing a new set of

164 *Special topics on innovation*

assumptions as well; after all, learning elevates the overall comprehension of the customers' problems and how to solve them [9, 18]. This process encompasses all the key components of customer development such as customer discovery, customer validation, market creation, and building the business itself and is depicted in Figure 12.2 under the customer development step.

Building minimum viable products (MVPs)

As part of validating the requirement assumption and advancing customer development, the innovators must build their first product that is envisioned in their business model with the salient features. It is not all-encompassing, but just enough to give the customer a feel for the solution that will solve their problem. This is called MVP and, per Ries, it is "a version of the product that enables a full turn of the build-measure-learn loop with a minimum amount of effort and the least amount of development time." [9].

An agile product development methodology is used to develop the first prototype with active customer engagement. The agile development method is an iterative one, unlike a liner method, and involves planning the approach, analyzing customer requirements, designing the solution, building MVP, testing, and validating with active customer engagement. Figure 12.2 illustrates the agile development process. MVP allows the innovators to test some of their hypotheses, which were created when there were uncertainties, and with customer validation, perhaps new features or functions can be added to the product and the ones that do not create value or contribute to meaningful learning, also called waste, can be eliminated as well [9, 18]. Weekly team meetings are conducted to review the progress and solicit feedback. The goal is to have a validated learning that allows refinement to the business model and the solution itself.

Persevere with or pivot from the current course of action

The validated learning through customer development and MVP-based hypothesis testing is an iterative process, perhaps involving additional hypotheses to be defined and tested. After such experimentation and testing, the innovator may decide whether to pursue the current approach or adjust or pivot to a new business model with alternative solutions. In the context of lean startup, a pivot is a "structured course correction designed to test a new fundamental hypothesis about the product, strategy, and engine of growth" [9]. It is paramount that such decisive and timely pivoting occurs to gain traction with customers and not lose market opportunity. This is also called adaptability to customer expectations.

The above defined building block steps are not independent and invariably will have cross interactions. There is a tightly coupled feedback mechanism between the activities, and the goal is to orchestrate an accelerated MVP development and get customer validation. The interesting outcome from all these in addition to the MVP is establishment of greater customer insight and their rapport, which will further solidify the acceptability and usefulness of the products among customers and the larger market itself. The design thinking approach, empathizing with/listening to customers, defining/understanding customer problem, generating ideas/solutions, prototyping solutions fast, and validating and testing solutions, which we reviewed in the previous

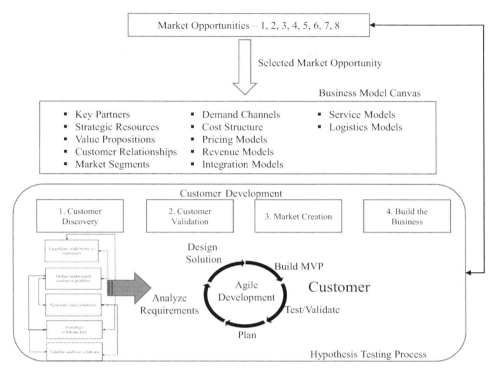

Figure 12.3 Design thinking interactions on lean startup.
Gruber, M., & Tal, S. (2017). Where to play: 3 steps for discovering your most valuable market opportunities. Pearson.
Adapted from Components of Lean Startup Framework [13]

chapter, finds its relevance in the lean startup framework and is at the core of the customer development step as illustrated in Figure 12.3.

12.4 Success Stories – Where lean thinking advanced innovation

12.4.1 *Pixar Animation Studios*

Pixar Animation Studios, founded in 1986 in Richmond, California, is a pioneer in computer-generated animated feature film productions and was acquired by the Walt Disney Company from Steve Jobs in 2006. Some of the successful movies produced by Pixar include *A Bug's Life*, *Toy Story 2*, *Monsters, Inc.*, *Finding Nemo*, and *The Incredibles*.

One may wonder how lean fits into the creative world of Pixar, as they seem to be at diametrically opposite ends of a spectrum. It is interesting that many of the processes that Pixar put in place as method and culture to fund and produce a successful animation movie emulate what a lean startup advocates as principles. These include open communication, transparency, value focus, iterative improvements, MVP, customer

166 *Special topics on innovation*

empathy, mutual respect, and collective creativity [19]. Some of the parallels between lean startup and Pixar are discussed below.

Preproduction

In a typical startup we have founders or visionaries. In the case of Pixar we have directors who have the vision like the startup founder. The directors are skilled artists who can visualize their animation dream movie and develop a persuasive narrative to convince their internal top leadership that their idea is a great one and will be a spectacular commercial success, requesting to fund their project. They use storyboards, which are nothing more than sequential pictorial illustrations, hand-sketched or using some computer application to tell the story. This is one of their primitive MVPs.

After securing the initial approval, the directors need to develop details for their original idea and start onboarding talented team members. Together as a team they conduct field research and strengthen the storyline. As they learn and engage customers or spectators, including having open dialogue with their teams, their story trajectory can change for the better until the directors are comfortable with the one that is compelling and exciting. This detailed product is shared with the top leadership, a persuasive pitch is made, and budget is secured for the entire movie production, which is analogous to securing funds by a startup through several rounds of venture capital or other financing mechanisms [20].

Production

Producing an animated movie takes a lot of time and resource. Now that budget is secured, the director organizes the production team that is onboarded with the necessary orientation to the movie details. The team includes many other artists and technical experts who are well versed with detailing movie characters and producing a film. Some of the key steps include modeling, surfacing, rigging, layout/set dressing/animation preparation, character animation, lighting, editing, sound mixing, etc. [21].

As the movie is produced, it goes through continuous evaluation and feedback solicitation from a brains trust that consists of peer directors and other key individuals, who may or may not be associated with the project. At Pixar, they use "dailies," which are a way to share and measure progress and is like the MVP or work-in-progress in the lean startup. The brains trust actively reviews such dailies and without any inhibition asks questions such as "have you considered X," or "have you thought about Y?" [20]. This is an open forum and no punitive consequence for questions asked by the members of the brains trust. This is done in keeping with the best interest of the movie and the brand and everyone understands it. It is akin to weekly meetings conducted in lean startup for validated learning to make course correction or pivot to a new solution, as necessary.

As the lean startups research the field and get closer to the customer as they develop solutions, Pixar conducts what is called the research trip. They use these trips to gain real-world experience and apply them to the animation that they build so that the experience is more real. For example, the Pixar producers experienced scuba diving in Hawaii when they produced *Finding Nemo* and physically drove cars on Route 66 (US Highway 66, the nation's first all-weather original highway linking Chicago to Los Angeles, established in 1926, but now replaced by other highways) when they made the movie *Cars* [20].

Postproduction

Pixar is good at conducting a formal postmortem review once the movie is produced to make sure the lessons learned are captured and reflected on immediately so that findings can be applied in future movies. This benefits all the directors and projects independent of whether they were involved in the subject movie. Again, organizational interest is given a priority as the knowledge capital is built within Pixar. In the lean startup framework, successful product launch is followed up with a formal lessons learned meeting as well.

There are quite a few parallels between lean startups and the processes within Pixar as they develop highly creative animated movies.

12.4.2 Dropbox

Dropbox has its headquarters in San Francisco, California, and it is known for shared file hosting services, leveraging cloud resources and employs more than 2,500 personnel. It was founded by MIT student Drew Houston in 2007 and later joined by Arash Ferdowsi, who was so excited after reviewing the initial idea in the form of a video. Their initial investor, Y Combinator, considers Dropbox one of their best investments [22, 23]. It is now a $10B market cap company traded on NASDAQ with more than 400 million outstanding shares.

What started off as a tool to help Drew Houston's personal file storage needs using a cloud infrastructure at a MIT dormitory has grown to dominate the world in not only file storage and sharing but also for seamless team collaboration and productivity improvement through what is called "smart workspace," a digital environment that minimizes unnecessary communication clutter. The key features of Dropbox's offerings allow storing and accessing files from anywhere, bringing all teams' digital contents together in one centralized place, and working smarter from one's desktop.

Dropbox offers its service in the form of popular mobile and desktop apps, communication channels, and project management systems that can be deployed on disparate hardware systems that run on most of the popular operating systems with always-on settings.

During their startup years, Dropbox mastered lean startup in a way that further simplified the approach to get customer value validation by developing the MVP that was distributed as a video [24]. The MVP was not even a developed product for potential customers to touch and feel, but to see and evaluate the product through a three-minute video posted on the platform Digg that was popular among the technology user community (https://youtu.be/7QmCUDHpNzE). The interest for their beta release skyrocketed from a mere 5,000 to 75,000 people within a few days, which gave Dropbox engineers more confidence to build the full-scale product for commercial release. The video contained a demonstration of Dropbox features that really mattered to the customers and added value, but not loaded with bells and whistles that otherwise would have diluted the purpose. Lean startup components can be applied in a lot of different ways to develop customers and learn their needs before the final product is developed and Dropbox is a great example.

168 *Special topics on innovation*

12.4.3 *Zappos*

Zappos.com is an online retailer based in Las Vegas, Nevada, founded in 1999 by Nick Swinmurn, a software engineer from California, who was frustrated with the lack of availability of a pair of Airwalks (shoes) in his local store and decided to start an online platform for shoes [25]. After a decade of growth, Amazon found significant complementary value in it and acquired it in 2009 for $1.2B. Although it had a focus on shoes, etc. when they started, it has now morphed into a popular destination for clothing, handbags, and accessories, in addition to major shoe brands. Their website boasts their purpose of "to live and deliver WOW," which is unique in the way they connect with their customers [25].

Nick Swinmurn's original vision was to create an online site with a wide selection of shoes with a rich online retail experience, and directly dropship to customers. However, to realize this vision, he would have to prove first his ability to set up strategically located warehouses, establish partnerships with logistics providers and major shoe manufacturers, build inventories of varying shoe designs, brands, and sizes, and demonstrate sales growth. It perhaps would have taken a lot of time, coordination, investments, and human capital if he had stuck with the then conventional process of preparing a business plan, executing the plan, and waiting for the results. Success would be still illusive and uncertain as there would be no customer feedback early on to fine-tune the business.

Swinmurn recognized the challenge and wanted to test his idea before scaling up. He approached the problem differently, drawing on the principles of lean that found traction in many industry verticals. He decided to leverage local shoe stores for his business experiments. Swinmurn visited some of the local shoe stores, took pictures of the shoes he wanted to present as a catalog, and published them online on his e-commerce website. Customers reviewed the online shoe options and some placed orders. After receiving the orders, Swinmurn provided drop ship delivery dates and would immediately go to the same local shoe stores, purchase them, and ship them to customers [26]. He was also keeping a shoe inventory list from the local stores that he could leverage to ship.

The approach was Swinmurn's way of building MVP and testing his business idea of online storefront before perfecting and scaling it up with automation and significant financial commitments. This approach, although having limitations to test the end-to-end process, including viability of financials, particularly profitability of the business model, did provide ample opportunity to assess the nature of online traffic and learn user preferences for his products as customers shopped online. This firsthand feedback loop from the customer shaped Zappos' business trajectory as they scaled up their effort, increased investments, and expanded their portfolio of offerings. Zappos did not have to rely upon external market research firms to understand customer preferences to shape its business strategy at the early stages as it was no comparison to the raw data they were able to harvest and learn from their own online store.

12.4.4 *General Electric (GE)*

An American icon, General Electric Company was founded in 1892 and is headquartered in Boston, Massachusetts. The company has a leadership position in many market segments: oil and gas, healthcare, power, renewable energy, aviation, transportation, energy connections and lighting, and venture capital and finance. Its annual revenue exceeds $76B as of 2020 with a market cap of $115B and is traded in the New York Stock Exchange [27, 28].

For an organization that takes pride in leading market segments in which it competes, it is no surprise how open they are in embracing innovative methods to bring new products and services to the market. When Eric Ries, author of the lean startup approached GE's management in 2013 to explore the possibility of applying his methodology in making turbines and jet engines, to his pleasant surprise, GE was overwhelmingly excited and asked him to train the new product introduction teams at its Crotonville, New York, the company's management development institute. This institute, started in 1956, is famous for imparting its global employees on experiential leadership and functional learning. GE's website boasts that this institute is the "epicenter of GE culture and an ideal that connects heritage and vision to performance. We unleash imaginations and deepen connections here, fostering personal discovery to connect who you are to how you lead [28]." The training was significant given GE's belief that lean startup can help its design and manufacturing, although lean startup has its roots in the software industry that leveraged the agile development process with sprints cycles.

After discussing with Eric Ries, on the merits of lean startup, GE set up a program called FastWorks to adapt lean startup within GE and committed 80 leaders who were then trained by Eric Ries as coaches. The FastWorks program's focus was to involve customers from the beginning of product design, develop and share with the customer a MVP in the form of prototype, validate iteratively the form factors, features and functions, learn from the feedback and pivot to an improved solution that aligned with customers who would eventually value and pay for it. It emphasized empowering and inspiring each other, allowing customers to determine GE's success, staying lean, learning from customers, adapting to suggestion, and delivering value.

GE was historically set up to take a structured path for product development and its organizational processes, including performance management, were architected to support such static processes. Annual goal-setting, incentives for objectives-based accomplishments, etc. did not support experimentation and risk taking, which are the central tenets of lean startup, now FastWorks' approach [29]. For a century old global company like GE, it was a herculean task to change the organizational processes and its culture to pivot to the new model, but GE's senior leadership was very committed to move forward with FastWorks on a global basis. GE trained an additional 1,000 executives on lean startup principles to show its pathbreaking new product introduction approach and had further plans to train another 5,000 global executives [30].

As an experiment, GE went ahead with a GE appliances business unit where FastWorks was introduced first to create a refrigerator with French doors. The then CEO gave a mandate to the product development team to develop a customer-appealing functional refrigerator within three months and a subsequent production version within a year, while limiting the budget to the bare minimum. The cross-functional FastWorks team took that as a challenge, owned the program, and developed MVP within the expected timeline and engaged the customer from the beginning. The entire team worked from a conference room, interacted with customers frequently,

170 *Special topics on innovation*

conducted their market research, developed several versions of the product, visited GE's design centers in New York and Chicago to test their in-progress prototypes, solicited feedback from other designers and expanded customers, and continuously adapted their design to the expectation of the customers based on their feedback. Some of the feedback included the color of the stainless steel and quality of the interior lighting, which made good sense as there was someone willing to buy if the changes were made. The team was empowered to make the necessary changes while working with the customer, bypassing the traditional bureaucratic approval process. The mandated French door refrigerator was produced within half the typical cost and development time [31]. Moreover, this product was sure to succeed as the customer co-created and was on board.

FastWorks put GE appliances on a faster annual cycle for new products introduction instead of releasing them once every five years. Speed to market and customer collaboration for product development catapulted GE to a premier position, ahead of its competitors [30].

12.5 Concluding remarks

Innovation leaders embrace lean startup principles and techniques with open arms to allow numerous possibilities for solution development. They recognize the importance of customer validation during the problem definition, solution development, and validation before scaling up for broad market consumption. Constrained budgetary situations make it a necessity rather than a choice. Isolated solution development within the four walls of corporate R&D that keeps customers at bay is a recipe for failure as customers are changing quickly given the pace of innovations across a broad market segment. Corporations must be nimble, adaptive, and willing to change their trajectory if the market forces dictate. Innovations in other industries have a knock-on effect in every business and pivoting to lean enterprise models will provide the necessary tools to be successful.

The lean startup approach may look little chaotic for linear-thinking businesses to begin with; nevertheless, once they experiment with a few innovation initiatives using the lean approach, they will start appreciating its strengths. It does have some structure, feedback loops, decision points for pivoting or persevering, etc. to get the solution developed and validated with hypotheses tested, all in close engagement with customers who are willing to pay for the innovation. After all, having proximity to customers reduces the unknowns, and the confidence level of the solution acceptability in the marketplace gradually increases as one progresses through the iterative process.

Interestingly, design thinking aligns well with the lean principles [32], and together they form a formidable innovation methodology that is risk-proof. However, businesses must prepare for such transition in an orderly manner, such as the P&G example that we discussed earlier, and should endure some initial challenges that they may experience within their context. Change management is the key for success as one embarks on the lean journey.

Lean enterprise and innovation   171

> ### Student activities (uses external source)
>
> 1. Review https://leanstartup.co/how-procter-gamble-uses-lean-startup-toinnovate/
> 2. List five learnings from this reading that allowed P&G to get ahead on innovation.
> 3. Relate them to some of the discussions we have in this chapter.
> 4. List potential change management issues when traditional businesses embrace a lean startup approach.

12.6 References

1. www.getvetter.com/posts/159-taiichi-ohno-an-intro-to-the-father-of-lean-manufacturing
2. www.villanovau.com/resources/six-sigma/six-sigma-vs-lean-six-sigma/
3. https://blog.masterofproject.com/pmp-certification-bible/
4. www.benchmarksixsigma.com/forum/topic/35195-skewness-and-kurtosis/
5. Emily Truelove, Linda A. Hill, and Emily Tedards, July 2020, "Kathy Fish at Procter & Gamble: Navigating Industry Disruption by Disrupting from Within," Harvard Business Review, 9-421-012.
6. www.marketingweek.com/pg-makes-gillette-merger-work/
7. https://hbr.org/podcast/2021/06/procter-s-lean-innovation-transformation
8. Steve Blank, 2013, "Why the Lean Startup Changes Everything," Harvard Business Review," 91(5), pp. 63–72.
9. Eric Ries, "The Lean Startup: How Today's Entrepreneurs Use Continuous Innovation to Create Radically Successful Businesses," Crown Books, 2011.
10. Alexander Osterwalder, and Yves Pigneur, "Business Model Generation: A Handbook for Visionaries, Game Changers, and Challengers," John Wiley & Sons, 2010.
11. https://journals.sagepub.com/doi/pdf/10.1177/1042258719899415
12. Steve Blank, 2019, "How to Stop Playing Target Market Roulette: A New Addition to the Lean Toolset," Retrieved May 25, 2019, from https://steveblank.com/2019/05/07/how-to-stop-playing-target-market-roulettea-new-addition-to-the-lean-toolset/
13. Marc Gruber, and Sharon Tal, "Where to Play: 3 Steps for Discovering Your Most Valuable Market Opportunities," Pearson, 2017.
14. Sharon Tal-Itzkovitch, Marc Gruber, and Uzi De Haan, 2012, "From Snipers to Scanners: Market Entry Decisions in Emerging Organizations," In Academy of Management Proceedings (Vol. 2012, pp. 13679). Academy of Management.
15. Marc Gruber, Ian C. MacMillan, and James D. Thompson, 2008, "Look Before You Leap: Market Opportunity Identification in Emerging Technology Firms," Management Science, 54(9), pp. 1652–1665.
16. Andrea Ovans, January 23, 2015, "What Is a Business Model?" Harvard Business Review.
17. https://canvanizer.com/new/business-model-canvas
18. Steve Blank, and Bob Dorf, "The Startup Owner's Manual: The Step-by-Step Guide for Building a Great Company, K&S Ranch, 2012.
19. www.pipefy.com/blog/lean-pixar-where-creativity-meets-performance/
20. https://steveblank.com/2015/10/27/pixar-artists-founders-and-corporate-innovation/
21. www.artella.com/index.php/2017/09/21/animation-production-step-step-guide-making-3d-animated-movie/
22. www.dropbox.com/
23. https://en.wikipedia.org/wiki/Dropbox_(service)

172 *Special topics on innovation*

24. https://medium.com/@LoganTjm/how-uber-airbnb-dropbox-released-mvps-to-achieve-rapid-growth-d823ac6eaed5
25. www.zappos.com/
26. https://medium.com/rocket-startup/how-zappos-built-a-product-by-faking-it-d3fd692a1fed
27. CNBC.COM
28. GE.COM
29. www.collectivecampus.io/blog/how-ge-saved-80-in-development-costs
30. https://hbr.org/2014/04/how-ge-applies-lean-startup-practices
31. https://academy.nobl.io/how-ge-implemented-fastworks-to-act-more-like-a-startup/#:~:text=To%20become%20more%20innovative%2C%20General,with%20customers%20and%20solicit%20feedback
32. www.bmc.com/blogs/design-thinking-vs-lean-vs-agile/

13 Sustainability-focused innovation

"Companies that persist in treating climate change solely as a corporate social responsibility issue, rather than a business problem, will risk the greatest consequences."
- Michael E. Porter and Forest L. Reinhardt

13.1 Introduction

Sustainability has been a hot topic for quite some time and garnered a lot of interest from many segments of society and many businesses. There are numerous definitions and understandings of this term, often confusing, misused, and abused, particularly when corporate initiatives are launched for publicity as a marketing ploy. Cambridge dictionary defines it as "the quality of being able to continue over a period of time." [1]. Professor Graham H. Pyke from Australia, a leading authority on sustainability, defines it as follows: "Sustainability is doing (all) the things we do today, in ways such that we (including future generations) can continue to do them tomorrow, and into the future [2]." In the context of business, Alexandra Spiliakos, in her *Harvard Business Review* article, defines sustainability as "doing business without negatively impacting the environment, community, or society as a whole [3]." The EPA in the US defines it thus: "Sustainability is about meeting today's needs without compromising the ability of future generations to meet their needs. It is about taking action to protect our shared environment – air, water, land, and ecosystems – in ways that are economically viable, beneficial to human health and well-being, and socially just in the long term. In practice, sustainability refers to efforts to align economic development with environmental protection and human well-being [4]."

According to the World Health Organization estimates, more than 12.6 million people die from environmental health issues annually, and 25% of the diseases in general are attributed to environmental pollution [5]. The National Institute of Environmental Health Sciences in the US reports that such diseases include allergies and asthma, birth defects, cancer, fertility problems, goiter, immune deficiency, kidney diseases, mercury poisoning, lead poisoning, nervous system disorders, and reproductive disorders [6].

Businesses that contribute to the environmental disasters are on notice and a growing number of environmentally conscious customers in many geographies are making their purchasing decisions driven by their progressive values. Customers are also concerned about how certain demographics are not represented within the businesses they interact with and demand diversity and inclusiveness transparency. We

DOI: 10.4324/9781003190837-20

174 *Special topics on innovation*

hear of customers boycotting popular global brands if they do not seem to practice social inclusion [7, 8, 9].

The McKinsey Global Survey reveals that many of the business leaders, little over 2,711, who responded to the survey were establishing formal sustainability programs and prioritizing diversity and inclusion. The shift toward these priorities is noticeable compared to previous decades and is primarily driven by the growing sustainability awareness among customers and employees and the firms' necessity to recalibrate their alignment between actual business practices and their publicly stated goals, missions, or values. The survey also provides some insights into how the businesses are tackling sustainability priorities. They seem to use innovations from the traditional areas such as energy-efficient equipment as well as fourth industrial digital tools such as internal and external social media, IoT, AI, big data, and machine learning. However, businesses have challenges in mustering value through a standalone sustainability initiative, and some are integrating such sustainability efforts into their core business functions that have the potential to enhance the overall value realized [10, 11].

In essence, in the context of business and taking a holistic view, sustainability refers to practices to produce products and services that create value for customers using natural resources, ethical business processes, and inclusive and diverse organizational resources. The approach should be benign to the environment and people while making sure the present and future generations can sustain. Social inclusiveness and business ethics are part of social responsibility. Nonetheless, we believe they should be included as part of the sustainability effort as well as there is a strong relationship between environment and social responsibilities and they must be addressed together.

> In the context of business and taking a holistic view, sustainability refers to practices to produce products and services that create value for customers using natural resources, ethical business processes, and inclusive and diverse organizational resources. The approach should be benign to the environment and people while making sure the present and future generations can sustain.

Recognizing the value potential of sustainability, many businesses are not only integrating sustainability goals into their core business functions but are also internalizing them through calibrated enterprise culture and applying best practices for consistency and endurance.

After all, businesses are unique and have strategies that are customized to their situation. However, sustainability goals can find common ground across many businesses. For example, in the case of manufacturing businesses, ethical sourcing is an important concern for sustainable businesses. Many developing Asian countries have been under the microscope for quite some time as they were questioned for child labor in appalling conditions, not conforming to internal labor standards. London-based Overseas Development Institute, in its 2016 survey, found that children as young as six were employed for 100 to 110 hours a week on an average wage of $2 a day [12]. Also, in early 2021, The US started cracking down on cotton, tomato, coal, chemicals, sugar, and polysilicon, a solar panel raw material imported by the US retailers from one of the major economies in Asia, citing alleged human rights violations and the widespread use of forced labor in some regions of the producing country. Companies such as Patagonia, Marks and Spencer, and H&M are just a few that quickly responded, recognizing that, if indeed true, these are unsustainable practices and they tried to distance themselves from such supply chains [13, 14].

By leveraging technology innovations such as blockchain technology that can provide authenticity and the provenance of the supply chain, businesses can operate efficiently and sustainably by not only complying with local laws but also conforming to their established organizational values.

Another sustainability example is to reduce greenhouse emissions. Greenhouse gases in the earth's atmosphere trap heat from the sun while allowing sunlight to pass through the atmosphere. Some of these gases include carbon dioxide, nitrous oxide, methane, ozone, and nitrous oxide [15]. The longer-term effect of such gases is that planet earth is warming up, causing unpredictable widespread natural disasters and ecological imbalance. One of the major activities that increases greenhouse gases in our environment is burning fossil fuels for transportation, electricity, industry, and heat generation [16]. The EPA in the US estimates that just over 6,558 million metric tons of carbon dioxide equivalent was produced in 2019 in the US, which is not sustainable [17].

Businesses that value sustainable practices, could perhaps source their electricity from producers who use less carbon-intensive natural gas and renewables instead of coal. They can also generate electric power on-site with cost-effective renewable energy innovations such as rooftop solar panels and solar water heating [18]. Getting LEED (Leadership in Energy and Environmental Design) certification for office buildings is another approach that can leverage the LEED framework to design and build healthy, highly efficient, and cost-saving green buildings [19].

Businesses can leverage technology innovations and offer energy-efficient products. For example, Toyota's Prius, the first mass-market hybrid car, was interdicted in 1997, overcoming many engineering challenges with the goal of reducing the carbon footprint and Toyota continues to push the envelope with innovative designs to lower carbon emissions across all its product offerings. The popular Celebrity Cruise's *Solstice* ship has all its LED lighting system powered by onboard solar panels and has an onboard filtration system that recycles and cleans 100% of its wastewater. Starbucks, the well-known coffee chain, aims to eliminate plastic straws by 2020 by redesigning its cold drink cups without straws and has already piloted this in the US and Canada [20].

On the topic of diversity and inclusiveness, recognizing significant value, there are several leading corporations internalizing and practicing them with top-level leadership support. For example, Johnson & Johnson, the medical devices, pharmaceutical and consumer packaged goods, a US company, has a vision to maximize the global power of diversity and inclusion, to drive superior business results and sustainable competitive advantage. Their diversity officer reports directly to the CEO and chairman, and they achieve impactful business results through employee resource groups, mentoring programs and "Diversity University," to promote working collaboratively. To their credit, *U.S. Veterans Magazine* recognized them as "Best of the Best" for achievements made in diversity efforts. Johnson & Johnson is one of only two companies that has been on the Working Mother 100 Best list for the past 28 years [21].

Mastercard, a US-based financial services corporation, another great example, has consistently made the top ten of Diversity Inc.'s 50 best companies diversity list, which is a great honor. Mastercard believes that diversity is the backbone of

176 *Special topics on innovation*

innovation accomplished through better insights, decisions, and financial products. One of their programs launched recently, "YoPros" BRG (the Young Professionals Business Resource Group), provides "Social Media Reverse Mentoring – younger to older generation" a one-on-one training program, which has been a great success. This demonstrates how much Mastercard cares about the older generation as much as the digital native younger generation and goes the extra mile to bridge the digital divide within the corporation [21].

Novartis International AG, a Swiss-based multinational pharmaceutical company, is committed to promoting diversity, not only in the workplace but also among its diverse patient population who are physically challenged. To serve its patients well and to understand their unique needs to serve them better, it is promoting innovative inclusive methods. They use the term "diverseability" instead of disability to recognize diverse skills and proficiencies of such people. Their hiring methods include training their staff on concepts such as unconscious bias, inclusive leadership, compensation/pay equity, etc. [21].

There are numerous other corporations making significant progress in social inclusion and the list is growing. The simple truth is there is significant value to be harnessed through these programs. The McKinsey study on diversity, encompassing 15 countries and more than 1,000 large companies, corroborates this observation [22].

13.2 Evolving market orientation toward sustainability – Gen Z

There has been a growing influence of Gen Z (those born on and after 1997 approximately) shoppers on corporations to embrace sustainable products and services more than other generational shoppers. First Insight, a leading shopper experience management platform, confirms the observation through its study that reveals that Gen Z shoppers prefer to buy sustainable brands even if the products and services are a little expensive as their purchasing decisions are driven by their personal, social, and environmental values. Gen Z love healthy environments, want to stay fit, are technology natives, value experience, and are concerned about the effects of pollution and other social issues [23, 24, 25, 26, 27, 28]. They are expressive, quick, and use digital tools to communicate, advocate, and collaborate in their ecosystem to promote and influence sustainable practices at the businesses and governments they interact with. Their connectedness through digital media and fearless ability to speak up to advance their beliefs arms them with an immense capacity never heard of. The sheer size of Gen Z, more than 60 million in the US alone as of 2018 [29], and over 50.5% of the world's population of 7 billion, is remarkable. It is also interesting to see the asymmetry of people under 30 on a global map – 89.7% of people live in emerging and developing economies, and more than 754 million live in Asia alone [30], where generally environmental concerns are getting headline notoriety.

Interestingly, Gen Z has the power of influence over other generations, both at the family level and at the community level – Gen Y (those born 1982–2002), Gen X (those born 1961–1981), and Baby Boomers (those born 1943–1960), given their native digital skills with their predisposed traits of being optimistic and socially responsible [31]. Innovations on the technology front such as Facebook, Instagram, Twitter, Snapchat, YouTube, WhatsApp, Messenger, WeChat, TikTok, etc. and Gen Z have a symbiotic relationship, as they feed off each other for their sphere of influence and growth.

Marketers recognize the unique role played by Gen Z as well as their values and expectations and try to leverage digital tools and sustainable products and services that offer attractive value propositions to such customers. The trend is getting more attention and importance across the globe, and businesses are incorporating sustainability in their business strategy.

13.3 Sustainability – A new secular growth driver

Designing a business strategy that anchors sustainability at its core is no longer an option but a necessity, and businesses are recognizing them as secular growth drivers. They offer much-needed complementary support to traditional cyclical drivers that many businesses depend on. Businesses are increasingly integrating sustainability considerations with their mainstream product and service offerings, and examples are plenty. Recyclable packaging to use of renewable energy sources to carbon footprint reduction in designing last-mile delivery logistics are just a few. However, business cases for such sustainable portfolio developments require a different approach. Prof. Dr. Stefan Schaltegger at the Centre for Sustainability Management, Leuphana Universität Lüneburg, Scharnhorststr suggests that pivoting to a more structured approach instead of relying on a checklist for sustainability business cases is imperative. Sustainability offers both opportunities and challenges and thus requires a balanced yet a careful approach that captures both market and non-market factors for business success.

Market factors are the ones that are directly determined by market forces based on efficiency of the competition, customer preferences alignment, government compliance, etc. For example, managing efficiently the end-to-end value chain cost structure can provide competitive advantage in a marketplace. As for the customer preferences alignment, producing products that bode well with customer expectations is important as they directly impact revenue and income goals as seen in consumers in Western Europe boycotting genetically modified food products [32]. In terms of government compliance, for example, the European Union is setting up a legal framework that provides a directive for product and service design for businesses to improve the environmental performance of products, such as refrigerators, washing machines, and microwave ovens [33]. This compliance may require additional resources and product features that may be expensive, and failure to comply will erode the market share. But, if done carefully and creatively, it will certainly benefit the business performance.

Non-market factors are the ones that typically emerge due to social and environmental activism by consumers and may indirectly influence the performance of businesses. Consumer backlash due to unacceptable business practices, often perceived unethical or inconsistent with consumer values, triggers boycotting of certain products and services from the businesses that could negatively impact the business performance. For example, alleged child labor and sweat shop practices at some of the contractors that worked for Nike caught many non-governmental organizations' attention and global media widely covered these exploitations, demanding immediate correction [32].

Social concerns and pushback from consumers and other agencies have far-reaching consequences on business performance, which has the potential to erode the brand image as well. If the businesses are sensitive to the prevailing value system of their consumers and commit to their own beliefs and purpose they stand for, the reward

178 *Special topics on innovation*

and loyalty they could expect from their customers will be profound. Starbucks, for example, soon after a racial bias experienced by two of its customers at its shop in Philadelphia [34], voluntarily closed more than 8,000 stores for a day to run racial bias training for their barristers on May 29, 2018 [35], which was further internalized as part of its ongoing training programs. The stature of Starbucks has only gone up and its performance got better as the company is known to be flag-bearer of social values. Business practices that are inconsistent with the expectations of the society are unsustainable.

Businesses that are proactive and internalize social values such as the demand for sustainability, and approach them comprehensively with a culture that fosters such priorities, are set to reap the benefits. Sustainability-related growth drivers will continue to trend higher, and businesses should not be blindsided. Market and non-market factors are critical for business strategy development, although there could be some overlaps, and that is the beauty of the world we live in.

13.4 Success stories – Sustainability-focused innovation

13.4.1 The Procter & Gamble Company (P&G)

P&G is a branded consumer-packaged goods company with a presence in more than 180 countries that generates more than $74B in annual revenue as of 2021. The major business segments where it operates include beauty, grooming, health care, fabric and home care, and baby, feminine and family care. Some of the well-known brands include Head & Shoulders, Olay, Old Spice, Pantene, Rejoice, Venus, Cascade, Mach3, Prestobarba, Dawn, Febreze, Mr. Clean, Bounty, and Charmin [36]. The most recent example for sustainability innovation at P&G Oral Care is the shift that happened in Jan 2021 from conventional non-recyclable packaging to recyclable packaging in its toothpaste brands, Crest, Oral-B, and Blend-a-med. This shift increases the level of recyclability of its toothpaste tubes, as part of the P&G Ambition 2030 commitments of achieving 100% recyclable or reusable packaging. Toothpaste tubes are used by billions of consumers every day; however, its multi-material construction poses a challenge for recycling facilities around the globe. The solution to this is the HDPE (High-Density Polyethylene) tube, which provides the same product protection as current tubes and has been certified by North American and European recycling bodies to be compatible with existing recycling technologies. These HDPE tubes can be recycled where collection programs exist [37]. Viridor, a UK recycling and energy recovery company, will supply P&G with HDPE materials, which is expected to save the equivalent of 200 million bottles of plastic over the next five years [38]. This is a big deal given how sensitive the plastic container topics are both in Europe and the US. P&G is recommitting itself to be socially sensitive and adapt its business strategy to align with consumer sentiments, and it will be a great win both for P&G and its customers.

13.4.2 Patagonia

Patagonia, Inc. is a US-based clothing company founded in 1973 and inspired by a band of climbers and surfers and the minimalist style they promoted in their lives and their sports [39]. It has physical store footprint in more than ten countries [40,

Sustainability-focused innovation 179

41] with a manufacturing supply chain connecting more than 16 countries [42]. It is known for its products such as fleece jackets, sleeping bags, and backpacks. Their website boasts their recognition that everything they make has an impact on the planet and hence they want to be responsible as they navigate their business.

As a business, they are accomplishing their sustainability goals through innovation programs such as materials and environmental and social programs. For example, 64% of their fabrics used in clothing and other apparels during the 2021 season were made with recycled materials. Although synthetic materials such as polyesters and nylon are widely used in the industry, Patagonia prioritizes organic cotton, recycled cotton, recycled polyester, recycled nylon, natural rubber, etc. where possible. They claim that 100% of their virgin down (down is a byproduct in the food industry) is certified to the advanced global traceable down standard. This ensures down in their clothing and apparel products comes from a responsible source that respects animal welfare and the supply chain can be fully traced [43].

Patagonia's Supply Chain Environmental Responsibility Program is another flagship initiative that is geared toward reducing environmental impacts of manufacturing Patagonia products and materials, including at their supplier sites. They have identified a range of impacted areas, including chemicals, water use, water emissions, energy use, greenhouse gases, and waste. The program leverages tools, such as the Higg Index, and certification programs, such as the bluesign® system. This allows suppliers to demonstrate their environmental compliance [39].

The company is known for its commitment to protecting the earth and its visible support for campaigns against ecosystem-destroying dams, oil drilling, pipelines, deforestation, and governments that deny climate change [44]. Patagonia supports public activism for social causes and provides a sizable portion of its income directly to such activism groups who are in the trenches of the issues, raise awareness across the stakeholders, and fight for policy change both at the corporate and governmental levels. This extended ecosystem model to advance its own core values, leveraging external advocates, has been well received by its customers and Patagonia is able to thrive on their customer loyalty for its products and services.

By championing innovative sustainability programs that care about the environment and social responsibility, and demonstrating visible engagement with stakeholders, Patagonia is able to lead the industry with a positive impact that is significantly benefiting its overall business performance in addition to strengthening its global image. It is known to promote anti-consumerism, fair trade, and environmental causes even by advertising with a one-page advertisement in the *New York Times* on the busiest Black Friday – "Don't Buy This Jacket." It did so because it wanted to be honest with its customers and raise their sustainability awareness by letting them know what it takes to produce one jacket – many times its weight of greenhouse gases, considerable material scrap, and large amounts of scarce fresh water. The company is still growing with an annual revenue of more than a billion dollars as of 2018 [45, 46].

13.4.3 Braskem (Brazil)

Brazilian petrochemical giant Braskem was formed through the merger of six companies from Odebrecht Group and the Mariani Group in 2002. Their portfolio is very extensive and rich with products such as polyethylene, polypropylene, and polyvinylchloride (PVC) resins as well as chemical raw materials such as ethylene,

180 *Special topics on innovation*

propylene, butadiene, benzene, toluene, chlorine, soda, and solvents. They are vertically integrated with extracting raw materials such as naphtha, condensate, natural gas, and ethanol, producing first-generation petrochemicals that are further used in second-generation resin products. The resins are used by many other corporations for third-generation consumer and industrial plastic products such as bottles, containers, etc. They have global manufacturing operations in Brazil, Germany, Mexico, and the US, with a customer base in 70 countries. On an annual basis, they produce 16 million metric tons of thermoplastic resins and other chemical compounds [47].

Braskem prides itself as a sustainable solutions corporation that leverages technology and continuous innovation. Their view of sustainable development is to conduct their business that meets the needs of all stakeholders, current and future. Their product development approach is guided by the UN Sustainable Development 17 Goals for 2030 (Table 13.1), the Paris Agreement on Climate Change, Materiality Matrix, and continuous risk management analysis of their business. Their three pillars of sustainable business strategy are: 1. Sustainable processes and resources; 2. Sustainable product portfolio; and 3. Sustainable integrated solutions [47].

Table 13.1 United Nations sustainable development – 17 goals

1. No Poverty – End poverty everywhere, in all its forms.
2. Zero Hunger – End hunger, achieve food security and improved nutrition, and promote sustainable agriculture.
3. Good Health and Well-being – Ensure healthy lives and promote well-being for all at all ages.
4. Quality Education – Ensure inclusive and equitable quality education and promote learning opportunities for all.
5. Gender Equality – Achieve gender equality and empower all women and girls.
6. Clean Water and Sanitation – Ensure availability and sustainable management of water and sanitation for all.
7. Affordable and Clean Energy – Ensure access to affordable, reliable, sustainable, and modern energy for all.
8. Decent Work and Economic Growth – Promote sustained, inclusive, and sustainable economic growth, full and productive employment, and decent work for all.
9. Industry, Innovation, and Infrastructure – Build resilient infrastructure, promote inclusive and sustainable industrialization, and foster innovation.
10. Reduced Inequalities – Reduce inequality within and among countries.
11. Sustainable Cities and Communities – Make cities and human settlements inclusive, safe, resilient, and sustainable.
12. Responsible Consumption and Production – Ensure sustainable consumption and production patterns.
13. Climate Action – Take urgent action to combat climate change and its impacts.
14. Life Below Water – Conserve and sustainably use the oceans, seas, and marine resources for sustainable development.
15. Life on Land – Protect, restore, and promote sustainable use of terrestrial ecosystems, sustainably manage forests, combat desertification, halt and reserve land degradation, and halt biodiversity loss.
16. Peace, Justice, and Strong Institutions – Promote peaceful and inclusive societies for sustainable development, provide access to justice for all, and build effective, accountable, and inclusive institutions at all levels.
17. Partnerships for the Goals – Strengthen the means of implementation and revitalize the global partnership for sustainable development.

https://sdgs.un.org/goals

Among many sustainability programs, the most ambitious one is their commitment to be the global petrochemical leaders in greenhouse gas emissions through carbon capture by leveraging production of materials with renewable, bio-based raw materials. Their vision is to by 2030 reduce scope 1 and 2 greenhouse gas emissions by 15% and to achieve carbon neutrality by 2050, which is a tall order. The global greenhouse gas protocol corporate standard classifies a company's greenhouse gas emissions into three "scopes."

Scope 1 emissions are direct emissions from owned or controlled sources, which have four use cases:

- Stationary combustion of fossil fuels (e.g., natural gas, fuel oil, propane, etc.) for comfort heating or other industrial applications
- Mobile combustion in all vehicles owned or controlled by a firm burning fuel (e.g., car, vans, trucks)
- Fugitive emissions or leaks from greenhouse gases (e.g., refrigeration, air conditioning units)
- Process emissions released during industrial processes and on-site manufacturing (e.g., production of CO_2 during cement manufacturing, factory fumes, chemicals)

Scope 2 emissions are indirect emissions from the generation of purchased energy.

Scope 3 emissions are all indirect emissions (not included in scope 2) that occur in the value chain of the reporting company, including both upstream and downstream emissions [48, 49].

Braskem has accomplished several milestones to promote sustainability and some of them are listed below.

In 2007, Braskem launched the first polyethylene made with 100% renewable resources and the first ethylene made with sugar cane. In 2010, it launched the green ethylene plant. It also deployed the Aquapolo and Aqua Viva projects, one of the largest water treatment and reuse systems in Brazil. In 2012, it launched the Ser+ (to be+) program for waste collectors to collect and recycle waste. It is included in the Dow Jones Sustainability portfolio in 2013 and received recognition from Fast company in 2014 for its excellence in bio-based products.

Continuing its quest to be the leader in advancing sustainability priorities, it launched "I am green" recycled resins in 2015, which was simply unthinkable with conventional practices. This feat was made possible by its relentless research effort and application of innovative technologies. To raise consumer awareness on the post-consumption of plastics, in 2017 it initiated the Plastianguis program that has been very successful since. In 2019, Braskem collaborated with Denmark-based Haldor Topsoe and demonstrated the development of monoethylene glycol (MEG) from sugar. This was a significant renewable plastic innovation that allowed just sugar as a raw material instead of traditional fossil fuels, paving the way for renewable MEG on an industrial scale [50]. In 2020, Braskem continued its sustainability pursuit in a much bigger way by expanding its green and recycled products.

Here is a corporation that demonstrates how it can sustain its growth by tightly integrating sustainability goals in its business strategy to produce innovative products that have less negative effect on the environment. Braskem is global and is able to adapt and adjust its business practices to meet global and regional sustainability compliance standards and the expectations of the global governance bodies such as the

182 *Special topics on innovation*

United Nations and international accords such as the Paris Agreement on Climate Change.

13.4.4 Colorifix (UK)

Colorifix is a UK-based private corporation that develops organic dyeing technology to make bio-degradable fabrics. It was founded by three ecologically focused individuals who were involved in developing biological sensors to monitor heavy metal contamination in drinking water in rural Nepal. They soon recognized the source of such contamination, which was essentially the textile dyeing waste. Nepal was supplying textiles to other countries and became the producers of such toxic pollutants. This problem motivated the founders to not only identify the source of the problem, but also to develop a solution to fix the problem that could help the textile industry to use an environmentally friendly dyeing process and flourish.

Interestingly, they adapted the same monitoring approach of using microorganisms that change color with different pollutant levels to develop colors for textiles. This natural method is environmentally friendly, does not use toxic chemicals, and reduces carbon footprint. Their technology uses sugar molasses and converts them into pigments of different colors as dyes for textiles. Manufacturers and designers such a H&M use these natural colors to produce textiles to meet global demand [51].

Colorifix's experimentation with producing organic dyes starts in their laboratories to find a color that is created by a living thing, a microorganism that can be seen in an animal, plant, or other microbes. They use DNA sequencing to understand what makes a pigment or color, then engineer synthetic microorganisms, which are used to grow and transfer the color. In essence, it is a field called synthetic biology. Their fermentation partners use such color-specific synthetic microorganisms to grow the color, like beer, using by-products of the sugar production industry. The microorganisms are fueled by sugar as well as naturally available nitrogen to develop colors at scale. The grown microorganisms are subsequently shipped to textile or fabric manufacturers where the color organisms directly replace traditional toxic chemicals. The process requires no special equipment to apply the colors onto fabrics unlike the chemically based dyeing process that requires heavy metals or organic solvents.

The Colorifix approach consumes one-tenth of the natural water that the textile manufacturers would otherwise consume. Interestingly, they can apply the color at 37 degrees Celsius on many of the fabrics, requiring no additional heating, saving a lot of energy costs [52]. The process is akin to ancestral methods of using natural pigments that has been practiced for thousands of years. Unfortunately, in the modern era with mass textile production, for fear of color inconsistency through organic methods with potential supply chain delays, the textile industry abandoned perfecting the organic method of dyeing textiles and adapted easier methods that used toxic chemicals with no regard to the environmental damage.

Colorifix partners with the Fashion for Good accelerator to leverage their technical expertise as well. Also, Colorifix is hugely benefited by their investment partners SAGANA, Cambridge Enterprise, Primera Impact, and H&M CO: LAB. The company recently won the Andam Innovation Prize award as well [52].

H&M, a multinational clothing retail company known for its fast-fashion clothing, operates in 74 countries with over 5,000 stores and is taking the lead in pivoting to the natural dyeing process for its textiles. It has a mission toward a circular fashion future that amplifies its sustainability goals. Its recent Innovation Stories collection, Color Story, celebrates more sustainable methods of working with color. It collaborates with innovators and has created a selection of contemporary clothing designs with natural colors that bring awareness to the dyeing and printing process environmental impacts. More recently it worked with Colorifix as well to use its sustainable coloring technology [53].

"Working with such interesting innovators and their wonderful ideas has been an incredible journey. Colorifix, for example, is the first company to use a natural, biological process to produce and fix pigments onto textiles. They are launching worldwide with this collection. We're thrilled that despite its state-of-the-art manufacture, the collection feels effortlessly modern and fresh." – Ella Soccorsi, Concept Designer at H&M [53]

Colorifix internalized sustainability in its strategy and developed its product offerings, leveraging biotechnology. They provide alternative natural dyeing choices to the global textile industry, which is estimated to be \$1,000.3B in 2020 with a CAGR of 4.4% from 2021 to 2028 [54]. The sustainability impact will be very significant if the textile industry warms up to the natural dyeing process. As the consumer awareness and sentiment is growing on the sustainability front, the textile industry is put on notice. Using the lead of H&M, we hope that other companies will soon follow suit.

13.5 Concluding remarks

Sustainability, finally, is getting the recognition it deserves. Society and businesses are placing exponential demand on limited natural resources and the environment is becoming polluted more than ever. Social values are changing toward diversity and inclusiveness at the workplace. It is no surprise that the businesses are beginning to respond to these developments to sustain their own existence. As society becomes connected by the fourth industrial revolution technologies, technology-savvy Gen Z takes the lead in advocating sustainability values. Business dependency on technology innovations is more pronounced in the past decade and they are forced to adapt to the changed realities. If they do not embrace sustainability values, customers will shun them. VW is a most recent example, which was imposed billions of dollars' fine for violating environmental laws in the US after a series of public protest [55].

Leading industry studies, including from McKinsey and Gartner [11, 22, 56], reveal the value propositions of enabling the sustainability cause; nonetheless, there is a cost associated with such initiatives. Businesses that are introvert and short-term focused will not endure advancing sustainability challenges as the effort requires longer-term commitment and external focus. Internalization of sustainability measures is the key for success and often comes with significant change management challenges. Through proper planning and disciplined execution, businesses can make strides on the sustainability front. Many governments are incentivizing sustainability pursuits, and a good example is the tax credit extended to automotive companies to switch from fossil-fuel-based to electric vehicles.

184　*Special topics on innovation*

> **Student activities**
>
> 1. Select the Patagonia, Timberland, and Ecovative Design company cases from Part VIII.
> 2. Review the details and understand their business models and motivations to be a sustainable business.
> 3. Discuss their sustainability approach to innovate and develop solutions.
> 4. Apply the TRIAL© framework based on your analysis and identify gaps. Review online resources including their corporate websites to gather additional supporting data.
> 5. Also answer the questions listed at the end of the cases.

13.6 References

1. https://dictionary.cambridge.org/us/dictionary/english/sustainability
2. https://mahb.stanford.edu/blog/what-does-sustainability-really-mean/
3. https://online.hbs.edu/blog/post/what-is-sustainability-in-business
4. www.epa.gov/report-environment/sustainability-and-roe
5. https://nielseniq.com/global/en/insights/analysis/2018/global-consumers-seek-companies-that-care-about-environmental-issues/
6. www.niehs.nih.gov/health/assets/docs_a_e/environmental_diseases_environmental_diseases_from_a_to_z_english_508.pdf
7. www.change.org/p/cisco-systems-boycott-of-businesses-that-lack-black-corporate-diversity
8. https://chainstoreage.com/four-10-consumers-currently-boycotting-company
9. www.businessbecause.com/news/insights/7504/millennial-gen-z-diversity-and-inclusion
10. www.mckinsey.com/business-functions/sustainability/our-insights/sustainabilitys-deepening-imprint
11. www.mckinsey.com/~/media/mckinsey/dotcom/client_service/sustainability/pdfs/mck%20on%20srp/srp_11_biz%20sustainability.ashx
12. www.npr.org/sections/goatsandsoda/2016/12/07/504681046/study-child-laborers-in-bangladesh-are-working-64-hours-a-week
13. www.reuters.com/article/us-usa-trade-china-xinjiang-trfn/u-s-retailers-told-to-target-forced-labor-in-china-after-cotton-import-crackdown-idUSKBN29L00X
14. www.nytimes.com/2021/01/13/business/economy/xinjiang-cotton-tomato-ban.html
15. https://climatekids.nasa.gov/greenhouse-cards/
16. IPCC, "Summary for Policymakers," in "Climate Change 2007: The Physical Science Basis. Contribution of Working Group I to the Fourth Assessment Report of the Intergovernmental Panel on Climate Change," Solomon, S. D., Qin, D., Manning, M., Chen, Z., Marquis, M., Averyt, K.B., Tignor, M., and Miller, H.L., (eds.), Cambridge University Press, Cambridge, UK, and New York, NY, USA, 2007.
17. www.epa.gov/ghgemissions/sources-greenhouse-gas-emissions#t1fn1
18. www.c2es.org/content/what-we-can-do/#:~:text=Greenhouse%20gas%20emissions%20can%20be,renewable%20hydrogen%2C%20and%20geothermal%20energy.
19. www.usgbc.org/help/what-leed
20. www.forbes.com/sites/blakemorgan/2019/08/26/101-companies-committed-to-reducing-their-carbon-footprint/?sh=9b44294260ba
21. www.socialtalent.com/blog/diversity-and-inclusion/9-companies-around-the-world-that-are-embracing-diversity

Sustainability-focused innovation 185

22. www.mckinsey.com/featured-insights/diversity-and-inclusion/diversity-wins-how-inclusion-matters
23. Kimberly Lanier, 2017, "5 Things HR Professionals Need to Know About Generation Z," Strategic HR Review, 16(6), pp. 288–290.
24. Varsha Jain, Reshma, Vatsa, and Khyati Jagani, 2014, "Exploring Generation Z's Purchase Behavior Towards Luxury Apparel: A Conceptual Framework," Romanian Journal of Marketing, 2, pp.18–29.
25. Sidian Lan, 2014, "An Importance-Performance Analysis of Multigenerational Preferences in Guestroom Technology," UNLV Theses, Dissertations, Professional Paper, available at https://digitalscholarship.unlv.edu/cgi/viewcontent.cgi?article=3621&context=thesesdissertations, referred on 14/12/2018.
26. D.C. Dabija, B.M. Bejan, and C. Bălgărădean, 2017, "Practici de sustenabilitate în retailul modern," Working paper, [Sustainability practices in modern retail, in Romanian].
27. Elena-Mâdâlina Vătămănescu, Bogdan G. Nistoreanu, and Andreea Mitan, 2017, "Competition and Consumer Behavior in the Context of the Digital Economy," Amfiteatru Economic, 19(45), pp. 354–366.
28. D.C. Dabija, B.M. Bejan, and V. Dinu, (2019), "How Sustainability Oriented is Generation Z in Retail? A Literature Review", *Tran* l. 18, No 2 (47), pp.140–155.
29. K. Claveria, , 2008, "Generation Z Statistics: New Report on the Values, Attitudes and Behaviors of the Post-Millennials, Retrieved October 10, available at www.visioncritical.com/generation-z-statistics, referred on 05/05/2018.
30. www.unesco.org/new/en/unesco/events/prizes-and celebrations/celebrations/international-days/world-radio-day-2013/statistics-on-youth/
31. Denisia Dunmore, 2013, "Has Technology Become a Need? A Qualitative Study Exploring Three Generational Cohorts' Perception of Technology in Regards to Maslow's Hierarchy of Needs," (Ph.D., Capella University), retrieved from ProQuest Dissertations and Theses.
32. Stefan Schaltegger, "Sustainability as a Driver for Corporate Economic Success: Consequences for the Development of Sustainability Management Control," Centre for Sustainability Management (CSM), 03/20, ISBN - 978–3-935630-89. Can also be accessed at http://fox.leuphana.de/portal/de/publications/sustainability-as-a-driver-for-corporate-economic-success(33d43fba-9aef-4c82-9a71-385eca065ecd).html
33. https://ec.europa.eu/growth/industry/sustainability/product-policy-and-ecodesign_en
34. www.inquirer.com/philly/news/starbucks-philadelphia-arrests-black-men-video-viral-protests-background-20180416.html
35. Dominic Rusche, 2018 (April 17), "Starbucks to Close 8,000 US Stores for Racial-Bias Training," The Guardian, retrieved from www.theguardian.com/business/2018/apr/17/starbucks-racism-training-close-stores-may-us
36. https://us.pg.com/
37. https://consumergoods.com/procter-gamble-oral-care-starts-shift-more-recyclable-packaging
38. https://packagingeurope.com/p-g-and-viridor-agree-five-year-hdpe-deal/
39. www.patagonia.com
40. Will Yakowicz, (March 16, 2020), "At Billionaire-Owned Patagonia Outdoor Clothing Chain, Employees to Be Paid Despite Store Closures Amid Coronavirus," Forbes, retrieved May 17, 2021.
41. Lauren Thomas, (March 13, 2020), "Patagonia is Closing All of its Stores and Shutting Down its Website Because of the Coronavirus," CNBC, retrieved May 10, 2021.
42. "Patagonia: What to Know About the Outdoor Brand," Highsnobiety, retrieved May 10, 2021.
43. https://d2evkimvhatqav.cloudfront.net/documents/su_traceble_down_q_a.pdf
44. https://thecorrespondent.com/424/the-more-patagonia-rejects-consumerism-the-more-the-brand-sells/56126501376-a30f2daa

186 *Special topics on innovation*

45. www.referralcandy.com/blog/patagonia-marketing-strategy/
46. www.patagonia.com/stories/dont-buy-this-jacket-black-friday-and-the-new-york-times/story-18615.html
47. www.braskem.com.br/sustainabledevelopmentstrategy
48. https://ghgprotocol.org/sites/default/files/standards_supporting/FAQ.pdf
49. https://plana.earth/academy/what-are-scope-1-2-3-emissions/
50. www.biofuelsdigest.com/bdigest/2019/02/10/mega-meg-braskem-and-haldor-topsoes-monoethylene-glycol-from-sugar-hits-the-scene/
51. https://pitchbook.com/profiles/company/229191-40#overview
52. https://colorifix.com/colorifix-solutions/
53. https://about.hm.com/news/general-news-2021/h-m-s-colour-story-collection-puts-a-contemporary--sustainable-s.html
54. www.grandviewresearch.com/industry-analysis/textile-market
55. www.reuters.com/article/us-volkswagen-usa/vw-faces-billions-in-fines-as-u-s-sues-for-environmental-violations-idUSKBN0UI1QP20160105
56. www.gartner.com/en/newsroom/press-releases/2021-04-27-gartner-says-cfos-must-embed-corporate-sustainability-in-their-firms-investment-proposition

Part VIII

Case studies*

Case 1: Amgen – Biosimilar Innovations – by Kavya Sivan	189
Case 2: FedEx – Innovation Through Sustained Adaptability – by Alaina Gregory	195
Case 3: Reliance Jio – From 4G to Digital Innovation – by Hursh Motwani	204
Case 4: Stryker Case Study – Design Thinking Response to COVID-19 – by Kyle Geiger	214
Case 5: The Whirlpool Corporation in 2020: Whirlpool – A History of Sustained Innovation from Within – by Malik Abbasi	225
Case 6: Apple's Swift – A Programming Language Innovation for the Future – by Maxwell Cornellier	232
Case 7: Microsoft – The Age of Nadella – by Serena Wang and Minnie Sun	240
Case 8: The Procter & Gamble Company – A Unique Innovation Approach – by Minnie Sun and Serena Wang	247
Case 9: Timberland – Sustainable Innovation – by Drew Arnson	253
Case 10: Zara-Inditex – Fast Fashion Done Right – by Rocco Pelà	260
Case 11: Patagonia – Leader of a Sustainable Business – by Suzanna Yik	267
Case 12: Amazon – Head in the Cloud: Transformation Through Leadership's Lens – by William McCrone	275
Case 13: Ericsson's Innovation Through M&A – by Derek Kuo	282
Case 14: Samsung's New Age Innovation Using Organization and Culture – by Derek Kuo	288
Case 15: Sun Pharmaceutical Industries – Innovation Through Specialty Acquisition Strategy, Technology, Leadership, and Culture – by Katie Kuhlman	294
Case 16: Ecovative Design – Organizing for Innovation in Sustainable Biomaterials – by Daniel Meeks	305

*All the cases were written under the book author's supervision.

Case 1: Amgen – Biosimilar Innovations

Kavya Sivan

Stephen M. Ross School of Business, University of Michigan
ksivan@umich.edu

Introduction

Amgen is one of the world's leading biotechnology companies headquartered just outside Los Angeles in Thousand Oaks, California. In the early 1980s, Amgen started with a small group of creative individuals who were passionate about creating cancer-related drugs. Today, Amgen is a global pharmaceutical powerhouse with 2020 revenues of over $25B with over 20 approved drugs [1, 2].

In 1983, a team led by some young Amgen researchers was tasked with finding and cloning the erythropoietin gene, which is known to promote red blood cell production. The task seemed nearly impossible – finding a gene on a single portion of DNA, which laid aside 1.5 million fragments of the human genome. However, after diligently working for two years, they were able to map it! The groundbreaking research allowed them to discover, develop, and market one of the most successful drugs in biotech history – Epogen. A few years later, a second groundbreaking finding led them to produce Neupogen, a drug that helps the body make white blood cells after cancer treatment [3].

Epogen and Neupogen became highly successful, with Epogen even being named the "#1 Product of the Year" by *Fortune Magazine* in 1989 [4]. Soon after, Amgen created an array of new drugs and went international. They also established a European headquarters in Switzerland. The company became one of the largest biotech companies in the world and is still viewed as the leader in oncology. By the early 2000s, this small biotech company had blossomed into a $15B annual revenue firm employing 14,000 people around the globe [5]! Their growth and success attracted multiple entrants and with that came competition. By 2009, the growth of both Epogen and Neupogen had slowed considerably. With patents for both drugs set to expire in 2013, researchers at Amgen were on edge to investigate new streams of revenue growth.

Exhibit 1.1 shows Amgen's revenue for their two most popular drugs as well as their total revenue. The years leading up to 2009 show declining growth. While total revenue grows, the amount of revenue the two drugs contribute declines or remains stagnant.

Challenge: Introduction of biosimilars

As Exhibit 1.1 shows, the years leading up to 2009 came with stagnant or negative growth. Amgen was facing declining revenues due to the patent expiry for both of their leading drugs. A few key competitors had also started working on replica

DOI: 10.4324/9781003190837-22

190   *Case studies*

Year	2001	2002	2003	2004	2005	2006	2007	2008	2009
Epogen Revenue	2,109	2,261	2,435	2,601	2,455	2,511	2,489	2,456	2,569
% Change	-	7.2%	7.7%	6.8%	-5.6%	2.3%	-0.9%	-1.3%	4.6%

Year	2001	2002	2003	2004	2005	2006	2007	2008	2009
Neupogen Revenue	1,346	1,844	2,522	2,915	3,504	3,923	4,227	4,659	4,643
% Change	-	36.9%	36.7	15.6%	20.2%	12.0%	7.8%	10.2%	-0.3%

Year	2001	2002	2003	2004	2005	2006	2007	2008	2009
Total Company Revenue	4,016	5,523	8,356	10,550	12,430	14,268	14,771	15,003	14,642
% Change	-	37.5%	51.3%	26.3%	17.8%	14.8%	3.5%	1.6%	-2.4%

Exhibit 1.1 Annual growth trend (in millions) [6]
Source: Amgen Investors Website.

versions (known as biosimilars) of Amgen's blockbuster drugs. Biosimilars are essentially drugs that are very similar to another already approved biological medicine [7, 8, 9, 10, 11]. Biosimilars are replacement/replica drugs to existing FDA-approved drugs and usually appear after a patent expiry.

In addition to the patent expiry threat, Amgen also faced a push from the patterns of the nation at large. In the US, the implementation of the Affordable Care Act in 2010 included a new and shortened development/approval procedure to encourage biosimilars [12]. The Act led to an increasing push by healthcare providers to drive down drug costs through biosimilars [13, 14, 15]. It also meant a larger push for biosimilars [16, 17]. As a leader in the biotech field, Amgen was facing a lot of media attention. With Europe providing approval for biosimilars a few years before the US, research and investments were already underway [18, 11].

Rather than being threatened by the development of competing biosimilars, Amgen viewed it as a business opportunity. They knew they had the resources and facilities to be a leader in the biosimilar drug field. Amgen knew they needed to explore alternative avenues and find a new source of revenue for the company. They saw this as an opportunity to innovate and become a pioneer in the field of biosimilars.

However, certain executives and employees within Amgen disagreed with the idea to enter the biosimilars market. They felt that Amgen should continue to focus on pioneering new drugs rather than use its resources toward developing biosimilars. The FDA approval process for biosimilars was long and arduous and came with lawsuits and litigation battles with competing drugs [9, 10]. Many were concerned that the company may not have the resources to fully engage in the development of new drugs as well as biosimilars. On the other hand, some believed that biosimilars were a strong way for Amgen to take an aggressive approach and become one of the pioneers in the field, thereby giving them strong diversification.

The disagreement between the two parties caused tension within the organization. Would entering the biosimilars market slow the pursuit of new drugs? Or would entering the biosimilars market allow for increased diversification revenue and recognition for the company?

Solution: Commitment to R&D

Amgen explored the avenue of biosimilars through a structured approach, which included three prongs: Culture, priority coordination, and internal strategy analysis.

Culture

Amgen looked to the first value on their mission statement: "**Compete** Intensely and Win." They believed that winning required taking risks and wanted to choose an avenue that put them at an edge over their competitors. Amgen knew that few key competitors were exploring entering the field of biosimilars. Some players in the arena such as Merck and AstraZeneca also started experimenting with biosimilars in their pipeline. These replica drugs were also a hot new area in Asia where some Korean and Singaporean "big-Pharma" companies were collaborating to invest and start a biosimilar portfolio.

Amgen also wanted to make sure that their final decision would be **creating value** for their patients. Amgen knew that biosimilars would expand patient access to critical drugs and provide expanded options in the healthcare system.

However, Amgen also valued the diverse opinions of their employees and understood that some employees had reservations. Amgen acted true to their first **core value** of "science-based thought." They wanted their decision to be based on quantitative thought and looked to apply scientific methods in all parts of their organization. They stayed true to their mission statement, which emphasized the importance of "collecting and analyzing data for rational decision making." This led them to perform a numerical and timeline analysis.

Priority coordination

After assessing their values, Amgen solved the biosimilar dilemma with a clear strategic thinking model. The company wanted to use research to see if they could find objective and quantitative-based evidence to enter the biosimilars field to bolster their value-based arguments. The company mapped the various cost requirements for developing a new drug versus a biosimilar and considered elements such as clinical trials, process development, capital requirements, etc. Amgen also performed extensive quantitative analysis on which avenue to develop biosimilars in, by using factors such as number of competing products, volume penetration, and price level. They also used modeling to estimate likely revenue/profitability and used sensitivity models to assess potential risks.

Internal strategy

As a company that valued quantitative planning, Amgen made a series of long- and short-term plans to take on the new venture. They created a plan to enter the US

192   *Case studies*

market by releasing five drugs by 2019 and estimated that this would be a $3B revenue opportunity [19]. This strategy was important for the success of the drugs because of the tight timeline and strict procedures of the biosimilar adoption process. They planned the five biosimilar drugs they wanted to release and crafted specific timelines and release dates. Amgen found that biosimilars would take around eight years to develop and cost between $100M and $200M compared to an estimate of $2.6B for developing a new drug [20].

Through their three-pronged structured approach, Amgen concluded that entering the biosimilars arena would be a smart decision for the business. They had numerical evidence to show the large growth potential of biosimilars. They began working on discovering, developing, and marketing these new drugs [21].

Financial outcome

Around 2018, Amgen started reaping the financial benefits of their decision. Just as the company hoped, biosimilars became a huge success story for Amgen. Mvasi (colorectal cancer biosimilar) and Kanjinti (breast cancer biosimilar) became two of Amgen's most successful biosimilar drugs [22]. Both drugs combined generated $234M million in sales during their first quarter of 2019. Mvasi had $115M in total sales (up 27% from 2019 Q4) and Kanjinti had $119M in total sales (up 16%) [23, 24]. Growth of these biosimilars was impressive and the US market shares for Mvasi and Kanjinti were 33% and 27%, respectively. In terms of their overall growth, biosimilars generated $173M in the third quarter of 2019, up from $82M in the second quarter of 2019 [23]. Amgen is now able to establish a very strong foothold in the biosimilar market and has found that biosimilars were also much more cost-effective to develop [25].

As of January 2020, there were only 12 approved and marketed biosimilar drugs in the US. Of these 12, Amgen was responsible for two of the most popular drugs [26]. The biosimilar approval process is complicated and arduous; however, Amgen was able to roll out two very successful drugs. With the system and expertise under their belt, Amgen worked on developing more and currently have two more biosimilars on their pipeline approval process.

Societal/growth outcomes

Apart from strong financials, Amgen gained many new substantial scientific insights through their biosimilar research. Amgen learned more about how the biological structure of a drug impacts its function. Through experiments in biosimilars they found how subtle changes in the drug process can change its performance and structure. These insights are now used in the development of their new pioneer drugs. Margret Karow, Execute Director at Amgen, stated, "The lessons we've learned in overcoming our biosimilar challenges are having a ripple effect across Amgen's whole pipeline," [27]. Many scientists at the company were interdepartmental. The insights gained through biosimilar development were quickly making their way into the development of other novel drugs. Through the process of mapping competitors' drugs for biosimilar development, mapping Amgen's own molecule became much easier. Furthermore, the biosimilar experience made them better at controlling variables in their own processes and testing.

Biosimilars not only created value for Amgen, but also for patients and healthcare systems. Biosimilars will lead to expected cost savings of about $150B in direct spending on biologic drugs over the next six years [13]. Biosimilars also increase the access to drugs and biologics within the healthcare system. They allow expanded options for patients across the board. This stays true to Amgen's core value of creating value for patients and the healthcare system.

Conclusion

Amgen solved the dilemma and disagreement between their employees through a structured and well-organized, three-prong process. They first assessed which option would align most with their core values and mission statement to ensure they were staying true to the goals of the organization. Next, they assessed entry through an extensive quantitative analysis, focusing on volume penetration, price level and revenue predictions. Lastly, they mapped out their long-term and short-term internal strategy to analyze the timeline of development and release. This approach eased all large concerns and led them to pursue entry into biosimilars [2].

This framework and decision-making model led Amgen to become a strong innovator in a new field. They became a large player in the field of biosimilars while also using the knowledge they gained across their whole drug pipeline.

Case questions

1. How did Amgen use a combination of culture, priority coordination, and internal strategy to aid them through a risky decision-making process?
2. What potential risks could have emerged if Amgen had not entered the field of biosimilars?
3. How did Amgen create value both internally as well as externally within the broader healthcare system?
4. Use external supporting data, including Amgen's corporate online system and annual reports, to assess their current biosimilar situation and discuss whether their biosimilar foray and the innovation approach is prudent and sustainable.

References

1. Eric Sagonowsky, Mar 29, 2021, "The Top 20 Drugs by Worldwide Sales in 2020," FiercePharma, www.fiercepharma.com/special-report/top-20-drugs-by-2020-sales
2. Robin Walsh, May 18, 2016, "A History of Amgen," Pharmaphorum, https://pharmaphorum.com/views-and-analysis/a_history_of_amgen/
3. Ian W. Mackenzie, June 5, 2015, "Amgen Inc: Pursuing Innovation and Imitation? (A)," Harvard Business School, 9-714-424.
4. Amgen Inc., "Amgen History," Amgen Inc., www.amgen.com/about/amgen-history
5. Amgen Inc., "Our Pipeline," www.amgenbiosimilars.com/products/our-pipeline/, accessed November 25, 2019.
6. Amgen Inc. Mar 31, 2020, "Annual Reports," Amgen Inc., investors.amgen.com/financial-information/annual-reports
7. Amgen Inc., "BioEngage Inside Biosimilars," What Are Biosimilars? www.amgenbiosimilars.com/bioengage/what-are-biosimilars

194   *Case studies*

8. Center for Drug Evaluation and Research, Feb 2, 2020, "Biosimilars," U.S. Food and Drug Administration, www.fda.gov/drugs/therapeutic-biologics-applications-bla/biosimilars

9. Zwebb, www.zwebb.com, Apr 22, 2011, "The History of the US Biosimilar Regulatory Pathway Posted 22/04/2011," Generics and Biosimilars Initiative, https:// gabionline.net/ Biosimilars/General/The-history-of-the-US-biosimilar-regulatory-pathway

10. Office of the Commissioner, Sept 14, 2017, "FDA Approves First Biosimilar for the Treatment of Cancer," U.S. Food and Drug Administration, www.fda.gov/news-events/ press-announcements/fda-approves-first-biosimilar-treatment-cancer

11. Amgen Inc., Oct 21, 2020, "Where Biosimilars Are Headed in the U.S," RSS, www.amgen.com/stories/2020/10/where-biosimilars-are-headed-in-the-us#:~:text=Biosimilars%20 are%20FDA%2Dapproved%20for,biosimilar%20and%20its%20reference%20product

12. Elizabeth Richardson, Oct 10, 2013, "Biosimilars: Health Affairs Brief," Health Affairs, www.healthaffairs.org/do/10.1377/hpb20131010.6409/full/

13. Spencer Case, 2018, "Biosimilar Cost Savings in the United States," RAND Corporation, www.rand.org/pubs/periodicals/health-quarterly/issues/v7/n4/03.html

14. Kave Niksefat, Biosimilars Update: 2019 Report, 6th Edition, Amgen Inc.

15. Lydia Ramsey Pflanzer, Dec 7, 2015, "There's a New Type of Medicine That Could Save the US Billions over the next Decade – but Not Everyone Wants That to Happen," Business Insider, www.businessinsider.com/what-is-a-biosimilar-and-how-does-it-work-2015-12

16. U.S. Food and Drug Administration, October 23, 2017, "Biosimilars: More Treatment Choices and Innovation," www.fda.gov/consumers/consumer-updates/biosimilars-more-treatment-choices-and-innovation, accessed December 11, 2019.

17. The Atlantic, "FDA Approved Biosimilars Offer More Treatment Options," The Atlantic, Atlantic Media Company, www.theatlantic.com/sponsored/amgen-2019/biosimilars/3265/

18. Jeff Yant, and Art Hewig, Sept 25, 2018, "Better Science Through Biosimilar R&D," Amgen Science, www.amgenscience.com/features/better-science-through-biosimilar-rd/

19. Amgen Inc., Mar 31, 2020, "Annual Reports," Amgen Inc., investors.amgen.com/financial-information/annual-reports

20. Erwin A. Blackstone, and P. Fuhr Joseph, Sept 2013, "The Economics of Biosimilars," American Health & Drug Benefits, Engage Healthcare Communications, LLC, www.ncbi.nlm.nih.gov/pmc/articles/PMC4031732/

21. Ed Silverman, Dec 20, 2011, "A Puzzling Amgen Move Into Biosimilars," Forbes Magazine, www.forbes.com/sites/edsilverman/2011/12/20/a-puzzling-amgen-move-into-biosimilars/ ?sh=18ee683bff8a

22. Amgen Biosimilars, July 18, 2019, "Amgen and Allergan's MVASI™ (bevacizumab-awwb) and KANJINTI™ (trastuzumab-anns) Now Available in the United States," www.amgen.com/media/news-releases/2019/07/amgen-and-allergans-mvasi-bevacizumabawwb-and-kanjinti-trastuzumabanns-now-available-in-the-united-states/, accessed November 25, 2019.

23. The Center for Biosimilars, Sept 8, 2020, "Amgen Sees Biosimilar 'Give and Take'," The Center For Biosimilars, www.centerforbiosimilars.com/view/amgen-sees-biosimilar-give-and-take-

24. Tony Hagen, Oct 29, 2020, "Mvasi, Kanjinti Add Heft to Amgen's Third-Quarter Sales," The Center For Biosimilars, www.centerforbiosimilars.com/view/mvasi-kanjinti-add-heft-to-amgen-s-third-quarter-sales

25. Eric Sagonowsky, Oct 29, 2020, "Amgen Exec: Biosims May Have Lagged in the U.S., but Now They're Paying Off," Fierce Pharma, www.fiercepharma.com/pharma/ biosims-have-been-slow-to-pick-up-u-s-but-amgen-starting-to-see-their-potential

26. Greg McFarlane, Aug 28, 2020, "How Amgen Makes Billions on Just a Few Drugs," Investopedia, www.investopedia.com/articles/markets/110514/how-amgen-makes-billions-just-few-drugs.asp

27. Jeff Yant, and Art Hewig, Sept 15, 2018, "Better Science Through Biosimilar R&D," Amgen Science, www.amgenscience.com/features/better-science-through-biosimilar-rd/

Case 2: FedEx – Innovation Through Sustained Adaptability

Alaina Gregory

Stephen M. Ross School of Business, University of Michigan
alainaeg@umich.edu

History

Innovation and disruption have been at the forefront of FedEx ever since its founding in 1971 by Yale student Fred Smith. He first developed the concept for FedEx as a term paper that imagined a global logistics company that would be the direct competitor to USPS. The term paper allegedly received a below average grade with marks that questioned the feasibility of the idea. Interestingly, FedEx became the first of many successful technology companies to be told their groundbreaking innovation was initially infeasible. Not deterred by his critics, Smith eventually came back to his idea and raised $91M in venture capital.[1] Surprisingly, he actually credits the straightforward need for his idea with the success in venture capital, saying, "FedEx proposition came along when the venture-capital business was really looking for more prosaic types of investments where you didn't have to create a product and a market all at the same time."[2] Despite the surplus of funding, the company took heavy losses from 1971–1976 before eventually turning a large profit.

Back in the 1960s, the global logistics industry was a monopoly owned solely by the United States Postal Service due to the need for heavy resources and scale. When FedEx was founded in 1971, it sought to increase efficiency and offer other delivery solutions to companies. It began a series of acquisitions of smaller logistics companies including Gelco and Tiger and continues to utilize that strategy to the present day.[3] It explicitly added value to consumers through express deliveries and global markets. This was largely B2B before the wider adoption of e-commerce technology and internet boom.

Macroeconomic environment

Presently, the global logistics industry is largely defined by e-commerce giants like Amazon, Alibaba, JD.com, Walmart, eBay, Shopify, and Rakuten. FedEx President Raj Subramaniam described the e-commerce trend: "The rise in demand for e-commerce goes beyond peak. It's a year-round phenomenon and we are ready to meet that demand."[4] Furthermore, FedEx has projected the US volume of small-sized packages to double by 2026.[5] Additionally, due to the coronavirus pandemic, demand for e-commerce has grown upward of 76%.[6] FedEx has been a partner to multiple e-commerce giants including Amazon. However, recently this partnership has ended with FedEx CEO Fred Smith citing the e-commerce giant as a direct competitor as Amazon continues to build their own logistics chain. Last year, Amazon launched

DOI: 10.4324/9781003190837-23

196   Case studies

a delivery service partners program that relies on a mix of UPS and its Flex delivery platform that is modeled after Uber utilizing a series of third-party contractors.[7] Additionally, Amazon added "transportation and logistics services" to its competitor's filing.[8] This indicates that while the e-commerce space is increasing demand for FedEx services it is also inviting increased competition.

Despite the threat of increased competition from a known disruptor, Amazon, CEO Smith responded by saying, "We basically compete in an ecosphere that's got five entities in it. There's UPS, there's DHL, there's the US Postal Service, and now increasingly, there's Amazon. That's who we wake up every day trying to think about how we compete against and give the best services to our sales force."[9] Additionally, there has been increased pressure to compete on the B2C e-commerce end to counter the 64% profit loss in May that was largely due to B2B impacts.[10] In fact, in Q4 FY2020 alone, FedEx US e-commerce volume rose 72% versus 56% a year ago.[11]

Pivot

Due to the increasing pressures of competition, FedEx's pre-pandemic strategy was "laser-focused on 5 areas of e-commerce; international profitability; market-leading revenue quality; B2B growth; and operational excellence and innovation."[12] When the coronavirus pandemic forced all businesses to rethink what rapid pivot and innovation means for their industry, FedEx was in many ways able to maintain its previous strategy toward e-commerce. CEO Fred Smith summarized the pivot as, "while our strategic course at FedEx was plotted long before COVID-19 entered the picture, in many ways, the world accelerated to meet our existing strategy."[13] He also acknowledged that FedEx still had to make major changes following the 2019 fiscal period in order to shift to be "all in" on e-commerce.

Oftentimes, larger companies have a hard time shifting in the face of rapid change and disruption. However, FedEx immediately adapted new initiatives to focus on e-commerce and the shifting environment. Foremost, FedEx made significant changes to FedEx Ground, which will largely increase share and profitability in the e-commerce industry. The new FedEx Ground includes extending residential deliveries to seven days a week year-round.[14] FedEx Ground will also be collaborating with FedEx Express to increase efficiency of day-definite residential express shipments.[15] Furthermore, with more emphasis on B2C, FedEx is increasingly focused on the last-mile optimization. Normally, the last mile of the package delivery is the most inefficient and expensive. To optimize, Fed-Ex is using dynamic route optimization and is increasing package density by taking on more FedEx SmartPost packages previously given to USPS.[16] CFO Alan explains, "As we continue to grow Ground and its densities, we are lowering costs at a rapid clip."

Innovation-based partnership

Furthermore, larger and more expansive innovation is being implemented in FedEx to support B2C transactions. Leadership is also focusing on forming multiple strategic partnerships with technology companies in order to propel the latest logistic innovations. For instance, FedEx has partnered for innovation with Alphabet in the creation of Wing Aviation LLC, a subsidiary of Alphabet. This service would directly optimize residential deliveries and increase profit margins in the e-commerce space.

Starting in October 2019, FedEx began a pilot program for the small package drone delivery service.[17] Wing Aviation was the first drone service to be certified to deliver packages long distances by the federal aviation administration. Wing Aviation utilizes the newest drone technology, which enables cloud connectivity on LTE networks to constantly provide real-time updates on location and ETA.[18] FedEx implementing this technology will lead to benefits such as lowered carbon footprint, reduction in package delivery time by two to three days, and less risk for package theft and/or damage. It could be possible for drones to deliver small packages within hours of ordering. Drone delivery is considered the future of the logistics industry due to its ability to avoid increasingly congested roads and target rural areas efficiently. Expanding on the Wing Aviation partnership Don Colleran, FedEx Express President, states that "FedEx is constantly innovating and testing solutions to meet growing customer needs, and we are excited to add this pilot to our portfolio of first-in-kind innovation."[19]

Another unique partnership that helped propel FedEx's innovation and efficiency is FedEx OnSite. This partnership utilized third-party FedEx pick-up and drop-off locations. Specifically, 7,500 Walgreens sites in every state. Adding to this, Raj Subramaniam says, "This holiday season, 80% of the US population is within nine minutes of a FedEx hold location."[20] Due to the success of the idea, FedEx Executive Vice President and Chief Information Officer, Rob Carter, won the 2019 Forbes CIO Innovation Award.[21] This partnership utilizes the vast storefronts of Walgreens to increase FedEx presence without significant capital investment.

Finally, FedEx recently announced FedEx Surround. This technology evolved from a strategic partnership with FedEx and Microsoft that allows businesses to "enhance visibility into its supply chain by leveraging data to provide near-real-time analytics into shipment tracking, which will drive more precise logistics and inventory management."[22] The synergy of this relationship stems from innovation by combining the scale of FedEx with the reliability and ubiquity of Microsoft cloud technology infrastructure service Azure. Smith comments that "together with Microsoft, we will combine the immense power of technology with the vast scale of our infrastructure to help revolutionize commerce and create a network for what's next for our customers."[23] With this technology, customers will have access to real-time insights down to the zip code on the movement of physical inventory.

Innovative technology

Investing in business technology and information like FedEx Surround is a continuing initiative at FedEx. For instance, Smith recently commented on the utilization of blockchain technology by saying, "We believe blockchain and its insight into an authentic chain of custody will completely change worldwide supply chains."[24] FedEx currently is developing blockchain for parcel deliveries. Blockchain would enable international deliveries to be tracked using secure ledgers that are accessible to all parties involved in the transaction. This allows it to be an absolutely true record of the package delivery information. Furthermore, this could prevent fraudulent and criminal activity by ensuring that the blockchain hash is needed to pick up packages for delivery. By investing in technology like blockchain, FedEx is on the cusp of the future for the logistics industry. FedEx CIO and EVP of FedEx Information Services, Rob Carter has collaborated with Don Tapscott, co-author of *Blockchain Revolution* to understand the key advantages of blockchain in FedEx's supply chain.

198 *Case studies*

Furthermore, FedEx joined Industry Coalition's Blockchain in Transportation Alliance and Blockchain Research Institute.[25]

Additionally, FedEx has been focused on its innovation, Sense Aware. Sense Aware is a "sensor-based logistics device that provides real-time tracking of a package location while it's in the FedEx Express network using Bluetooth Low Energy."[26] It utilizes IoT technology to monitor fragile or high-value items. This technology is available to customers for an extra charge. It enables a package's location, temperature, humidity, pressure, shock, and light to be tracked at any moment. Due to this, it has been successfully trialed in the healthcare shipping industry with temperature-sensitive items such as medicines and vaccines. Healthcare is a targeted industry as pharmaceutical cold chain logistics is a $12.6B global industry.[27] It was expected to be fully rolled out by September 2020 and would be instrumental in increasing reliability in the logistics industry.

Other current internal innovations include investments in driverless eco-friendly delivery vehicles. Specifically, FedEx recently unveiled the FedEx SameDay Bot. This small autonomous bot was designed specifically for residential and last- mile deliveries in mind. FedEx is working with Walgreens, Walmart, and Target because more than 60% of these companies' customers live less than three miles from FedEx's location.[28] Brie Carere, Chief Marketing and Communications Officer at FedEx, noted the need for the bot in the e-commerce industry by saying, "The bot represents a milestone in our ongoing mission to solve the complexities and expense of same-day, last-mile delivery for the growing e-commerce market in a manner that is safe and environmentally friendly."[29] FedEx used DEKA Development & Research Corp. to develop the ideal bot from their base iBot model, for the internal innovation idea.[30]

People

The leadership of FedEx has always been differentiated compared to other companies. Founder of FedEx, Fred Smith, still remains the CEO and president of the board after almost 50 years. It is uncommon for founders of companies to remain CEO after the IPO and even rarer for them to be successful for almost half a century. Smith was also known for his emphasis on long-term strategy. He consistently speaks about 10–15 years out during shareholder meetings and constantly underscores the importance of innovation in the logistics industry. The evident talent of Smith has led to a strong structure of lower management with a clear vision.

Smith has segmented the company in an organized way into several different strategic units. These units are FedEx Express, FedEx Ground, FedEx Freight, FedEx Office, FedEx Custom Critical, FedEx Trade Networks, and FedEx Services.[31] Each of these units have presidents who oversee the general performance. However, there are initiatives to promote collaboration and avoid siloed communication among the units.

For instance, to promote continuous innovation that scoped from front to back end, FedEx utilized Corporate Business Services technology in partnership with Deloitte and Oracle. FedEx used as-a-service (aaS) and baked it into its current structure.[32] Chris Wood, Vice President Business Transformation, FedEx Services described the technology as "an agile, adaptive Digital Foundry framework that helps deliver greater value and build the organization of tomorrow."[33]

More holistically, FedEx has the PSP People-Service-Profit philosophy at the forefront of their organization. This "is based on the belief that by creating a positive

FedEx   199

working environment for employees, they will provide better service quality to customers, which would then lead to customers using FedEx products and services."[34] To action this, FedEx instituted a promotion from within policy to invest in their human capital and talent. They give complete priority and preference to internal candidates to support employee development. The employees are set up to be successful for these promotions from internal professional development programs such as AiM (Advance into Management Program) and APAC e-learning.[35] Furthermore, monetary investment in employees is available through a robust tuition assistant program designed to enhance career advancement opportunities within FedEx. All these people-oriented programs allow FedEx to propel internal innovation through talent retention and internal development.

Outcomes

The coronavirus pandemic has been difficult for most companies as countries are estimated to lose an average of 2.4% of their GDP.[36] It has been especially trying for a global company such as FedEx. They had just incurred a huge economic hit a month earlier, with the loss of their largest e-commerce business, Amazon. Further, they had heavy ties with China. As illustrated in Exhibit 2.1, it is evident FedEx was already feeling economic pressures after cutting ties with Amazon in early August 2019, well before the start of the coronavirus pandemic. FedEx began to rally back the revenue in time for Q2 2020 but still struggled to increase other key numbers. Just as they were recovering from losing relations with Amazon, COVID-19 hit China in December 2019. FedEx felt the effects of the pandemic earlier than other companies due to its sizable logistics and trade relationship with China. In February, cases peaked in China and began to start in the US, leading to worsening performance in Q3 and Q4 of 2020. In only nine months, operating margin had fallen from 7.4% to 2.4% and FedEx stock plummeted.

However, FedEx had already begun to pivot and utilize its culture of innovation for the following months. As mentioned previously, FedEx implemented multiple ideas to increase package density and promote the B2C sector. These included an emphasis on last-mile optimization, extension of residential deliveries, and SmartPost packages. Multiple of these ideas had already been tested in certain sectors of FedEx. Due to the expansive network and unlimited market options for FedEx, trial-based implementation of innovations is both convenient and a normal part of the process. In the pandemic crisis scenario, the constant testing of innovative ideas coupled with agile information systems allowed FedEx to implement immediately. Moreover, FedEx's long-term investment in the newest logistics technology and innovation through Wing Aviation and blockchain further strengthens the company in turbulent times. Finally, building off a culture focused on people first, FedEx provided direct aid by shipping more than 200,000 surgical masks to global hospitals and deploying two medical shelters and equipment to Martin Luther King, Jr. Community Hospital for the underserved communities of California.[37]

These direct actions of FedEx resulted in increased financial performance for Q4 over Q3 by increasing operating income, operating margin, and net income. Surprisingly, FedEx was able to turn around their performance through the peak months of the pandemic in the US. Additionally, in the past few months, the share price has skyrocketed from $90 to over $200. It is now higher than it was before both

200 Case studies

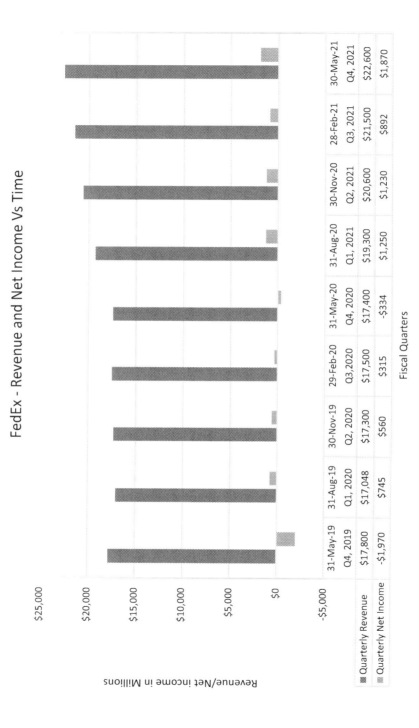

Exhibit 2.1 FedEx financial performance.
Data Source: https://investors.fedex.com/financial-information/quarterly-results/default.aspx

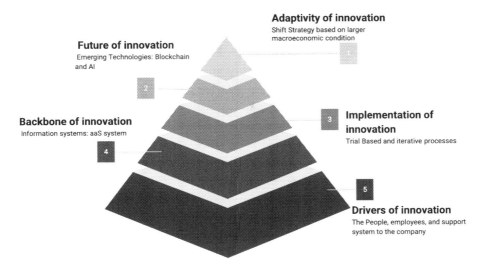

Exhibit 2.2 The pyramid of organizational innovation.

the Amazon exit and the pandemic. These metrics speak to the adaptivity of FedEx as a company. They also highlight how supporting innovations throughout multiple dimensions of a company can increase its performance even during a crisis. The innovation building blocks that FedEx leveraged to strengthen its overall performance are depicted in Exhibit 2.2.

Questions

1. FedEx's large economy of scale was a barrier to entry that protected them against competition for many years. As mentioned in the case, tech behemoth Amazon and other e-commerce giants are now entering into the logistics industry. How do you think FedEx's latest emphasis on innovation and development protects against new competitors such as Amazon?
2. Do you believe that turbulent macroeconomic conditions can be an opportunistic time for greater innovation?
3. How was FedEx able to apply technologies such as blockchain, IoT, and agile work streams to fuel its innovation?
4. What does FedEx do to emphasize social and environmental innovation? Why is this imperative to the company's success?
5. In what ways is FedEx's leadership unique? Is it common for a founder and CEO to continue to be innovative for decades? What can we learn from Fred Smith's continued success?
6. How do the "building blocks" of innovation pictured in Exhibit 2.2 contribute to FedEx's success? Why is it important to innovate on multiple dimensions of a company? What does this say about ingraining innovation as a culture?

202 *Case studies*

Notes

1 www.bloomberg.com/news/articles/2004-09-19/online-extra-fred-smith-on-the-birth-of-fedex
2 Ibid
3 https://investors.fedex.com/company-overview/Acquisition-History/default.aspx
4 www.commercialappeal.com/story/money/industries/logistics/2019/06/10/how-e-commerce-has-changed-fedex-past-year-amazon/1409208001/
5 www.dcvelocity.com/articles/30775-parcel-carriers-evolve-as-e-commerce-explodes
6 www.digitalstrategyconsulting.com/countries/usa-digital-marketing-research-tips-and-news-for-marketers/us-shopping-trends-ecommerce-sales-rise-76-on-last-year/49990/
7 www.cnbc.com/2019/02/05/amazon-10k-adds-transportation-and-logistics-services-to-competitors.html
8 Ibid
9 Ibid
10 https://investors.fedex.com/news-and-events/investor-news/news-release-details/2019/FedEx-Corp-Reports-Fourth-Quarter-and-Full-Year-Earnings/
11 https://s1.q4cdn.com/714383399/files/doc_financials/quarterly/2020/q4/FedEx-Earnings-Transcript-Q4-FY20.html
12 http://s1.q4cdn.com/714383399/files/doc_financials/quarterly/2020/q2/Earnings-Transcript-Q2FY20.pdf
13 https://investors.fedex.com/financial-information/Chairmans-Letter/
14 https://newsroom.fedex.com/newsroom/fedex-to-optimize-last-mile-residential-deliveries-position-for-continued-e-commerce-growth/
15 Ibid
16 Ibid
17 https://newsroom.fedex.com/newsroom/wing-drone-deliveries-take-flight-in-first-of-its-kind-trial-with-fede
18 Ibid
19 https://newsroom.fedex.com/newsroom/drone-deliveries-coming-soon-as-wing-unveils-plans-for-first-of-its-kind-trial-with-fedex-and-walgreen/
20 https://newsroom.fedex.com/newsroom/fedex-package-pickup-and-drop-off-now-available-at-more-than-7500-walgreens-locations-in-all-50-states/
21 www.forbes.com/sites/peterhigh/2019/04/08/fedex-cio-rob-carter-wins-the-2019-forbes-cio-innovation-award-with-fedex-onsite/#1501b8b271d6
22 https://martechseries.com/sales-marketing/b2b-commerce/microsofts-intelligent-cloud-drives-fedex-surround/#:~:text=FedEx%20Surround%2C%20the%20first%20solution,precise%20logistics%20and%20inventory%20management.
23 https://news.microsoft.com/2020/05/18/fedex-and-microsoft-join-forces-to-transform-commerce/
24 https://investors.fedex.com/financial-information/Chairmans-Letter/
25 www.fedex.com/en-us/about/policy/technology-innovation/blockchain.html
26 https://investors.fedex.com/financial-information/Chairmans-Letter/#:~:text=Furthermore%2C%20we%20have%20launched%20SenseAware,network%20using%20Bluetooth%20Low%20Energy.
27 https://pharmaceuticalcommerce.com/latest-news/us-drug-2016-sales-450-billion-moderate-single-digit-growth/
28 http://sustainability.fedex.com/FedEx_2020_Global_Citizenship_Report.pdf
29 Ibid
30 https://newsroom.fedex.com/newsroom/thefuturefedex/
31 https://ukdiss.com/examples/frederick-w-smith-fedex-case-study.php?vref=1
32 www.wired.com/wiredinsider/2020/05/fedex-baked-continuous-innovation-enterprise/

33 Ibid

34 https://newsroom.fedex.com/newsroom/fedex-attributes-success-people-first-philosophy/
#:~:text=The%20People%2DService%2DProfit%20philosophy%20(P%2DS%2DP)%20
is%20based,using%20FedEx%20products%20and%20services.

35 Ibid

36 www.statista.com/statistics/1102991/covid-19-percent-change-gdp-country/

37 https://fedexcares.com/stories/delivering-good-help-combat-covid-19/
international-medical-corps-prepares-covid-19-surge

Case 3: Reliance Jio – From 4G to Digital Innovation

Hursh Motwani

Stephen M. Ross School of Business, University of Michigan
hmotwani@umich.edu

Introduction

While enjoying his morning tea with his wife from his luxurious penthouse, Mukesh Ambani receives his daily morning call from his Chief Financial Officer Alok Agarwal. There has been no stopping for Mukesh Ambani, the Chairman and Managing Director of the Indian conglomerate Reliance Industries Limited (RIL). Despite the challenges that COVID-19 offers, Mr. Ambani has been able to make blockbuster agreements with multinational and private equity firms worldwide. It all started on April 22, 2020, when RIL decided to sell a 10% stake of Reliance Jio to Facebook for $5.7B [1, 2]. Subsequently, the management team of Reliance Jio made independent deals with global investors such as Silver Lake, Vista, General Atlantic, Mubadala, Abu Dhabi Investment Authority (ADIA), TPG Capital, and L. Catterton. This is followed by a $4.5B-dollar investment in Reliance Jio by Google and an earlier $2.5B-dollar investment by Microsoft [1, 2]. Having successfully completed these mega deals, the astute Mukesh Ambani is feeling good that he has partnered with the right organizations to achieve his vision of a "Digital India." Mr. Ambani asks Mr. Agarwal to call a virtual meeting of the core management team to discuss their next steps. At this meeting, the group discuss RIL's strategy to move from oil to digital, and what steps Reliance Jio needs to take to ensure success.

The telecom industry in India

The Indian telecom industry, comprising wireless or mobile communications and fixed lines, has grown significantly over the years, and has now become a necessity of every Indian. The initial growth in this industry can be attributed to the liberalization of the Indian economy in 1991, which opened the door for private service providers, the passing of the National Telecommunications Policy in 1994 and the formation of the Telecom Regulatory Authority of India (TRAI) Act 1997 [3]. With a subscriber base of more than 1.2 billion and total internet users of more than 700 million, India is the world's second-largest telecommunications provider in the world [4]. Also, tele-density, a crucial measure of the penetration of Indian telecom, has increased tremendously over the years in both the rural and urban markets. The overall growth in this sector can be attributed to the proactive and liberal government policies, strong consumer demand, affordable tariffs, easy market access to telecom equipment, increased internet accessibility and speed, increased competition among service providers with an emphasis on 4G network, roll out of mobile number portability, and deregulation

DOI: 10.4324/9781003190837-24

	Vodafone Idea Limited	Reliance Jio Limited	Bharti Airtel Limited	Bharat Sanchar Nigham Limited	Mahanagar Telephone Nigham Limited (MTNL)
Ownership	Partnership between Aditya Birla Group and Vodafone Group	Wholly owned by Reliance Industries	Bharti Group (45.7) Pastel Ltd (15.57 percent), LIC India (4.3 percent)	Government (100%)	Government (56.3%)
Product offerings	India Voice and Data services across 2G, 3G, and 4G platforms.	Does not offer 2G or 3G serv ice, and instead uses voice over LTE to provide voice service on its 4G network	2G, 3G and 4G wireless services, mobile commerce, fixed line services, high-speed home broadband, DTH, enterprise services	Provides both fixed line telephones and mobile telephony services on GSM and CDMA platforms	Fixed telephone service, GSM (including 3G services) CDMA based Mobile service, Internet, Broadband, ISDN, and Leased Line services
Subscribers as of March 31, 2019	368.3 million	over 322.99 million	over 403 million customers globally	About 115.89 million	3.527 million

Exhibit 3.1 Comparative analysis of India's top five telecommunications service providers [8, 9, 10]

of Foreign Direct Investment (FDI) norms resulting in large FDI inflow [5, 6]. It is projected that the Indian telecom industry today contributes to 8.2% of India's GDP and that the telecommunications industry in India will add 500 million new internet users over the next five years due to an increase in mobile phone penetration and reduction in data costs [7].

Currently, due to major consolidation, three major private companies and two state-owned companies dominate the telecom industry in India. Prior to the disruptive launch of Reliance Jio in 2016 there were 10 to 12 service providers in every circle or service area. The private companies include Vodafone Idea Limited (31.5% market share), Reliance Jio (30.8% market share), and Bharti Airtel Limited (27.5% market share), while Bharat Sanchar Nigham Limited (BSNL) with a market share of 9.9%, and MTNL with a market share of 0.29% are the two-state owned companies [8, 9, 10]. Exhibit 3.1 provides a comparative analysis of these major providers.

Lockdowns on account of COVID-19 are also having a positive impact on the Indian telecom industry since it is pressing Indians to embrace online platforms for entertainment, gaming, banking, education, and work-related activities. As a result, the demand for broadband has spiked, and is expected to remain high even after the pandemic as Indians get more confident with conducting business virtually [11].

Reliance Jio's 4G entry and success

In the mid-1980s, an extremely small portion of the Indian population (0.001%) owned a telephone. However, by July 2016, almost every Indian possessed a mobile telephone with text messaging features because of 2G and 3G technology [12]. Seeing the potential opportunities for disruption, Mukesh Ambani decided to refocus Jio's

206   *Case studies*

entry into the Indian telecom industry using 4G technology. With an initial investment of Rs 150,000 Crore or $22B in a 4G network, Mr. Ambani wanted to transform the highly competitive Indian telecom sector from voice call-centric to data-centric[13]. This change in focus was truly a game changer as it made the existing strategy of competitors obsolete. Also, by providing free voice and data services as part of an introductory offer to its customers, Reliance Jio's cost leadership strategy was able to further intensify the existing price war. Here are some other ways Jio was able to penetrate and grow its market share in a highly competitive market.

Marketing strategy of Reliance Jio

Price: The cost leadership strategy that Reliance Jio implemented was truly a game changer and was instrumental in Reliance Jio capturing a significant market share from its competitors. In the four different 4G LTE data plans (1GB, 2GB, 3GB, and 4GB), Reliance Jio's plans were significantly less than that of their competitors. For example, prior to Jio, customers were paying $0.1/min for voice calls and $4/GB for data on average. On the other hand, Jio's introductory price ranged from $0.3 to $80 a month [14]. The competition had no choice but to restructure and lower their pricing strategies to compete with Jio.

Product: In addition to Jio's 4G voice and data offerings, additional products that Jio offered included voice telephony and peripheral services such as instant messaging, music streaming, and digital payments platform. While the competitors offered independent data and voice packages, Jio started bundling them into their bandwidth and data plans. To increase the customer acquisition rate, Jio also started free delivery of subscriber identity module (SIM) cards to their customers in December 2016.

Promotion: Jio developed an assertive and aggressive promotion strategy that involved all forms of media, including social media like Facebook, Instagram, Twitter, and YouTube. Top celebrities and film industry icons like Amitabh Bachchan and Shahrukh Khan also frequently appeared in their commercial advertisements and served as Jio's ambassadors and influencers. This turned out to be a winning strategy as the masses were able to relate these stars to the Jio brand. To increase the number of LYF (pronounced "life" and is an Indian brand of Jio smartphones) smartphone users, Jio placed an offer of free Jio SIM and unlimited internet services for a year. This strategic move helped Jio increased their customer base by migrating customers from other networks.

Place: Jio's products were mainly sold through the Reliance retail channels, mainly Jio stores and dealers located in cities across India, and an e-commerce site, which was launched and managed by Reliance Retail [12,14, 15, 16, 17].

Technology strategy

Their investment in the latest 4G LTE technology and voice over LTE technology has made Jio a leader both in terms of speed and coverage. Investment in an optical fiber network, which enjoys ten times more data and voice capacity than traditional cable network capacity, was a brilliant move by Mr. Ambani and his team. As of September

2016, Jio's fiber network spanned more than 270,000 kilometers, compared to 200,000 of Airtel, and 160,000 of Vodafone. Jio also did a smart thing by partnering with Hindustan Futuristic Communications Limited to manage their optical fiber network [18, 19, 20].

People strategy: Leadership team and style

The Reliance Jio team was led by the transformational, charismatic, and result-oriented leader, Mr. Mukesh Ambani. Mr. Ambani's mantra has always been: "Leadership is not about following anybody; it is about setting new standards that nobody else has set [21]." This mantra is very appropriate because Mr. Ambani's vision of introducing 4G technology in the Indian telecommunications industry and his dream of "Digital India" is disruptive and innovative. Exhibit 3.2 depicts a couple of inspirational quotes made by Mr. Mukesh Ambani that showcase his leadership style. In addition to being visionary, Mr. Ambani is also execution-focused and result-oriented. He is determined to achieve his vision and takes all the necessary steps to ensure that the goals and milestones are achieved. For example, to ensure a successful launch of 4G technology in a short time, Mr. Ambani and his leadership team hired a lot of experienced expatriates from around the world to change Jio's fortunes. At any given time, 15% of the 20,000 employees working at the Jio Navi Mumbai campus were expatriates, many of them holding key positions. Mr. Ambani also believes and has instilled in his leadership team the importance of flat organizational structure, empowered employees, and open plan offices.

Reliance Jio's people-centric business strategy has been designed around a fractal business model that focuses on the customers and provides empowerment to its employees so that they are able to make quick decisions using real-time information. Mr. Ambani is also a true believer of the "team of teams" operating model to help a large organization like Reliance Jio stay nimble, growth-focused, efficient, and effective. To strengthen its ties with its employees, Reliance Jio has built an entire

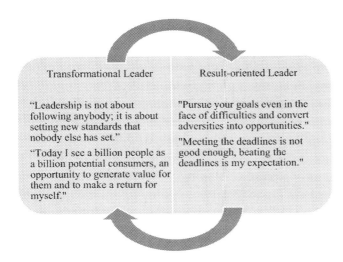

Exhibit 3.2 Leadership style of Mr. Mukesh Ambani as depicted by his inspirational quotes [21].

208   *Case studies*

human-centric management platform that matches workdays and critical success factors. To help Reliance Jio stay innovative and fast-moving, the management team of Jio is always looking for new performance measurement and development tools, in addition to more efficient hiring, onboarding, and training practices. Reliance Jio has also designed and implemented a network-based operating business model to ensure that key functional groups such as sales and service teams, although operating independently, stay connected with the mother ship (i.e. Jio Corporate) seamlessly and can access up-to-date sales and financial information to better serve their customers [21, 22, 23].

Profitability and financial success

Since the launch of 4G in 2016, Reliance Jio has been extremely profitable and has been very successful in capturing a significant market share in a very competitive environment. Reliance Jio is said to have acquired 100 million users in less than the first six months of 4G network introduction. This number is supposed to be even higher than those reported by Facebook and WhatsApp. For the year ending March 31, 2020, Reliance Jio increased its net profits by $737.5M or 88% [24]. The company also reported a 26% increase in its number of subscribers. The total number of subscribers has now reached 387.5 million, and the monthly revenue per user is $1.73 [24]. Over the years, the company has also witnessed an exponential growth in data and voice usage. In the past year, data usage increased by 34%, while voice usage increased by 21%. Each user consumed about 11.3 GB or 771 minutes of data per month [24]. As Mr. Ambani starts to fulfill his dream of "Digital India" with the introduction of 5G, profitability and the number of users is expected to grow exponentially in the future [25, 26].

Is Reliance Jio ready to move from 4G to digital?

Though Reliance Jio has been extremely successful in the past four months in building partnerships, raising significant capital, and becoming a debt-free company, will this be enough for Mr. Ambani to fulfill his dreams of a "Digital India?" To respond to this question, we decided to perform a partial SWOT analysis, which is presented in Exhibit 3.3.

The major strengths of Reliance Jio include: (1) Strong foundation and backing of parent company Reliance Industries Limited, which is a highly credible global brand; (2) Strong leadership team that is forward-thinking and disruptive. Led by Mr. Mukesh Ambani the leadership team is very experienced, influential, and well connected; (3) Strong and growing customer base. With a total number of subscribers of 387.5 million, Reliance Jio has a very strong and loyal customer base; (4) Continuous investment in state-of-art technology. Jio's investment in 4G LTE technology allows it to grow its network faster and wider. This technology is also capable of supporting 5G and 6G technologies that are critical for Jio to go digital; (5) Great promotion and brand management strategies. The use of celebrities in advertising, along with the effective use of social media have paid off for Reliance Jio and will be even more useful for its growth in the future.

Though Reliance Jio made a late but successful foray into the Indian telecommunication industry, it does have two potential weaknesses that may need to be addressed.

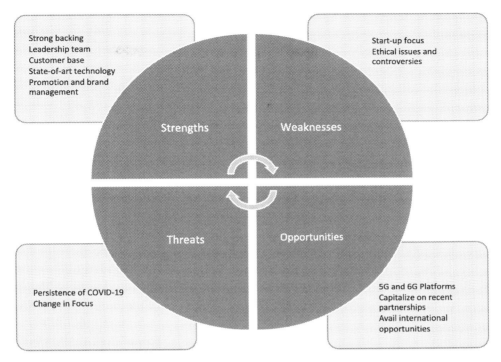

Exhibit 3.3 Reliance Jio's SWOT analysis [27, 28].

(1) Reliance Jio is very startup focused. Jio Platform is currently working with over 20 startups to build progressive technologies for the future. Will these startups deliver? (2) Ethical issues and controversies. Reliance Jio has been widely criticized for lack of transparency, undercutting competitive prices, and undisciplined financial management. Will this come to eventually haunt Reliance Jio?

As far as opportunities are concerned, Reliance Jio can disrupt the Indian telecommunications industry further in the future. Specifically, here are three: (1) Will Reliance Jio be able to successfully launch 5G and 6G platforms to broaden their bandwidth and fulfill Mr. Ambani's dream of a "Digital India?" (2) Will the leadership team of Reliance Jio be able to capitalize on the partnerships and agreements they have signed with multinational companies and private investors? (3) In spite of focusing solely on the Indian market and Mr. Ambani's dream to create a "Digital India," will the leadership team of Reliance Jio capitalize on the future international opportunities that will arise?

The potential threats that could arise in the future include: (1) The persistence of COVID-19, which may slow down the national economy and could have an adversarial impact on the telecommunications sector in India. (2) Change in focus. Reliance Jio's low-cost strategy and providing freebies have been very successful, but will they be able to continue to implement this strategy going forward or will they change their focus and potentially lose a portion of their customer base to emerging and existing competition [15, 27, 28]?

Next steps for Reliance Jio

Despite the negative impact of COVID-19 on businesses worldwide, Reliance Jio has been extremely fortunate that the year 2020 has been lucky for them so far. With record profits and number of subscribers, and with the signing of major agreements and global technology leaders' partnerships, Reliance Jio is well positioned to fulfill Mr. Ambani's dream of a "Digital India." Will Reliance Jio be able to capitalize on its technology, human capital, and strategic partnerships to digitally empower India's 1.3 billion population? Time will tell.

Innovation goals and takeaways

Reliance Jio's successful journey toward achieving its long-term lofty innovation goals of "Digital India," can be attributed to Reliance's innovative culture, strong leadership and new leadership models, unconventional paths to design and innovation, and strategic partnerships. It will be interesting to see if Reliance Jio can achieve the same degree of success in its efforts to launch 5G and 6G platforms.

There are several takeaways from this case. First, do not be afraid to think big. Mukesh Ambani, the Chairman and Managing Director of the Indian conglomerate RIL, is a true dreamer, innovator, and a strategic thinker. He genuinely believes in being a leader and setting his own standards and taking big risks, rather than being a follower and playing catch-up. Second, ambitious vision and big dreams must be followed through with a well-thought-out strategy and disciplined execution. Reliance achieved this through well-defined marketing, technology, people, and financial strategies, and laser-focused execution. This case highlights the importance of people and culture to Jio's overall success. Lastly, Jio's ability to build strategic partnerships and challenge them to perform at a higher level with a sense of urgency, certainly contributed to their enviable success. Despite COVID-19, Mr. Mukesh Ambani was able to make blockbuster partnership agreements with multinational, investment, and private equity firms worldwide, which resulted in Reliance Jio's triumph and accomplishments.

Reflection

As we look back on Reliance Jio's success and its future vision, we can ask ourselves the following three questions: 1) Would Reliance Jio have been as successful without Mr. Mukesh Ambani? 2) Was it a good idea for Reliance Jio to enter into so many partnerships and agreements that they did in the past six months? 3) What additional steps and transformational changes will Reliance Jio and Mr. Ambani have to make to achieve the vision of a "Digital India?" We believe that Reliance Jio will be challenged to do a better job of managing its growth in the future with less criticism that we discussed earlier.

Discussion questions

1. Discuss Reliance Jio's innovation approach and the critical factors that led to its impressive growth.

Reliance Jio 211

2. Mr. Mukesh Ambani's mantra has always been: "Leadership is not about following anybody, it is about setting new standards that nobody else has set." Did Mr. Ambani follow through on this mantra. Evaluate Mr. Ambani's leadership style based on his decision-making abilities and his inspirational quotes in the context of innovation.
3. Is Reliance Jio ready to take the next steps and achieve Mr. Ambani's vision of a "Digital India?" What are potential obstacles that Reliance Jio may encounter?

Looking at the case through the lens of the TRIAL© framework

Summary Matrix	1 (low)	2	3	4	5 (High)
Did technology play a role?					X
This case is technology-focused. It discusses Reliance Jio's significant role in the Indian telecom industry, Jio's entry and success with 4G, and Jio's vision of a "Digital India."					
Did they have unique leadership? If so, what?					X
The success of Reliance Jio can be attributed to its Chairman and Managing Director Mr. Mukesh Ambani. Mr. Ambani is truly a charismatic leader, strategic thinker, risk taker, deal maker, and result-oriented. He believes in thinking big and is always wanting to set standards that no one has set.					
What resources (talent and other resources) did they use?				X	
Reliance Jio's people-centric business strategy has been designed around a fractal business model that focuses on the customers and provides empowerment to its employees so that they are able to make quick decisions using real-time information.					
Did they have an imaginative and achievement culture?			X		
Reliance Jio did have an imaginative and achievement culture. Mr. Ambani's mantra has always been "Leadership is not about following anybody, it is about setting new standards that nobody else has set." Ambani's vision of transforming India from 3G to 4G to 5G and ultimately of a "Digital India" shows how imaginative the culture of the organization is.					
In addition to being visionary, Mr. Ambani is also result-oriented. He is determined to achieve his vision and takes all the necessary steps to ensure that the goals and milestones are achieved. This illustrates that the culture is also achievement-focused.					
What else contributed to their success?			X		
The financial stability of the company, the "team of teams" operating model, the human-centric management platform, the emphasis on customer engagement, and the partnerships that they continuously established were critical elements that contributed to Reliance Jio's growth and success.					

References

1. Grady McGregor, June 20, 2020, "11 Deals for $15 Billion in 10 Weeks: Why India's Jio Platforms Is on an Investment Spree," Fortune, fortune.com/2020/06/20/mukesh-ambani-jio-platforms-deals/
2. Chris Duckett, May 5, 2020, "Reliance Jio Gets ₹5,656 Crore from Private Equity Firm Silver Lake," ZDNet, www.zdnet.com/article/reliance-jio-gets-5656-crore-from-private-equity-firm-silver-lake/
3. Rajni Gupta, Nov 7, 2016, "Telecommunications Liberalisation: Critical Role of Legal and Regulatory Regime," Economic and Political Weekly, www.epw.in/journal/2002/17/special-articles/telecommunications-liberalisation.html
4. "Brand India," IBEF, www.ibef.org/industry/telecommunications/showcase
5. K. Reddy Sai Sravanth, K. Reddy Sai, et al., 2019, "PEST Analysis of Present Indian Telecom Sector," International Journal of Innovative Technology and Exploring Engineering Regular Issue, 9(2), pp. 4938–4942, doi:10.35940/ijitee.b6384.129219.
6. Ashish Kumar, 2017, "Turning Red Ocean More Red: Impact of Entry of Reliance Jio in Hyper-Competitive Indian Telecommunication Industry," Jaipuria International Journal of Management Research, 3(2), p. 86, doi:10.22552/jijmr/2017/v3/i2/162948.
7. ET Bureau, July 4, 2019, "Telecom Industry May Contribute 8.2% to GDP by 2020 by Leveraging 5G," The Economic Times, https://economictimes.indiatimes.com/industry/telecom/telecom-news/telecom-industry-may-contribute-8-2-to-gdp-by-2020-by-leveraging-5g/articleshow/70071849.cms?from=mdr
8. Manish Singh, June 19, 2020, "How Reliance Jio Platforms Became India's Biggest Telecom Network," TechCrunch, https://techcrunch.com/2020/06/19/how-reliance-jio-platforms-became-indias-biggest-telecom-network/
9. Aditya Gupta, Kushagra Raghav, and Parth Dhakad, 2019, "The Effect on the Telecom Industry and Consumers after the Introduction of Reliance Jio," International Journal of Engineering and Management Research, 9, pp. 118–137, 10.31033/ijemr.9.3.16.
10. Raveend, et al., Aug 5, 2020, "List of Top 5 Telecom Companies in India 2020," Indian Companies. in, https://indiancompanies.in/top-telecom-companies-in-india-market-share/
11. Gagandeep Kaur, June 9, 2020, "Who's Invested What (and Why) in India's Jio Platforms?" Light Reading, www.lightreading.com/asia/whos-invested-what-(and-why)-in-indias-jio-platforms/d/d-id/761548
12. Vijay Govindarajan, and Gunjan Bagla, Dec 27, 2016, "Doing Business in India Requires a Mobile-First Strategy," Harvard Business Review, hbr.org/2016/12/doing-business-in-india-requires-a-mobile-first strategy
13. Vidhi Choudhary, Mar 30, 2016, "Reliance Jio Initial Investment at Rs 150,000 Crore: Mukesh Ambani," Livemint, www.livemint.com/Companies/ncT04NLRTtEMDEHAWdMPGN/Reliance-Jio-initial-investment-at-Rs150000-crore-Mukesh-A.html
14. Aditya Narayan, "Disrupting the Telecom Industry – Reliance Jio: Market Entry Strategy," www.linkedin.com/pulse/disrupting-telecom-industry-reliance-jio-market-entry-narayan
15. Neelam Tyagi, "Reliance Jio and JioMart: Marketing Strategy, SWOT Analysis, and Working Ecosystem," Analytics Steps, www.analyticssteps.com/blogs/reliance-jio-and-jiomart-marketing-strategy-swot-analysis-and-working-ecosystem
16. www.ciim.in, Sep 8, 2016, "Reliance Jio's Marketing Strategy and Case Study," Chandigarh Institute of Internet Marketing – Ciim.in, www.ciim.in/reliance-jios-marketing-strategy-case-study
17. https://Theresearchershub.com/Wp-Content/Uploads/2018/08/Dissertation-on-Telecom-Industry.pdf
18. Online, ET, Mar 30, 2018, "Reliance Jio: Airtel: Jio vs Airtel vs Vodafone Offers: Choose the Best 4G Data Plan," Economic Times, https//economictimes.indiatimes.com/news/company/corporate-trends/jio-vs-airtel-vs-vodafone-offers-choose-the-best-4g-data-plan/articleshow/63480951.cms

19. Newley Purnell, Sep 5, 2018, "Two Years Ago, India Lacked Fast, Cheap Internet-One Billionaire Changed All That," The Wall Street Journal, Dow Jones & Company, www.wsj.com/articles/two-years-ago-india-lacked-fast-cheap-internetone-billionaire-changed-all-that-1536159916
20. JioFiber, Feb 8, 2020, "Jio Fiber Optic Cable Network Map," JioFiber.Info, https://jiofiber.info/jio-fiber-optic-cable-network-map/
21. Alok Soni, May 31, 2014, "13 Inspiring Quotes by Dhirubhai Ambani Teaching You How to Dream Big," YourStory.com, https://yourstory.com/2014/05/dhirubhai-ambani-quotes
22. Sunny Sen, Jan 30, 2018, "Mukesh Ambani's Army of Expats at Jio," Livemint, www.livemint.com/Industry/lHFD4WXCoWs4BPdiYgdFKJ/Mukesh-Ambanis-army-of-expats-at-Jio.html
23. Josh Bersin, Feb 14, 2020, "Reliance, One Of The Largest Companies In India, Takes HR Very Seriously," Josh Bersin, https://joshbersin.com/2020/02/reliance-one-of-the-largest-companies-in-india-takes-hr-very-seriously/
24. Chris Duckett, May 1, 2020, "Reliance Jio Sees 2020 Net Profit Jump by 88%," ZDNet, www.zdnet.com/article/reliance-jio-sees-2020-net-profit-jump-by-88/
25. "Reliance Jio's Q4 Net Profit Soars to Whopping 177.5% at Rs 2,331 Cr, Revenue Jumps 27% to Rs 14,835 Cr – Business News, Firstpost," Apr 30, 2020, Firstpost, www.firstpost.com/business/reliance-jios-q4-net-profit-soars-to-whopping-177-5-at-rs-2331-cr-revenue-jumps-27-to-rs-14835-cr-8317841.html
26. Itu Rathore, et al., May 8, 2020, "Reliance Jio Average Monthly Data and Voice Usage in India," Dazeinfo, https://dazeinfo.com/2019/12/18/reliance-jio-average-monthlydata-and-voice-usage-in-india-graphfarm/
27. Hitesh Bhasin, Dec 18, 2018, "SWOT Analysis of Reliance Jio – Reliance Jio SWOT," Marketing91, www.marketing91.com/swot-analysis-of-reliance-jio/
28. Rajesh Kurup, "Three Years After Launch, Reliance Jio Is Ready with More Disruptions," @Businessline, The Hindu BusinessLine, Sep 5, 2019, www.thehindubusinessline.com/info-tech/three-years-after-launch-reliance-jio-is-ready-

Case 4: Stryker Case Study – Design Thinking Response to COVID-19

Kyle Geiger

Stephen M. Ross School of Business, University of Michigan
kpgeiger@umich.edu

Overview of the problem

Devastation following the coronavirus outbreak continues, reaching 21,250,743 confirmed cases and 766,648 deaths worldwide as of August 15, 2020[1]. What does this mean for companies operating within the medical sector? Companies – and healthcare professionals alike – are hurrying to stay ahead of the rising trend of cases and ever-growing curve. The US – in less than a three-week period – recorded nearly a million new cases, surpassing five million on August 9, 2020, and resting at 5.3 million as of August 15, 2020[2]. This need for quick innovation is only further exacerbated by areas of high case counts – such as Texas – facing the reality of overcapacity and resulting shortages; an antiviral drug that "shows promise for treating COVID-19 patients" is in jeopardy of shortage; hospitals have nearly exhausted their supply of ventilators and are considering the use of older, less optimal models; and with space and hospital beds running low, hospitals are forced to perform patient care in lobbies and conference rooms[3].

Introduction to Stryker

Stryker Corporation, operating within the industry of medical technology, is tied to the solution. Founded in 1941 by Dr. Homer Stryker of Kalamazoo, Michigan, the company was born out of dissatisfaction with current medical products. Initially named the Orthopedic Frame Company, Dr. Stryker prided himself in innovation. With innovations such as the Wedge Turning Frame, which enabled spine immobilization as patients with serious back injuries were turned, and the patented oscillating saw, sales reached one million by 1958[4].

Switching names in 1964 to Stryker Corporation once his son took over, the company continued to climb in success. Within 15 years of the name change, Stryker hit over $17.3M in sales and went public in 1979. Since going public, Stryker has consistently landed on the Fortune 500 list since 2003 and passed $10B in sales in 2016[5].

Despite the success, Stryker's mission stays fixed. With quality first in mind, Stryker is "driven to make healthcare better for its customers by providing innovative products and services that meet regulatory requirements through its effective quality system."[6] Further bolstered by the values of integrity, accountability, people, and the ability to grow talent, and performance, Stryker created a company successful in financials and people diversity. In the 2019 Annual Review, $14.9B in sales were made; 44% came

DOI: 10.4324/9781003190837-25

from the medical and surgical subsector; 21% came from neurotechnology and spine; and 35% came from orthopedics. With the industry of medical technology making $407B in sales[7], Stryker's market share is approximately 3.7%. In terms of diversity success, Stryker's board of directors is considered one of the most diverse within the industry with 40% female representation and 50% non-white representation[8].

Response to COVID-19

Although the information surrounding the outbreak changes daily in its magnitude and overall effect, Stryker commits itself to be a source of stability. Stryker is responsible for the availability of treatments performed by healthcare professionals. To maintain the mission of putting people first, President and COO Timothy J. Scannell released a statement reassuring that "meeting service and supply needs"[9] is of extreme focus. The pandemic opens an opportunity up for Stryker to showcase its innovation channels. These channels have long been part of Stryker's strategy to fortify its three main segments. To better the conditions for healthcare professionals, Stryker developed a response effort that has the following concentrations: "Caregiver safety, data solutions, increased volume, and patient outcomes."[10] "Caregiver safety" focuses on implementing barriers of protection against exposure and minimizing time in contact with those exposed; "data solutions" deals with increasing the ease of patient data collection using software and using the provided software to create an effective prognosis for treatment. "Increased volume" streamlines the supply chain to better production efficiencies, providing healthcare professionals with the needed beds, stretchers, defibrillators, and surgical technologies. In addition to the increased production of pre-existing products, Stryker has created "a low-cost, limited-edition bed" called the Emergency Relief Bed. Its purpose is to allow responders and caregivers more efficient patient movement and closes the growing gap of beds needed. This product is a testament to Stryker's powerful internal innovation, as the Emergency Relief Bed took just two weeks "from design to launch"[11] to bring to the frontlines. Stryker also pledges to "manufacture 10,000 beds per week,"[12] which displays supply chain strength. Finally, "patient outcomes" increases the production of "hygiene, disinfecting, and surgical protection products."[13] With this four-pronged response in effect, it makes a stranger to Stryker wonder this: What enables Stryker to react quickly in the face of disaster?

Approach to innovation

At Stryker, acquisitions and internal innovations are central to the ascent in annual growth rates; Stryker continues to grow in annual sales growth – reaching 40 years of straight growth – as well as a compounded annual growth rate (CAGR) of 16.2%[14] within those 40 years. Despite there being two components to Stryker's innovation strategy, the financial benefit is not evenly distributed. As seen on the 2019 Annual Review, Stryker reported a sales growth of 9.4%. Of that 9.4%, 2.6% yielded from acquisitions and 9.0% yielded from increased unit volume and product choice; foreign exchange negatively impacted the 11.6% increase by 1.3%, and lower prices contributed a hit of 0.9%[15]. Seeing the discrepancy in gain, it makes you wonder just how Stryker distinguishes an opportunity as an acquisitional or innovational gain. According to John Daniel – Vice President of Stryker's Neurovascular Research & Development – "proof-of-concept phases drive decisions on whether Stryker makes or

216 Case studies

buys new technologies."[16] Taking on a sort of "hybrid innovation," those taking part in Stryker's R&D assess the competencies and technologies needed for the proposed solution. If outside ideas and resources present themselves as meritorious, M&A may be the course of action. However, if an opportunity presents itself that is both realistic with internal capacity and solves unmet needs and clinical challenges, Stryker will employ an internal innovation operation using design thinking. Innovation is so central to Stryker's operations that it continues to invest "north of 6% of sales [on R&D]"[17] and has not canceled any of its R&D projects.

Design thinking

Started at Stanford University, design thinking is pivotal to innovation at Stryker. This methodology is revered so much that the process is institutionalized within the creative thinking process. Now what exactly is design thinking? Design thinking is a social technology. It helps to rid human biases and behavioral norms from the framing and experimentation processes that block untapped creativity[18] when brainstorming. Working to the benefit of Stryker, design thinking works best when utilized by a diverse team. Voted as the best workplace for diversity in the US by Forbes and Great Place to Work, the diversity of Stryker adds lasting value. By having a wide diversity of thought, groupthink is lessened, forcing the employees to expand talents creatively and analytically. This growth taps into the founding value of people at the company. Stryker founded the workshop Think Twice to further emphasize the worth of design thinking, directly challenging unconscious biases. Since launching, over 4,000 employees and 16 countries have taken part[19].

A more open mind leads to more efficient partnerships with customers – most often physicians in the case of Stryker. Creating a network composed of close relations, Stryker can tap into the "immersion" process of customer research, "taking the time to listen to customers' needs and shaping decisions by translating those inputs into product design."[20] In the case of the coronavirus pandemic, Stryker identified through its personal connections within the healthcare profession that medical materials and bedding were running low and hospital expenditures were at a high. This need for higher volume and a more budget-conscious alternative for medical supplies became more evident as elected officials, healthcare providers, and healthcare systems "requested additional resources and financial support."[21] Governor Gretchen Whitmer of Michigan made public her letter directed at President Trump that sought federal funding for the distribution of medical supplies.

Continuing along the steps of design thinking, Stryker entered the stage of "alignment," skipping the stage of "sense making" as the looming pandemic created a common database of insights and next steps[22]. Stryker did not constrain itself to simply producing the most cost-effective hospital bed. Instead, it focused on the possibility of a versatile product. Of use in "triage centers and pop-up areas of care, to the emergency department, and in-patient hospital general departments,"[23] Stryker mass-produced an ideal product; varying levels of respiratory distress were even accommodated with the angled design of the head of the bed. These features had the intended purpose and alignment for frontline workers to worry less on medical supply levels and focus more on the treatment of their patients.

The Emergency Relief Bed offers a complementary product that connects the "caregiver safety" and "increased volume" components of Stryker's response to COVID-19.

The complementary product – called the Emergency Relief Patient Cover – can be used on any bedding or stretcher to reduce exposure of "airborne particulates"[24] between patient and healthcare provider. In conjunction with required Personal Protective Equipment (PPE), the patient cover serves to add an additional layer of protection, easing the minds of those on the frontlines – a positive externality to its design.

Due to the compressed timeline of both innovations, Stryker's design thinking, as illustrated in Exhibit 4.1, underwent a rapid progression and adjustment within the remaining phases of "generate idea" and its "test experience."[25] "Deliberation" within the "generate idea" step was simple. For the launching of a new hospital bed and thus the expansion of the medical and surgical equipment portfolio to be justifiable, conditions of a heightened need must be presented. Primarily using direct feedback from healthcare professionals and customers, Stryker gained an irrefutable perspective of need for a product design that was both simple in construction and versatile in use. Even though the company started in 1941, the Stryker teams of today still hold the following ideology at the core of operations and innovations: "If your tools do not work, make them work. If you cannot make them work, make some that do."[26] With large metropolitan areas like Atlanta forced to reactivate temporary medical centers to accommodate for patient overflow, time became a constraint on the ideation cycle like never before[27].

Emergency Relief Bed: From concept to launch

The concept began on Friday, March 2020 at almost midnight[28]. The Director of Advanced Operations at Stryker's Medical Division, Dean Birkmeier, was working. The need for beds was apparent; however, none of Stryker's existing product lines could be mass-produced in a timely manner due to bottlenecks associated with customization. According to Birkmeier, the Medical Division needed to figure out a solution that streamlined logistics and the supply chain, all while using "readily available materials"[29] to minimize waste associated with wait times. With an unprecedented emphasis on the speed of the deliverable, Stryker ventured into the unknown terrain of disruptive supply chain and iterative product innovation.

Stryker conceptualized the bedding innovation in a team of 120, comprised of the medical, instruments, and joint replacement divisions[30]. To stay close to its customers and remain independently creative in thought, Stryker employs a "decentralized approach to R&D."[31] With time ticking by seen as a waste of resources and negligent toward its healthcare customers, Stryker's decentralization offers immediacy within response[32]. This immediacy proved pivotal in the backdrop of COVID-19. According to Birkmeier, "Everything from manufacturing to regulatory filings needed to be carefully orchestrated to run concurrently in an extremely curtailed time frame."[33] It is also important to note that with decentralized operations, coordination failure can occur due to lack of communication, and misaligned incentives and priorities.

With alignment of the product solidified – as discussed previously – Stryker quickly designed a prototype of the bed and developed a vertically integrated supply chain that enabled regional manufacturing to increase global market penetration. As the incentive behind this product innovation was identical among involved parties – creating an affordable and available solution to COVID overcrowding – Stryker was able to avoid coordination failure and nonoptimal supply chain performance. Though

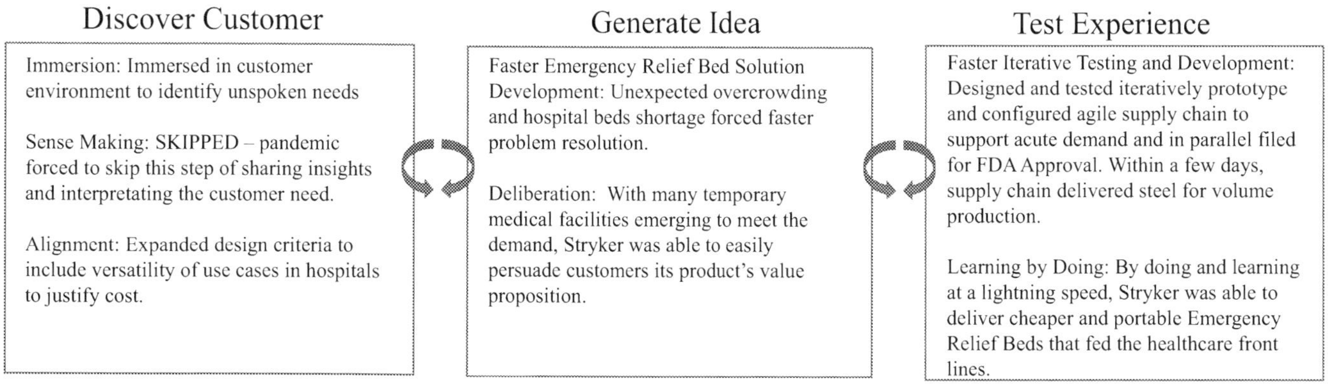

Discover Customer

Immersion: Immersed in customer environment to identify unspoken needs

Sense Making: SKIPPED – pandemic forced to skip this step of sharing insights and interpretating the customer need.

Alignment: Expanded design criteria to include versatility of use cases in hospitals to justify cost.

Generate Idea

Faster Emergency Relief Bed Solution Development: Unexpected overcrowding and hospital beds shortage forced faster problem resolution.

Deliberation: With many temporary medical facilities emerging to meet the demand, Stryker was able to easily persuade customers its product's value proposition.

Test Experience

Faster Iterative Testing and Development: Designed and tested iteratively prototype and configured agile supply chain to support acute demand and in parallel filed for FDA Approval. Within a few days, supply chain delivered steel for volume production.

Learning by Doing: By doing and learning at a lightning speed, Stryker was able to deliver cheaper and portable Emergency Relief Beds that fed the healthcare front lines.

Exhibit 4.1 Design thinking: Stryker's Emergency Relief Bed [23,26]. Adapted from https://hbr.org/2018/09/why-design-thinking-works

iterative experiences are a characteristic of design thinking, Stryker's truncated production schedule sped up physician feedback regarding product performance. On March 27, 2020, seven days after the idea's introduction, Stryker completed the limited-release Emergency Relief Bed. Learning in action, the company identified an issue in the current supply chain and manufacturing of medical supplies – specifically bedding. The revered technological savviness of Stryker was for once a hindrance in the production of necessary supplies, as customization increased wait times. In a period where increased wait times result in fatal endings, unsafe overcapacity, and diverted attention in attending professionals, Dean Birkmeier and his team engaged in abridged design thinking. As a technology company, it can be easy to overlook simple solutions. Through the implementation of design thinking, Stryker allowed itself to overcome individualistic human biases[34] and instead turn toward the strong partnerships it has built with physicians and healthcare professionals. The usage of an iterative approach based on feedback increases employee and customer buy-in and drives home the mission: "Together with our customers, we are driven to make healthcare better."[35] The social technology garners a company-wide commitment to change and enforces a learning process within innovation, which Stryker embraces. To Stryker, innovation is a conversation between two parties; it is a conversation that consolidates the four core values: 1) Integrity – doing what is right; 2) Accountability – doing what is promised; 3) People – shaping innovators through collaboration; and 4) Performance – giving back fully to those directly affected by innovators' actions[36].

That is not to say, however, that Stryker's innovation did not run into obstacles.

Roadblocks

In the case of Stryker's response efforts to COVID-19, the company experienced two main issues: The availability of required materials and Food and Drug Administration (FDA) approval. Based out of the US, Stryker's initiative to create a low-cost, readily available solution to serve those battling the influx of COVID hospitalization relied on the usage of steel. However, in a project of this magnitude, sourcing for this input proved difficult. Stryker has a weekly manufacturing target of 10,000 Emergency Relief Beds. Coupled with the announcement of donating more than "22,500 Emergency Relief Bed Kits to Project C.U.R.E."[37] that released on August 13, 2020, the project requires more steel than from "New York to Dallas."[38] To make matters worse, Stryker had to innovate within a shrinking economy. From February to March 2020, national unemployment rose from 3.5% to 4.4%[39], restricting operational steel sources. To combat this, Stryker expanded its search to steel mills and service centers in the US and Canada and eventually secured sources for the project.

FDA approval has been granted for the limited release of the Emergency Relief Bed, however the Patient Cover has yet to be cleared. The cover is "authorized for use by healthcare providers in contact with patients known or suspected to have COVID-19 under the Emergency Use Authorization for Protective Barrier Enclosures."[40] With review of applications taking anywhere from six months if under Priority Review to ten months if under Standard Review[41], Stryker has encountered a time lag due to bureaucracy. While the FDA offers timely review through the "Accelerated Program," the Patient Cover was not deemed as novel enough to fill an unmet medical need in the treatment of illness[42]. Although innovation was quick due to the pressurized situation

220 *Case studies*

	Three Months			Six Months		
	2020	2019	% Change	2020	2019	% Change
Net Sales	$2,764	$3,650	(24.3)	$6,352	$7,166	(11.4)
Cost of Sales	1,216	1,270	-	2,473	2,503	-
Gross Profit	$1,548	$2,380	(35.0)	$3,879	$4,663	(16.8)
R&D Expenses	233	246	-	487	471	-
SGA Expenses	1,225	1,282	-	2,555	2,685	-
Recall Charges	-	117	-	(6)	130	-
Amortization of Intangible Assets	110	122	-	228	236	-
Total Operating Expenses	$1,568	$1,767	(11.3)	$3,264	$3,522	(7.3)
Operating Income (Loss)	$(20)	$613	(103.3)	$615	$1,141	(46.1)
Other Income (Expenses), Net	(67)	(48)	-	(112)	(96)	-
Earnings (Loss) Before Income Taxes	$(87)	$565	(115.4)	$503	$1,045	(51.9)
Income Taxes	(4)	85	-	93	153	-
Net Earnings (Loss)	$(83)	$480	(117.3)	$410	$892	(54.0)

Exhibit 4.2 Stryker's statement of earnings

Source: https://s22.q4cdn.com/857738142/files/doc_financials/2020/q2/50330860-6cdd-4189-a8af-dbe8f6661a27.pdf

of a pandemic, governmental regulations and regulatory systems have lengthened the process and production cycle.

Outcome

These bounds toward innovation are seen within Stryker's Statement of Earnings as illustrated in Exhibits 4.2 and 4.3.

Although Q1 of 2020 was seen with lower research, development, and engineering expenses, Q2 surpassed that of 2019 by 3.3%. It is important to note that despite falling sales, Stryker is continuing to push a culture of innovation. However, Stryker's continuing trend of declining sales in Q2 is not an isolated incident within the competitive landscape. While Stryker sales have fallen 11.4% from $7,166M in Q2 of 2019 to $6,352M in Q2 of 2020, competitors have also experienced similar decreases in sales and profitability, pointing toward COVID-19 as a negative macro trend. Johnson & Johnson report a decline of 10.8% in sales[43]; another medical device manufacturer – Boston Scientific – took an even bigger hit, with sales showcasing a 23.9% decline[44]. The environment of COVID-19 has negatively impacted

	Three Months			Six Months		
	2020	**2019**	**% Change**	**2020**	**2019**	**% Change**
Orthopedics						
Knees	$241	$440	-	$673	$879	-
Hips	216	343	-	532	679	-
Trauma & Extremities	330	394	-	722	790	-
Other	107	96	-	189	175	-
Orthopedics Total	$894	$1,273	(29.8)	$2,116	$2,523	(16.1)
MedSurg						
Instruments	$328	$504	-	$841	$965	-
Endoscopy	316	480	-	771	950	-
Medical *Only line to outperform 2019	632	542	16.6	1,219	1,073	13.6
Sustainability	48	75	-	115	140	-
MedSurg Total	$1,324	$1,601	(17.3)	$2,946	$3,124	(5.7)
Neurotechnology & Spine	**$(20)**	**$613**	**(103.3)**	**$615**	**$1,141**	**(46.1)**
Neurotechnology	$369	$484	-	$852	$953	-
Spine	177	292	-	438	562	-
NS Total	$546	$776	(29.6)	$1,290	$1,515	(14.9)
TOTAL SALES	**$2,764**	**$3,650**	**(24.3)**	**$6,352**	**$7,166**	**(11.4)**

Exhibit 4.3 Stryker's net sales by product Line

Source: https://s22.q4cdn.com/857738142/files/doc_financials/2020/q2/50330860-6cdd-4189-a8af-dbe8f6661a27.pdf

customer sales due to declining confidence in the economy. According to McKinsey, "discretionary categories are 30–60% net intent when compared to pre-COVID."[45] As a result of the pandemic's drain on hospitals, demand for elective surgeries and equipment are minimized.

Positively, Stryker's MedSurg division performed the best during the pandemic. With most innovations attributed to the medical product line like the Emergency Relief Bed, Q1 2020 outperformed 2019 by 16.6% and maintained a 13.6% outperformance in Q2. These metrics, when analyzed individually rather than collectively, attest to Stryker's strength in innovation. With social technology, internal innovation demonstrated needed flexibility in the presence of a crisis. Dr. Homer Stryker's legacy began "with a bed and a commitment to innovation."[46] Stryker's adherence to that legacy is unremitting. Whether it is quick innovation to serve the frontlines of a crisis or the newest stroke care technology, Stryker innovates effectively while never changing its core message: making healthcare better every day.

Takeaways

So, what can we learn by looking at how Stryker dealt with the bedding crisis regarding COVID-19? Stryker, through its close relationships with its clients on the frontlines of healthcare, was able to identify an opportunity for innovation. This innovation stemmed from a global crisis, though for simplicity we are looking at the crisis through the lens of the US. To fulfill this unmet need, Stryker created the Emergency Relief Bed. However, in creating this low-cost, versatile model, Stryker had to modify its approach to design. Stryker has a strength in the customization of hospital equipment; given the landscape of COVID-19, customizable parts for mass production and quick operations was infeasible. This yielded a relatively simple iterative medical innovation and made Stryker agile within its innovation.

By utilizing design thinking during the planning process, Stryker was able to address the main purposes of its product innovation: Quick distribution and versatile function as temporary facilities, hallways, lobbies, and many other locations open and fill up with patients.

Summary of key events

- Problem: Hospitals became overcrowded and ran out of supplies and beds
- Solution: Create a simple and affordable hospital bed design that can be produced quickly and sent to healthcare facilities
- Approach: Eliminate custom design and parts, show flexibility in solution response
- Process: Focus on the insights gathered during customer discovery and deliberate the solution quickly. Reconfigure supply chain to be nimble and responsive
- Roadblocks: Try to source steel in a contracting economy. Receive FDA approval just for the bed and not for the complementary patient cover
- Workaround: Source steel locally – US and Canada
- Delivery: Within seven days, idea to solution realization. Shipped to non-US markets as well

Questions

1) What synergies exist between Stryker's diverse workforce and design thinking? Why do you think that is, and how does it facilitate innovation?
2) How did the COVID-19 pandemic encourage Stryker to fully embrace iterative and agile thinking in the context of the Emergency Relief Bed?
3) In the context of a pandemic/crisis, are the linear steps of design thinking helpful to innovation? If so, why? If not, why not? Would you choose to keep any aspects in your modified decision-making framework?
4) How has Stryker's mission to make healthcare better with its customers influenced decisions made in response to the COVID-19 outbreak?
5) How was Stryker able to grow its medical product line when consumer confidence has fallen? Was Stryker's approach to innovation and its customers related to this growth?
6) What enabled Stryker to expedite its innovation cycle? How was the company able to avoid time being wasted – one of the seven types of muda (Japanese term for waste)? (Hint: Think about the "three rights to expect.")

Notes

1 www.cnn.com/interactive/2020/health/coronavirus-maps-and-cases/
2 www.nationalgeographic.com/science/2020/05/graphic-tracking-coronavirus-infections-us/
3 www.texastribune.org/2020/07/14/texas-hospitals-coronavirus/
4 www.stryker.com/us/en/about/history.html
5 Ibid
6 www.stryker.com/us/en/about.html
7 www.forbes.com/sites/brucejapsen/2019/09/23/report-medical-technology-sales-soar-but-rd-fails-to-link-patients/#68b098152b32
8 www.stryker.com/us/en/about/our-board-of-directors.html
9 www.stryker.com/us/en/covid19/coo.html
10 www.stryker.com/content/stryker/us/en/covid19.html
11 http://bi.gale.com.proxy.lib.umich.edu/global/article/GALE%7CA624352740?u=umuser
12 www.stryker.com/us/en/acute-care/products/emergency-relief-bed.html
13 www.stryker.com/us/en/covid19/product-focus.html
14 https://s22.q4cdn.com/857738142/files/doc_financials/2019/SYK_AR19_v16_IR-site.pdf
15 https://s22.q4cdn.com/857738142/files/doc_financials/2019/SYK_AR19_v16_IR-site.pdf
16 www.stryker.com/us/en/about/news/features/innovation--design--and-a-look-to-the-future-of-stroke-technolog.html
17 http://bi.gale.com.proxy.lib.umich.edu/global/article/GALE%7CA624352740?u=umuser
18 https://hbr.org/2018/09/why-design-thinking-works
19 https://s22.q4cdn.com/857738142/files/doc_financials/2019/SYK_AR19_v16_IR-site.pdf
20 www.stryker.com/us/en/about/news/features/innovation--design--and-a-look-to-the-future-of-stroke-technolog.html
21 www.healthaffairs.org/doi/full/10.1377/hlthaff.2020.00426
22 https://hbr.org/2018/09/why-design-thinking-works
23 www.stryker.com/us/en/acute-care/products/emergency-relief-bed.html
24 www.stryker.com/us/en/emergency-care/products/emergency-relief-patient-cover.html
25 https://hbr.org/2018/09/why-design-thinking-works
26 www.stryker.com/us/en/about/news/features/from-concept-to-launch-in-7-days--new-emergency-relief-bed.html
27 www.fox5atlanta.com/news/georgia-world-congress-center-to-be-reactivated-for-covid-19-patient-overflow-as-case-numbers-rise
28 www.stryker.com/us/en/about/news/features/from-concept-to-launch-in-7-days--new-emergency-relief-bed.html
29 Ibid
30 Ibid
31 www.stryker.com/us/en/about/news/features/innovation--design--and-a-look-to-the-future-of-stroke-technolog.html
32 https://hbr.org/2017/12/when-to-decentralize-decision-making-and-when-not-to
33 www.stryker.com/us/en/about/news/features/from-concept-to-launch-in-7-days--new-emergency-relief-bed.html
34 https://hbr.org/2018/09/why-design-thinking-works
35 www.stryker.com/us/en/index.html
36 www.stryker.com/us/en/about.html
37 www.stryker.com/us/en/about/news/features/stryker-donates-22-500-emergency-relief-bed-kits-to-project-c-u-.html
38 www.stryker.com/us/en/about/news/features/from-concept-to-launch-in-7-days--new-emergency-relief-bed.html
39 www.bls.gov/opub/ted/2020/unemployment-rates-rose-in-29-states-and-the-district-of-columbia-in-march-2020.htm

224 *Case studies*

40 www.stryker.com/us/en/emergency-care/products/emergency-relief-patient-cover.html
41 www.fda.gov/drugs/development-approval-process-drugs
42 www.fda.gov/media/82381/download
43 www.investor.jnj.com/johnson-johnson-reports-2020-second-quarter-results
44 https://news.bostonscientific.com/2020-07-29-Boston-Scientific-Announces-Results-For-Second-Quarter-2020
45 www.mckinsey.com/business-functions/marketing-and-sales/our-insights/survey-us-consumer-sentiment-during-the-coronavirus-crisis
46 www.stryker.com/us/en/about/news/features/from-concept-to-launch-in-7-days--new-emergency-relief-bed.html

Case 5: The Whirlpool Corporation in 2020

Whirlpool – A History of Sustained Innovation from Within

Malik Abbasi

Stephen M. Ross School of Business, University of Michigan
abbasima@umich.edu

Summary

The Whirlpool Corporation is the world's largest manufacturer and producer of home "white-goods" – kitchen and laundry appliances. Currently led by CEO Marc Bitzer, Whirlpool manufactures goods in 13 countries, and sells products in nearly every corner of the world, with revenues of approximately $20B in 2019. Major competitors in the space include Samsung, LG, Electrolux, Philips, GE and more. Since being founded in 1911, Whirlpool has made major strides globalizing its supply chain and creating new products for customers. However, competition has risen alongside Whirlpool, challenging their market share and profitability. To combat increasing competition, stagnating revenues, and scarcely differentiated products around the year 1999, an innovation revolution occurred inside the corporation. The internal mantra behind R&D was completely changed to be inclusive of all employees, always, in all functions. Whirlpool adopted open innovation models within the company, encouraging employees to think of ways to better serve customers' unspoken desires. The changes were successful and, since 1999, Whirlpool has continued to dominate the home appliances market through product innovations and strategic partnerships.

Background

Very few companies can boast the accomplishment of being in business for over 100 years. Major innovation and adaptation responding to market charges are needed for an organization to have a lifespan of over a century. The Whirlpool Corporation is one such corporation that has endured and thrived over the past century. Founded in 1911 in Benton Harbor, Michigan, Whirlpool was founded after Lou Upton patented an electric-motor-driven washing machine. After the cast-iron transmission gear failed in each one of the 100 washers sold in their first order, Upton set a precedent for customer service and innovated by replacing each part with a new steel gear. For the next 100 years, Whirlpool has continued to innovate to make life easier and more efficient in homes of consumers around the world. Today, the Whirlpool Corporation is the world's largest global manufacturer of home, kitchen, and laundry appliances, including washers, dryers, refrigerators, freezers, and more. The company produces goods in 13 countries and sells products in nearly every corner of the world. The company has enjoyed a 130% stock price increase since 2010, the last recession when the

DOI: 10.4324/9781003190837-26

financial market meltdown was experienced, and now has a market capitalization of $14.5B and more than $21.7B in 2021 revenue.

Problem

Business has not always been as prosperous as in recent years. In the late 1990s, the home appliance market was beginning to stagnate, and Whirlpool's growth slowed. Companies in the home appliance space were beginning to fight over even fractional percentage point improvements in market share not only in the US, but as they expanded out into the global market. Manufacturers competed to improve their products' quality, add new features, and become more energy-efficient. Despite these innovations, to gain market share Whirlpool had to sell their machines for the same price as others, not raise them, to remain competitive. Profit margins shrank, and combined with rapid globalization by competitors, Whirlpool was left at a defining moment. Exhibit 5.1 illustrates net sales over time. Ex-CEO Jeff M. Fettig was quoted as saying the following: "By 1999 it was clear to us at Whirlpool that there was "something" critical missing in our strategy. Growth rates were flat, average selling prices were going down, and margins had become a cost game. We somewhat reluctantly concluded after deep soul searching that the "something" was innovation." [1]

Solution

To combat stagnating revenues and increasing competition in the global market, an innovation revolution was launched inside the corporation. Ex-CEO David Whitwam believed Whirlpool could gain a sustainable advantage in the home appliance industry by focusing on fulfilling unarticulated customer needs. "[Whitwam] called this a Brand-Focused Value Creation Strategy, which would emphasize creating new platforms. The key to sustainable competitive advantage would be setting a new pace of innovation for the industry." [2] David Whitwam then appointed Nancy Tennant Snyder, Chief Innovation Officer, to spearhead reimagining the internal strategy of the 90-year-old manufacturing company. By attempting to embed innovation into every facet of the company, Whirlpool would become more lean, agile, and competitive. They would

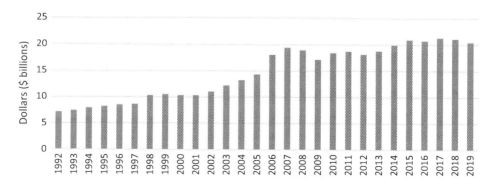

Exhibit 5.1 Whirlpool net sales.
Data Source: Whirlpool Earning Reports and 10-K Filings [5–30]

be able to create products that pushed the boundaries of what customers knew. This would not be an easy feat; embedding innovation across a corporation as large as Whirlpool would take many years to accomplish, and the process would never be truly done – if it were, then would the company truly be committed to innovation?

Rather than funding a specific "innovation division" that would consist of engineers and businesspeople out to think up the next best thing, Whirlpool encourages participation from everyone in the company. By creating tools and frameworks for general innovation, any department can devise new ways to push the envelope and better serve customers. Some of these are tangible tools, such as company-wide forums for innovative thought sharing. They include dashboards created for executives to track the latest and greatest innovations as they develop. Other tools are intangible and come in the form of knowledge transmitted through "I-mentors." I-mentors are specifically trained individuals within Whirlpool that excel at facilitating innovation within their teams. I-mentor skills can include structured brainstorming sessions, making proper business cases for new products, capitalizing on opportunity, and more. By getting the knowledge of proper innovation tactics out into the open, Whirlpool began the first phases of embedding innovation with I-mentors.

Once the concepts and ideas of innovation began to make their rounds within the company, leaders had to make criteria and define what innovation should mean to Whirlpool. After all, the corporation was encouraging innovation everywhere, but without standards for what it should look like, money and energy might be wasted. The criteria are as follows:

1. Create a unique and compelling solution valued by our customers (end users) and aligned to our brands
2. Create competitive advantage, be part of a sustainable migration path (successive generations of a product, service, or idea that deploys over many years), or both
3. Create differentiated shareholder value [3]

This working definition, combined with the facilitation training of I-mentors, are the foundation of innovation within Whirlpool. An idea created by anybody could be expanded on and developed, then put into the internal innovation pipeline, the "I-pipe." This system is a data collection tool that makes it possible for individuals to look up details of specific projects, active or canceled, to learn from them. Innovation challenges are posted to employees: "We also have tools like an online forum that is a portal that employees and businesses alike can use. Challenges are posted there, and employees are encouraged to create and participate in dialogues." [3] Tools like these embedded innovation from the bottom up, involving every level of employee by crowd-sourcing idea generation and development. At the end of the pipeline, innovation is seen from the opposite direction – the top down. Innovation boards, or "I-boards," are placed to allocate human and capital resources, where decisions are made as to which innovations are worth investing into. Here, long-term strategy and priorities set by executives make their way into the innovation cycle, furthering its embeddedness in Whirlpool.

After these initiatives to ingrain innovation within every fiber of the company were in place for a few years, progress and growth were seen. Nancy Tennant Snyder, CIO at the time, wrote that in 2005 the breakthroughs were apparent within Whirlpool. Tangible results could be measured based on performance of innovations that had reached the market. Reported after the fact was the following: "In 2006, innovation projects created $1 billion of new revenues, out of a total of about $18 billion. In 2007, that figure rose to $2.7 billion out of $19.4 billion. In 2008, it was $4 billion out of $19 billion. Growing revenues from innovation are allowing Whirlpool to maintain its top-line corporate revenue level." [2] There were also intangible results of these efforts: Company culture had become far more collaborative, and new ideas were always encouraged. Whirlpool began attracting talented employees simply because of the embedded innovation; people wanted to work for an innovative company, and for transformative leaders. This, of course, has had a far larger impact than sales growth, because it has carried over to what the company is today.

Fast forward to 2020, and Whirlpool's investment into embedded innovation continues to pay massive dividends. While many competitors took the traditional route of cutting costs and trying to increase margins to stay relevant, Whirlpool invested in the company's future by restructuring. Increased spending on R&D (aka innovation), as presented in Exhibit 5.2 indicates that Whirlpool has no plans of slowing down. Annual reports cite a 3% YoY target for net sales growth fueled by innovation.

Whirlpool today

By embedding innovation within the corporation, Whirlpool has seen a great deal of success following its restructuring and revamp. This can be seen by looking at the rapid increase in net sales from 2000 onward.

Contributing toward increased net sales are many factors that take advantage of embedded innovation. One of these is international sales growth fueled by partnerships and acquisitions. In 1995, Whirlpool purchased Kelvinator of India, and added it to its portfolio of companies. Kelvinator, having been established in India, understood their customers' demographics and preferences well. Kelvinator's expertise in the market, combined with Whirlpool's global manufacturing power, allowed Whirlpool to increase sales in India. By synergizing with this smaller company's resources, Whirlpool was able to penetrate a foreign market much better than it could have

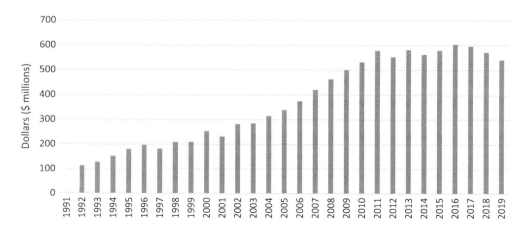

Exhibit 5.2 Whirlpool R&D spending.
Data Source: Whirlpool Earning Reports and 10-K Filings [5–30]

hoped to without them. As different markets have different consumer preferences and competitors, having an established company's viewpoint is invaluable. By taking advantage of the agility that embedded innovation brings, and working with a partner organization, Whirlpool was able to increase international sales.

Whirlpool found similar success in the Latin American market through a different type of innovation model. Instead of partnering with a company who knew the intricacies of Latin American customer demographics, Whirlpool ventured out to redesign an age-old product for a new market – the oven. An excerpt from an interview with Whirlpool Corporation Cooking Designer Wesley Mendez describes their thinking: "All those [Latin American] countries – most of their cuisine is based on the surface, so everything is fried or heated, but now people are willing to invest more in the oven – maybe to roast, maybe to bake." [4] He goes on to explain that redesigning an oven to open outwardly like a refrigerator, rather than downward, would be more appealing and inviting to local customers. He cites it as giving them more control over what is being cooked. Mendez also talks about the unique glass backsplash added to the product for the Latin American market for aesthetics and customer preferences. He concludes by saying, "The combination of improving the design, craftsmanship, fit and finish, touchpoint materials, and this disruptive way of opening the door backed by our focus on usability-improvement – I think that is what makes this new [oven] from Whirlpool Corporation a winning product in the market." [4] Whirlpool's international market growth is presented in Exhibit 5.3.

Most recently, Whirlpool announced a partnership with tech giants Amazon and Google to bring smart-home technology to their products. Integrating Amazon Alexa and Google Home technologies with appliances such as microwaves and washing machines will provide huge time savings and usability benefits for customers. For example, one would be able to check the time remaining on their washing cycle on their phone, or even more easily by asking Alexa. Someone living alone could preheat their oven or use the defrost setting on their microwave before they even reach home. This demonstrates Whirlpool's willingness to innovate alongside partners and

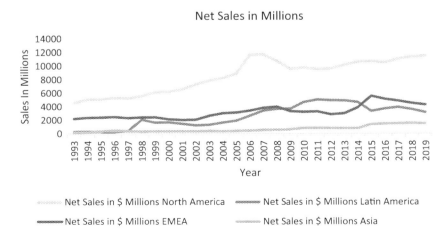

Exhibit 5.3 Whirlpool's international market sales growth.
Data Source: Whirlpool Earning Reports and 10-K Filings [5–30]

230   *Case studies*

the ways in which they can adapt to existing technology and consumer preferences to keep themselves relevant in a competitive market.

Conclusion

The Whirlpool Corporation's enlightenment around innovation during the turn of the millennium created a workplace and organization that fostered growth and new ideas. For the last 20 years, they have been able to take advantage of their innovation pipelines, company culture, and product ideation to learn, grow, and continue doing what they do best: Creating new products to serve their customers better. Expanding their global footprint and product base was the catalyst for Whirlpool's growth to their current size, and relentless commitment to innovation has helped sustain its success.

Takeaways from Whirlpool's innovation revolution include the importance of flexibility, embedded culture, and strong leadership models. By leveraging a long-term strategy that began at both the top and bottom of the company, leaders and employees within Whirlpool were continually exposed to new ideas and innovations, eventually leading to innovation being embedded in the Whirlpool culture. In any organization, large or small, having aligned goals between all stakeholders makes that organization more efficient, attractive, and sustainable. Discovery and invention are bolstered by a supportive environment that allows a group of intelligent professionals to collaborate as efficiently as possible. Furthermore, allowing for experimentation through workplace flexibility was an excellent tactic used by Whirlpool that can be applied to any number of fields.

Case questions

1) Explore and apply the TRIAL© framework and identify possible gaps to sustain innovation. Leverage any online source, including corporate websites for the analysis. Please use TRIAL© framework worksheets by accessing Digital Learning Resources provided with this book.
2) Highlight some of the future challenges that Whirlpool is faced with given the global competition and suggest a few prioritized action items for the CEO to advance and sustain innovation.

References

1. Nancy T. Snyder, and Deborah L. Duarte, "Unleashing Innovation: How Whirlpool Transformed an Industry," Jossey-Bass, 2008.
2. Robert C. Wolcott, October 18, 2010, "Whirlpool: Building an Innovation Culture," www.businessinsider.com/whirlpool-building-an-innovation-culture-2010-10
3. Peter P. Roosen, and Tatsuya Nakagawa, July 14, 2008, "Innovation 101: Whirlpool's Spin on Innovation," IndustryWeek, www.industryweek.com/leadership/companies-executives/article/21933039/innovation-101-whirlpools-spin-on-innovation
4. Whirlpool Corporation, 2020, February 4, "Whirlpool Innovation: Opening New Doors," www.whirlpoolcorp.com/whirlpool-innovation-opening-new-doors/
5. Whirlpool Corporation, 1995, "Form 10-K 1994," https://investors.whirlpoolcorp.com/financial-information/sec-filings/default.aspx

6. Whirlpool Corporation, 1996, "Form 10-K 1995," https://investors.whirlpoolcorp.com/financial-information/sec-filings/default.aspx
7. Whirlpool Corporation, 1997, "Form 10-K 1996," https://investors.whirlpoolcorp.com/financial-information/sec-filings/default.aspx
8. Whirlpool Corporation, 1998, "Form 10-K 1997," https://investors.whirlpoolcorp.com/financial-information/sec-filings/default.aspx
9. Whirlpool Corporation, 1999, "Form 10-K 1998," https://investors.whirlpoolcorp.com/financial-information/sec-filings/default.aspx
10. Whirlpool Corporation, 2000, "Form 10-K 1999," https://investors.whirlpoolcorp.com/financial-information/sec-filings/default.aspx
11. Whirlpool Corporation, 2001, "Form 10-K 2000," https://investors.whirlpoolcorp.com/financial-information/sec-filings/default.aspx
12. Whirlpool Corporation, 2002, "Form 10-K 2001," https://investors.whirlpoolcorp.com/financial-information/sec-filings/default.aspx
13. Whirlpool Corporation, 2003, "Form 10-K 2002," https://investors.whirlpoolcorp.com/financial-information/sec-filings/default.aspx
14. Whirlpool Corporation, 2004, "Form 10-K 2003," https://investors.whirlpoolcorp.com/financial-information/sec-filings/default.aspx
15. Whirlpool Corporation, 2005, "Form 10-K 2004," https://investors.whirlpoolcorp.com/financial-information/sec-filings/default.aspx
16. Whirlpool Corporation, 2006, "Form 10-K 2005," https://investors.whirlpoolcorp.com/financial-information/sec-filings/default.aspx
17. Whirlpool Corporation, 2007, "Form 10-K 2006," https://investors.whirlpoolcorp.com/financial-information/sec-filings/default.aspx
18. Whirlpool Corporation, 2008, "Form 10-K 2007," https://investors.whirlpoolcorp.com/financial-information/sec-filings/default.aspx
19. Whirlpool Corporation, 2009, "Form 10-K 2008," https://investors.whirlpoolcorp.com/financial-information/sec-filings/default.aspx
20. Whirlpool Corporation, 2010, "Form 10-K 2009," https://investors.whirlpoolcorp.com/financial-information/sec-filings/default.aspx
21. Whirlpool Corporation, 2011, Form 10-K 2010," https://investors.whirlpoolcorp.com/financial-information/sec-filings/default.aspx
22. Whirlpool Corporation, 2012, "Form 10-K 2011," https://investors.whirlpoolcorp.com/financial-information/sec-filings/default.aspx
23. Whirlpool Corporation, 2013, "Form 10-K 2012," https://investors.whirlpoolcorp.com/financial-information/sec-filings/default.aspx
24. Whirlpool Corporation, 2014, "Form 10-K 2013," https://investors.whirlpoolcorp.com/financial-information/sec-filings/default.aspx
25. Whirlpool Corporation, 2015, "Form 10-K 2014," https://investors.whirlpoolcorp.com/financial-information/sec-filings/default.aspx
26. Whirlpool Corporation, 2016, "Form 10-K 2015," https://investors.whirlpoolcorp.com/financial-information/sec-filings/default.aspx
27. Whirlpool Corporation, 2017, "Form 10-K 2016," https://investors.whirlpoolcorp.com/financial-information/sec-filings/default.aspx
28. Whirlpool Corporation, 2018, "Form 10-K 2017," https://investors.whirlpoolcorp.com/financial-information/sec-filings/default.aspx
29. Whirlpool Corporation, 2019, "Form 10-K 2018," https://investors.whirlpoolcorp.com/financial-information/sec-filings/default.aspx
30. Whirlpool Corporation, 2020, "Form 10-K 2019," https://investors.whirlpoolcorp.com/financial-information/sec-filings/default.aspx

Case 6: Apple's Swift – A Programming Language Innovation for the Future

Maxwell Cornellier

Stephen M. Ross School of Business, University of Michigan
maxwcorn@umich.edu

Pre-Swift: Apple and Objective-C

The story of Steve Jobs and Steve Wozniak founding Apple Computer Inc. in 1976 and building the Apple I computer in the garage of Jobs' childhood home in Los Altos, California is well known. Less obvious is the fact that nearly a decade later in September 1985 neither of the founding duo were still with Apple. Steve Jobs had decided to resign as chairman of the company following a tumultuous relationship with then CEO John Sculley. With his departure, Jobs announced that he was founding a new computer company focused on powerful workstation computers for academia. However, Jobs also recruited several employees from Apple to leave with him for his new company, NeXT Inc. This led Apple to file a suit against Jobs for poaching the employees, fearing that they would use their knowledge of Apple technology in competition against them. The suit was settled in January 1986 and barred NeXT from using Apple software, operating systems, and requiring that it only make more powerful computers to avoid competition in the consumer segment.

In 1988, Steve Jobs' new company licensed the Objective-C programming language from a company called Stepstone. This language was used to build NeXTSTEP, the operating system that powered NeXT's workstation computers. This is an important moment in Apple's history as the operating systems of Macs, iPads, and iPhones are all fueled in part by applications of this late-20th century operating system. NeXT bought the total rights to the Objective-C programming language in 1995 from Stepstone. In 1996, Apple, which faced low sales and angry investors, purchased NeXT and brought Steve Jobs back to the company he founded in hopes of restoring its market value. Apple also gained the rights to Objective-C with the purchase and the operating system that had been built on it. The operating system developed by NeXTSTEP was the foundation used to build the original macOS and later all of Apple's other current operating platforms: iOS, iPadOS, tvOS, and watchOS. All these platforms and their applications were programmed entirely in Objective-C, first created in 1984, until 2014 and all still include some use of the relatively ancient language in 2020.

When consumers purchased the first Apple iPhone in 2007, they were limited to the apps pre-downloaded onto their device. These included standard native applications found on iPhones today such as the calculator, the safari browser, and the nostalgic YouTube app. Then in July 2008, Apple premiered the App Store with 500 applications available for download. At this point all these native and third-party apps were

DOI: 10.4324/9781003190837-27

written entirely in Objective-C. As of the first quarter of 2020, Apple's App Store had almost 1.85 million applications available for download. However, these applications were not all built with Objective-C; many were built with the foundations for a new chapter in Apple's history, a coding language named "Swift."

Apple Inc. history

Apple has been a strong player since it entered the market for consumer electronics in 1977, today it has risen to one of the top market leaders in the global smart-phone industry as well as the tablet sector for enterprises. The remaining decades in the 20th century saw product growth for the company, a successful initial public offering, but also some mishaps as competition grew. These mishaps caused rotation in the company's leadership, even causing one of its founders, Steve Jobs, to depart the company. Steve Jobs did eventually return to the company as interim CEO in 1997, becoming the full CEO once again 2000. With the full return of Steve Jobs, the 21st century also brought a new page of growth for the company.

Apple's desktop and laptop products continued to develop with new operating systems and the availability of Intel processor chips in 2005. As with many Apple products, the Mac computers are known for their speed and power, used often by developers, producers, and college students alike. Due to their high price point, Apple's consumer computer market share is often below 8% [1]. Still, they are an important and iconic product in Apple's brand, making up about 10% of revenue in 2019 [2]. In 2011, Apple introduced an App Store specifically for Mac operating systems to increase their productivity and differentiation. This innovation has also allowed for more connectivity among the growing family of Apple products. Apple seeks to further strengthen the connectivity and power of the Mac by transitioning to Apple silicon processors. This departure from the Intel processors was announced at the 2020 Apple Worldwide Developers Conference (WWDC) and will make app development more seamless across Apple's multiple software platforms.

This period in Apple's history is most remembered by the release of the original iPod in 2001, and the first iPhone in 2007. The birth of these two influential, disruptive products into the overall Apple ecosystem cemented the legacy of Steve Jobs as a visionary and as an innovator. The iPhone proved to be Apple's most successful product, dominating the market and leading Apple's revenue drivers, making up 54.7% of net sales in 2019 [2]. The iPhone consistently is rated high among US consumers; the iPhone 8, X, and SE all received American Customer Satisfaction Index scores of 83 in 2019, trailing just behind Samsung's Galaxy Note 9 that led with a score of 86 [3]. Samsung is a main competitor of Apple due to its lower price point, which allows it to lead in lower income markets internationally. However, Apple has dominated the North American smartphone market continuously over the last decade as the largest manufacturer. Apple faces success globally as well, being the third-largest seller of smartphones in the first quarter of 2019, despite declining sales in key markets such as China [1].

Despite declining sales and some signs of Apple's growth slowing, investors remain confident in the corporation due to its history of performance and innovation and are optimistic in the growth of its services segments [1]. When Steve Jobs passed away in 2011 following his battle with cancer, some feared for the future of the company. These fears have been proven needless as Job's successor, Tim Cook, has led the company to new heights as Apple became the first public company to reach a market

234 *Case studies*

valuation of $1T in 2018. Apple remains ahead of Alphabet as the US's largest publicly traded company by market capitalization exceeding the $2T mark during 2021.

Apple: Designed in California, powered by a 1984 programming language

The smartphone industry in the US and internationally grew toward saturation as many companies entered the market with low-cost products. While Apple has introduced the more budget-friendly iPhone SE, it is not able to compete with the prices of competitors around the world. Still, the iPhone continues to win over its consumers with quality, innovation, and the value of its brand. The iPhone has strong brand loyalty and recognition that keeps its consumers buying each new iteration of the device for the newest features. With competitors being able to offer similar features and even some new innovations before Apple at a lower cost, Apple started to see smartphone market share erosion.

To combat this, Apple sought to leverage its operating system and exclusive offerings, namely the Apple App Store. To build the best apps and experience for consumers, Apple needed to encourage the best developers and companies to put their software applications on Apple's platform as opposed to the Android Google Play Store. The trouble was that the foundation on which all this growth was being built was using a programming language from the 1980s, Objective-C. Developers, including Apple's internal teams, still use this language today but it is not the best option to harness the potential of Apple's hardware and other software. Chris Lattner, an Apple engineer at the time, recognized the downsides of using Objective-C to support the expansion of Apple. So, in July 2010 he started working on a new programming language that he named Swift [4]. This was the first time Apple had created its own programming language, one that is optimized to enable the full capabilities of Apple's hardware. Swift is more attractive to iOS developers than other modern languages such as Google's Go, an open-source programing language, as it was initially designed specifically for Apple devices, is fully compatible and offers more power [4].

Implementation and evolution of Swift

Swift was built to be easier to learn, faster to use, and to unleash more power on Apple's operating platforms. Subsequently, Lattner introduced the language and continued its development with a few key people at Apple in 2011. Further development continued in 2013 with the Apple Developer Tools team, and finally the first version of the language was announced to the world at the 2014 WWDC.

Throughout this entire creation process the innovation was only known by a small group of people within Apple, in line with the controversial culture of super secrecy inside the company [4]. By limiting the team developing the language at first, Apple was able to construct the core of the language how it envisioned without outside pressure. But once the language was released, the new question was whether people would be excited and adopt the new language. Although biased, its creators were confident that developers would be open to their new language over time due to the benefits that it offered. The benefits mainly were improvements in efficiency, safety, and power over Apple's former designated programming language, Objective-C. These advantages targeted the complaints iOS developers had with Objective-C, as well as others such as the language's confusing syntax [5]. Accordingly, Swift was created with a standard, modern syntax, which allows developers to learn and implement the code safer in a shorter amount of time.

Swift also features an interactive visualization of its code in a program called Swift Playground, available through Xcode (Apple's integrated development environment) on Mac computers or the iPad. This allows developers to visually see what they are coding as they type in real time without recompiling the entire stack. This makes mastering the language faster as it assists in learning what the code does through instant visualization and feedback [4]. Swift Playground is possible due to the ability of Swift to both compile and execute code at fast speeds [4]. This advantage makes it a more efficient tool for developers than Objective-C as it can decrease total build times [5].

Swift open source

A year after its initial release, Apple announced Swift 2.0 at its 2015 WWDC and that the language would become open source with an Apache 2.0 license. This meant that developers would be able to own the copyright to their code and use Swift with very minimal restrictions from Apple. Becoming open source was a major steppingstone for Swift on its journey to becoming a widely adopted coding language, as stated by then VP of Software Engineering, Craig Federighi. In an interview Federighi stated, "[Apple]… saw open sourcing as a critical element to make Swift reach its potential to be the language, the major language for the next 20 years of programming in our industry [6]."

Within the first week of Apple placing the open-source code on GitHub, a popular platform for software developers to collaborate and exchange codes with version controls, the language code had already been cloned around 60,000 times [6]. Early successes such as this were due to a key element of Swift becoming open source. This key element is the ability for developers to port their code outside of the Apple eco-system onto other systems such as Linux. This brings new developers from other programming environments to Swift with a potential to add more quality applications to Apple's App Store. This second offering of the Swift language shows its nature as a growing language that can be nurtured by more outside contributions. Although the portability of the code to other platforms was very limited when the language first transitioned to open source, the nature of open source allowed it to expand. As a result of open source, external and internal contributions have made the language usable with other platforms such as Android and officially with Linux. Hand in hand with this, the overall community, and thus contributors to the language, grew simultaneously. This expansion continued when Apple announced version 5.3 of Swift in March 2020 with official support for Windows operating systems.

These innovations were possible due in part to the dedicated teams working within Apple to increase the power of the language. However, they would not be possible without the input from the development community who use the open-source code. The open-source code and library for Swift is hosted for Apple on Github. Apple also uses Github's community features to improve its code. First, anyone can contribute to a discussion of ideas about the evolution of the language on a forum dedicated to that purpose. Once a thorough discussion has taken place, users are encouraged to submit their ideas as a pull request using the framework laid out in the Swift Programming Language Evolution guide. These requests are then reviewed by teams inside of Apple who decide whether to approve and distribute them with the next version of the language. These ideas can be anything from bug fixes, improvements to make the language faster and stronger, or support on new and existing operating platforms. The forums allow for troubleshooting of problems, bug identification, and, most importantly, a direct line of communication between Apple and those who are using its language. This direct communication and collaboration between Apple and the community has allowed Swift to grow rapidly in a short period of time.

Lyft and Swift open source

Outside the forums, Apple works directly with corporations that use the language to help them leverage it while identifying improvements to be made. An early key example of this was when Lyft decided to rebuild their entire iOS app using Swift in early 2015. The software engineers and programmers at Lyft using Swift started as an experiment with one coder. Its base in the company quickly expanded to their entire iOS development team once the benefits of using the language were realized. The quick adoption of the language inside Lyft is also thanks to how easy it is to learn the language. This was evident for them with Lyft engineers learning the language well enough to implement it in just two to three weeks [7].

The first Swift rebuild of the app required a third of the lines of code written for the original version with Objective-C. Project times were drastically cut down by Swift and the overall app grew as developers were able to use their time more efficiently [7]. The implementation of Swift was a large success for Lyft as it improved the stability, features, and expansion of their application. Lyft's use of language at this early stage also benefited Apple's Swift teams, who received feedback on the language from Lyft's software engineers. There was direct collaboration between the teams inside Apple and Lyft in identifying bugs in the young language and in implementing it [7]. This partnership approach was also taken with others such as Uber and Airbnb, who also built their iOS app with Swift. These improvements in the language helped it spread rapidly into the repertoire of other iOS developers. As of March 2020, there were over 500,000 applications on the Apple App Store that included Swift programming in their build [8].

Spreading Swift through education

However, Apple has much ground to cover before Swift becomes a widespread language used over multiple operating systems. Swift can leverage its quick learnability and the tools offered by Apple, namely Playground, to become a more popular language. Another goal of Apple is to make coding more accessible for everyone through education programs that teach programming languages, including Swift.

Apple launched their Community Education Initiative in 2019 with their "Everyone Can Code" curriculum in schools across the country [9]. This initiative supports communities in need by helping to fund technology costs (iPads) and by implementing STEM into school curriculums to increase education and career opportunities. Apple further expanded this initiative by adding partnerships with ten more Historically Black Colleges and Universities (HBCUs) into its network, which includes a total of 24 locations currently [9]. These HBCUs will serve as regional hubs for coding in their areas that will host programs to support coding, technology, and creativity education

Apple's Swift 237

for people of all ages. These partnerships will help to break down the lack of diversity in STEM careers and will help to introduce a new generation into coding through partnerships with other community agencies and K-12 schools.

Apple has been working closely with Tennessee State University for over two years to support the school's HBCU C^2 program that aims to spread coding programs to all HBCUs nationwide [9]. These programs are also potentially beneficial for Apple as they help to widen the base of developers that create applications for their platforms and use Apple devices. Most importantly, it is an example of the mission of Apple to improve the lives of its shareholders.

Financial impact

As a publicly traded, for-profit company, Apple's motivation to spread Swift is not purely altruistic. Swift is designed to run the best on Apple devices and is made to support applications that are run on Apple's operating systems. In supporting the education and adoption of Swift, Apple is creating a larger number of developers that can create applications for their App Store. A superior offering of apps gives Apple an advantage over Android-powered smartphones in consumer, enterprise, and academic segments. Additionally, an increase in the number of apps being built and bought by consumers on the App Store leads to an increase in revenue for Apple. An Apple Developer account, a $99 annual membership, is required for developers and companies to list their apps on the App Store.

Apple also gains revenue from the app store via the 30% cut they collect from the purchase price of applications sold on the App Store. The other 70% goes to the companies that develop and list the application. In January 2020, Apple revealed that it has paid a total of $155B to developers since it opened the App Store in 2008 [10]. Based on the 70/30 purchase price split between vendors and Apple, this would result in over $65B of revenue for Apple from the App Store [11]. Revenue from services like the App Store have increased over the past several years and made up just under 18% of total net sales in 2019 [2]. An increase in net sales from their service categories is important for Apple as product sales have declined in recent years (down 14% between FY18 and FY19) [2]. Apple can continue to use Swift to grow the iOS developer base to increase the quality and quantity of App Store applications.

For Apple CEO Tim Cook, the mission of Apple is not centered around the stock price. Cook states that, "it's about products and people. Did we make the best product, and did we enrich people's lives? If you are doing both of those things – and obviously, those things are incredibly connected because one leads to the other – then you have a good year." [12] This has allowed Apple to be consistently named as the most innovative company year after year and is why Swift has been able to flourish. If Apple were only focused on profits, it could have kept Swift closed instead of releasing it as open source where it could be used to increase platforms, like Android, of their competitors. Instead, Apple saw Swift as an opportunity to advance coding not just for Apple's benefit but for everyone. This motivated their decision to make the language open source, resulting in an influx of contributors and users of the language. When questioned about Apple's process for creating hardware for developers, Tim Cook stated, "We try to continually push ourselves to do more and more, not just on the hardware side but also in terms of developers' tools so they can take advantage of the hardware that is there, in the best way. That is the heart of what the coding

238 *Case studies*

software Swift is about. We've created the language and our hope was that you can get a lot more people coding, and then secondly have people push more to take advantage of the latest hardware." [13] These comments reveal the culture of innovation within Apple and Swift's role in their "Everyone Can Code" mission.

Future of Swift

Swift continues to grow as a language inside and outside of the Apple ecosystem. Internally, Apple has increased the usage of Swift in the development of its operating systems and native applications. For instance, iOS 13 featured twice the number of binaries written with Swift than present in iOS 12 [14]. Adoption of the code is also evident in its use to build the latest versions of many of its native applications in iOS 13. For developers who build iOS applications, a 2019 survey found that 53% use Swift only, 31% use both Swift and Objective-C, and only about 15% use Objective-C exclusively [15]. Further, of the 31% that use both, 61% said that most of their codebase is written in Swift [15]. Swift has gained popularity outside of the Apple ecosystem, being listed as the sixth most-loved programming language [16]. Nevertheless, Swift has work to be done before it is used as a widespread programming language across all operating systems. Work will continue to be done to achieve this goal by the overall Swift community in collaboration with the dedicated teams within Apple. Together they have improved the language and released version 5.3 in early 2020. Swift 5.3, the most recent iteration of the language comes just six years after its initial release. In this time, Swift has managed to become the dominant programming language for iOS developers. Its growth will continue due to its strengths over its predecessor and as a programming language for wider use. In short, this successful, modern programming language is thanks to the culture of innovation within Apple and its ability to collaborate with external partners in support of its goals.

Questions to consider for case analysis

1. Apple's new programming language Swift was created after recognizing the need for more powerful and easy to use language. Why did Apple not recognize this need sooner and had to wait? Do you think open innovation, as opposed to conducting everything internally in a secretive manner, perhaps could have provided the structure and environment to continuously seek out the best relative to the market?
2. What could have been the primary reasons for making Swift an open-source after developing it exclusively for internal use? Does open-source catapult Swift into a more market dominant programming language? What could be some of the challenges for Apple posed by innovation through open-source?
3. Discuss Apple's innovation culture in general based on the Swift development experience as portrayed in this case. Compare and contrast with your own personal innovation experiences at your present organizations.
4. To what extent did leadership play a role in this case to bring out the Swift innovation?
5. What do you think is the type of innovation discussed here? Why do you think so? The first few chapters of this book may be reviewed to answer this question.

References

1. A. Zimmermann, L. Wallin, and R. Cozza, July 28, 2020, "Vendor Rating: Apple," retrieved 2020, from www.gartner.com/document/code/721784?ref=ddisp&refval=721784. ID: G00721784
2. Apple Inc, 2019, "2019 10-K Annual Report," https://investor.apple.com/sec-filings/sec-filings-details/default.aspx?FilingId=13709514
3. ACSI, June 4, 2019, "American Customer Satisfaction Index Scores for Smartphone Models in the United States in 2019," [Graph], Statista, retrieved August 10, 2020, from www-statista-com.proxy.lib.umich.edu/statistics/1014060/american-customer-satisfaction-index-for-smartphone-models/
4. Cade Metz, July 14, 2017, "Why Apple's Swift Language Will Instantly Remake Computer Programming," retrieved 2020, from www.wired.com/2014/07/apple-swift/
5. Chris Lattner, (n.d.), Chris Lattner's Homepage, retrieved 2020, from www.nondot.org/sabre/
6. John Gruber, December 14, 2015, "Transcript of Craig Federighi and John Gruber on The Talk Show Episode 139," retrieved 2020, from https://daringfireball.net/thetalkshow/139/transcript
7. Harry McCracken, September 10, 2015, "Lyft Goes Swift: How (and Why) it Rewrote its App from Scratch in Apple's New Language," retrieved August 14, 2020, from www.fastcompany.com/3050266/lyft-goes-swift-how-and-why-it-rewrote-its-app-from-scratch-in-apples-new-lang
8. Rosalie Chan, March 10, 2020, "Here's What You Need to Know About Why Developers Love Swift, the Apple Programming Language that Developers Are Using to Build Most New Iphone Apps," retrieved 2020, from www.businessinsider.com/developers-love-swift-apple-programming-language-ios-apps-2020-3
9. Rachel W. Tulley, July 16, 2020, "Apple Teams Up with Hbcus to Bring Coding and Creativity Opportunities to Communities Across the US," retrieved 2020, from www.apple.com/newsroom/2020/07/apple-teams-up-with-hbcus-to-bring-coding-and-creativity-opportunities-to-communities-across-the-us/
10. Katie Alsadder, January 8, 2020, "Apple Rings in New Era of Services Following Landmark Year," retrieved 2020, from www.apple.com/newsroom/2020/01/apple-rings-in-new-era-of-services-following-landmark-year/
11. Kif Leswing, January 8, 2020, "Apple's App Store Had Gross Sales Around $50 Billion Last Year, but Growth is Slowing," retrieved 2020, from www.cnbc.com/2020/01/07/apple-app-store-had-estimated-gross-sales-of-50-billion-in-2019.html
12. Robert Safian, July 30, 2018, "Why Apple is the World's Most Innovative Company," retrieved 2020, from www.fastcompany.com/40525409/why-apple-is-the-worlds-most-innovative-company
13. David Phelan, February 10, 2017, "Apple CEO Tim Cook: As Brexit Hangs Over UK "Times Are Not Really Awful, There's Some Great Things Happening," retrieved 2020, from www.independent.co.uk/life-style/gadgets-and-tech/features/apple-tim-cook-boss-brexit-uk-theresa-may-number-10-interview-ustwo-a7574086.html
14. Nate Swanner, October 10, 2019, "Apple Doubled Down on Swift in iOS 13. Are iOS Developers Doing the Same?" retrieved 2020, from https://insights.dice.com/2019/10/10/swift-ios-13-apple-developers/
15. A. Chumak, August 13, 2019, "Swift & Objective-C 2019 – The State of Developer Ecosystem in 2019 Infographic," retrieved 2020, from www.jetbrains.com/lp/devecosystem-2019/swift-objc/
16. Stack Overflow Developer Survey 2019, retrieved 2020, from https://insights.stackoverflow.com/survey/2019

Case 7: Microsoft – The Age of Nadella

Serena Wang and Minnie Sun

Stephen M. Ross School of Business, University of Michigan
wangse@umich.edu; mxsun@umich.edu

Company background

Microsoft is one of the most widely recognized names in technology across the globe. Founded in 1975 by Bill Gates and Paul Allen, Microsoft quickly rose the ranks in 1980 when it landed its first major business deal as IBM PC's operating system producer [1]. Since its humble beginnings as a computer software company, it has expanded to become a leader in software development and computer hardware, consumer electronics and services, cloud computing, and much more.

When the word "Microsoft" is mentioned, people may think of the iconic four-tile logo. That logo was the trademark symbol of the Windows operating system, a product that propelled Microsoft into the spotlight. Since then, the company has developed an incredible array of products in a variety of other areas. These include business (Office 365, Skype for business, Azure), office (Microsoft Teams, Outlook, OneDrive, Word, Excel, PowerPoint), devices (Surface, PC accessories, Xbox), developer/IT (Visual Studio, SQL Server, SharePoint server), applications (Microsoft Edge, Skype), and more (Bing, MSN explorer, movies/TV, PC gaming). This enormous breadth of products is a testament to the company's creativity, diversity, and stability [2].

However, Microsoft was not always as stable and prosperous as it is today. The company has survived and thrived through periods of incredible developments in modern technology, from the rise of mobile devices to cloud computing. It has not always been able to anticipate those developments and make proactive investments to maintain itself at the top, especially during the early 2000s [3]. Microsoft has only had three CEOs since its inception: Bill Gates (founding – 2000), Steve Ballmer (2000 – 2014), Satya Nadella (2014 – present) [4]. Under the leadership of Satya Nadella, Microsoft made aggressive moves into cloud computing and services [5]. This has kept Microsoft in every field, if not at the forefront of many of those fields, even as the technological landscape shifts and advances. All this information contextualizes the innovation challenges and solutions Microsoft has experienced to become the mammoth it is today.

Major innovation: Challenge or business problem

As Microsoft saw a change in leadership from Steve Ballmer to Satya Nadella, the company also decided to enter a new sector of the technology space growing in popularity: Cloud computing. Microsoft's primary cloud service is called Azure. The current innovation challenge with their cloud products is figuring out how they

DOI: 10.4324/9781003190837-28

can become the largest cloud computing provider. As of now, Microsoft has a strong second-place position, capturing 17.6% of the public cloud services market (Google Cloud holds the third position at 6%) but is facing a formidable competitor with Amazon Web Services (AWS) in first-place position, claiming about 32.4% of the public cloud services market [6]. Though Microsoft has gained a significant share of the cloud computing market, its Q3 2019 reports for Azure showed slower growth at 59% compared to the 76% growth rate in the prior year that capped Microsoft's overall gains [7]. This suggests to investors that, although Azure is promising, it still has a long way to go before it can claim cloud computing dominance. For Microsoft to achieve its goal as a market leader of cloud computing, Nadella has made many changes to the company to foster innovation.

Problem solutions

Company restructuring

In 2018, Nadella reorganized Microsoft into three main divisions: "Experiences & Devices," "Cloud + AI," and the existing branch of "Microsoft Research." [8] The Experiences & Devices division will now cover Windows, Office 365, new technology, and enterprise management, all of which used to be separate divisions. The Cloud + AI Platform division will include Azure cloud, AI for businesses, and the AI tools for developers to build their apps. This restructuring is intended to bring greater consistency across all Windows software and devices by using cloud and AI. Compared to the previous company structure, Microsoft under Nadella has shifted away from consumer technology toward business services such as cloud computing.

The old structure replaced innovation with bureaucracy and teamwork with internal politics, with Nadella describing the different divisions as "warring gangs." [9] According to Nadella, "We can't let any organizational boundaries get in the way of innovation for our customers. Each one of us needs to push on what technology can do for people and our world." [8]. By eliminating the bureaucratic boundaries between the numerous previous divisions, Nadella hopes this restructuring will emphasize the development of Microsoft's Azure enterprise cloud platform. This decision was not for short-term financial gain, because even though cloud services have been a steady growth factor in Microsoft's bottom line, Windows and Office 365 still make the company more money. Instead, this restructuring is intended to promote growth in the long term. Creating a division entirely focused on Cloud + AI allows Microsoft to drive more innovation within that industry and use these advancements to improve the other divisions [10]

Improving company culture

Nadella believes that changing the company's culture to support innovation will also help promote cloud development. When Nadella was named Microsoft's CEO, he told the employees that "renewing [the] company's culture would be [his] highest priority." [11] Under his leadership, Microsoft was able to shift the internal culture from an outdated technology producer to a cloud powerhouse. The key to this culture shift is a concept that is now a mantra at Microsoft: The growth mindset. Compared to the previous cutthroat culture at the firm, which was less accommodative of experiments

242 *Case studies*

and failures, Microsoft now has opened many opportunities for innovation by encouraging employees to be open about failure.

When Nadella was doing an in-depth analysis within the company employees to understand the issues he soon he recognized that there was a widespread misconception that failure was something to be avoided. This culture of aversion toward mistakes inhibits the company from growing. Especially in a culture where employees struggle to admit any shortfalls, innovative ideas that are riskier by nature are rarely explored. Nadella recognized this issue and decided to encourage a growth mindset of accountability. Rewarding individuals who brought the company closer to its goal of innovation through both failures and successes reduces the inhibitions for change. An example of this is when the Chief People Officer Kathleen Hogan made a mistake with implementing a new HR program. Hogan was anxious about her error and sent an email to Nadella to apologize sincerely. His response showed not upset at all and said, "You're overly apologetic. You've acknowledged the mistake, stated what you've learned and how you intend to fix it. Now move on." [12] Nadella's upholding of the growth mindset, even in tough situations, sets himself as a role model and shapes a culture of learning from failure. A company that can learn from its mistakes to get to the desired results, in the end, is the form of accountability that pushes a company to become forward-thinking [12].

Company partnerships

The last key solution to Microsoft's innovation challenge was an increased investment in gaining strong partnerships and nurturing current partnerships. Nadella had a clear vision for where he wanted Microsoft to be under his leadership, and cooperation was at its center. The CEO had often been quoted as saying he would compete fiercely, but he would also cooperate where it made sense because customers demanded it – and it was all about the customer.

Cooperation and partnerships were promoted internally and externally. Internally, in tandem with the company culture shift, developers saw massive growth as the company mindset shifted from an overly hostile and competitive environment to share ideas and exchange experiences. This massively increased productivity and satisfaction, as people finally had sufficient access to the physical and intellectual resources they needed. Externally, Microsoft found ways to innovate by identifying customers' real pain points and partnering with other companies to resolve them when it made sense. In the age of the cloud and interconnectedness, that cooperation is more important than ever because customers expect nothing less. They expect open application programming interfaces, developer-friendly platforms, and much more innovation – and Microsoft delivered [13].

Outcomes

Due to all the changes Nadella implemented to encourage innovation, Microsoft was successful in its efforts to improve its cloud computing technology. This success can be seen through Microsoft's victory of the $10B Joint Enterprise Defense Infrastructure (JEDI) cloud computing contract with the government. This contract set off a showdown among Amazon, Microsoft, Google, and other companies for the right to develop and transform the US military's cloud computing systems. Though there are many competitors for this contract, the Pentagon announced that only Amazon and Microsoft met the technical requirements to qualify for the contract, essentially eliminating all other competitors, with Google also deciding to drop out of the race because the military work conflicted with its corporate principles [14, 15].

The decision to go with Microsoft was shocking because Amazon was considered the front runner because it was the dominant player in the cloud computing industry and had already built cloud services for the CIA. Though not the largest cloud computing player, Microsoft was considered in the lead for many other government cloud programs. Though the decision to award Microsoft with the contract is partially due to Amazon's political implications, there are significant implications for Microsoft and the cloud computing industry. Receiving this JEDI contract gives Microsoft the likely potential to earn roughly $40B in federal government expenses on cloud computing over the next few years. Under the leadership of Nadella, Microsoft was put in the prime position to compete with its largest competitor and successfully claim a contract that can bolster its cloud development over the next few years. Continuing the company's innovative direction will allow Microsoft to utilize this advantage better and successfully become the dominant player in the cloud computing industry [14].

Financials

Microsoft reported a 2020 annual revenue of $143.02B for its July–June fiscal year. This is a 13.95% growth rate from its previous year and is consistent with its growth over the past five years. With this increase in sales, Microsoft also accrued an increased cost of goods sold and depreciation and amortization by 7.38% from 2019, which is lower than the growth rates from previous years. Because Microsoft was able to achieve increased revenues while decreasing costs, it was able to achieve a total gross income of $96.94B with a 17.37% growth rate that is higher than in previous years. Microsoft also reported earnings before interest, taxes, depreciation, and amortization of $65.76B, which grew at a normal growth rate of 21.28%. This data reveals that Microsoft was able to achieve a higher level of operating efficiency as well as maintain similar growth in 2020 compared to the past five years. Microsoft's 2016–2020 financial performance is presented in Exhibit 7.1.

Beyond Microsoft Azure and Office 365, Microsoft has also been investing in many initiatives that have the potential to strengthen the key lines of business, such as cloud computing and its Office suite. Microsoft has invested in a total of 139 technology companies with its most recent investment in Kano, a coding platform for app development, on July 14, 2020 [16]. This recent investment activity shows that Microsoft is actively looking for new technology companies to support, breeding more innovation within the technology space.

With its investment portfolio, Microsoft has had 37 exits, some of the more notable companies being Facebook, Apple, and Uber [17]. In addition to its investments, Microsoft has also been actively acquiring innovative technology companies, acquiring 232 different organizations. Its most recent acquisition was Orions Systems, a seed-stage digital management solution platform for healthcare companies, on July 8, 2020. Its acquisitions range across a wide range of technology companies, from healthcare to information systems. These acquisitions target smaller companies and are intended to diversify the technology spaces in which Microsoft is operating. In both Microsoft's

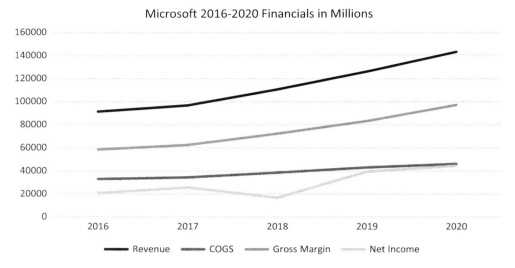

Exhibit 7.1 Microsoft's 2016–2020 financial performance.

investment and acquisition activity, it seems Microsoft is interested in capturing the innovation beyond its own company [18].

Setbacks and growth

Microsoft would not be the company it is today without its fair share of challenges and obstacles. Most of its largest obstacles happened under the leadership of the previous CEO, Steve Ballmer, with strings of product launch failures that dealt a huge blow to the company's financial standing and a blow to employees who consistently saw their time and energy go into a failed product. These failed products highlighted the needs and benefits for Microsoft to change position [19].

Although it was a highly trial-and-error oriented process, Microsoft eventually learned its lesson and grew through experiencing its lowest points. It developed a consumer-oriented mindset, highly in tune with customers' shifting needs, to ensure it would never experience such a string of ill-implemented products again. It began turning its focus internally to develop a culture of collaboration and clarify what its company mission was. It became the Microsoft we know today, with its array of successful products and services catering to consumers, and no shortage of ideas.

Key takeaways

1. Visionary leadership can change the course of an entire company, no matter how big or small it may be.
2. Connecting with consumers and understanding their needs and pain points is a critical step in innovating toward the right direction.
3. Innovation is not just about the products themselves, but also the creative culture that fuels their development.

Microsoft 245

4. Microsoft capitalized on many key growing technologies, such as cloud computing.
5. Satya Nadella created a much more innovation-driven culture, rather than competition-driven.
6. Microsoft restructured its organizational structure to better facilitate innovation.
7. Microsoft leveraged the talent of their employees and re-energized them to work toward new future technological goals.

References

1. Mark Hall, Microsoft Corporation, Encyclopedia Britannica, Inc., Nov 12, 2020, www.britannica.com/topic/Microsoft-Corporation
2. "Current Versions of Microsoft Products," Techsoup.org, Aug 28, 2020, www.techsoup.org/current-versions-of-microsoft-products
3. Barry Ritholtz, Sept 6, 2013, "What's Behind Microsoft's Fall from Dominance?" The Washington Post, WP Company, www.washingtonpost.com/business/whats-behind-microsofts-fall-from-dominance/2013/09/05/b0e5e91e-157b-11e3-804b-d3a1a3a18f2c_story.html
4. Malathi Nayak, Feb 4, 2014, "Timeline: Microsoft's Journey: Four Decades, Three CEOs," Reuters, www.reuters.com/article/us-microsoft-succession-timeline/timeline-microsofts-journey-four-decades-three-ceos-idUSBREA131R720140204
5. Greg McFarlane, Feb 8, 2020, "The Real Secret to Microsoft's Success," Investopedia, www.investopedia.com/stock-analysis/032014/real-secret-microsofts-success-msft-aapl-goog-ibm.aspx
6. "Incremental Growth in Cloud Spending Hits a New High While Amazon and Microsoft Maintain a Clear Lead," Synergy Research Group, Feb 4, 2020, www.srgresearch.com/articles/incremental-growth-cloud-spending-hits-new-high-while-amazon-and-microsoft-maintain-clear-lead-reno-nv-february-4-2020
7. Annie Gaus, Jan 3, 2020, "Microsoft's 3 Biggest Challenges for 2020," TheStreet, www.thestreet.com/investing/microsoft-3-biggest-challenges-2020
8. Dave Gershgorn, Mar 29, 2018, "Microsoft Reshuffles to Bring More AI into Products," Quartz, https://qz.com/1240855/microsoft-ceo-satya-nadella-is-reorganizing-the-company-to-bring-more-ai-into-products/
9. Satya Nadella, et al. "Hit Refresh: The Quest to Rediscover Microsoft's Soul and Imagine a Better Future for Everyone," Harper Business, an Imprint of HarperCollinsPublishers, 2019.
10. "Microsoft Expands Artificial Intelligence (AI) Efforts with Creation of New Microsoft AI and Research Group," Microsoft News Center, Sept 29, 2016, https://news.microsoft.com/2016/09/29/microsoft-expands-artificial-intelligence-ai-efforts-with-creation-of-new-microsoft-ai-and-research-group/
11. "PRESENTING: Satya Nadella Employed a 'Growth Mindset' to Overhaul Microsoft's Cutthroat Culture and Turn It into a Trillion-Dollar Company – Here's How He Did It," Business Insider, Mar 7, 2020, www.businessinsider.com/microsoft-ceo-satya-nadella-company-culture-shift-growth-mindset-2020-3
12. Ron Carucci, Oct 15, 2019, "Microsoft's Chief People Officer: What I've Learned About Leading Culture Change," Forbes Magazine, www.forbes.com/sites/roncarucci/2019/10/14/microsofts-chief-people-officer-what-ive-learned-about-leading-culture-change/
13. Ron Miller, Feb 4, 2019, "After 5 Years, Microsoft CEO Satya Nadella Has Transformed More than the Stock Price," TechCrunch, https://techcrunch.com/2019/02/04/after-5-years-microsoft-ceo-satya-nadella-has-transformed-more-than-the-stock-price/
14. Kate Conger, et al., Oct 25, 2019, "Microsoft Wins Pentagon's $10 Billion JEDI Contract, Thwarting Amazon," The New York Times, www.nytimes.com/2019/10/25/technology/dod-jedi-contract.html?auth=login-google1tap

15. Shelly Kramer, Sep 8, 2020, "Microsoft Wins Department of Defense JEDI Contract Award – For Now Anyway," Futurum Research, https://futurumresearch.com/research-notes/microsoft-wins-department-of-defense-jedi-contract-again-for-now-anyway/
16. Microsoft Financial Statements 2005–2020: MSFT. Macrotrends, www.macrotrends.net/stocks/charts/MSFT/microsoft/financial-statements
17. "Microsoft – Funding, Financials, Valuation & Investors," Microsoft Crunchbase, www.crunchbase.com/organization/microsoft/company_financials
18. "Investment History," Microsoft, Dec 23, 2020, www.microsoft.com/en-us/Investor/investment-history.aspx
19. Hiten Shah, Mar 13, 2020, "The Most Important Turning Points in Microsoft's History," FYI, https://usefyi.com/microsoft-history/

Case 8: The Procter & Gamble Company – A Unique Innovation Approach

Minnie Sun and Serena Wang

Stephen M. Ross School of Business, University of Michigan
mxsun@umich.edu; wangse@umich.edu

Company background

The Procter & Gamble Company, commonly known as P&G, was founded in 1837 by William Procter and James Gamble. They made a name for themselves during a time of financial crisis, selling soap and candles at lower prices but retaining a high-quality product. From those humble beginnings, P&G has become a global consumer goods powerhouse with a strong foothold in nearly every segment of personal/home care product. P&G's consumer packaged goods portfolio consists of over 60 brands, including international leaders in their respective markets such as Crest, Gillette, Tide, Olay, Pampers, and more.

P&G built its empire upon a long string of acquisitions, ranging from Old Spice to Duracell. These acquisitions were later followed by a long string of dropped brands, as P&G sought to streamline its product offerings. In late 2014, the company dropped nearly 100 smaller brands in favor of focusing on the core 60-some brands seen today that bring in most of P&G's revenue. This was considered a highly sensible decision, as it allowed P&G to focus on brands that brought in most of the company's profits and made brand management significantly more efficient. They were a very strong company in the products that they currently managed so P&G believed that rapidly expanding their product base would result in a profit boost as well.

When discussing innovation, things like dish soap and toothpaste are not what most people would initially consider as relevant, and most people will not even recognize P&G as a company responsible for producing these. However, P&G has truly distinguished itself as an international leader through its consistent innovation in markets that seem most counterproductive to it. They have single-handedly created new markets and expanded on old ones, staying keenly in touch with consumer needs to anticipate any changes in tastes. With a string of highly dedicated and innovative leadership, including its current CEO David Taylor, P&G has made innovation the cornerstone of the company.

Major innovation challenge or business problem

P&G has always benefited from selling products with relatively inelastic demand, such as toothpaste and soap, allowing the company to stay afloat even during times of recession and financial hardship. However, continuing to grow the company by selling these basic products through inorganic acquisitions or organic efforts also proved to be the company's most significant innovation challenge.

DOI: 10.4324/9781003190837-29

248   *Case studies*

In the early 2000s, P&G was simply not meeting their profitability and revenue targets. In fact, only 15% of their products were as profitable as the company hoped. Around this time, the then-CEO Durk Jager resigned in 2000 after a woefully failed restructuring effort to boost profitability. This downturn in the company was reflected in the company's stock price, where the internal issues in the company began hitting the company's bottom line. During this time, P&G stockholders became wary of the company's overall direction and began selling shares to avoid losing more money in fear the company would continue this downward trajectory with the company's stock price dropping to below $30. The management of P&G quickly got together to resolve its internal issues, which would also solve its external issues with customers and other stakeholders.

They came up with an effort named "Organization 2005" that was aimed to boost revenue by introducing a large variety of new products and decrease costs by shutting down numerous plants. However, rather than boosting profitability, the initiative put the company into its first profitability decline in eight years [1]. Thus far, P&G had been known for its stable earnings and conservative leadership. "Organization 2005" tried to do too much too quickly and spread the company thin by attempting to expand product lines in too many of its brands. Expenses skyrocketed, while sales did not grow nearly enough to justify the increased investments.

This was a clear indication that the company needed to make significant internal changes to grow overall, rather than stay stagnant or even shrink. P&G had attempted to innovate in a certain way – by trying as many new things as possible, as quickly as possible. This tactic failed them miserably, continuing the company in this downward spiral. The company's stock price continued to remain around its low price, around $30, as stockholders continued to be wary about the company's profitability.

Market forces were working against them as well; competition was rising steadily with many new generic brands that produced cheaper alternatives to P&G's premium offerings. Compared to P&G, stockholders were more comfortable investing in its competitors as they offered stronger potential for growth. Leadership knew that innovation had to be the answer, but it had to take a different form than their previous failed approach. P&G needed to better define what its competitive advantage was and continue building upon its strategic advantage, rather than pursuing a strategy that the company itself was not suited for.

Problem solutions

Taking all the lessons learned from the failed "Organization 2005" to heart, P&G took it slowly in its next attempts. Led by new CEO, A.G. Lafley, these attempts at innovation laid down a critical, organic growth-driven foundation for the company. P&G's future innovation efforts were built upon three categories: Building up a strong internal capability for organic innovation, increasing demand within existing product categories, and creating entirely new business models and markets.

Building the internal foundation

Before P&G could begin innovating, they needed to restructure first. As mentioned before, in 2014, P&G cut down their 165-brand portfolio into just 65 brands. Lafley believed this would make P&G a simpler, streamlined company that would enable more efficient management, streamlined operations, and sustainable growth [2]. The dropped brands brought in only 3% of the company's overall profits combined, and thus allowed the company to focus on making its most profitable brands even more so. However, they not only dropped brands that were less profitable, but also brands that did not fit the "image" of P&G's traditional personal and family care products. For example, Duracell, a battery manufacturer, was sold to Berkshire Hathaway for $2.9B [3].

As with any major restructuring like P&G's, there was a heavy impact on employees, with more than 4,000 jobs eliminated [4]. This streamlining proved to be financially and strategically beneficial for the company, but it did not come without its price. In 2018, P&G also revamped its management structure by reducing the number of business units from ten to six, as well as giving heads of units the power to oversee regional sales teams (a function previously delegated to other management) [5]. P&G's restructuring was all about streamlining.

This restructuring was helpful for the company because it allowed P&G to further its most profitable segments, rather than waste money on product segments that lost money quarter over quarter. This product rationalization will allow P&G to maintain and increase profitability as it is able to focus more of its management and development on these fewer products that make up more of the company's profit.

As restructuring was underway, the company was also turning its attention toward growth. A key takeaway from "Organization 2005" was that the company needed to be transparent to its employees about the overall goals of the company. With such a broad portfolio even after streamlining, with some products overlapping in customer bases, trying to force innovation upon each team was extremely ineffective and counterproductive. Leadership implemented new initiatives to foster more sustainable innovation by focusing not on the end products themselves, but rather how to better the process of building and supporting new ideas. These initiatives included:

- Developed new organizational structures to support innovation, such as subunits within specific departments focused solely on growth initiatives
- Leveraged organizational restructuring to link innovation developments with broader company strategy assessments, fostering better transparency and company unity
- Instilled growth mindset values in senior management to foster trickle-down ideation
- Formed group of new growth business guides called P&G Ventures, made up of entrepreneurs who understood the process of introducing new markets and could create new business models, products, and solutions for consumers [6]
- Decentralized R&D efforts so instead of one massive research department separate from other product departments, there were smaller R&D groups integrated into each brand
- Produced process manuals and training guides to guide future innovation

These initiatives, among others, created a systematic process for creative ideation that valued the process of innovation above all. By investing in bettering the process, P&G began to see more successful products come to the market.

250   *Case studies*

Increasing current demand

Armed with new tools for developing products in tune with consumer wants and needs, P&G then turned its attention to applying that process. They honed in on how to deliver new benefits in existing product categories. One clear example of this was through its oral hygiene line, Crest. Crest had been the clear market leader until Colgate, its now biggest competitor, entered the scene in the early 2000s. Oral hygiene is an industry with relatively inelastic demand, so how does one stimulate demand for toothpaste? Looking to regain the lead, Crest introduced innovation to their traditional product mix by introducing Crest Whitestrips, Crest Pro-Health, Crest 3D White, and a variety of other targeted products. These efforts created a sustained disruption in the overall market by taking various benefits of the tooth-brushing experience – from whiter teeth, to fighting cavities, to bad breath, and more – and distinguishing them in different products. This stimulated demand in their current customer base and regained some of the customers lost to Colgate previously.

Creating new markets

In some cases, however, more drastic innovation and brand overhauls were necessary to bring P&G back to the top. One of the clearest examples of this was with Tide. Tide originated as a simple laundry detergent. The brand has now grown to include an unrivaled product mix in the laundry cleaning industry. However, not only did Tide expand their product lines, but also their entire business model.

The introduction of Tide Dry Cleaners, an on-demand laundry service, represented a completely new segment of the brand. P&G researchers found that customers were heavily dissatisfied with existing dry-cleaning options in terms of hygiene, accessibility, and ease of use. Tide Dry Cleaners established attractive storefronts with capabilities for every type of customer looking to wash/dry clean. The introduction of Tide Dry Cleaners represented a disruption beyond increasing current demand. Tide captured the growing demographic of populations moving into urban areas living in smaller apartments, many of which did not have in-unit laundry. P&G acutely found a pain point in their consumers' laundry habits, the annoyance of transporting a heavy detergent bottle, and provided them with the simple solution in the form of a Tide pod. Establishing itself as the reliable neighborhood laundromat, while using Tide's newly expanded product lines to wash clothes, propelled Tide to the status of an undeniable market leader and one of P&G's top-performing brands [7].

The major changes made to Tide did not happen out of luck or chance. They were the successful results of systematic and structured innovation that were a response to thorough research, which helped them understand shifting trends and needs. The strong internal foundation, mentioned earlier, was critical in helping them both grasp the true wants of their customers, and develop the best solutions possible to meet those needs.

Financials

Due to the changes made to the internal structure, increased demand, and new markets, among other things, P&G has seen clear, strong financial growth. From 2016 to 2019, the company has seen slow gross profit growth of about $100M every year

The Procter & Gamble Company   251

[8]. This averages to about a 2% increase compared to each respective previous year. Though the growth is modest, it is notable due to the ability for such a large company to consistently attain, which can be attributed to its innovation strategies. This trend changed in 2020 when the company reported around $2.8B increase in gross profit in one year alone [8]. Compared to the modest 2% increase in growth margin, 2020 was able to achieve almost 5% growth from previous years. This growth can be attributed to the growth in revenue of about $3B and only a $1B increase in cost of goods sold. Both factors, being able to drive sales as well as maintaining low cost of materials, can be financially linked back to the significant growth. The innovative changes set the company up to achieve this growth, despite economic concerns stemming from the pandemic.

Outcome

Due to the rationalization of product lines, P&G has become a more efficient and stronger company. This change allowed P&G to focus on the product segments that sold and let go of the ones that were not as popular. Because of this, P&G was more adaptable to changing consumer needs and developed products that have changed the markets, such as Tide pods. Many companies make the mistake of losing focus of their strategic business advantage and fail to recognize changes in their customers' demands and adjust their offerings.

Questions

1. What do you think was the justification for why P&G decided to pursue a strategy of producing many new product lines?
2. Do you think that P&G's solution was the right one? What else could they have done?
3. Why do you think creating hundreds of different variations of a single product is not appealing from the lens of a consumer? From the lens of P&G?
4. Identify what P&G's competitive advantage is and how their strategy involved with "Organization 2005" strayed away from their strategic strength.
5. Do you think the design thinking approach was in essence what P&G introduced by listening and empathizing with customers and aligning the product offerings to meet customers' changed expectations?

Key takeaways

1. Innovation is not only about having the newest products, but also creating out-of-the-box business models, finding new twists on old products, and beyond.
2. Sometimes, innovation cannot take place until a company makes room for new ideas by removing poor-performing ideas.
3. Sustained innovation does not merely come from "light bulb" moments and trying to do everything new at once, but rather systematic approaches and strong infrastructures to support consistent innovation and growth.
4. P&G leveraged key analytics to identify poor-performing products and make way for new products.

252 *Case studies*

5. Their leadership went through trial-and-error processes of best practices for sustained innovation.
6. They implemented groups of entrepreneurs within product segments to specifically drive innovation.
7. P&G practiced a highly imaginative culture, even while selling very basic household items.

References

1. Cable News Network, (n.d.), "P&G CEO quits amid woes," CNNMoney, https://money. cnn.com/2000/06/08/companies/procter/#:~:text=8%2C%202000&text=NEW%20 YORK%20(CNNfn)%20%2D%20The,the%20company%27s%20ongoing%20 profit%20woes
2. Rachel Abrams, August 1, 2014, "Procter & Gamble to Streamline Offerings, Dropping Up to 100 Brands," The New York Times, www.nytimes.com/2014/08/02/business/procter-gamble-to-drop-up-to-100-brands.html
3. "Procter & Gamble sells Duracell to Berkshire Hathaway for $2.9 billion: Experience," (n.d.), Jones Day, www.jonesday.com/en/practices/experience/2016/02/procter-amp-gamble-sells-duracell-to-berkshire-hathaway-for-29-billion#:~:text=Procter%20%26%20 Gamble%20sells%20Duracell%20to%20Berkshire%20Hathaway%20for%20 %242.9%20billion,-February%202016&text=Jones%20Day%20advised%20The%20 Procter,for%20%242.9%20billion
4. Emily Glazer, and Paul Ziobro, February 2012, "P&G to Cut Over 4,000 Jobs," The Wall Street Journal, www.wsj.com/articles/SB1000142405297020391830457724145187064 5894
5. Aisha Al-Muslim, November 9, 2018, "P&G Moves to Streamline Its Structure," The Wall Street Journal, www.wsj.com/articles/p-g-moves-to-streamline-its-structure-1541713822
6. Kimberly A.Whitler, April 30, 2019, "Big Firms Can't Innovate: How P&G Ventures Is Dispelling the Myth," Forbes, www.forbes.com/sites/kimberlywhitler/2019/04/13/how-pg-ventures-is-dispelling-the-big-company-myth/?sh=40d31baf6f66
7. Nathaniel Meyersohn, February 20, 2019, "Who Knew, Tide Does Dry Cleaning. Now it's Expanding the Business," CNN Business, www.cnn.com/2019/02/20/business/tide-cleaners-laundry-service/index.html
8. "Procter & Gamble Financial Statements 2005–2021: PG," (n.d.), Macrotrends, www. macrotrends.net/stocks/charts/PG/procter-gamble/financial-statements

Case 9: Timberland – Sustainable Innovation

Drew Arnson

Stephen M. Ross School of Business, University of Michigan
drewarn@umich.edu

Timberland was founded in 1952 after Nathan Swartz bought out his partners in Abington Shoe Company and moved operations to Newmarket, New Hampshire. In 1968, Timberland began using injection molding technology on their shoes, a first in the industry [1]. Silicone-infused leather was then fused to the sole without any stitching, creating the first-ever waterproof work boot. Their "yellow boot" [1] was branded as the Timberland in 1973, and it gained traction with northeastern construction workers year-round as well as college students trudging to class in the winter. Built to be adaptable to snowy winters, pounding rain, and blistering summers, the shoes continued to grow in popularity, attracting outdoor enthusiasts and people looking for dependable everyday footwear too. The boots were so groundbreaking and brand-defining they changed the name of the company to Timberland in 1978 [1].

Furthering their separation from other work boot makers, Timberland was the first to create a national ad campaign for their boots [2]. By putting their now-famous tree logo on the outside of the boot and following the example created by sneaker companies like Nike and Adidas, the Timberland brand grew rapidly through their national advertising. Not only was the boot functional and durable, but it also became an increasingly fashionable choice.

Now based in Stratham, New Hampshire, Timberland's CEO is Jeffrey Swartz, grandson of founder Nathan Swartz. Timberland became a subsidiary of VF Corporation after being purchased in 2011 for $43 per share, which gave the company a valuation of around $2B [3]. VF Corporation owns 19 other apparel brands including Dickies, Vans, and The North Face. They break down their brands into "Outdoor," "Work," and "Active" categories. They are valued at over $23B, with FY ending March 2020 revenues of $10.5B across all brands. Within the Outdoor segment, Timberland earned just under $2B, showing its importance to the VF conglomerate. Timberland PRO is in the Work category, which earned $886M in sales at a 5.7% profit margin [4]. As a subsidiary, Timberland no longer publicly reports detailed financial statements, but annual reports have shown stagnant revenue growth the pre-COVID 19 pandemic, despite VF steadily increasing profitability [4, 5]. Despite this, Timberland is maintaining their steadfast commitment to sustainability, believing in the longevity and long-term value of this strategy.

VF Corporation's 2020 10-K describes Timberland as a brand that offers "outdoor, adventure-inspired lifestyle footwear, apparel and accessories that combine performance benefits and versatile styling for men, women and children." [4] The Timberland PRO line offers "work and work-inspired products that provide comfort, durability and performance." [4] While a smaller revenue driver, the company believes the PRO

DOI: 10.4324/9781003190837-30

254   Case studies

brand will experience substantial growth globally by expanding into retail and "work-inspired lifestyle" products [4]. Timberland shoes and apparel are available through almost every consumer channel. Products are sold online through timberland.com and through partnerships with other retailers. Timberland also has a global brick and mortar presence, with 230 VF-operated retail stores as well as strategic partnerships with chain and department stores [4].

Timberland grew in popularity in the 1990s when they became a fashion statement in American hip-hop culture, with rappers and fans alike wearing the iconic yellow boot nationwide. The company rode this wave to increase its market capitalization "eight-fold" to $1.6B in 2005 [3]. After a stagnation in sales from 2006–2011, executives realized Timberland's international image was not consistent, so the company sought to better understand its customer base. After being purchased by VF Corporation, Timberland created a survey that was sent to 18,000 customers across eight countries. This reassessment of the global brand showed that the primary Timberland customer of the 2010s is "an urban dweller with a casual interest in the outdoors." The company was able to adjust their product offerings and branding to attract this new target demographic, more efficiently classified as the "outdoor lifestyler," [6] and saw an associated uptick in sales.

To correspond with the modern Timberland consumer, the company has also created a modern brick and mortar experience called "flex retail." [7] These pop-up locations allow for decor and inventory to be customized based on location and demographics in the area. These locations can be open and closed within days, giving shoppers a unique experience tailored to their specific location. It also allows Timberland to capitalize on the seasonality of their product offerings. This openness to change and innovation has been a hallmark of Timberland's identity since its inception. The corporate history of innovation and trend setting creates an atmosphere where employees are encouraged and expected to push boundaries of what an apparel company can be.

Timberland's recent innovations have focused on making their end products, production processes, and supply chains all more sustainable, with the goal of having a net positive on the impact by 2030 [8], meaning they hope to take more carbon out of the air than they put in. Such a dramatic reduction in carbon emissions requires innovative solutions both in how to stop producing carbon and how to remove it. Timberland uses both strategies, but this case focuses on how they can innovate to achieve that ambitious 2030 goal.

In addition to their carbon goals, they hope to only produce circular products by 2030, meaning that each product can be recycled back into a new production process, eliminating waste and emissions from producing virgin materials [9]. Timberland's shift from only quality innovation to sustainable *and* high-quality innovation required a clear mission from senior leadership, corporate infrastructure that supports sustainable innovations, and an openness to partnerships to efficiently scale up the level of positive impact on the environment. These commitments have driven Timberland's corporate evolution, making them a notable example of how a company maintains its innovative excellence while adjusting for the environmental realities of the time.

Cultural commitment to sustainable innovation

When Jeffrey Swartz became CEO in 1998, he not only wanted to improve Timberland's financial performance, but also bring environmental performance to the forefront. The company began writing corporate social responsibility (CSR) reports in the 1990s, matching the ideals of their nature-oriented consumers. However, Swartz brought a culture of service and responsibility to every aspect of the business. His terminology of "commerce and justice" [10] serves as a guiding vision for himself and his employees, showing how they are the same goal, not two contradictory objectives. Swartz believes the key element to a successful implementation of his vision is transparency: "If you want to make the assertion that commerce and justice are not divorceable notions, then you need to demonstrate that in a constant, open, and inspectable way." [10]

Their institution of "strong, yet achievable goals" [11] forced improved accountability in their global supply chain and required a high standard of environmental impact reporting. The importance of clear goal setting from company leadership is supported by generalized research as well. Corporations positively impact their performance when they institute credible goals and discuss them transparently [12]. Corporations also are more likely to achieve their CSR-related goals when they regularly measure and publicly report their results [13]. Timberland's innovative decision to not only state their goals but then publicly hold themselves accountable against those goals [14] highlights how they implement best practices in the sustainability space. Timberland has been using that position of transparency to inspire innovation internally as well as in the industry.

Motivated by their clearly defined mission of producing high-quality, sustainable products, Timberland brought a new level of transparency to their supply chain in 2006 by developing an internal "green index" [15] to measure the sustainability of their products. The idea of the index was to create a consistent, objective measure of sustainability across suppliers and materials. Bringing the concept of an environmental "nutrition label" [15] to their products was a level of transparency that was not commonplace in the 2000s, but their business did not suffer due to the heightening of their environmental focus.

Betsy Blaisdell, a senior manager of environmental stewardship at Timberland, said, "I think these programs have just been in place for so long that they've kind of proven themselves. Business units are adopting them because they see an opportunity to fulfill our business model, which is doing well by doing good. But there are typically cost savings or complexity reduction opportunities associated with these initiatives." [15] Blaisdell also cited Timberland's creation of the Leather Working Group, which created standards for leather tanneries. Timberland only sources from gold- and silver-rated tanneries [16], which may seem more expensive, but reducing supply chain complexity while adding consistency to their high-quality products has proven itself valuable in the long run.

The effectiveness and utility of the Green Index caught the attention of REI, a major outdoor retailer in the US, and they were enthused by the idea of an objective measure of sustainability that could be used in their stores. Spurred by Timberland's initial innovation, a coalition of over 200 outdoor brands collaborated to develop the "Eco Index." [15] After a collaboration with Nike, the Index tool was adapted for every type of apparel and became the Higg Index in 2012. The Higg Index is now used by retailers like Nike and Gap, as well as manufacturers like DuPont and Gildan to measure the sustainability of their production choices [17]. The initiative from Timberland to hold themselves accountable and be transparent has snowballed into the adoption of three different Higg Index tools by hundreds of retailers, manufacturers, and governments [18].

256 Case studies

Infrastructure for sustainable innovation

While it is critical that corporate leadership verbally touts their commitment to sustainability and has processes in place to measure their achievements, there still needs to be infrastructure within the firm to facilitate the sustainable innovations needed to reach those lofty goals. Timberland has successfully fostered a culture of sustained innovation by repeatedly allocating resources and talent toward innovation-driven divisions. In the early 2000s, the creation of the "Invention Factory" led to revolutionary products like the TravelGear line of customizable shoes, and the highly successful PreciseFit insoles [2]. A clear directive to take risks and seek unique sources of inspiration allowed for Timberland designers to work creatively without the fear of taking risks. The designated structure enabled and increased the pace of innovative design. Since the Invention Factory was separate from the standard design and marketing teams, there were tensions when rolling out the new products [2]. Managers across teams came together to create a collaborative integration process, again showing the benefits of formalized systems that foster innovative thinking.

As time progressed, Timberland recognized the need to double down on its sustainability efforts. In 2013, the VF Corporation saw an opportunity to rejuvenate innovation across all its brands, specifically in technical apparel, jeans, and footwear, by establishing three "Global Innovation Centers" nationwide, with the footwear center located at Timberland headquarters in New Hampshire [19]. The centers are staffed with "scientists, engineers, technical designers and key talent who will combine proprietary insights with consumer needs and a deep understanding of technology and new materials" with the goal of developing "breakthrough products" that improve brand equity and revenue growth [19]. Since the creation of the new footwear center, Timberland designers have taken the strategy of "SPG: Style, Performance, and Green." [20] This "truly ownable design formula" not only encourages but mandates that sustainability is woven into the innovative practices of the company. Products that have been produced since the advent of the center include ReBOTL fabric, made from recycled plastic bottles; Hoverlite outsoles, which use 34% recycled rubber; Timberdry linings, which use 50–100% recycled plastic depending on the product; and Cordura fabric, made entirely out of recycled plastic [21]. All these efforts have led to differentiated products that have either maintained or raised Timberland's existing level of quality. Over 345 million bottles have been used by Timberland since 2009 across their products, showing the effectiveness of their sustainability practices [21]. These differentiated products have had room to sprout and grow due to the resources provided from a formalized innovation infrastructure.

Innovation through collaboration

The internally driven innovation at Timberland is remarkable for its consistency and longevity, but their leadership knows that a company with global supply chains cannot truly achieve its profitability or sustainability goals without the cooperation of all stakeholders. Timberland has a goal of achieving circularities for all its products by 2030, so its suppliers need to be involved partners to achieve innovative sustainability strategies across the entire supply chain [22]. Circular, or closed loop, economic systems, are "restorative by intent or design," [23] as opposed to linear systems, which generate unsustainable waste.

The most extensive and impactful collaboration that Timberland has utilized is that of the Leather Working Group (LWG). The LWG is a membership organization that consists of tanneries, final product manufacturers, chemical distributors, and more [24]. As a founding member, Timberland was a key driver in bringing transparency and sustainable practices to the industry. By creating a rating system and in-depth audit, Timberland revolutionized the leather industry, and made their products eco-friendlier by sourcing 96.7% of their leather from LWG gold- or silver-rated suppliers [25]. This long-term collaboration allows Timberland to not only reduce their Scope 1 emissions, but also their Scope 2 and 3 emissions, as well as bringing regenerative practices to their suppliers, helping the long-term viability of those businesses too. Scope 2 and 3 emissions are different categorizations of carbon emissions related to distance from the primary operations of an organization [14]. Partnerships with sustainable agriculture nonprofits such as the Savory Institute and Other Half Processing have increased the reach of Timberland's efforts as well [9]. That showcases innovation in a nontraditional sense – implementing industry-wide changes to achieve the company's own mission.

Timberland also pursues partnerships to create innovative individual products. A partnership with Thread, a company that produces a canvas fabric made from 100% recycled plastic, has given Timberland another pathway into designing more new products that also achieve their sustainability goals [26]. New boots, backpacks, and shoes were all able to be introduced after making the choice to start using an alternative supplier with an innovative approach to material production. Sticking with circularity, but moving out of the clothing industry, Timberland partnered with Omni United tires to design and produce Timberland Tires, which were designed to efficiently be recycled into boot outsoles at the end of their product life [27]. While a seemingly ridiculous idea for a clothes company to start producing car tires, Timberland was able to leverage a partnership to lower their sourcing costs, source more sustainable materials, and open a new revenue stream. This partnership was an example of designing a process with sustainability in mind, a key differentiation compared to retroactively trying to minimize the environmental impact of traditional, unsustainable processes.

Conclusion

Timberland helped initiate a global phenomenon of transparency and measurement with their company-wide devotion to a cause of "doing well by doing good." [28] Companies are benefiting financially from setting goals and using peer-to-peer benchmarking with the Higg Index; most users dramatically reduce their electricity, water, and fuel costs. In addition to the direct cost savings, increasing consumer demand for sustainable goods provides boosts in revenue and consumer perception. In 2011, Timberland redefined their target consumer – the outdoor lifestyler – allowing them to innovate their product development and refocus their marketing [6]. Even before that, Timberland redefined how they approached their CSR reporting by pushing the boundaries of what corporate transparency looks like. By integrating a cohesive culture throughout the company, sustainable innovation was not seen as a one-off task but a continual commitment to bettering the brand. By following through on that culture by providing infrastructure for innovation and seeking out creative partners, Timberland has continued to elevate themselves in the realm of sustainable

258   *Case studies*

innovation. They not only talk the talk but walk the walk of working toward being more sustainable, stimulating a culture of innovation at all levels.

Case questions

1. Which factors were most important in creating a culture of innovation?
2. How did Timberland balance advancing their business interests with their sustainability goals?
   a. Try to think of a current manufacturing process or product that is designed, from its outset, to fit into a closed loop, or circular economy.
   b. Try to think of a process or product that could be reimagined and redesigned to incorporate sustainable principles.
3. Regarding the Leather Working Group, are there ethical concerns about companies partnering to create organizations that audit themselves?
4. What technological advancements came from these innovation processes?
5. What are other examples of individual companies making strategic decisions that affect entire industries?
6. What are potential drawbacks of putting structure around creative/innovative processes?

References

1. "Our Story," Timberland, VF Corporation, 2020, www.timberland.com/about-us/our-story.html
2. Rosabeth Moss Kanter, and Ryan L. Raffaelli, February 2, 2015, "Innovation at Timberland: Thinking Outside the Shoebox," Harvard Business Review, Case Study.
3. Elizabeth Holmes, June 14, 2011, "Sale Gives Timberland Leg Up," The Wall Street Journal, Dow Jones & Company, www.wsj.com/articles/SB10001424052702303848104576383230037744242
4. "Annual Report Fiscal Year 2020," Annual Reports, V.F. Corporation, Mar 28, 2020, https://d1io3yog0oux5.cloudfront.net/_e3788fc7d2c93cd26de1a6fae9c5ae49/vfc/db/409/70380/annual_report/VF_FY2020 ShareholderLetter-DIGITAL-FINAL.pdf
5. "Annual Report Fiscal Year 2019," Annual Reports, V.F. Corporation, Mar 30 2019, https://d1io3yog0oux5.cloudfront.net/_e3788fc7d2c93cd26de1a6fae9c5ae49/vfc/db/409/66586/annual_report/VF_FY2019_AR_Design-052919-FINAL_Digital.pdf
6. Sarah Halzack, Jan 2, 2015, "How Timberland Used Customer Data to Reboot Its Brand," The Washington Post, WP Company, www.washingtonpost.com/news/business/wp/2015/01/02/how-timberland-used-customer-data-to-reboot-its-brand/
7. Pamela N. Danziger, Sept 22, 2017, "Timberland Blazes a New Trail in Retail," Forbes Magazine, www.forbes.com/sites/pamdanziger/2017/09/22/timberland-blazes-a-new-trail-in-retail/
8. "Responsibility – Making Things Better," Timberland, VF Corporation, 2020, www.timberland.com/responsibility.html
9. "All Timberland Products to Be 100% Circular, Net Positive by 2030," Sustainable Brands, Sept 1 2020, https://sustainablebrands.com/read/product-service-design-innovation/all-timberland-products-to-be-100-circular-net-positive-by-2030
10. Jennifer Reingold, Nov 2005, "Walking the Walk," Fast Company, https://Search proquestcom.proxy.lib.umich.edu/pqrl/docview/228749051/fulltextPDF/E94DDDDC18CD4AF7PQ/2?accountid=14667
11. James Ovenden, Sept 1, 2016, "Supply Chain Case Study: Timberland," Innovation Enterprise, https://channels.theinnovationenterprise.com/articles/supply-chain-case-study-timberland

Timberland   259

12. George A. Shinkle, et al., 2019, "On Establishing Legitimate Goals and Their Performance Impact: JBE," Journal of Business Ethics, 157(3), pp. 731–751.
13. Laura Motel, 2016, "Increasing Diversity Through Goal-Setting in Corporate Social Responsibility Reporting," Equality, Diversity, and Inclusion: An International Journal, 35(5), pp. 328–349.
14. "Technical Guidance for Calculating Scope 3 Emissions," Greenhouse Gas Protocol, World Resources Institute & World Business Council for Sustainable Development, 2013, www.ghgprotocol.org/sites/default/files/ghgp/standards/Scope3_Calculation_Guidance_0.pdf
15. Nina Kruschwitz, Nov 2012, "New Ways to Engage Employees, Suppliers and Competitors in CSR," MIT Sloan Management Review, 54(2), https://search-proquest-com.proxy.lib.umich.edu/pqrl/docview/1266763120/3BBD9657A0B4409EPQ/3?accountid=14667
16. "Better Product," Timberland, VF Corporation, 2020, www.timberland.com/responsibility/product.html
17. "10 Ways the Higg Index Creates Business Value," Higg Index, Apparel Coalition, 2015, https://apparelcoalition.org/wp-content/uploads/2015/08/Higg_BusinessValue_Oct22_FINAL.pdf
18. "The Higg Index," Sustainable Apparel Coalition, 2021, https://apparelcoalition.org/the-higg-index/
19. "VF to Establish Three Global Innovation Centers to Accelerate its Innovation Platform," Business Wire, Aug 26, 2013.
20. "Annual Report Fiscal Year 2013," Annual Reports, VF Corporation, Mar. 2013, https://d1io3yog0oux5.cloudfront.net/_e3788fc7d2c93cd26de1a6fae9c5ae49/vfc/db/409/66565/annual_report/2013.pdf
21. "ReBOTL Recycled Technology," Timberland, VF Corporation, 2020, www.timberland.com/rebotl.html
22. Arthur Friedman, 2020, "Steps in the Right Direction: How Timberland Aims to be Net Positive by 2030," Sourcing Journal (Online).
23. Ellen MacArthur Foundation, May 2015, "Circularity Indicators," Ellen MacArthur Foundation, www.ellenmacarthurfoundation.org/assets/downloads/insight/Circularity-Indicators_Methodology_May2015.pdf
24. "About Us," Leather Working Group, 2020, www.leatherworkinggroup.com/who-we-are/about-us
25. Timberland, 2020 Quarter 3 CSR Full Report, VF Corporation, 2020, https://images.timberland.com/is/content/TimberlandBrand/Responsibility/downloads/2020/q3/All_Q3_2020.pdf
26. "Thread x Timberland Partnership," Timberland, VF Corporation, 2018, www.timberland.com/blog/values/timberland-thread-partnership.html
27. "Timberland and Omni United Launch First-of-its-Kind Cross-Industry Partnership – Unveiling Timberland Tires: Timberland Tires Will be the First Line of Tires Purposely Created to be Recycled into Footwear Outsoles at the End of their Life on the Road," PR Newswire, Nov 3, 2014.
28. Jeff Swartz, Sep 1, 2002, "Doing Well and Doing Good: The Business Community and National Service," Bookings Institution, www.brookings.edu/articles/doing-well-and-doing-good-the-business-community-and-national-service/

Case 10: Zara-Inditex – Fast Fashion Done Right

Rocco Pelà

INSEAD
rocco.pela@insead.edu

"Fast fashion" is the term used to describe clothing designs that move quickly from the catwalk to stores to meet the latest trends [1]. The fast fashion global industry, as of 2019, was valued at $36B [2]. This industry has seen several players come and go over the years; while some have managed to reap sizable gains, others have collapsed under the pressure of the fierce competition. European giants Zara and H&M, among a select few others, have seen consistent success over the past few decades. In particular, Zara and its parent company Inditex have emerged as true leaders in the industry, displaying outstanding operational efficiency thanks to continuous innovation. Over the past two decades, Inditex's annual net sales growth has often exceeded 10%, reaching €26.1bn in 2018. Inditex's net profit margin of 10% to 14% has been the envy of mass-market rivals [3]. Meanwhile, several competitors have struggled, with California retailer Forever 21 filing for bankruptcy in December 2020, and Gap posting a record $932M loss for the 2020 financial year [4].

Originally founded in 1974 by Spanish entrepreneur Amancio Ortega [5], Zara has grown into a world-renowned brand. Today, Inditex is the largest fashion group in the world, operating over 7,200 stores in 96 markets, with Zara alone accounting for over 2,000 of those [6]. While Zara clearly stands out as Inditex's flagship brand, notable sister brands owned by the Spanish group include Massimo Dutti, Bershka, Stradivarius, Oysho, Pull&Bear, and Uterque.

Opening its first store in 1975 in the small Spanish town of A Coruña, Zara's unusual approach toward fashion proved to be quickly appreciated by the Spanish market, as the firm was able to expand to the biggest cities in Spain within its first eight years [5]. In 1985, Inditex was incorporated as a holding company, laying the foundations for the supply chain developments that are widely considered to be the key success factor in Zara's growth. Amancio Ortega strongly believed that Zara needed a dynamic supply chain in order to stand out in an industry that was dominated by large multinational firms [7]. Ortega devised simpler design, manufacturing, and distribution processes, reducing lead times and allowing Zara to quickly react to new consumer trends; he called this process "Instant Fashion." [7] Between 1985 and 1995, Zara aggressively expanded to the global market, opening stores in Portugal, the US, France, Mexico, Greece, Belgium, Sweden, Malta, Cyprus, Norway and Israel [5]. The international expansion continued over the course of the following decades, ultimately reaching the current count of 96 markets.

The Zara empire is built on two basic rules: "Give customers what they want," and "get it to them faster than anyone else." [7] To do so, Zara has regularly implemented innovative

DOI: 10.4324/9781003190837-31

approaches, ranging from revolutionary manufacturing and distribution processes, to the use of RFID tags to improve inventory management. Zara's rapid adoption of technology, especially in the 2010s, is a large reason for its recent financial performance, which has brought the brand value from $7.6B in 2010 to $14B in 2020 [8].

Ultimately, Zara's success story is the result of several factors. The firm's culture of innovation, lean operations and first-in-class supply chain efficiency have allowed it to succeed in an industry rich in fierce competition. The following analysis will provide insight into the key inflection points and factors behind Zara's success. It will evaluate the Spanish firm's core strengths, discussing the current and upcoming challenges faced by the company.

Zara's super-agility

Introduction

The secret to Zara's success lies in its super-agility. In particular, it displays an outstanding ability to keep up with the dynamic nature of the fashion industry, adapting to changing trends by releasing brand-new collections with very little delay. Zara's founding principle remains the same as today: Make speed the driving force [9]. Zara's unique approach has allowed it to transform from a local retailer to a global leader, spearheading fast fashion apparel.

Customer-centric approach

From the very beginning, Zara identified a significant gap in the market that no other firms were addressing: To keep pace with the latest trends, while still offering clothing collections that are made of high-quality garments and relatively affordable [7]. As a result, Zara revolutionized the standard practices that had characterized the fashion industry for centuries. Traditionally, designers and creative directors ideate designs, which are then manufactured and delivered to stores, in hopes that they will satisfy consumer taste and sell well. Conversely, at Zara, market signals are what drives manufacturing decisions. Customer preferences are extracted based on the items that sell at trade shows and in stores. This information is then forwarded to designers, who work backward to create products based on these insights. As a result, Zara introduces new collections on a bi-weekly basis.

To put this approach into perspective, fast fashion competitors such as Mango or Gap renew their collections "only" six times a year [10]. Most retailers determine 50% of their designs six months in advance, with 80% of the inventory committed by the beginning of each season. Conversely, Zara determines only 20% of a season's line six months in advance, adopting its just-in-time production at short notice [11]. If a design fails to sell well, it is swiftly withdrawn, removed from future orders, and replaced by a new one. This rapid turnover provides a sense of urgency for customers to buy an item that they are interested in, as they are aware that it will be permanently unavailable within a few weeks. Additionally, this business strategy allows the company to sell more items at full price because of the sense of scarcity and exclusiveness that the brand exudes [12].

Zara collects extensive qualitative data from its frontline interactions with customers, as it specifically trains its employees to be receptive to customer behaviors

262   *Case studies*

[7]. Before the start of each workday, floor staff and store managers gather to discuss customer insights; a report is made containing best-selling items, pieces returned by customers, shopper feedback, as well as general trends that staff have identified [13]. Associates and store managers intently listen and note down customer comments, ideas for cuts, fabrics, or a new line, and keenly observe styles that customers are wearing that have the potential to be converted into unique Zara apparel [7]. Through the use of point-of-sales data, Zara can then accurately forecast consumer demand by style, color, and size. All of Zara's employees provide input, the aggregation of which results in insightful human intelligence that Zara uses to adjust its production and rapidly move from concept to product.

This attention to detail appears to be appreciated by Zara's customers, as shopper frequency at Zara is two to three times higher than traditional women's apparel, indicating super-loyalty to the brand [14]. In Spain, an average high-street store expects customers to visit thrice a year, but for Zara, customers tend to visit approximately 17 times per year [7]. Moreover, this high frequency further reinforces Zara's need to regularly reinvent its product offering to retain its customers' interest.

Thanks to its customer-centric data collection, Zara is able to tailor its product offering to address unique specifications that shoppers around the world may have. Factors such as physical, climate, or cultural differences all dictate design decisions for each market. For example, stores in Japan offer smaller-sized clothes, while stores in Latin America adopt lighter garments to address differences in seasonality [7]. For a company that allocates only 0.3% of sales to advertising, Zara has a remarkably close relationship with its customers [15]. By putting the customer at the core of its design decisions, Zara works to deliver exactly what consumers are looking for.

Supply chain efficiency

It is important to acknowledge that Zara's customer-centric approach is only possible thanks to the firm's first-in-class supply chain. Zara's super-responsive supply chain outputs garments 24 hours, 365 days a year, shipping new products to stores twice per week [7]. The primary distribution center in A Coruña inspects, sorts, tags, and loads clothing into trucks, delivering them within 48 hours. This vertically integrated system is responsible for the production of over 450 million items each year [12].

Rather than focusing on product margin, once again, Zara focuses on speed. Zara condenses the lead time from design to placement on store shelves to a mere three or four weeks by forcing its design and production teams to work with a limited range of fabrics and material [16]. Although these restrictions inevitably affect creative freedom, they crunch lead times, enabling the swift operations that Zara is known for. By accelerating this process, Zara dramatically reduces its demand uncertainty, as it needs to forecast its sales over a much shorter span of time, allowing the firm to quickly adapt to the latest shifts in consumer preferences [17].

Despite producing a significant portion of its products in the A Coruña facility, Zara also makes extensive use of its factories in Turkey, Morocco, and Asia. In order to reap the benefits of the higher economies of scale and lower production costs that these alternate markets provide, Zara allocates its production in a unique way. Fashionable, riskier products that require testing and piloting are produced in Spain. Conversely, "standard" products that have highly predictable demand are produced in factories outside of Spain. These garments are less complex and can be produced in significantly larger quantities. By splitting its production, Zara incurs significant lower costs [7].

Technological innovation

Under the hood, Zara uses several technologies to make this near-flawless system a reality.

Zara-Inditex's recent investments in technology have largely focused on big data. The data analytics performed by the Spanish firm is unparalleled in the industry, resulting in a phenomenal predictive capacity. The company tracks data from each of its global stores. A myriad of inputs is collected, ranging from sales data to the ambient temperature and energy consumption of each store, as well as social media engagement. The data is then processed at Zara's data processing center in Spain, which runs 24 hours a day, drawing insightful relationships that drive the company's decisions. These extensive analytics allow Zara to reach eerily specific conclusions about its customers. For example, the company is able to deduce the average weight of residents in each neighborhood of its stores [6]. As a result, it can better determine garment sizes than will need to be shipped to those locations.

A further example of technological implementation in Zara's operations is the use of RFID, which is now a staple of the brand's automated replenishment system. Each garment sold in stores includes an RFID chip, which allows individual identification of each item by means of radio waves. By using this technology, Zara has been able to evolve its supply chain and establish an accurate and automated inventory tracking system. The data provides real-time size availability, reducing excess stock and maintaining the firm's lean operations [18].

In 2018, Zara introduced a radically innovative technology to improve its in-store experience: Augmented Reality (AR) [19]. Since then, stores around the world have been equipped with AR displays that allow customers to visualize models wearing selected looks from Zara's ranges by simply using the smartphone camera system. The same 3D scanning technology allows a similar experience through Zara's e-commerce platform, enabling models to pop-up on packages of online purchases delivered to customers, showing alternative outfits [32].

Zara's frequent adoption of new technology has been aligned with its mission to deliver quality garments at a phenomenal speed. By leveraging innovative inventions to emphasize its core values, Zara has been able keep its lead on the rest of the industry.

Organizational culture

Zara and Inditex's unique philosophy is the result of a carefully crafted organizational culture. Its employees are among the youngest in the field, with 62% of its employees aged under 30 [20]. Further, the relatively flat organizational structure, which lacks a chief designer, empowers its staff to make data-driven decisions, fostering an entrepreneurial mindset. Due to its rapid operations, the company requires a dynamic, driven workforce – the word "impossible" does not exist at Zara. This is reflected in the compensation structure, as store managers receive up to 50% of their compensation as a variable component, making floor-level staff heavily incentive-driven [21].

Further, Zara's organizational culture is one that encourages its management to proactively think about risks and challenges that it might face. For example, although

264 *Case studies*

the fast fashion industry has regularly faced scrutiny for the environmental impact of these firms' operations, Zara has consistently been an early mover in this respect. Zara has regularly worked with local universities in Spain to identify eco-friendly approaches to reduce its environmental footprint [7]. By 2019, 100% of the brand's fleet of stores were eco-efficient "eco-stores." These stores use at least 20% less electricity and 40% less water than conventional stores [22]. Additionally, Inditex annually publishes extensive CSR and climate change reports to display the group's commitment to these domains. This has resulted in the 'Carbon Disclosure Project' naming Inditex as a fast fashion leader in this regard.

Challenges ahead

The year 2020 proved to be a challenging one for firms across all industries, with retail and fast fashion being among the most severely affected by lockdowns and social distancing measures. These events forced mass migration to e-commerce platforms, which Zara followed. At Inditex, e-commerce shopping rose 50% in Q1 2020 following the temporary closure of 6,000 of its 7,000 stores. As a result, Inditex announced plans to invest $3B in its e-commerce operations [23]. The changing landscape of the retail industry suggests that there may be fresh, incoming challenges for Zara and Inditex.

(1) Zara has historically kept its advertising expenses to a minimum, relying on its physical stores and their locations as the primary means of marketing. With the accelerating transition to e-commerce and Inditex recently announcing that it will be shutting down 1,200 stores, one wonders whether this approach, in the long run, will be sufficient to remain popular and stay atop of the fierce competition [24].

(2) Zara's strategy of offering affordable prices is currently a key advantage over its competitors. Nevertheless, as new players enter the industry and fight to catch up to Zara, cutting prices and refining their business models, this gap is likely to diminish soon, especially on European soil, with competitors such as H&M and Mango heavily expanding. Zara may need to review its strategy and focus on other qualities that make its garments stand out.

(3) The next in line for the title of chairman at Inditex is set to be Amancio Ortega's daughter, Marta Ortega. This transition of power will prove to be a crucial inflection point. It will be of paramount importance for the next generation of leadership to effectively adapt to the industry, while staying true to the founding principles, values, and organizational culture that have made it the giant it is today.

Conclusion

Zara has shown itself to be a pioneer and stellar innovator in the field of fast fashion. Its customer-centric approach, technological innovation, supply chain responsiveness, and organizational culture have combined to create a super-agile company that rapidly adjusts to the dynamic nature of the retail industry. Nevertheless, the COVID-19 pandemic has introduced fresh challenges for Zara. As the Spanish firm faces increasing digitalization of retail, fierce competition, and a transition of power, how will it react?

Case questions

1. What is Zara's value proposition to its customers?
2. What makes Zara stand out against its fast fashion competitors?
3. How do customers benefit from Zara's innovation?
4. What are the benefits and drawbacks that Zara faces by restricting the creative output of its design team?
5. Zara practiced achievement-based culture by placing more than 50% of staff compensation as variable or performance-based. Can you discuss this, applying the TRIAL© framework?
6. Zara was closer to customers and demonstrated its ability to adapt to dynamic changes in consumer preferences. Can you discuss this, applying the TRIAL© framework?
7. What are some new and evolving technology innovations that can be leveraged by Zara to tackle its upcoming challenges?

References

1. Investopedia, 2021, "How Fast Fashion Works," [online], Investopedia, available at www.investopedia.com/terms/f/fast-fashion.asp, accessed January 29, 2021.
2. Statista, 2021, "Fast Fashion Market Value Forecast worldwide 2009–2029 | Statista," [online], Statista, available at www.statista.com/statistics/1008241/fast-fashion-market-value-forecast-worldwide/#:~:text=In%202019%2C%20the%20global%20market, was%2036%20billion%20U.S.%20dollars, accessed January 29, 2021.
3. Financial Times, 2021, "How Extreme Agility Put Zara Ahead in Fast Fashion," [online], Financial Times, available at www.ft.com/content/3f581046-cd7c-11e9-b018-ca4456540ea6, accessed January 29, 2021.
4. CNN, 2021, "The Gap Posts a Record $932 Million Loss," [online], CNN, available at https://edition.cnn.com/2020/06/04/business/gap-loss/index.html, accessed January 29, 2021.
5. Inditex, 2021, "Our Story – inditex.com," [online], Inditex.com, available at www.inditex.com/about-us/our-story, accessed January 29, 2021.
6. Jessica Jones, 2021, "How Zara Took Over the World's High Streets," [online], CultureTrip, available at https://theculturetrip.com/europe/spain/articles/how-zara-took-over-the-worlds-high-streets/, accessed January 29, 2021.
7. Martin Roll, 2021, "The Secret of Zara's Success: A Culture of Customer Co-creation," [online], Martin Roll, available at https://martinroll.com/resources/articles/strategy/the-secret-of-zaras-success-a-culture-of-customer-co-creation/, accessed January 29, 2021.
8. Statista, 2021, "Brand Value Comparison of H&M and Zara Worldwide 2010 – 2020," [online], Statista, available at www.statista.com/statistics/1071147/brand-value-comparison-of-handm-and-zara-worldwide/, accessed January 29, 2021.
9. Fashionista, 2021, "Fashion History Lesson: The Origins of Fast Fashion," [online], Fashionista, available at https://fashionista.com/2016/06/what-is-fast-fashion, accessed January 29, 2021.
10. IE, 2021, "Zara: Technology and User Experience as Drivers of Business," [online], IE Insights, available at www.ie.edu/insights/articles/zara-technology-and-user-experience-as-drivers-of-business, accessed January 29, 2021.
11. HBS Digital, 2021, "Digitalization of Zara and Fast Fashion – Technology and Operations Management," [online], Technology and Operations Management, available at https://digital.hbs.edu/platform-rctom/submission/digitalization-of-zara-and-fast-fashion/, accessed January 29, 2021.

266   *Case studies*

12. TradeGecko, 2021, "Zara Supply Chain Analysis – the Secret Behind Zara's Retail Success," [online], Tradegecko.com, available at www.tradegecko.com/blog/supply-chain-management/zara-supply-chain-its-secret-to-retail-success, accessed January 29, 2021.

13. Straits Times, 2021, "Zara's Secret to Success Lies in Big Data and an Agile Supply Chain," [online], Straits Times, available at www.straitstimes.com/lifestyle/fashion/zaras-secret-to-success-lies-in-big-data-and-an-agile-supply-chain, accessed January 29, 2021.

14. Forbes, 2021, "Why Zara Succeeds: It Focuses on Pulling People In, Not Pushing Product Out," [online], Forbes, available at www.forbes.com/sites/pamdanziger/2018/04/23/zaras-difference-pull-people-in-not-push-product-out/?sh=57029d5923cb, accessed January 29, 2021.

15. Retail Gazette, 2021, "How Does Zara Survive Despite Minimal Advertising?" [online], Retailgazette.co.uk, available at www.retailgazette.co.uk/blog/2019/01/how-does-zara-survive-despite-minimal-advertising/#:~:text=%E2%80%9CZara%20only%20spends%20about%200.3,Zara%20builds%20massive%20brand%20loyalty.%E2%80%9D&text=And%20while%20it%20is%20a,shoppers%20are%20likely%20to%20visit, accessed January 29, 2021.

16. Forbes, 2021, "Zara Uses Supply Chain to Win Again," [online], available at www.forbes.com/sites/kevinomarah/2016/03/09/zara-uses-supply-chain-to-win-again/, accessed January 29, 2021.

17. Md Afzalul Aftab et al., 2021, "Super Responsive Supply Chain: The Case of Spanish Fast Fashion Retailer Inditex-Zara," [online], available at www.researchgate.net/publication/324702528_Super_Responsive_Supply_Chain_The_Case_of_Spanish_Fast_Fashion_Retailer_Inditex-Zara, accessed January 29, 2021.

18. Inditex, 2021, "Inditex Deploys RFID Technology in its Stores," [online], Inditex.com, available at www.inditex.com/article?articleId=150174&title=Inditex+deploys+RFID+technology+in+its+stores, accessed January 29, 2021.

19. Econsultancy, 2021, "How Zara is Using In-Store Tech to Improve its Frustrating Shopper Experience," [online], Econsultancy, available at https://econsultancy.com/how-zara-is-using-in-store-tech-to-improve-its-frustrating-shopper-experience/, accessed January 29, 2021.

20. Forbes, 2021, "Zara Stores Target Millennials with Augmented Reality Displays," [online], Forbes, available at www.forbes.com/sites/emmasandler/2018/04/16/zara-stores-targets-millennials-with-augmented-reality-displays/?sh=5af4c5852315, accessed January 29, 2021.

21. Inditex, 2021, "Annual Report," [online], Static.inditex.com, available at https://static.inditex.com/annual_report_2017/assets/pdf/c2_en.pdf, accessed January 29, 2021.

22. Inditex, 2021, "Ecoefficient-Stores," [online], Inditex.com, available at www.inditex.com/our-commitment-to-the-environment/climate-change-and-energy/eco-stores, accessed January 29, 2021.

23. Digital Commerce, 2021, "Zara Owner Plans to Invest $3 Billion in Ecommerce Operations," [online], Digital Commerce 360, available at www.digitalcommerce360.com/2020/06/10/zara-owner-plans-to-invest-3-billion-in-ecommerce-operations, accessed January 29, 2021.

24. Business Insider, 2021, "Zara's Owner Says it Will Close as Many as 1,200 Stores as it Doubles Down on Online Shopping," [online], Business Insider, available at www.businessinsider.com/zara-inditex-invests-in-online-shopping-post-pandemic-2020-6?r=US&IR=T), , accessed January 29, 2021.

Case 11: Patagonia – Leader of a Sustainable Business

Suzanna Yik

Stephen M. Ross School of Business University of Michigan
yiksuzy@umich.edu

Overview

"Ethical, environmentally friendly, and outdoors" are words that come to mind when one hears Patagonia. Founded in 1973, Yvon Chouinard combined his passion for sustainability with his love of being in the great outdoors [1]. Now a well-known brand, Patagonia is a leading outdoor apparel company focused on environmental conservation and activism [1]. In the 2020 Fashion Transparency Index, Patagonia was ranked 7th out of 250 apparel companies [2]. With just 37 stores and a presence in the US, Europe, Japan, Argentina, Chile, and more, the sustainable company has kickstarted progressive actions that radically change how we now think of the fashion industry [3].

Patagonia is famous for two components of their business model: (1) Having a purpose-driven mission; and (2) Being at the forefront of advocating for environmental causes [4].

The company's original mission is to "build the best product, cause no unnecessary harm, [and] use business to inspire and implement solutions to the environmental crisis." [4] The company focuses on creating high-quality products while minimizing their environmental impact. Today, Patagonia has revised their statement to be evermore clear and impactful: "Patagonia is in business to save our home planet." [4]

In 2011, Patagonia became a benefit corporation [5]. The company declared their commitment to sustainability and their employees by documenting it in their articles of incorporation. Since then, Patagonia completed their B Impact Assessment, examining their impact on customers, workers, communities, the environment, and governance [6]. This highlights the push to continuously improve and enforce change. The company also supports activists by donating at least 1% of annual sales to organizations for natural environment preservation and restoration efforts as shown in Exhibit 11.1 [7, 8, 9, 10, 11]. Named 1% for the Planet, these grassroots environmental organizations use the donations to integrate parts of Patagonia's business model into their own [4]. Another related program the company has is Patagonia Action Works. As an interactive website, customers input their location and the webpage outputs names of local community environmental organizations that Patagonia supports. This platform connects Patagonia and their customers to an ecosystem of other environmentally conscious partners who help foster positive community engagement.

DOI: 10.4324/9781003190837-32

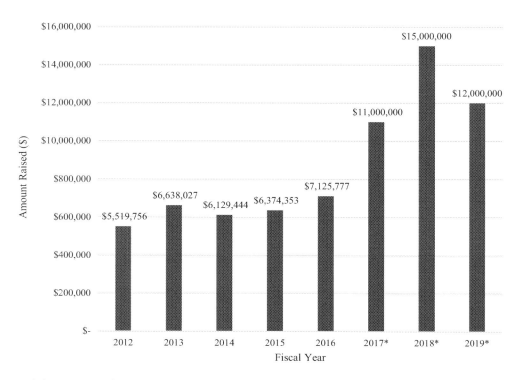

Exhibit 11.1 1% for the Planet Initiative.

Social responsibility into company

Introduction

The secret to Patagonia's success lies within their focus on social responsibility as a foundation to establish and grow a company [12]. Patagonia continuously adapts to the social climate by constructing their operational model to minimize their environmental impact and implementing marketing tactics to inform and foster accountable conversation among customers. Patagonia's efforts in retail innovation and social change are accomplished through their business practices and activism. Combined with their purpose-driven mission, the company is a leader within the outdoor apparel industry and is transforming how businesses view sustainability.

Product lifecycle management

From the beginning, Patagonia's business model is rooted in "four core values: quality, environmentalism, integrity, and innovation." [12] All four values are configured in their operational model, specifically in their product lifecycle management process. It is based on the four Rs – reduce, repair, reuse, and recycle [12]. Termed Worn Wear, the program is a toolset that connects customers to Patagonia to extend the life of Patagonia products [13]. The trade-in program allows customers to send in their used Patagonia clothing to get repaired and resold. The recycled material offers great quality products with low impact inputs, appealing to environmentally conscious customers. In 2018, 11,300 US tons of clothing occupied the landfills, while only 2,510 US tons were recycled [13]. Worn Wear aims to combat this statistic by reducing the number of clothes thrown out each year.

ReCrafted is another stellar implementation of product lifecycle management. Unlike Worn Wear, where used clothing is repaired and resold, ReCrafted items are clothes made from other clothes. Each piece is composed of multiple used Patagonia items that enter warehouses and are beyond repair [13]. ReCrafted clothing is a one-of-a-kind product. This initiative attracts upcycle junkies and environmentally conscious consumers [13]. ReCrafted further reduces the amount of clothing waste that ends up in landfills.

A notable marketing strategy run by Patagonia was their advertisement during the 2011 Thanksgiving season [14]. The company thought it would be hypocritical of them to work toward environmental change without acting upon their words [15]. They needed to encourage customers to think before they buy. The "Don't Buy This Jacket" flyer campaign reinvigorated the "Rs" of environmentalism and reinforced the benefits of reduce, reuse, repair, recycle and reimagine when it comes to their products, which subsequently turned into the Common Threads Initiative [16]. The flyer depicts a popular fleece jacket and encourages customers to reconsider before purchasing the product, and instead opt for a used Patagonia product. The four Rs are listed and described, emphasizing the importance of each R, and how Patagonia can help viewers accomplish each. Even though Patagonia encourages consumers to rethink not buying full-priced, new products, the company follows through with their mission and purpose with their actions. The advertisement was successful and generated conversation around Patagonia's product lifecycle management tactic. It caused "revenues to grow about 30% to $543M in 2012, followed by another 5% growth in 2012. By 2017 the company reached $1B in sales." [14]

Supply chain management and transparency

What does supply chain transparency mean and look like? The *Harvard Business Review* states that "Supply chain transparency requires companies to know what is happening upstream in the supply chain and to communicate this knowledge both internally and externally." [17] Patagonia does just that. The well-known sustainable company strives to be sustainable by sourcing materials to ensure products are made under safe, fair, legal, and human working conditions. The textile industry releases "more than 1.2 billion US tons of CO_2 emissions into our atmosphere every year." [18] Additionally, 10% of the world's global greenhouse gases emitted are due to clothing and footwear industries [18]. Being part of this industry, Patagonia has created initiatives to source, manufacture, and transport sustainability [18]. Nearly 70% of all Patagonia products are made from recycled materials, including plastic bottles [11]. The company also uses hemp and organic cotton to green their supply chain [11]. Patagonia's environmental initiatives and their commitment to protecting the Earth led Patagonia to be "awarded the United Nations' flagship environmental honor for entrepreneurial vision." [11] Although these practices tend to be more costly, a study from the MIT Sloan School of Management finds that consumers are

270   *Case studies*

willing to pay 2% to 10% more for products with greater supply chain transparency [17]. As the retail industry grows increasingly competitive, customers desire more supply chain transparency from companies to make informed decisions about their purchases. Businesses in the fashion and textile industries are expected more than ever to green their supply chain and be more sustainable.

Patagonia plays a significant role in sourcing new suppliers and in keeping current suppliers accountable for their green supply chains. Each supplier must be screened for quality, social standards, environmental impact, and product and material sourcing [12]. Patagonia thoroughly inspects their suppliers' entire production line from farming through the supplier to Patagonia facilities to ensure the supply chain upholds the highest standards of quality while minimizing environmental impact [12]. Additionally, Patagonia maintains internal controls within their facilities to avoid last-minute order changes or demand price changes, which could impact worker conditions [12]. The company also has veto power to stop partnerships with those who fail to meet Patagonia's standards, demonstrating that Patagonia walks the talk [5]. In the fall of 2015, Patagonia ramped up their Fair Trade Certified apparel [19]. They now work with Fair Trade USA to help integrate certified apparel with partners in India and to help workers get living wages in factories in Thailand, Vietnam, Columbia, and Mexico [17]. The Fair Trade Certification requires commitment, trust, and transparency, all of which Patagonia practices as a role model corporation [19].

The sustainable company kickstarted The Footprint Chronicles [20]. Launched in 2007, this interactive website shows a Google map with pinpoints of factories around the world [13]. Individuals click on each pin to learn more about the specifics of that factory and products produced there for Patagonia [13]. The exact social and environmental conditions of the supply chain are also detailed, including what goes into vendors' operations and staffing [17]. This highlights how transparent Patagonia is, not only to their business partners but also to their consumers.

From using materials that are mostly recycled to creating The Footprint Chronicles, Patagonia is termed to be an innovator in the categories of adopters as shown in Exhibit 11.2 [17, 21]. Innovators are the first people to bring fresh ideas and to take on the risk of pursuing them [21]. Patagonia fully discloses transparency and achieves all the transparency milestones. Their supply chain scope has progressed from greening internal operations to direct and indirect suppliers and now raw materials [21]. Patagonia is the epitome of a purpose-driven mission aligning with their supply chain transparency. Although they have had great success thus far, Patagonia has increased their electricity usage as shown in Exhibit 11.3 [10]. Going forward, the company strives to reduce their environmental footprint and be carbon neutral by 2025 by prioritizing energy efficiency and renewable electricity [18].

Organizational management and culture

Newly appointed Patagonia CEO Ryan Gellert discusses recent executive restructuring. It is "aimed at more clearly aligning its various business units with its mission and outdoor sports communities." [22] He champions strengthening business with more environmental protection and fighting climate change through the power of Patagonia's core values and employees [22]. Decentralized workplace departments allow for sustainability and corporate responsibility at every step of the business process – from product development to marketing and sales [12].

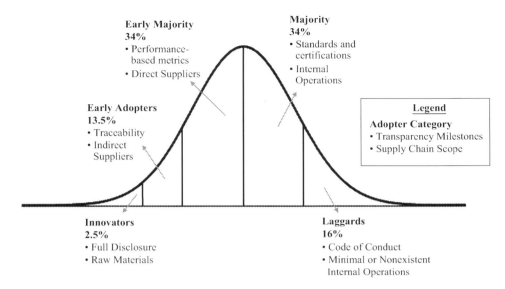

Exhibit 11.2 Supply chain transparency in innovation adoption categories. Adapted from [17, 21].

Electricity Use (KWH)		
Region	FY18	FY19
North America	5,500,624	8,671,027
Japan	1,275,256	1,387,022
Europe	622,205	605,402
Australia	142,343	216,311
South Korea	174,571	182,658
South America	92,457	89,606
Total	7,807,456	11,152,026

Exhibit 11.3 Patagonia's electricity usage around the world [10]

Employee culture rates as one of the company's best practices [5]. Their people live up to the term "work-life balance" while focusing on physical and mental health [5]. Patagonia's headquarters even offer exercise class options and on-site childcare. These perks allow employees to be their best selves at work without having to worry about their children or if they can squeeze in time for a workout. Patagonia's internship program fosters professional and personal growth while supporting environmental causes [5]. Opportunities such as these advance the company's mission statement to better the planet – both environmentally and their people.

The people and their collaborative collectivism are also leading innovative changes [22]. In Europe, Patagonia employees create environments where people can get involved above and beyond their roles [22]. Employees work together more

272 *Case studies*

than ever before. They came to work for Patagonia because of their fondness for the company's mission statement [22]. Each person brings great ideas, passion, and inspiration, pushing Patagonia to improve and live up to their mission statement to save the planet.

Challenges ahead

2020 was a hectic and challenging year for most apparel businesses with lockdowns and social distancing requirements forcing companies to file for bankruptcy or cease in-store shopping experiences. Patagonia's sales have dropped significantly since March 2020 [23]. As the pandemic continues into 2021, the clothing industry and Patagonia may face more challenges soon.

(1) The pandemic has disrupted production; as a result, supply chains shut down [24]. However, as more people stay at and work from home, sales of different products fluctuate. Gyms are closed and more individuals are turning to nature, causing outdoor athletic clothing sales to rise. More sales are now made on e-commerce rather than brick and mortar stores due to lockdowns and store capacity limits [23]. With supply chains shut down or delayed, Patagonia needs to navigate how to keep up with the demand for athletic clothes and online sales.
(2) One of Patagonia's goals is to become carbon neutral by 2025 [18]. As climate change becomes an ever more pressing issue, the company needs to utilize their resources more sustainably and efficiently to combat climate change threats. Factories are under severe pressure to ration their water [25]. How will Patagonia alleviate this issue? Patagonia is also under pressure to find ways to help local populations where their products are made – to improve living conditions and implement disaster relief promises [6].
(3) CEO Ryan Gellert newly stepped into his role. He seeks to invest money and manpower to influence environmental policy both in the US and abroad [4]. His transition to power during a pandemic and new policies being enacted under the Biden administration will be difficult to navigate. It is critical that Ryan Gellert can lead the company, adapt to the current climate, and strive toward his vision for Patagonia's future while staying true to the company's mission statement and core values of sustainability.

Conclusion

Patagonia shows itself to be an industry leader and outstanding innovator in the outdoor apparel and clothing industries. Their mission statement and core values are present in everything they do. Their product lifecycle management, supply chain management and transparency, and organizational management and culture work together to demonstrate that social responsibility can be the foundation to a sustainable and successful business. Patagonia's radical passion for environmental activism and initiatives inform consumers on the importance of sustainability and being environmentally conscious, and how to act upon it. The COVID-19 pandemic has created challenges; however, with the company's collectivism and people, Patagonia will innovate and develop ways to combat them.

Patagonia   273

Case questions

1. What innovation value does Patagonia create by being a benefit corporation?
2. What role do customers play in Patagonia's mission statement?
3. How do suppliers (direct and indirect) benefit from Patagonia's green supply chain standards?
4. What are the benefits and drawbacks that Patagonia faces by having multiple programs and initiatives for customers to be environmentally conscious and involved?
5. How will COVID-19 affect Patagonia's operations and revenue (for 1% for the Planet)?
6. How can Patagonia help grassroots environmental organizations further their sustainability efforts?

References

1. Corporate & Social Responsibility History, (n.d.), Patagonia, www.patagonia.com/our-footprint/corporate-social-responsibility-history.html
2. K.R. Whitely, March 1, 2021, "Outdoor Trend Report: Why Transparency Among Outdoor Companies Is On the Rise," Outside Business Journal, www.outsidebusinessjournal.com/the-magazine/features/outdoor-trend-report-transparency-the-voice/
3. Environmental Protection Agency, October 7, 2020, "Textiles: Material-Specific Data," EPA www.epa.gov/facts-and-figures-about-materials-waste-and-recycling/textiles-material-specific-data
4. Veronika Sonsev, November 27, 2019, "Patagonia's Focus On Its Brand Purpose Is Great For Business," Forbes, www.forbes.com/sites/veronikasonsev/2019/11/27/patagonias-focus-on-its-brand-purpose-is-great-for-business/?sh=3168d56954cb
5. Elissa Loughman, February 10, 2020, "Benefit Corporation Update: Patagonia Passes B Impact Assessment, Improves Score to 116," Patagonia, www.patagonia.com/stories/benefit-corporation-update-patagonia-passes-b-impact-assessment-improves-score-to-116/story-17871.html
6. Christopher Marquis, May 15, 2020, "Lessons From Patagonia: Stay Outspoken On Climate And Policy For Success And Social Change," Forbes, www.forbes.com/sites/christophermarquis/2020/05/15/lessons-from-patagonia-stay-outspoken-on-climate-and-policy-for-success-and-social-change/?sh=414239f15418
7. Patagonia, 2016, "Annual Benefit Corporation Report 2016," www.patagonia.com/on/demandware.static/-/Library-Sites-PatagoniaShared/default/dwbe159047/PDF-US/2016-B-CorpReport-031417.pdf
8. Patagonia, 2017, "Annual Benefit Corporation Report 2017," www.patagonia.com/static/on/demandware.static/-/Library-Sites-PatagoniaShared/default/dw824fac0f/PDF-US/2017-BCORP-pages_022218.pdf
9. Patagonia, 2018, "Annual Benefit Corporation Report 2018," www.patagonia.com/on/demandware.static/-/Library-Sites-PatagoniaShared/default/dw825bc0a0/PDF-US/2018-B-CorpReport.pdf
10. Patagonia, 2019, "Annual Benefit Corporation Report 2019," www.patagonia.com/on/demandware.static/-/Library-Sites-PatagoniaShared/default/dwf14ad70c/PDF-US/PAT_2019_BCorp_Report.pdf
11. "US Outdoor Clothing Brand Patagonia Wins UN Champions of the Earth Award," UN Environment, September 24, 2019, www.unep.org/news-and-stories/press-release/us-outdoor-clothing-brand-patagonia-wins-un-champions-earth-award

274 *Case studies*

12. Kelley, December 9, 2015, "Patagonia – Turning Social Responsibility into Company Business," Technology and Operations Management, https://digital.hbs.edu/platform-rctom/submission/patagonia-turning-social-responsibility-into-company-business/
13. "Better Than New," (n.d.), Worn Wear, https://wornwear.patagonia.com/faq
14. Poonkulali Thangavelu, January 23, 2021, "The Success of Patagonia's Marketing Strategy," Investopedia, www.investopedia.com/articles/personal-finance/070715/success-patagonias-marketing-strategy.asp
15. "Don't Buy This Jacket," November 25, 2020, Patagonia, www.patagonia.com/stories/dont-buy-this-jacket-black-friday-and-the-new-york-times/story-18615.html
16. B. Christin, July 24, 2020, "Patagonia: A Focus on a Sustainable Model," harlem hue, www.harlemhue.com/index.php/2020/07/24/patagonia-the-1b-powerhouse-with-an-anti-growth-strategy/
17. Alexis Bateman, and Leonardo Bonanni, January 20, 2021, "What Supply Chain Transparency Really Means," Harvard Business Review, https://hbr.org/2019/08/what-supply-chain-transparency-really-means
18. "Supply Chain Environmental Responsibility Program," (n.d.), Patagonia, www.patagonia.com/our-footprint/supply-chain-environmental-responsibility-program.html
19. "Patagonia Ramps Up Fair Trade Certified Apparel," October 1, 2015, just-style.com, http://bi.gale.com.proxy.lib.umich.edu/global/article/GALE%7CA463856596?u=umuser
20. Lisa Polley. February 10, 2020, "Introducing the New Footprint Chronicles on Patagonia.com," Patagonia, www.patagonia.com/stories/introducing-the-new-footprint-chronicles-on-patagoniacom/story-18443.html
21. W. LaMorte, September 9, 2019, "Behavioral Change Models," Diffusion of Innovation Theory, https://sphweb.bumc.bu.edu/otlt/mph-modules/sb/behavioralchangetheories/behavioralchangetheories4.html
22. Jeff Beer, September 23, 2020, "Exclusive: Patagonia's New CEO Talks About the Future of the Beloved Brand," Fast Company, www.fastcompany.com/90553967/exclusive-patagonias-new-ceo-talks-about-the-future-of-the-beloved-brand
23. Kim Bhasin, December 16, 2020, "Patagonia's New CEO Plots a Post-Trump Future for the Activist Brand," Bloomberg.com, www.bloomberg.com/news/features/2020-12-16/patagonia-s-new-ceo-plans-to-keeping-up-climate-fight-at-clothing-brand
24. Judith Magyar, January 19, 2021, "SAP BrandVoice: How COVID-19 Is Nudging The Fashion Industry To Go Circular," Forbes, www.forbes.com/sites/sap/2021/01/12/how-covid-19-is-nudging-the-fashion-industry-to-go-circular/?sh=4728e5cb2a63
25. "Climate Change and the Fashion Industry – How Patagonia is Fighting Back," November 15, 2017, Technology and Operations Management, digital.hbs.edu/platform-rctom/submission/climate-change-and-the-fashion-industry-how-patagonia-is-is-fighting-back/

Case 12: Amazon – Head in the Cloud: Transformation Through Leadership's Lens

William McCrone

Stephen M. Ross School of Business, University of Michigan
WMcCrone@UMich.edu

Looking back

Jeff Bezos sat down at his desk at the end of the first quarter 2021 looking back on the empire he had built. His goal of creating Earth's most customer-centric company had blossomed from a simple book retailing company into a technology behemoth literally changing how the world does business. He thought back to his 1997 shareholder letter. This letter, reprinted in every annual report, declares "this is Day 1" as the Amazon ethos [1]. Jeff pondered how he would ensure a successful leadership transition. The worry was becoming a "Day 2" company, which he said in 2016 was marked by "… stasis. Followed by irrelevance. Followed by excruciating, painful decline. Followed by death [2]."

Thinking back to the early days of Amazon, where he would sit on the floor while packing books only to drive them himself to be shipped, Jeff knew the company had come too far [3]. He quickly grabbed a pen to write down what he considered important to lead the company away from this tragic end.

Culture

Amazon has several cultural cornerstones for their operations to provide for their customers. Among these cornerstones are a long-term focus, working backward, and leadership principles. The long-term focus of Amazon is best demonstrated by the fact that despite starting in 1994, their first profitable year was in 2003 [4]. Jeff Bezos believes that placing long-term bets that may take years to grow will produce significant results, and continuous innovation through these bets will prevent the company from requiring a major change that could cost its existence [5]. This focus was also present in the flywheel business model that Jeff embraced from Jim Collins whereby a few key choices in the business cycle can begin to create momentum to the point that the cycle of operations produces compounding returns and grows a business rapidly [6]. Jeff had his top lieutenants use it to build out the retail business. The cycle for the Amazon flywheel was laid out in The Everything Store as follows: Lower prices led to more customers; more customers increased sales volume; larger volume attracts third-party sellers that pay a commission; this commission allows Amazon to reduce fixed costs; reducing fixed costs reduces prices [7]. Increasing any part of the cycle feeds the wheel and produces growth.

DOI: 10.4324/9781003190837-33

276 *Case studies*

Growth opportunities are guided by identifying the needs of the customer and working backward. The goal of the process is to empower small groups to produce something of value by imagining the result, and how it will be embraced [8]. The next step is to analyze the value produced by the opportunity through feedback and decide if it is worth building [9]. Once the decision is made to produce it, a roadmap is made [10]. Finally, the process begins with identifying what work needs to be done to build the product [11]. The whole goal is to figure out what products would actually make the customer happy and solve their problems instead of just creating a new invention.

Leadership principles are one of the most important tools. These principles provide a way to settle arguments within Amazon's small teams, known as two-pizza teams, with a goal to be no larger a group than can be fed by two pizzas [12]. A close group focused on collaboration may create points of contention or groupthink that ensure harmony. These principles exist to act to define the merit of ideas for the teams. They consist of 14 different principles that should define all actions taken at Amazon and this is illustrated in Exhibit 12.1. While many of the principles feel natural in a business setting, there are two that stand out and allow the company to function as an innovation center. The first is principle 13 – "have backbone; disagree and commit [13]." Amazon believes that submitting to someone else's idea is detrimental; this groupthink in the name of civility prevents growth of other ideas that may produce better outcomes. However, once the disagreement is noted and the team decides on a path, everyone should commit to prevent any further issues. This is a novel concept to prevent resentment and encourage innovation in an office setting. The other principle of note is 4 – "are right a lot [14]." Jeff himself noted that this principle often surprises people [15]. However, it is important to understand the purpose of this principle. The belief is that with practice people can get better at being right, and the right people do this by listening and changing their opinions when presented with new information [16].

Technology transition

Around the year 2000, the company decided to pursue an option to act as a platform for companies that had pure brick and mortar presences, Amazon wanted to provide the option to host a company's website with the technical backing of an e-tail native [17]. However, upon realizing the code that had propped the company up since 1994 was mostly spaghetti, they decided not to pursue it. Jeff and his team began realizing that they needed to advance their engineering quality and they untangled the code for each division and created well-documented APIs to redirect the company [18]. This change in engineering mindset was the nucleus of what has become Amazon Web Services (AWS), whereby internal services were eventually turned into a set of common tools that any engineer could use.

As the years progressed, with little change to the original model of Amazon, the executives went to a retreat to identify the future of the company. In a meeting designed to last 30 minutes, Jeff Bezos and Andy Jassy realized that the company had built a significant competency in infrastructure services like compute, storage, database, and operating all their data centers at a low cost to meet their margin goals [19]. Through piecing these competencies and finding the opportunity to sell just compute power without the hardware necessary to run it, Jeff and Andy were able to identify what has become known as the "operating system for the internet" – cloud services [20].

Customer Obsession	Leaders start with the customer and work backwards. They work vigorously to earn and keep customer trust. Although leaders pay attention to competitors, they obsess over customers.
Ownership	Leaders are owners. They think long term and don't sacrifice long-term value for short-term results. They act on behalf of the entire company, beyond just their own team. They never say "that's not my job."
Invent and Simplify	Leaders expect and require innovation and invention from their teams and always find ways to simplify. They are externally aware, look for new ideas from everywhere, and are not limited by "not invented here." As we do new things, we accept that we may be misunderstood for long periods of time.
Are Right, A Lot	Leaders are right a lot. They have strong judgment and good instincts. They seek diverse perspectives and work to disconfirm their beliefs.
Learn and Be Curious	Leaders are never done learning and always seek to improve themselves. They are curious about new possibilities and act to explore them.
Hire and Develop the Best	Leaders raise the performance bar with every hire and promotion. They recognize exceptional talent, and willingly move them throughout the organization. Leaders develop leaders and take seriously their role in coaching others. We work on behalf of our people to invent mechanisms for development like Career Choice.
Insist on the Highest Standards	Leaders have relentlessly high standards — many people may think these standards are unreasonably high. Leaders are continually raising the bar and drive their teams to deliver high quality products, services, and processes. Leaders ensure that defects do not get sent down the line and that problems are fixed so they stay fixed.
Think Big	Thinking small is a self-fulfilling prophecy. Leaders create and communicate a bold direction that inspires results. They think differently and look around corners for ways to serve customers.
Bias for Action	Speed matters in business. Many decisions and actions are reversible and do not need extensive study. We value calculated risk taking.
Frugality	Accomplish more with less. Constraints breed resourcefulness, self-sufficiency, and invention. There are no extra points for growing headcount, budget size, or fixed expense.
Earn Trust	Leaders listen attentively, speak candidly, and treat others respectfully. They are vocally self-critical, even when doing so is awkward or embarrassing. Leaders do not believe their or their team's body odor smells of perfume. They benchmark themselves and their teams against the best.
Dive Deep	Leaders operate at all levels, stay connected to the details, audit frequently, and are skeptical when metrics and anecdote differ. No task is beneath them.
Have Backbone; Disagree and Commit	Leaders are obligated to respectfully challenge decisions when they disagree, even when doing so is uncomfortable or exhausting. Leaders have conviction and are tenacious. They do not compromise for the sake of social cohesion. Once a decision is determined, they commit wholly.
Deliver Results.	Leaders focus on the key inputs for their business and deliver them with the right quality and in a timely fashion. Despite setbacks, they rise to the occasion and never settle.

Exhibit 12.1 AWS culture

Source: Amazon. AWS Culture. Accessed on May 12, 2021. https://aws.amazon.com/careers/culture/

278 *Case studies*

AWS defines cloud computing as "the on-demand delivery of IT resources over the internet with pay-as-you-go pricing. Instead of buying, owning, and maintaining [your own data centers] [21]." Essentially, Amazon created infrastructure as a service. Servitization is nothing new and has existed in many arenas, including hardware, with Rolls-Royce starting "power by the hour" in 1962 [22]. The concept of providing a technically substantial product and only charging its use to de-risk customer ownership was not original. Shared IT services were also pioneered in the 1960s by Joseph Licklider, where he created a virtualized compute services – multiple users accessing a single computer – which led to the creation of the internet's precursor: ARPANet [23].

While both servitization of technology and virtualized computer services were not unknown, nobody had been able to bring the concepts together before Amazon. This innovation is novel, with one of Merriam-Webster's definitions as "original or striking especially in conception or style [24]." This novel idea is how Amazon was able to take their newfound core competencies of compute and storage and turn them into their first cloud offerings of infrastructure as a service in 2006 – Elastic Compute Cloud (EC2), and Simple Storage Service (S3) [25]. What this meant was, for the first-time, companies no longer needed to maintain an IT services division to maintain servers and data centers. This was crucial for startups or other small companies that did not have significant capital to purchase the systems themselves. By providing a pay-as-you-go model the companies could extend their runway of financing and treat storage and compute as operational expenses. While we may take it for granted in 2021, this was mind-blowing in the 2006 technology world that was still recovering from the dot.com bubble bursting. This was a game changer innovation and is seen with the public cloud computing market exceeding \$266B and 85% of businesses worldwide making use of the cloud [26].

Playing with fire

With the successful foray into establishing itself as a technology company between their cloud service and several successful Kindle devices, Jeff and Andy looked where to go next. In 2010 the world had shifted from the idea that computers were the dominating force on the internet to a new paradigm of mobile first [27]. There was pressure for Amazon to compete with the other platforms available to not get left in the dust, and thus the Fire Phone was announced in June of 2014 [28]. While the device was technically sound with some unique features, the sales were a bust. Fortunately, Jeff's strong belief in failure as a path to innovation saw this as just another step. With writing down \$170M, Jeff told the vice president in charge of the phone: "You can't, for one minute, feel bad about the Fire Phone. Promise me you won't lose a minute of sleep [29]." This is one of the bets that paid off because of the feedback Jeff provided to the engineering team about enjoying the smart assistant. Just a couple of months after the launch of the phone, the Echo speaker was launched with its personnel assistant Alexa [30]. This foray into smart homes launched a new ecosystem for Amazon in the era of the IoT. Amazon's net income has peaked in 2020 as illustrated in Exhibit 12.2.

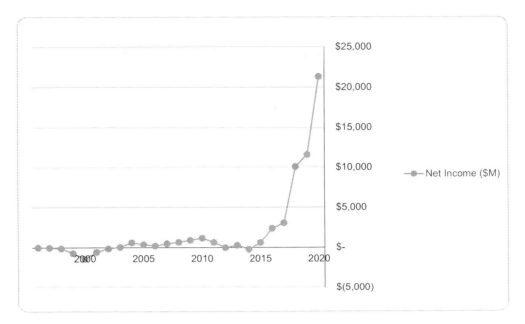

Exhibit 12.2 Amazon's annual net income.
Compiled from Amazon Annual Statements. Accessed May 12, 2021. https://ir.aboutamazon.com/annual-reports-proxies-and-shareholder-letters/default.aspx

Closing

Looking back on his time at Amazon, Jeff was worried. He saw technology companies become less innovative when the founder passed the mantle onto the next CEO and did not want the fate of Amazon to be the same. He needed to express the essential leadership traits necessary to continue his vision of Amazon as a 'Day 1' company and pass those lessons onto the new generation of leaders.

VASTEFA© leadership framework application

The VASTEFA© leadership framework [31] is a simple way to analyze the leadership innovation capacity and address any gaps. At Amazon, Jeff Bezos served as its leader from1994 until middle of 2021 with an incredible achievement. His ability to lead and navigate Amazon is quite inspiring to many, and Exhibit 12.3 illustrates how his leadership skills can be mapped to the VASTEFA© leadership framework.

References:

1. Jeff Bezos, amazon.com. Shareholder Letter, 1998, https://ir.aboutamazon.com/annual-reports-proxies-and-shareholder-letters/default.aspx
2. Jeff Bezos, amazon.com. Shareholder Letter, 2016, https://ir.aboutamazon.com/annual-reports-proxies-and-shareholder-letters/default.aspx

280 *Case studies*

Vision	Jeff truly believes in two things that the company will be the most customer centric one in existence, and that Amazon will forever be a Day 1 company. The belief in being customer centric shows in the leadership principles, where the first principle is customer obsession; and the method of working backwards from the customer to ensure it provides value. Being a Day 1 company is shown by reprinting the first annual letter to shareholders declaring the company is Day 1 and by expressing what happens to the company when it becomes Day 2.
Action	While his role has shifted over time Jeff has always been part of the business. In the early days he would be on the floor packing books into boxes himself, later on he would be interacting with his senior leadership on creating new opportunities like cloud, and he continually was used for feedback like creating Alexa.
Support	The focus on long-term growth and telling people not to worry about failures like the Fire Phone, allows freedom and provides support to develop an innovative company. Jeff empowered his top leadership to build out teams and supported their development like launching 2 new industries with cloud and smart homes even if he had to take a loss on risk of failure.
Team	Focusing on creating his two-pizza teams would prevent Jeff from building overly large organizations where people would coast. Knowing that there are issues in teams, the production of the 14 leadership principles became a way to ensure issues can be stopped and the company can continue to move forward.
Experiment	Focus on long-term success with creating bets early and not being afraid of failure. This is also seen in Exhibits 2 and 3 where there is no emphasis on short-term profits. When Jeff told his Senior VP to not let the failure of the Fire Phone make him feel bad it was because he knew that big bets are necessary to have breakthrough successes.
Feedback	By working backwards from what the customer wants and getting feedback from various teams and focus groups Amazon's leaders can ensure that innovations meet the needs of customers. Feedback is sought internally too, with Jeff providing feedback about the digital assistant that eventually became Alexa.
Adaptability	The greatest example is the progression of Jeff's adaptation from selling easily shippable books and slowly increasing categories to become the everything store. As Amazon grew it transitioned to a technology company spawning the cloud industry, creating electronic devices, and becoming a defining entity in the smart home ecosystem.

Exhibit 12.3 VASTEFA© leadership framework application

3. Michael Kozlowski, GoodEReader, May 9, 2018, "Amazon CEO Jeff Bezos talks about selling books in new interview," accessed May 13, 2021, https://goodereader.com/blog/business-news/amazon-ceo-jeff-bezos-talks-about-selling-books-in-new-interview
4. Juan Perez, 2004, "Amazon Records First Profitable Year in its History," Computerworld, www.computerworld.com/article/2575106/amazon-records-first-profitable-year-in-its-history.html
5. Devindra Hardawar, 2011, "How Jeff Bezos' Long-Term Thinking Paid Off Big for Amazon," Venture Beat, https://venturebeat.com/2011/09/09/jeff-bezos-long-term-amazon/
6. Jim Collins, "The Flywheel Effect," www.jimcollins.com/concepts/the-flywheel.html
7. Brad Stone, "The Everything Store: Jeff Bezos and the Age of Amazon," 2013.
8. ProductPlan, "Working Backwards (the Amazon Method)," www.productplan.com/glossary/working-backward-amazon-method/
9. ibid.
10. ibid.
11. ibid.
12. "Two-Pizza Teams," Amazon, accessed 13 May 2021, https://docs.aws.amazon.com/whitepapers/latest/introduction-devops-aws/two-pizza-teams.html
13. "Leadership Principles," Amazon, www.amazon.jobs/en/principles
14. ibid.
15. Taylor Locke, Oct 11, 2019, "Jeff Bezos: This is the One Amazon Leadership Principle that 'Surprises People' the Most," CNBC, www.cnbc.com/2019/10/11/jeff-bezos-amazon-leadership-principle-that-surprises-people.html

16. ibid.
17. Ron Miller, "How AWS Came to Be," Tech Crunch, https://techcrunch.com/2016/07/02/andy-jassys-brief-history-of-the-genesis-of-aws/
18. ibid.
19. ibid.
20. ibid.
21. AWS, https://aws.amazon.com/what-is-cloud-computing/
22. Rolls-Royce, "Rolls-Royce Celebrates 50th Anniversary of Power-by-the-Hour," www.rolls-royce.com/media/press-releases-archive/yr-2012/121030-the-hour.aspx#:~:text='Power%2Dby%2Dthe%2DHour'%2C%20a%20Rolls,per%2Dflying%2Dhour%20basis
23. Educba, "Introduction to History of Cloud Computing," www.educba.com/history-of-cloud-computing/
24. Merriam-Webster, Novel, adjective, www.merriam-webster.com/dictionary/novel
25. Christopher McFadden, "A Very Brief History of Amazon: The Everything Store," Interesting Engineering, https://interestingengineering.com/a-very-brief-history-of-amazon-the-everything-store
26. Jacquelyn Bulao, "How Many Companies Use Cloud Computing in 2020? All You Need To Know," TechJury, https://techjury.net/blog/how-many-companies-use-cloud-computing/#gref
27. Riley Longo, "Mobile First: What Does It Mean?" March 5, 2012, UX Matters, www.uxmatters.com/mt/archives/2012/03/mobile-first-what-does-it-mean.php#:~:text=Mobile%20First%3A%20A%20Paradigm%20Shift&text=Google%20surfaced%20their%20mobile%2Dfirst,Web%E2%80%94or%20any%20other%20device.
28. Matt Burns, "Amazon Announces the Fire Phone," June 5, 2014, TechCrunch, https://techcrunch.com/2014/06/18/amazon-announces-the-fire-phone/
29. Charles Duhigg, "Is Amazon Unstoppable?" Oct 10, 2019, The New Yorker, www.newyorker.com/magazine/2019/10/21/is-amazon-unstoppable
30. ibid.
31. Vijay Pandiarajan, "VASTEFA© Leadership Framework," WMBA Win 2021 Class Slides, Ross School of Business, The University of Michigan, 2021.

Case 13: Ericsson's Innovation Through M&A

Derek Kuo

Stephen M. Ross School of Business, University of Michigan
derekk@umich.edu

Ericsson overview

Telefonaktiebolaget LM Ericsson, otherwise known as Ericsson (NASDAQ: ERIC) was founded in 1876 by Lars Magnus Ericsson. Headquartered in Stockholm, Ericsson was originally established as a workshop for small engineering jobs, including repairs made to telegraph instruments. After the invention of the telephone, Lars Magnus Ericsson saw the potential possibilities in innovating on the telephone and created his own device – a new version of the telephone known as "the Swedish pattern." The firm first began manufacturing telephones in 1878, which would spur its growth from a mere 500 employees producing a little over 100,000 telephones into one of the world's largest multinational networking and telecommunications companies [1].

Over the years, Ericsson has continued to push the limits of innovation with telecom, which is a testament to Ericsson's purpose statement: "To empower an intelligent sustainable and connected world by relentlessly innovating technologies that are easy to adopt, use and scale." [2] For example, one of Ericsson's earliest innovations was in 1981 where the firm developed the Nordic Mobile Telephony (NMT 1G) a first-generation mobile telephone to lay the foundation for the communication revolution. Since then, it has created numerous industry-disruptive innovations: Erlang, a common programming language to build massively scalable, real-time system; GS88 or Penelope, the world's first "smartphone" ten years before Apple's iPhone, equipped with a QWERTY keyboard and touch screen; and Bluetooth connectivity, are all examples of Ericsson's innovation [2]. More recently, in 2002, Ericsson created the Wideband Code Division Multiple Access (WCDMA), which made broadband mobile and became the backbone of the first wave of 3G access [2]. By the end of 2014, WCDMA subscriptions had grown at 60% YoY and by 2020 would serve approximately 4.5 billion people [2]. In 2007, Verizon for the first time in its history, abandoned its own plans for a joint global standard and adopted Ericsson's LTE concept [2]. Each of these major breakthroughs in telecom are examples of the continuing culture of innovation at Ericsson.

Today, Ericsson is an international telecom company that focuses on using technology and innovation to create a more connected world. The firm operates through the following business segments: Networks, digital services, managed services, and other emerging businesses. Ericsson's network segment supports all radio-enabled

DOI: 10.4324/9781003190837-34

technologies for accessibility and transportation encompassing both hardware and software services. The digital services segment houses software services such as operating support systems, cloud communication, and cloud infrastructure for businesses worldwide. The managed services segment includes networks and IT-related services, network design and optimization, and application development and maintenance. The emerging business segment includes exploring new opportunities such as Iconectiv, Red Bee Media, and Media Solution [3].

To further explore the boundaries of Ericsson's innovative culture, this case looks more specifically at the 2013 acquisition of Microsoft MediaRoom by Ericsson and its most recent push for 5G revenue-driving-based innovation.

2000's rise of Internet Protocol Television (IPTV)

To better contextualize the 2013 acquisition of MediaRoom by Ericsson, the race for IPTV needs to be explained. Unlike TV with cable and satellite, IPTV sends shows and movies through standard internet connection. During the early 2000s, this was seen as the future of media streaming and media consumption [4].

According to Nevron, the delivery of TV through internet protocol (IP) networks achieved great success due to its ability to stream source media continuously and had numerous use cases ranging from residential to corporate to commercial. The ability to stream videos on demand, which was reliant on IPTV technology, would become prominent later with the rise of streaming services like Netflix, HBO, and Disney+ among others [5].

In the early 2000s, big-name telecom players such as AT&T, Sprint, and WorldCom all wanted an edge and competed to become the top industry player in the IPTV space [6]. As these three companies saw that the future of media consumption would compete in the IPTV space, analysts at Grand View Research found that the IPTV market would be worth over $117B by 2025 [4].

2013 Microsoft MediaRoom and Ericsson

In 2013, Microsoft MediaRoom was a legacy client/server IPTV architecture that was a platform that supported simultaneous recordings of multiple high-definition and standard-definition TV channels [7]. MediaRoom relied on low-cost setup boxes made by Motorola, Cisco, and Tatung running Windows 5.0, and the MediaRoom client software to communicate securely with back-end server farms hosted by service operator companies. The stored content was then streamed to the client's personal device. This system was able to showcase the power of Microsoft's ecosystem from end to end, which threatened the entire telecom industry as Microsoft began encroaching on the TV business [8].

At the same time, Ericsson was an established Swedish company with a strong presence as a maker of backbone equipment for cellular companies. Ericsson's next large influx of money would not arrive until the takeoff of 5G cellular technology, and the telecom space historically operated on very long timelines. The CEO at the time, Hans Vesberg, developed products for the media distribution space in hopes of expanding their business but did not see traction in the marketplace, especially with MediaRoom dominating [8].

284   *Case studies*

Ericsson's rapid acquisitions

As part of this effort, Ericsson acquired a wide range of media companies. In 2006, Ericsson signed a $2.1B deal to acquire Redback Networks, a telecommunications equipment company that housed 15 of the top 20 telephone carriers worldwide [9]. Then, in 2007, Ericsson looked toward the encoding company, Tandberg Television, for $1.4B, to further play a bigger role in the IPTV space [10]. Furthermore, in 2012, they acquired Technicolor's broadcast services division, a worldwide technology leader in the media and entertainment sector, for €19M, to broaden its managed services offerings for media broadcasters [11].

Unfortunately for Microsoft, the MediaRoom business did not grow into the $1B business that the firm once thought it was going to be. This is when Microsoft began looking for a buyer for the business. In the meantime, parallel to the continued evolution of MediaRoom, the engineering team also developed a cloud-based end-to-end IPTV product that would be hosted in the Azure cloud and serve content to internet browser-based clients [12].

In 2013, Microsoft ultimately provided Ericsson with an opportunity to gain an established product that was being used by many telecom companies that were synergistic to Ericsson's customer base. These were all consolidated under their Business Unit Support Solutions division, which was a consulting arm of Ericsson with headquarters in Texas [13]. With hopes of developing a stronger presence in Silicon Valley, Ericsson took over multiple floors in a new complex in Santa Clara and consolidated employees from MediaRoom, Tandberg, and Redback. Also created was a new demo and conference facility [14]. The hope was that all end-to-end media technologies could be leveraged to provide solutions ranging from network backbone equipment to full IPTV implementations.

To further reinforce their presence in the IPTV space and synergize with their acquisition of MediaRoom, in 2014, Ericsson also acquired Red Bee Media [15]. Red Bee was known for its end-to-end managed services offerings. Ericsson was able to capitalize on Red Bee's innovative solutions across the entire content delivery chain – covering live and remote production, managed OTT, distribution, media management, access services, content discovery, playout, and post-production. This acquisition showed Ericsson's continued commitment to innovating and competing with the IPTV industry.

Sell-off

However, in 2016, Ericsson began seeing high disruption in the IPTV space because of direct streaming videos on smartphones and laptops. Thus, in typical technology fashion, many customers were sold on the new upcoming cloud products and lost interest in legacy products. The development of the cloud products started to lag, and Ericsson was not seeing the payoff from a very expensive, highly skilled, engineering force in the expensive Silicon Valley [16].

As a result, Ericsson's main businesses slowed and they decided to retrench and focus on their core technologies and strengths. While Ericsson was at the forefront of tackling the challenges of streaming bandwidth and mobile viewing experiences through our end-to-end, cloud-based TV solutions, it saw a lack of potential for

MediaRoom's continued growth and decided to sell off the arm to better navigate and focus on the convergence of the IT, media, and communications industries and move quickly into 5G, cloud, the IoT, and other new, disruptive markets.

In January of 2019, Ericsson spun off the MediaRoom division, with One Equity Partners taking a 51% stake and Ericsson taking a 49% stake [16]. The new company was formed called MediaKind [17].

5G innovation

In tandem with the race for IPTV supremacy, telecom companies were also focused on delivering the best, most up-to-date mobile networking service. Since the early 1980s with the advent of 1G, delivered analog voice, to more recently in 2010, 4G LTE, firms like Ericsson have been innovating and competing to deliver the best service [18]. Today, 5G is on the line as the fifth generation of cellular networks that is capable of IoT connectivity, enhanced mobile broadband services, and VR/AR applications. Among its competitors, Ericsson has over 70 live 5G networks in 40 different countries placing it at the forefront of 5G expansion [19].

Ericsson acquires Cradlepoint

One of Ericsson's most recent acquisitions in the 5G space was that of Cradlepoint. In a similar fashion to its acquisition of MediaRoom, Ericsson looked to the US-based market leader in Wireless WAN Edge 4G and 5G solutions for the enterprise market [20].

Ericsson chose to acquire Cradlepoint due to its innovative solutions that synergized well with Ericsson's existing product offerings. Integrating Cradlepoint's infrastructure for vehicle, mobile, and workforce IoT to device connectivity, Ericsson will be capable of creating new revenue streams for its clients by supporting 5G-enabled services and further leverage their existing expansive 5G network. Additionally, Ericsson's global network will help accelerate Cradlepoint's solutions expansion internationally [21].

The acquisition was welcomed by both Ericsson and Cradlepoint alike as Ericsson maintained that Cradlepoint would operate as its own standalone subsidiary within the larger firm. Cradlepoint would simply be given additional resources, more data, and options for more advanced connectivity services with the larger firm [22].

As Cradlepoint was one of the larger and more famous 5G deals that Ericsson has signed in the last few months, other large firms have also looked to Ericsson for partnerships that may give them a leg up in the race for 5G [23].

Following in Cradlepoint's footsteps, T-Mobile announced a recent deal with Ericsson and Nokia. Following the T-Mobile and Sprint merger earlier last year, the joint entity signed an initial $3.5B deal to use Ericsson as the base for their 5G infrastructure. This past year they made a significant infrastructure upgrade to be able to "extend their 5G range as the 600MHz band now covers 280 million people across nearly 1.6 million square miles which T-Mobile has coined 'ultra-capacity' 5G. [21]"

Conclusion

Like the race for IPTV supremacy, Ericsson's latest push toward 5G all connects back to their culture of innovation. From its inception, the Ericsson management team has

286 *Case studies*

always searched for ways to continue to push the limits of telecommunications technology. Acquiring a multitude of businesses in the early 2000s to become a dominant force in the IPTV space and now focusing its efforts on the future of mobile broadband connectivity with 5G, Ericsson has proved repeatedly that it refuses to remain stagnant and continues to evolve.

Case questions

1. How did Ericsson leverage its resources to its advantage initially with the rise of IPTV and once again to adapt to the burgeoning 5G industry?
2. Through the rapid M&A processes that Ericsson conducted in the early 2000s, what technologies was Ericsson able to acquire?
3. How did Ericsson utilize innovation to maintain its position as a market leader in telecom?
4. In what capacity did Ericsson use non-linear thinking to expand on their innovation strategies?
5. What are the potential gains and drawbacks to Ericsson's strategy of rapid expansion by way of acquisition in the IPTV and now 5G space?
6. What are some other examples of companies making similar decisions to Ericsson to either disrupt the industry or maintain its market position?

References

1. "Telefonaktiebolaget LM Ericsson," 2019, 2019 Annual Report, www.ericsson.com/495c1f/assets/local/investors/documents/2019/ericsson-annual-report-2019-en.pdf
2. Ericsson About Us, 2021, "Shaping History,"www.ericsson.com/en/about-us/history/shaping-history.
3. Ericsson Future Technologies, 2021. "Future Technologies For an Intelligent Society," www.ericsson.com/en/about-us/history/shaping-history
4. "What Is IPTV? Everything You Need To Know About The Future of Video," 2018, Uscreen, www.uscreen.tv/blog/what-is-iptv/
5. "What Is Internet Protocol Television Or IPTV? – Nevron Blog," 2018, Nevron Blog, www.nevron.eu/blog/iptv/
6. John Borland, 2021, "2000 Marked Tumultuous Times for Telecom Companies," CNET, available at www.cnet.com/news/2000-marked-tumultuous-times-for-telecom-companies/
7. "Microsoft Mediaroom IPTV and Multimedia Platform Debuts at Nxtcomm – Stories," 2007, Stories, https://news.microsoft.com/2007/06/17/microsoft-mediaroom-iptv-and-multimedia-platform-debuts-at-nxtcomm/
8. Microsoft Media Room SErver 1.1 SP3.2 Product Documentation, 2021, "Architecture of Microsoft Media Room," Scribd.com, available at www.scribd.com/document/397568676/Architecture-of-Microsoft-Mediaroom
9. Ericsson Company 2006, 2021, "Redback became a subsidiary of Ericsson," www.ericsson.com/en/about-us/history/company/the-consequences-of-expansion/redback-became-a-subsidiary-of-ericsson
10. "Ericsson Completes Next Step In Tandberg Television Acquisition | TV Tech," 2021, Tvtechnology.Com, www.tvtechnology.com/news/ericsson-completes-next-step-in-tandberg-television-acquisition, accessed July 3, 2021.
11. "Ericsson Closes Acquisition Of Technicolor's Broadcast Services Division," 2012, News Powered By Cision, https://news.cision.com/ericsson/r/ericsson-closes-acquisition-of-technicolor-s-broadcast-services-division,c2245877, accessed July 3, 2021.

12. Charlie Osborne, 2021, "Ericsson Completes Acquisition of Microsoft Mediaroom," ZDNet, available at www.zdnet.com/article/ericsson-completes-acquisition-of-microsoft-mediaroom/
13. Todd Bishop, 2013, "Microsoft Selling Mediaroom to Ericsson, Exiting IPTV Business to Focus on Xbox," Geekwire, www.geekwire.com/2013/microsoft-selling-mediaroom-iptv-business-ericsson/
14. Ericsson Blog 2016, 2021, "Experience Ericsson at New Santa Clara Facility in Heart of Silicon Valley," www.ericsson.com/en/blog/2016/10/experience-ericsson-at-new-santa-clara-facility-in-the-heart-of-silicon-valley
15. "Ericsson Completes Acquisition of Red Bee Media – Red Bee Media," 2021, Red Bee Media, www.redbeemedia.com/news/ericsson-completes-acquisition-of-red-bee-media/, accessed July 3, 2021.
16. Ericsson Press Releases, 2021, Ericsson Completes Divestment of Majority Stake in MediaKind," www.ericsson.com/en/press-releases/2019/2/ericsson-completes-divestment-of-majority-stake-in-mediakind
17. "Global Media Technology Solutions and Innovators," 2021, Mediakind, www.mediakind.com/
18. "Mobile Networking: 1G To 4G," 2021, Community.Jisc.Ac.Uk, https://community.jisc.ac.uk/library/advisory-services/mobile-networking-1g-4g
19. Ericsson 5G by Ericsson, 2021, "What is 5G?" www.ericsson.com/en/5g?gclid=Cj0KCQiAyJOBBhDCARIsAJG2h5f4naQTGtj-mK0noJVFG2Y6j-Ac0HCmKp4Q7r84cErpE5SYCls2SsUaAo8yEALw_wcB&gclsrc=aw.ds
20. Ericsson Discover 5G, 2021, "5G By Ericsson," www.ericsson.com/en/5g
21. Ericsson Press Releases, 2021, "Ericsson Completes Acquisition of Cradlepoint," web, www.ericsson.com/en/press-releases/2020/11/ericsson-completes-acquisition-of-cradlepoint
22. "Ericsson Closes $1B Cradlepoint Purchase with Eye on Enterprise," 2020, Fiercewireless, www.fiercewireless.com/wireless/ericsson-closes-1b-cradlepoint-purchase-eye-enterprise, accessed July 3, 2021.
23. "Bloomberg – Are You a Robot?" 2021, Bloomberg.com, www.bloomberg.com/news/articles/2020-09-18/ericsson-buys-cradlepoint-in-1-1-billion-deal-to-build-5g, accessed July 3, 2021.

Case 14: Samsung's New-Age Innovation Using Organization and Culture

Derek Kuo

Stephen M. Ross School of Business, University of Michigan
derekk@umich.edu

Samsung overview

Samsung is a South Korean electronics company and one of the world's largest producers of electronic devices including appliances, cellular devices, semiconductors, memory chips, and integrated systems. The firm was founded in 1938 by Lee Byung-Chul, originally as a trading company. Samsung did not enter the electronics market until 1969 with their first electronics product being black-and-white televisions, an incredible innovation at that time. In the 1970s and 80s Samsung further pushed into the technology sector by acquiring a 50% stake in Korea Semiconductor and created two R&D institutes that broadened the company's technologies into electronics, semiconductors, telecommunications, and aerospace among other industry verticals [1].

Following founder Lee Byung-Chul's retirement in the late 1980s Samsung separated into five business groups, Samsung Group, Shinsegae Group, CJ Group, Hansol Group, and Joongang Group. Samsung Group is the electronics company we all know of today. After the split, Samsung concentrated its efforts on mobile devices and semiconductors, which now are their more important sources of income [1].

The Samsung Galaxy, Samsung's flagship product, was born in 2000 as a byproduct of "fast-following." Seeing Motorola, IBM, and Apple furiously compete for dominance in the mobile phone industry, Samsung did not enter the conversation until the rise of smartphones began to take over the mobile phone market. Being able to quickly identify a critical shift in consumer demand to preference Apple's iPhones over other cellular devices, Samsung built the Galaxy as a direct competitor and set the stage for its success through innovation and strategy 20 years later [2].

Currently, while Samsung holds a strong position as one of the market leaders within the smartphone industry, the firm has begun to look at other markets and industries to expand into, with information technology, healthcare, biotechnology, and comfort being a few examples of Samsung's continued innovation. Among all of Samsung's recent innovations, their commitment to sustainability innovation stands out as a critical long-term goal for the firm.

Samsung management organization

Samsung's management and organization are built to further their mission to "enrich people's lives and social responsibilities, to contribute to sustainable future innovative technologies, product and the aspiration for the design inspiration for the future society" [3].

DOI: 10.4324/9781003190837-35

Exhibit 14.1 Samsung's business units structure [4].

Product-type divisions are core to the firm's organizational structure so each division that represents a product category can focus on technological innovation and product development [4]. Exhibit 14.1 illustrates how Samsung is organized based on business units.

The firm has worked to create a corporate culture that enables the long-term success of its competitive position in the electronics industry in multiple international markets. Core to the enterprise's values is the following main characteristics of Samsung's culture [5]:

1. Development of opportunities for all employees
2. Passion for excellence
3. Constant change
4. Ethical foundation for integrity
5. Emphasis on prosperity for all

As a part of the underlying strategy for Samsung, development opportunities for employees at every level help keep individuals motivated and interested in the day-to-day work at the firm [6]. The company ensures career development opportunities through both institutionalized programs as well as through encouraging employees to support each other with their career goals within the organization. Samsung's geographic and product-type divisional organizational structure helps support extensive innovation and technological progress in each products' development [7]. Furthermore, the geographic divisions help Samsung achieve high innovation in the cultural context of a geographic region, which allows them to have strong global branding tied to their products and room for specific local partnerships across the globe.

Samsung emphasizes a passion for excellence from the people they choose to hire. The firm puts a large emphasis on human resource development to ensure they recruit a high caliber of individuals who can contribute to the corporate culture of excellence [8]. Samsung's ability to both maintain and promote a high-achieving culture within

290 Case studies

the firm allows them to consistently innovate on advanced technologies to stay ahead of the curve [9].

Putting innovation at the center of their corporate culture, Samsung's proclivity toward constant change has helped the firm not only survive but retain its position as a global leader in technology [7]. As one of the core pillars of its culture, Samsung employees are taught to embody the idea that change is necessary to improve and compete against other high-achieving, innovative firms like Apple.

Ethics and foundational integrity are crucial aspects of Samsung's workplace culture. Executive officers at the firm understand the importance of compliance and morals. Through their strong leadership, Samsung's employees have also embraced this idea, which has helped minimize publicity issues, promoted brand image, and furthered the company's strategic objectives related to their shareholders and stakeholders [10]. Additionally, this specific cultural characteristic that promotes fairness, respect, and transparency, has led to the long-term tenure of many in upper-level management who have experience in recruiting and training high-quality talent.

Aside from the following internal cultural components of Samsung's workforce, the firm prides itself on extending its corporate culture beyond its own organization to include the community it serves as well [11]. Samsung places emphasis on long-term prosperity for the stakeholders and communities they serve. Management at the firm spend time ideating on innovative ways to bring Samsung's technologies to local communities to improve the quality of life for all its existing and potential customers [12]. One example of this is through the company's push to motivate workers to engage in corporate citizenship programs that provide solutions to large community problems through technology and involve the local communities in career opportunities with the firm.

Each of Samsung's cultural characteristics lends itself toward continued innovation at Samsung. This case will explore the continuation of these key characteristics in the Samsung Galaxy and Samsung's continued effort in sustainable innovation.

Samsung Galaxy

The Samsung Galaxy is one of Samsung's flagship products that has continually evolved over the past decade. Beginning in 2010, the Samsung Galaxy S was the first device of the third Android smartphone series produced by Samsung. The Galaxy S was able to catch the eye of the smartphone market as it had "perfect audio quality" and was a clear market leader in terms of innovation for Android-based phones [13]. With each iteration from the S2 to S10, Samsung kept improving both the phone's hardware (camera, screen, size), connectivity from 3G to 5G LTE, and interface experience with users [14].

Most recently, the Samsung Galaxy S21 and S21+ have a few key industry-leading innovations. First, the smartphone is foldable. Brian Ma, Vice President of the International Data Center, found that: "One of the big things that Samsung is betting on is foldables, which the rest of the industry does not quite have yet [15]. And Samsung's already on its second, moving into third-generation products now." Second, the transition between smartphone and tablet is virtually seamless. Like the iPad and iMac cross-screen integration, the Samsung Galaxy brings that innovation to the smartphone level. Additionally, the Samsung Galaxy goes above and beyond on battery life by including two separate batteries for the phone to have a longer single charge lifetime [15]. And finally, the Samsung Galaxy S21 offers six cameras for increased resolution and performance [16].

Samsung and sustainable innovation

Samsung's dedication to sustainable innovation is a new initiative that goes beyond the typical bounds of "innovating" to be competitive. Sustainable innovation is Samsung's next leap that will put them head and shoulders above other firms and they are dedicated to becoming socially conscious global citizens. As Samsung's Vice Chairman and CEO stated, "As we take our first steps into the next half-century, we are acutely aware of our obligations and roles in sustainable operations. As a global corporate citizen, Samsung Electronics will continue to create environmental and social values while achieving positive economic outcomes" [17]. From the 2020 Sustainability Report, Samsung plans on expanding its sustainable innovation initiative across all three of their major business lines.

On the Consumer Electronics Division, one example of a green initiative is with the Visual Display business. As the market leader for the global TV market capturing the largest share of the market at 30.9%, Samsung paves the way for other TV producers by introducing expanded resource recycling by upcycling a design that can revamp TV packaging boxes into small furniture or for pet use for minimized environmental impact [17]. Additionally, Samsung makes sure to use sustainable materials such as bioplastics and sustainably sourced paper as packaging materials [17].

In the IT & Mobile Communication Division, Samsung is a key player in the mobile phones and smartphone markets capturing 17.5% and 20.9% of the market, respectively [17]. Again, as a forerunner in the space, Samsung can further differentiate themselves from their competition by focusing their innovation efforts on sustainability. Using materials such as bioplastics and sustainably sourced paper while also developing a high efficiency charging technology with 86% charging efficiency, Samsung is taking strides to help reduce their carbon footprint on the world [17]. Furthermore, for their consumers, Samsung has developed security solutions such as Knox to protect their users' information, and curated digital well-being features such as App Timer and Samsung Kids to pioneer a new generation of immersive, intelligent, and secure experiences that seamlessly integrate with the other Samsung products, while building a sustainable future [17].

Finally, in the Device Solutions Division, Samsung has focused its efforts on green innovation in the industry's first third-generation 10-nanometer-class DRAM and sixth-generation V-NAND with a 100+ layer single-stack design, breaking through the previous limits of memory technologies [17]. While impressive, Samsung exceeded expectations by simultaneously designing and implementing a low-power circuit design that reduced the semiconductor chip operating voltage by 15% compared to the fifth-generation V-NAND, thereby reducing greenhouse gas emissions [17]. Additionally, by applying channel-hole etching and single-step etching technologies, they were able to further reduce their water and energy footprint [17].

Conclusion

Ultimately, through the culture, organization, and structure of Samsung, the firm has been able to survive and outperform their competitors over the years because

292   *Case studies*

of innovation. To stay relevant in the coming future, Samsung has shifted its priorities and focus to include sustainability not just for the survival of the company, but also for the betterment of the world we live in today. In the 21st century and going forward, it will be the responsibility of industry leaders like Samsung to continue to innovate and change with culture and technology, and if they fail, another company will quickly take their place as the new market leader in this competitive industry.

Case questions

1. Which factors were most important in creating a culture of innovation?
2. How did Samsung balance advancing their business interests with their sustainability goals? Do Samsung's sustainability goals provide the firm with any competitive advantages? You may use external current online resources as well to answer this question.
3. What are some other examples of companies making similar decisions to Samsung to either disrupt the industry or maintain their market-leading positions?
4. Does Samsung's organizational structure lend itself toward its innovative culture? Why or why not?

References

1. "Samsung | History & Facts," 2021, Encyclopedia Britannica, www.britannica.com/topic/Samsung-Electronics
2. "Samsung Electronics Joins Top 5 Most Innovative Tech Brands For 6 Consecutive Years," 2019, Businesskorea, www.businesskorea.co.kr/news/articleView.html?idxno=34647
3. Jay B. Barney, 1986, "Organizational Culture: Can it Be a Source of Sustained Competitive Advantage?," Academy of Management Review, 11(3), pp. 656–665.
4. "Samsung Strategy and Innovation Center," 2021, Samsung Strategy and Innovation Center, www.samsung.com/us/ssic/
5. P. L. Foster, 2015, "A Positive Corporate Culture Builds a Foundation for Innovation (and a Lot of Other Things)," Baylor Business Review, 34(1), p. 12.
6. Leandro A. Viltard, and Mario N. Acebo, 2018, "Corporate Culture: A key to Stimulate Innovation," Independent Journal of Management & Production, 9(3), pp. 869–888.
7. "Samsung's Generic Competitive Strategy & Intensive Growth," 2019, Panmore Institute, http://panmore.com/samsung-generic-strategy-intensive-growth-strategies-competitive-advantage
8. Dong Liu, Yaping Gong, Jing Zhou, and Jia-Chi Huang, 2017, "Human Resource Systems, Employee Creativity, and Firm Innovation: The Moderating Role of Firm Ownership," Academy of Management Journal, 60(3), pp. 1164–1188.
9. Andrea Taylor, Felix Santiago, and Rilla Hynes, "Relationships Among Leadership, Organizational Culture, and Support for Innovation," in "Effective and Creative Leadership in Diverse Workforces," pp. 11–42, Palgrave Macmillan, Cham, 2019.
10. Arkadiy V. Sakhartov, "Selecting Corporate Structure for Diversified Firms," in "Academy of Management Proceedings," vol. 2016, No. 1, p. 11521, Academy of Management, Briarcliff Manor, NY 10510, 2016.
11. Ron Ashkenas, Dave Ulrich, Todd Jick, and Steve Kerr, "The Boundaryless Organization: Breaking the Chains of Organizational Structure," John Wiley & Sons, 2015.
12. Mitchell J. Neubert, Emily M. Hunter, and Remy C. Tolentino, 2016, "A Servant Leader and Their Stakeholders: When Does Organizational Structure Enhance a Leader's Influence?" The Leadership Quarterly, 27(6), pp. 896–910.

13. "IT & Mobile Communications | Business | Samsung US," 2021, Samsung, Electronics America, www.samsung.com/us/aboutsamsung/business-area/it-and-mobile-communications/
14. "From Galaxy S To Galaxy S21: A Timeline of Samsung Phones," 2021, Pocket-Lint, www.pocket-lint.com/phones/news/samsung/136736-timeline-of-samsung-galaxy-flagship-android-phones-in-pictures
15. "7 Innovations that Help Samsung's Galaxy Fold Catch the Eye," 2019, South China Morning Post, www.scmp.com/magazines/style/tech-design/article/2187687/7-innovations-help-samsungs-galaxy-fold-smartphone-catch
16. "Latest Samsung Smartphone," 2021, Samsung Levant, www.samsung.com/levant/smartphones/
17. "A Journey Towards a Sustainable Future," 2020, Samsung Sustainability Report, https://images.samsung.com/is/content/samsung/assets/global/ir/docs/sustainability_report_2020_en.pdf

Case 15: Sun Pharmaceutical Industries – Innovation Through Specialty Acquisition Strategy, Technology, Leadership, and Culture

Katie Kuhlman

Stephen M. Ross School of Business, University of Michigan
kakuhlman@gmail.com

Case introduction

Sun Pharmaceutical Industries, "Sun Pharma," is one of the world's largest generic pharmaceutical companies, providing drugs and other pharmaceutical products to markets in over 100 countries [1]. Founded in 1983 by Dilip Shanghvi, the company originated in India and focused its initial efforts on building a unique route to market for its products that were already targeting an underserved Indian market [2]. They focused on doctor engagement with a two-pronged approach: Specialization and pipeline. The specialization approach required assigning field representatives per specialty drug, which assuaged future acquisitions with other specialty pharmaceutical companies and brand. The second pipeline approach focused on relationship-building upstream with medical students, not just current acting doctors and pharmacists. By establishing these two practices in the company's infancy, Shanghvi would be able to turn Sun Pharma into a multibillion-dollar company that continues to grow today. This case will dive into Sun Pharma's inflection period of the 2010s and how it has managed to successfully innovate within a highly competitive and saturated global pharmaceutical and manufacturing industry.

Industry overview

Sun Pharma is a member of the global generic pharmaceutical industry with a growing position in specialized drugs and treatment. Prior to 2010, Sun Pharma's revenues were driven by the Indian generics market. The global generic market is highly saturated – an industry with low concentration and high competition [3]. The following are some of Sun Pharma's largest global competitors, and none hold a market share higher than 5% as of 2020: Pfizer Inc., F. Hoffman-La Roche AG, Novartis AG, Johnson & Johnson Services Inc., Merck & Co. Inc., and Sanofi SA [3].

Within the generic pharmaceuticals industry, the average percentage of annual revenue invested in R & D of new drugs has decreased due to a phenomenon called "patent cliffs," or major losses in income for companies who had been able to exclusively sell their products until the patent expires [3]. The US generics market has also fallen prey to rapid price erosion, severely decreasing incumbents' margins on these generic products [4, 5]. The rising phenomena of patent cliffs and subsequent price

DOI: 10.4324/9781003190837-36

erosion have forced companies to look for other revenue and margin drivers if they want to continue operating in the US.

In 2020, global industry revenues for pharmaceutical manufacturing rose to $1.3T [3]. The US is the largest individual market for pharmaceutical demand; so-called developed markets have a consistent and/or growing demand for pharmaceuticals due to wavering demographics, access to healthcare and health insurance, and disposable income [6]. Japan and the EU are the second and third most dominant regions in the global generic pharmaceutical industry [3]. However, as countries like India and Brazil continue to grow their population and demand for pharmaceutical products, companies in the industry must also direct their attention to "Emerging Markets [3, 7]."

Sun Pharma operates in four geographical segments: India, the US, Emerging Markets, and Rest of the World [8].

"Complex generics" are a category of generic products that require more advanced technology to both develop and act effectively; these products also target more specific conditions than regular generics [5]. Complex generics offer an opportunity for differentiation and greater margins in the industry. The mandatory R&D investment in complex generics is also generally higher than typical generics, offering a barrier to entry for new entrants compared to incumbents like Sun Pharma with established R&D pipelines and manufacturing capabilities [5].

Growing global market share

In the 1990s, Sun Pharma expanded its manufacturing plants and research facilities outside India's borders [1]. By 2010 Sun Pharma had a footing in the pharmaceutical markets of 40 countries [9]. In these countries, Sun Pharma's presence was largely defined by its generic products borne of its R&D pipeline. Its sales were growing fastest in the branded generic sales category. At this point, the company was divided into four groups all within the Sun Pharmaceuticals Industries' umbrella: Indian branded generic drugs, US generics, other international branded generics, and API (active pharmaceutical ingredients). The US market only made up one quarter of the company's revenue and was not the fastest growing segment with Sun Pharma's current generics strategy [9]. In fact, the American generics industry would continue to decline in annual revenues, profits, and profit margin until 2021 [10]. It is obvious that specialty drugs had not been a public priority for Shanghvi, as they were not even granted their own business division in 2010.

Though he now had a stronghold over the Indian generics market, Shanghvi did not believe his company had accomplished all that was possible. He began asking how Sun Pharma could expand its global footprint and spread its revenues across even more lines. *Hint*: by 2015, Sun Pharma would be in 150 countries and growing.

Sun Pharma innovation capacity

R & D investment

The front page of Sun Pharma's website announces that they are "driven by innovation [1]." Sun Pharma regularly commits 7–8% of its annual revenues – not profits – to R&D investment each year, proving itself as more than just a generics manufacturer. The company structure also reflects this commitment to unique innovation. Of its

296   *Case studies*

36,000 global employees, 2,000 are scientists working exclusively on the R&D team. The R&D team was first formed in 1991, eight years after the company was initially established. This enables Sun Pharma to study, test, develop, and release its own mix of both specialty/complex and generic pharmaceutical products. Using innovation to drive its R&D developments is a self-proclaimed core strength of the business, made more effective and more efficient by its division of teams: Formulations, process chemistry, and analytical development. Some examples of different products that Sun Pharma has developed in-house include inhalers, nasal sprays, and anti-inflammatory drugs [11].

Though R&D in the pharmaceutical industry is a notoriously long and expensive process, Sun Pharma's R&D team serves as an innovative vertical integration for the company, enabling them to stay ahead of potential new specialty drugs and score the patent. The company's R&D pipeline has helped the company maintain a stronghold on the generic and complex generic pharmaceutical markets [12]. They have sought a balanced mix of organic developments internal to Sun Pharma and through outside acquisitions to grow their portfolio of generic and specialty drugs at a sustainable speed.

Since its inception in the 1980s, Sun Pharma has worked to expand its manufacturing capacity and capabilities [8]. In 1996, Sun Pharma continued to expand its manufacturing plants and research facilities and began to acquire related companies to increase its portfolio. This expansion strategy that focused on innovation capacity took off in the early 2010s.

Expanding the portfolio

The R&D required for developing, testing, and licensing generic drugs is both an expensive and long process, but the resulting generic product enables those R&D expenses to be spread across many consumers and markets [3]. Specialty drugs can target much more specific conditions, thus, consistent customers, especially those with chronic or long-term conditions. Specialty drugs are used to treat individualized symptoms and conditions in patients [5]. For example, someone reaching for the acetaminophen (generic) may have any number of reasons for their symptoms as opposed to someone seeking treatment for their chronic psoriasis (specialty) [13]. Relative to generics, developing specialty drugs involves less expensive R&D with target consumer groups who have high inelastic demand for your product, creating high margin opportunities. Sun Pharma recognized this opportunity to differentiate itself within the competitive and saturated generic pharmaceutical industry via high margin niche and specialty products.

Beginning around 2010, Sun Pharma shifted its global focus to specialty drugs. At this point in the company's journey, Sun Pharma continued to technologically innovate and work to develop new generics. However, they were also able to creatively identify gaps in the specialty market and went on an acquisition spree [8]. Now, Sun Pharma would not have to pay for years and years of R&D with the hopes they could secure a patent or create a new drug first; they would have exclusive access to already-existing specialty drugs with visible demand. By the early 2010s, Sun Pharma had enough money and likeminded leadership to begin its biggest period of global expansion via specialty acquisitions. As a result, total income for the company would double in just two years, and multiply over 6.5 times after just five years [11].

So, what exactly did Sun Pharma do to shoot its revenues into the stratosphere?

Innovation through acquisitions

Expansive acquisition timeline

The Indian generic pharmaceuticals company launched a spending spree of specialty manufacturers and products across the globe. Sun Pharma seemed to prioritize US-focused acquisitions, though this is unsurprising given the US's consistent market for pharmaceutical drugs (attractive market) and high number of pharmaceutical groups and companies that already existed (existing footprint makes for easier transition). Sun Pharma has prioritized expanding its selection of specialty products in ophthalmology (eyecare), dermatology (skin), and oncology (cancer) [11].

Acquisitions and investments of US companies, brands, and properties in early 2010s [8]:

- Manufacturing plant in Bryant, Ohio
- Chattem Chemicals Inc.
- Taro Pharmaceuticals
- Generic branch of URL Pharmaceuticals
- Dusa Pharmaceuticals
- Ranbaxy
- Pharamlucence
- InSite Vision

After securing the above initial US investments, Sun Pharma accelerated its pace and global footprint in 2015 with the following acquisitions, purchases, or launches [8]. The dates alongside the product name are when that product became commercialized in the stated market [11]. Specialty acquisitions post-2015 are also found in Exhibit 15.1.

- GSK's Opiates (Australia, 2015)
- Brands by Novartis (Japan, 2016)
  - Acquired 14 prescription brands
- Ocular Technologies (2016)
- Biosintez (Russia, 2016)
- BromSite (US, 2016)
  - Sun Pharma launched BromSite as its first *branded* ophthalmic product
- Odomzo (US, 2017)
  - Second specialized product launch in US during this period
- ILUMYA (US, 2019)
  - Third specialized product launch in US during this period
- YONSA (US, 2019)
  - Fourth specialized product launch in US during this period
- XELPROS (US, 2019)
  - Fifth specialized product launch in US during this period
- Pola Pharma (Japan, 2019)
  - Dermatology brand acquisition

298 *Case studies*

- Cequa (US, 2020)
  - Sixth specialized product launch in US during this period
- ILUMYA (Japan, 2020)

Sun Pharma's interest in ophthalmology, dermatology, and oncology products is reflected in the above acquisitions and launches. BromSite, for example, was Sun Pharma's first *branded* ophthalmic product that it released commercially in the US. BromSite fights pain and inflammation in the eyes following cataract surgery and can be used before and after the procedure. It is an NSAID, or nonsteroidal anti-inflammatory drug, and said to be the first USFDA-approved NSAID that targets and prevents pain specific to cataract surgery [14]. BromSite was launched as a part of Sun Pharma's growing ophthalmic business arm called Sun Ophthalmics [15]. It was branded and marketed under Sun Ophthalmics as well. BromSite's commercial launch was a big deal for Sun Pharma at the time because it was the first branded product that they launched in the US. Sun Ophthalmics operating as its own growing entity also demonstrates the company's approach to innovation via commitment to its specialty business divisions.

Financial impact

From 2010 to 2020, Sun Pharma had grown its specialty portfolio successfully to watch its revenue jump from 2010's $361.83M to 2020's $4.576B [9, 16, 17]. Its net profit after minority interest nearly quadrupled over those ten years, from $122.86M in 2010 to $514.7M in 2020 [9, 16, 17]. R&D expenditure and investment also saw a steep increase from 2010 to 2015 – £30.65M to $267.27M, respectively – and only a slight increase from 2015 to 2020 (net increase of only approximately £2M to $269.81M) [9, 16, 17, 18]. Exhibit 15.2 and Exhibit 15.3 outline revenue, profit, and R&D investment growth over the ten-year period.

Of the top ten generic pharmaceutical companies, by 2017 Sun Pharma rose to the fifth largest in the world, capturing 3% of global market share, as shown in Exhibit 15.4 [5]. Besides the top three players – none of whom break 10% of the global generics market – the remaining leaders all share the same relatively small percentage of the global market, between 1% and 4%. The top ten only make up 35% of the total global share, which is actually 1% less than it was five years earlier in 2012. This goes to show how, even as an industry leader in both market share and innovation, Sun Pharma is still fighting for a relatively small slice of the pie; they identified the value of high margin niche and specialty products to continue innovating and growing their portfolio in a very saturated market.

As of Q1 2021, nearly 32% of its total sales in India were driven from specialty products, 17% of total Emerging Market sales, and 14% of Rest of the World sales [19]. Specialty revenue in the US has dropped since 2020 due to legal issues and payouts relating to Taro Pharma, when this subsidiary was forced to pay almost $480M in the summer of 2020 due to criminal charges in the US that accused the group of drug price fixing [20].

Innovation culture

Sun Pharma's flashy specialty acquisition strategy across the 2010s caught the attention of multiple press and media outlets, catapulting their unique innovation culture into the spotlight. Forbes ranked Sun Pharma in the top 100 of most innovative companies on the planet in the years 2014, 2015, and 2018 [21]. During this period, Forbes celebrated Sun Pharma's three-pronged system for maintaining and growing its portfolio of pharmaceutical products. The three major divisions – manufacturing, development (including R&D), and marketing – operate uniquely compared to other major drug companies [22]. In 2014 and 2015, Sun Pharma was one of just six global pharmaceutical companies to make the list. Only four pharmaceutical companies made Forbes' top 100 in 2018 [23, 24]. Sun Pharma credits both its acquisitions and R&D pipeline for its continual innovation [6]. These two sources in particular enable Sun Pharma to continue growing its specialty portfolio while controlling the generic value chain. The R&D teams are also able to dedicate many resources toward complex generics. Their specialty business lines, on the other hand, have continued to grow and succeed following commercialization of a few major drugs within American markets.

The company's 2018 Letter to Shareholders calls out "nurturing specialty growth" on page 1 of 45, signaling the management-level commitment to specialty innovation [6]. Their commitment to ophthalmology, oncology, and dermatology are repeated, as well as treatment targeting the central nervous system. Managing Director Dilip Shanghvi outlined Sun Pharma's commitment as follows:

> We are developing our specialty products pipeline with a focus on improving patient outcomes either by addressing unmet medical needs or by enhancing patient convenience through differentiated dosage forms. Over the past two years, we have also focused on establishing the requisite front-end capabilities for our specialty business. This involves setting up a relevant sales force (for promoting these products to doctors), establishing the required regulatory and market access teams, along with support staff [6].
>
> Managing Director, Dilip Shanghvi

Annual reports and letters to shareholders released in the few years following 2018 include similar language to prove the company's commitment to diversifying its drug portfolio via R&D, generic and complex generic development, specialty business lines, and acquisitions of specialty products [11, 17].

Conclusion

Sun Pharma set the tone for a culture of innovation when it first began in the 1980s and built unique relationships with development opportunities and future doctors and pharmacists. Faced with high competition and a diverse global market, Sun Pharma identified an exclusive way to handle its four main targets – India, the US, Emerging Markets, and Rest of the World – while managing the dangerous patent cliff. The

300   *Case studies*

2010s saw major portfolio and profit growth as a result of its specialty acquisition strategy. This past decade of Sun Pharma's pursuit of high margin niche and specialty drugs has created a unique story of innovation within technology, leadership, and culture.

Looking through the TRIAL© framework

- Did technology play a role?
  Sun Pharma's established R&D pipeline and the technological resources available through each step of the value chain were the largest tech contributions to Sun Pharma's high margin success.
- Did they have unique leadership?
  Sun Pharma is unique in that its 1983 founder is still the Managing Director nearly 40 years later. To complete the many expensive purchases and acquisitions throughout the 2010s, leadership had to be extremely united in goals and priorities to make such investments.
- What resources (talent and other resources) did they use?
  Many financial resources were dedicated to the specialty acquisitions of the 2010s. Additionally, the establishment of specialty business lines (ex: Sun Ophthalmics) required Sun Pharma's human capital to be spread across divisions.
- Did they have an imaginative and achievement culture?
  The early establishment and continued commitment to Sun Pharma's own R&D division – dedicating approximately 8% of total revenues and thousands of full-time employees to its R&D team – demonstrate achievement-focused culture. This line also must be very creative in its pursuit of new drugs, both complex generic and generic, of which they can earn patents.
- What else contributed to their success?
  Maintaining its stronghold on the Indian pharmaceutical market is actively proving to be very beneficial for Sun Pharma among other Emerging Markets. Sun Pharma's specialty focus in oncology, dermatology, and ophthalmology has also accelerated their success in specialty markets by identifying the biggest gaps in product options for customers in dominant markets (ex: ophthalmology brand success in the US).

Case questions

1. How was Sun Pharma able to successfully identify market gaps in demand among underserved customer bases?
2. Are there other areas for growth toward which Sun Pharma should have devoted more attention (for example, the API market)?
3. Would Sun Pharma's 2010s acquisition spree have been as successful without forming separate specialty lines of business? Why or why not?
4. What was the most important decision Sun Pharma made to yield the successful innovations that it has?
5. How can Sun Pharma maintain an innovation mindset going forward?

Appendix

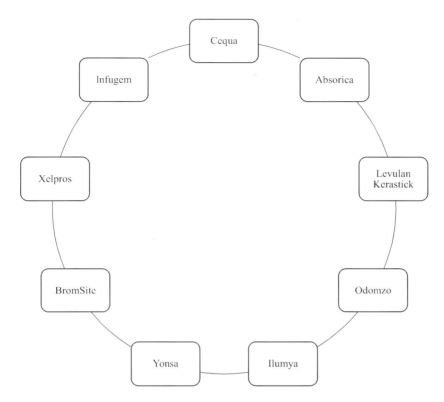

Exhibit 15.1 Specialty products added to Sun Pharma portfolio after 2015 [25]

Year	2010	2015	2020
Revenue	$361,830,000	$3,825,000,000	$4,576,000,000
Total Profit	$122,860,000	$620,590,000	$514,700,000
R&D Investments	$30,650,000	$267,270,000	$269,810,000

Exhibit 15.2 Financial impact of specialty Innovations – 2010, 2015, and 2020

Sources
2010 data: page 26 [9]
2015 data: page 2 [18]
2020 data: page 2 [17]
Rupees to USD conversion: [16]

302 Case studies

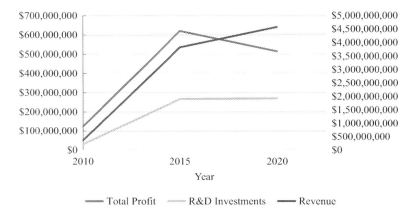

Exhibit 15.3 Specialty innovations-related financials trend – 2010, 2015, and 2020

Sources
2010 data: [9]
2015 data: [18]
2020 data: [17]
Rupees to USD conversion: [16]

Top-Ten Global Generic Pharmaceutical Companies	% of Global Market Share (2017)
Teva Pharma	9.10%
Sandoz	6.20%
Mylan	5.30%
Pfizer	3.80%
Sun Pharma	3%
Fresenius Kabi	2.10%
Lupin	1.80%
Sanofi	1.40%
Endo International	1.10%
Aurobindo Pharma	1.10%

Exhibit 15.4 2017 Global market share of pharmaceutical companies [5]

References

1. "About Us: Sun Pharmaceutical Industries Limited," May 9, 2021, Sun Pharmaceutical Industries Ltd., www.sunpharma.com/about-us/
2. J. Ramachandran, and Savithran Ramesh, "Sun Pharmaceutical Industries Limited: Disclosure Practices," Aug 16, 2020, Indian Institute of Management Bangalore, Harvard University.
3. Eva Koronios, "Global Pharmaceuticals & Medicine Manufacturing," Mar 2020, Industry Report C1933-GL, IBISWorld, https://my-ibisworld-com.libproxy.bus.umich.edu/download/gl/en/industry/720/1/0/pdf

Sun Pharma Industries 303

4. Kevin Kennedy, "Generic Pharmaceutical Manufacturing in the US," 2021, Industry Report 32541B, IBISWorld, https://my-ibisworld-com.libproxy.bus.umich.edu/download/us/en/industry/488/1/0/pdf.

5. Charles-André Brouwers, et al. "The Paths to Value for US Generics," 2020, Boston Consulting Group, https://image-src.bcg.com/Images/BCG-The-Paths-to-Value-for-US-Generics-Jan-2020_tcm9-237195.pdf.

6. Dilip Shanghvi, "Managing Director's Letter," May 25, 2018, Annual Report 2017–18, Sun Pharmaceutical Industries Ltd, https://sunpharma.com/wp-content/uploads/2020/12/Board-Report-and-Management-Discussion-_-Analysis.pdf

7. Manbeena Chawla, "AstraZeneca Announces Three Large-Scale Initiatives in China," Nov 8, 2019, BioSpectrum Asia Edition, www.astrazeneca.com/media-centre/press-releases/2019/astrazeneca-announces-three-large-scale-initiatives-in-china-to-advance-global-medicine-research-and-development-061120119.html

8. "Milestones & Recognitions: Sun Pharmaceutical Industries Limited," May 9, 2021, Sun Pharmaceutical Industries Ltd., https://sunpharma.com/milestones-recognitions/

9. Board of Directors, "At Work," May 2010, Annual Report 2009–10, Sun Pharmaceutical Industries Ltd., https://sunpharma.com/wp-content/uploads/2020/12/download-completeAnnualReport2.3MB-3.pdf

10. "Active Pharmaceutical Ingredient Market Research Report by Type, by Synthesis, by Manufacturer, by Therapeutic Application - Global Forecast to 2025 - Cumulative Impact of COVID-19," ReportLinker. Intrado Globe Newswire, www.globenewswire.com/en/news-release/2021/05/14/2229709/0/en/Active-Pharmaceutical-Ingredient-Market-Research-Report-by-Type-by-Synthesis-by-Manufacturer-by-Therapeutic-Application-Global-Forecast-to-2025-Cumulative-Impact-of-COVID-19.html

11. Board of Directors, "Specialty in Progress," Dec 2020, Annual Report 2018–19, Sun Pharmaceutical Industries Ltd., https://sunpharma.com/wp-content/uploads/2020/12/Complete-Annual-Report.pdf

12. Sun Pharma Board of Directors, "Annual Reports Presentations: Sun Pharmaceutical Industries Limited," June 16, 2021, Sun Pharmaceutical Industries Ltd., https://sunpharma.com/investors-annual-reports-presentations/

13. Sohini Das, "Sun Pharma to Launch Its First Innovative Product for Psoriasis in Japan," June 29, 2020, Business Standard, www.business-standard.com/article/companies/sun-pharma-to-launch-its-first-innovative-product-for-psoriasis-in-japan-120062901146_1.html

14. "BromSite Important Safety Information," 2020, BromSite, Sun Ophthalmics, www.bromsite.com/patient/

15. Frederick Castro, "Sun Pharma Launches First Branded Ophthalmic Product, BromSite™, in USA," 28 Nov. 2016, World Pharma Today, Leo MarCom Pvt. Ltd., www.worldpharmatoday.com/news/sun-pharma-launches-first-branded-ophthalmic-product-bromsite-in-usa/

16. "INR Exchange Rates," 2021, TransferWise Ltd, Wise.com, https://wise.com/us/currency-converter/currencies/inr-indian-rupee

17. Board of Directors, "The Transformation Journey," May 2020, Annual Report 2019–20, Sun Pharmaceutical Industries Ltd., https://sunpharma.com/wp-content/uploads/2020/12/SunPharmaAR2019-20-1.pdf

18. Board of Directors, "Growing Together," May 2015, Annual Report 2014–15, Sun Pharmaceutical Industries Ltd., https://sunpharma.com/wp-content/uploads/2020/12/completeannual-report.pdf

19. Ujjval Jauhari, "India Business, Speciality Products to Drive Growth for Sun Pharma," May 30, 2021, Mint, Livemint.com, www.livemint.com/market/mark-to-market/positive-speciality-portfolio-outlook-bodes-well-for-sun-pharma-11622181127346.html

20. Chris Kay, "Top India Drugmaker Profit Rebounds as Virus Impact Eases," Nov 3, 2020, Bloomberg.com, www.bloomberg.com/news/articles/2020-11-03/top-india-drugmaker-sees-profit-rebound-as-virus-impact-eases

304 *Case studies*

21. SyncForce, "Sun Pharmaceutical Industries," 2021, Ranking the Brands, www.rankingthebrands.com/Brand-detail.aspx?brandID=5455
22. Jeff Dyer, and Hal Gregersen, "How We Rank the World's Most Innovative Companies 2015," 24 Mar. 2016, Forbes Magazine, www.forbes.com/sites/innovatorsdna/2015/08/19/how-we-rank-the-worlds-most-innovative-companies-2015/?sh=6eeb13695f8c
23. "The World's Most Innovative Companies," 2018, Forbes Magazine, www.forbes.com/innovative-companies/list/
24. "Sun Pharma Industries," May 13, 2021, Forbes Magazine, www.forbes.com/companies/sun-pharma-industries/?list=innovative-companies&sh=3c40d13932e2
25. Nimish Desai, "Creating Lasting Value," Feb 2021, Investor Presentation - February 2021, Sun Pharmaceutical Industries Ltd., https://sunpharma.com/wp-content/uploads/2021/02/IR-Presentation-Feb-2021.pdf

Case 16: Ecovative Design – Organizing for Innovation in Sustainable Biomaterials

Daniel Meeks

Ecovative Design
dcmeeks@umich.edu

Company introduction

Ecovative Design, headquartered in Troy NY, is an innovative biotechnology company that harnesses the unique binding properties of mushroom mycelium to replace environmentally impactful products with more sustainable alternatives. The company's mission statement is to grow everyday materials that support and enhance spaceship Earth. In nature, fungi act as a recycling system, decomposing organic material into nutrients that are usable by other organisms, and therefore reintroducing these materials into the food web. Mushroom mycelium is the root structure that grows in soil and plant materials, digesting organic materials, and transporting the nutrients throughout the organism. Ecovative harnesses this essential natural process to create products that are self-assembling, require low external energy inputs, and are compostable at the end of their useful life. Ecovative uses this technology to develop products that can be used as a replacement for environmentally impactful materials and processes, providing a much-needed alternative for the purpose of lessening our collective impact on the earth.

Ecovative was founded by Eben Bayer and Gavin McIntyre, who developed the technology in an entrepreneurship and design course as undergraduate students at Rensselaer Polytechnic Institute. This course, called Inventor's Studio, was instructed by Professor Burt Swersey. Under Swersey's mentorship, Bayer and McIntyre founded the company after graduating in 2007 and began building the business in an incubator at RPI before expanding to an industrial facility in 2009. In the early days of the company, the small team sought to understand the capabilities of mycelium-based materials, tackling invention through an Edisonian approach of informed trial and error. This consisted of pairing feedstocks with species of mushrooms, which were biologically compatible, to create products with interesting and favorable performance characteristics. With the help of local mushroom experts and insights from the mushroom cultivation industry, the company began building a library of tested mushroom species and feedstocks. In addition to discovering the technical capabilities and potential applications for their newly developed materials, through this process Ecovative honed their understanding of the mycological practices, which would become the basis of their first commercial manufacturing efforts.

DOI: 10.4324/9781003190837-37

Exhibit 16.1 Ecovative cofounders Gavin McIntyre (CCO) and Eben Bayer (CEO) [1]

Initial commercial offering: Mushroom® packaging

In 2009, Ecovative announced their first commercial product, Mushroom® packaging, with the intent to stem the world's reliance on expanded polystyrene (EPS) packaging. EPS is a single-use product with disastrous environmental impacts during production, as well as at end of life. One cubic foot of polystyrene requires over half a gallon of petroleum to manufacture, making it an incredibly energy-intensive product [2]. EPS does not chemically decompose, but instead is mechanically broken down into increasingly smaller particles. It is estimated that in the late 2000s, EPS occupied 25% of the world's total landfills. Even more damaging is when these materials find their ways into our waterways and eventually to the ocean, where these microscopic particles are accumulated in the environment, and eventually into our food systems. Therefore, these materials are not only damaging to the environment, but they are also damaging to human health.

To address this problem, Ecovative developed their mycocomposite technology, a process that creates single-use materials that are compatible with earth's natural recycling system (see Exhibit 16.7, TRIAL© framework). Mycocomposite practices include inoculating crop wastes such as corn stalks and hemp pith with mycelium. The mycelium grows through the substrate, binding the individual particles into a cohesive composite material. Once dried, these materials are shelf stable and have comparable performance to many conventional protective packaging foams, but are fully compostable, meaning the embodied nutrients are returned to their environment at the end of their useful life. Additionally, Ecovative's mycocomposite system requires low energy inputs, where most of the external energy required for manufacturing is used to treat the crop waste substrates. Subsequently, the growing mycelium can be grown in standard warehouse conditions, without the need to maintain specialized environmental conditions.

Because the composite material retains the shape of the container it is grown within, Ecovative was able to create products with specified geometries by growing within preformed plastic molds. In Ecovative's production system, these plastic molds were reused dozens of times and were collected and recycled into new molds at the end of their useful life. By designing their production systems to utilize a standard tray size regardless of the product shape, Ecovative could service multiple protective packaging customers with differing product shapes and dimensions with minimal alterations to the manufacturing process.

Between 2010 and 2018, Ecovative manufactured Mushroom® protective packaging for several large customers, including those in the computer, housewares, and furniture industries. To support their growing manufacturing base, Ecovative's team of engineers designed and installed specialized machinery to automate this complex manufacturing process. At company headquarters in Green Island, NY, Ecovative designed and built their first production facility, producing a precursor material to protective packaging production, where substrate is inoculated with mycelium, then grown under conditions to colonize the substrate in a clean and sanitary environment, ensuring high-quality early-stage growth. This system also afforded Ecovative the ability to grow in a high-density growth environment, saving warehouse space and overhead costs.

Once fully colonized with mycelium, the substrate could be packed into growth forms for a second growth cycle to produce protective packaging parts. To support this process, Ecovative's engineering team designed an automated manufacturing system for filling trays of growth forms. This process adapted practices and machinery used in food production industries to ensure clean handling of materials and efficient cleaning of equipment at the end of each production run.

Despite the growth of Ecovative's production capacity, Ecovative knew that their current facility could not support the necessary scale to become cost competitive with conventional EPS. While they could not compete with EPS packaging for mature and globally distributed products, Ecovative's size and agility was an asset in terms of their ability to rapidly design and produce cost-effective prototypes. Riding the wave of new direct-to-customer distribution models, Ecovative began targeting small to medium enterprises who could not afford the expensive process of prototyping custom EPS packaging and were looking for packaging solutions that lowered their upfront business operations expenses and allowed them to get to market quickly and cost-effectively. This target customer identification process highlighted the resilience of Ecovative's team, as they closed out large accounts and began the process of acquiring an entirely new customer base (see Exhibit 16.7, TRIAL© framework).

Customers who meet these new criteria for target customer include Keap candles, Aplos, Shrine, Our Treaty, and Loli Beauty. Additionally, because of the low set-up costs in their operations, Ecovative could supply many unique protective packaging products within a single production run. This meant that their business could take on many smaller volume customers without substantially increasing operational expenses.

Reimagining the business model through the definition of core competencies

In 2018, after nine years of producing Mushroom® protective packaging, Ecovative's facility in northeast US had grown to support several small to medium enterprises.

308 *Case studies*

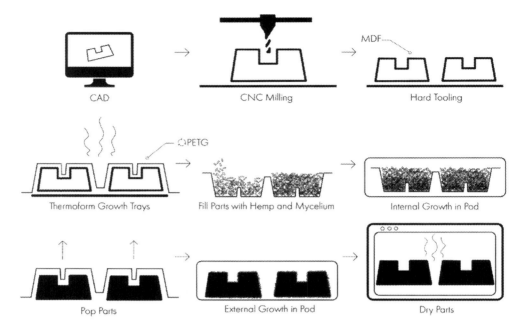

Exhibit 16.2 The Mushroom® protective packaging production process, from prototype tooling development to growth and drying to prepare for shipment [3]

However, they found that the revenue potential of their local customers was dwarfed by their customers on the west coast. This meant that most of their finished product had to be shipped across the country, only to then be shipped again to the final customer. Not only was this costly, it also did not meet the environmental vision of the company. Ecovative needed to decide what its role was in the value chain. Were they committed to scaled manufacturing and prepared to relocate their staff to California to produce protective packaging?

Ecovative determined that while they had previously manufactured internally, the company's true core competency was the development of mushroom mycelium-based technologies and their development into novel products. Based on this core competency, Ecovative redesigned their business model to focus on the development of products and manufacturing processes that could then be licensed to independent manufacturers around the globe. This would create an ecosystem of businesses capable of addressing geographically diverse customers, while leveraging Ecovative's intellectual property and expertise. Therefore, the company prepared the protective packaging business for licensing to an external manufacturer and began the process of identifying the next great mycelium-based product. In 2018, Ecovative licensed their US protective packaging business to Paradise Packaging, of Paradise, CA, and began identifying partners to expand their protective packaging business globally.

Simultaneously, Ecovative's R&D department set to work identifying the next product in Ecovative's technology development pipeline. The R&D group had a few ongoing Small Business Innovation Research grants, which were used to develop new applications of Ecovative's technology. Using this research as its starting point, Ecovative

Exhibit 16.3 Finished Mushroom® protective packaging parts being prepared for drying after growth [4]

Exhibit 16.4 Comparison of pure mycelium panel production at lab scale (left) and at pilot production scale (right) [9]

began to conduct an opportunity analysis for the next generation product that would become the future of the company. The criteria used to determine the company's direction were that (1) the product maintained Ecovative's core values of environmentalism by replacing or disrupting an environmentally impactful industry; (2) could provide a higher margin product where a smaller market share could prove profitable in the early stages of commercialization; and (3) technically superior to alternatives in the market by leveraging their patented mycelium technologies. Ultimately, Ecovative

310 *Case studies*

decided to focus the R&D department on pure mycelium products, which had shown promising development in several industries ripe for disruption.

Ecovative's pure mycelium products are grown in proprietary growth chambers under specific environmental conditions that produce mycelial growth directly out of the substrate to create large masses of white mushroom mycelium. This technology had previously been tested by Ecovative in several applications, including as performance foams, cosmetic applicators, and even as vegan leather. While these products were appealing for several reasons, the company believed that their mycelium technology could have even greater impact. Ecovative set its sights on redesigning the pure mycelium technology to develop a new product: Mushroom bacon.

Developing mushroom bacon

In the last decade, the plant-based meat industry has grown rapidly, both domestically and abroad. Changing consumer sentiments around the ethical and nutritional impacts of a high animal protein diet have led to a growing number of consumers opting to reduce or eliminate their consumption of animal protein and other animal products. This issue also resonated with Ecovative's environmental mission of replacing harmful materials and practices from the environment. To raise a single pound of beef in the US, conventional animal agriculture practices consume 2.2 gallons (13lbs) of gasoline and 610 gallons (5,080lbs) of water, and produce 22lbs of CO_2 equivalents [5, 6].

The growth of this new consumer sentiment has created a gold rush of companies seeking to develop new alternatives to animal protein, several whom have been acquired by conventional industry players seeking to capitalize on the trend. In the last decade, there has been $2.7B of venture capital invested in plant-based meats, with $1.9B in 2019 and Q1 2020 alone [7].

Led by companies such as Beyond Meat and Impossible Foods, the plant-based meat industry to date has focused primarily on ground meat alternative products, including burgers, sausages, and meatballs. Ground meat represents the minority of meat sold both domestically and globally. In fact, the most common ground meat product, ground beef, only accounts for 40% of the US beef market [8]. Ground meat alternatives have been the first products to reach the market in part because of the technical difficulty of replicating the texture and consistency of whole cut meat. Plant-based products generally derive their structure from plant ingredients, which has been suitable for ground products, but cannot supply the bite and consistency to replicate whole cut meat products.

Ecovative's pure mycelium technology has always focused on utilizing the network of mycelium fibers to create structure, making it the perfect product to address this market. Ecovative decided to focus its initial offering within the alternative meat industry on creating mushroom bacon, in part because of bacon's thin profile and small size relative to other products such as steak. Ecovative felt strongly that it could create a premium product for this segment by making further innovations in pure mycelium growth and manufacturing processes, and by developing a method for processing mycelium panels to mimic the taste and texture of bacon.

The plant-based bacon market includes soy-based products from Morningstar Farms (a Kellogg company) and Quorn (a Monde Nissin company). Despite the large and well-financed competition within the plant-based food industry that these soy-based products present, many are extruded products lacking inherent texture.

Ecovative's innovation challenge therefore became how to take their new pure mycelium platform, develop a product that meets the markets needs better than the incumbents, and can be scaled to a size at which it can serve the food industry quickly to address the current growth in the plant-based food market.

Organizing to facilitate rapid innovation

To accomplish this goal, Ecovative reorganized its company to meet the challenges ahead. While reorganizing the company was no small feat, the adaptability of the company and its ability to effectively manage change allowed the organization to quickly reorient around its new goals (see Exhibit 16.7, TRIAL© framework).

First, Ecovative segmented its R&D team into groups. The Pilot group would develop manufacturing processes to rapidly grow the technology from lab scale to full pilot scale. To meet an ambitious timeline, the Pilot operations team would take over lab-scale incubators to produce small-scale pilot production efforts and conduct process development trials. Fostering an environment of continuous improvement, the pilot operators would be tasked with determining the most efficient processes for manufacturing these materials at small scale. Materials produced at this stage were utilized internally to produce samples for investment and marketing purposes.

Leveraging the learnings from lab-scale production, the engineering team designed and installed new growth chambers, which expanded the current capacity by an order of magnitude, allowing for small-scale pilot manufacturing, and distribution to local grocery stores. Each time the engineering team commissioned a new capacity-increasing growth system, the operations team would take over production in that system, and continue to provide design feedback to improve systems as they scaled. Using this model, the Pilot team transitioned from lab scale to full pilot production scale, a nearly 500 times capacity increase, over the course of one year.

Because the basis of success for this relationship was effective continuous improvement, standard operating procedures were constantly re-examined and updated throughout this process. To accomplish this, the operations team must effectively manage change, and readily adapt to new procedures. Improvements were therefore treated as most important achievements provided by the Pilot operations team and were consistently communicated in terms of their effect on the profit and loss statements of future production systems (see Exhibit 16.7, TRIAL© framework).

Also, within the Pilot group, a Food Safe Manufacturing team was recruited from the greenhouse horticulture industry, to ensure that these newly developed systems followed the strict regulations of food production, which was a new constraint on Ecovative's manufacturing processes. This team would be embedded within the engineering teams to help inform the food safe facility constraints of new growth chambers and operations floor plans, as well as with the operations team to improve practices and procedures to meet these regulations. Obtaining this expertise within the team was a crucial resource as it entered an unfamiliar regulatory environment (see Exhibit 16.7, TRIAL© framework).

A second group that was developed from the existing R&D department was the Functional Biology team. This team of mycologists, microbiologists, and bioprocess engineers was tasked with providing scientific support to the Pilot group, by developing test methods to ensure product safety and to solve biological contamination issues. This team was also responsible for scaling down the pure mycelium

312 *Case studies*

process to develop bench-scale processes to enable fundamental research to inform future process development.

The Functional Biology team, along with the Bioengineering team, is also responsible for conducting fundamental and applied research required to determine the capabilities of Ecovative's materials. This provides two specific functions. First, bench-scale experimentation is conducted using internally designed highly controlled, high replicate growth systems to deepen Ecovative's understanding of how their technology functions, and what key properties Ecovative can leverage to improve the quality of their existing technologies. These research projects are generally requested by the Pilot team to overcome specific development hurdles for products in the development cycle, such as understanding optimal environmental conditions to elicit optimal mycelium growth. Second, as more is learned about the capabilities of the material, new functionalities are unlocked, which ultimately become the basis of new potential applications in the development pipeline. This second function by its nature is generally separate from ongoing development projects and is contingent on the inquisitive and imaginative nature of these researchers (see Exhibit 16.7, TRIAL[©] framework).

Additionally, Ecovative created a Product Development team, which was responsible for creating the final bacon product. This team was composed of biological scientists internal to Ecovative, as well as food scientists and product developers hired from industry. This team's responsibility was to take raw mycelium slabs produced by the Pilot team, and design handling and cooking processes to create the best and most authentic plant-based bacon. This team provided critical feedback, which helped to define the specifications of the manufacturing process. This segmentation of the R&D community into specific functional groups helped the team to better understand the scope of their responsibilities, build accountability to other groups by fostering internal customer relationships, and allow for a more focused approach to solve the technical challenges that this innovative team faced.

An important group in the company's reorganized structure was the R&D Operator group. The original members of the R&D Operator group were former members of

Exhibit 16.5 Sliced pure mycelium panels before post processing into MyBacon™ product (left) and MyBacon™ strips after cooking (right) [10]

Ecovative's production team. These individuals have a deep practical understanding of Ecovative's core mushroom technologies and had experience with working successful and efficient production environments. As Ecovative transitioned toward an R&D-focused organizational structure, this team received training to act as scientific support staff for all pilot-scale research activities. These combined skills allowed this team to support pilot research for new products leaving the lab and envision production systems, which would make them commercially viable at full-scale manufacturing. This unique prospective allowed Ecovative to ground their pilot research in operational realities and gave engineers direct access to direct feedback for design improvement.

As Ecovative reorganized, it began to innovate methods to increase agency and accountability, and foster collaboration within the team. One of the most important ways that the R&D operations team achieved this was by adopting a "process ownership" program. Process ownership paired operators with specific pilot operations processes, creating single point accountability for the operations' continued success. The responsibilities of process ownership included maintaining documentation, training team members, and creating a lean manufacturing environment. Each operator on the team was given ownership over a process and gained ownership of more impactful or difficult processes as their experience level increased. This program effectively enabled team-wide leadership at the operational level by giving agency and responsibility to each of the operators and helped to create a culture of accountability, which was built from within the operations team.

Design thinking

In 2018, Ecovative utilized design thinking to chart the course for MyBacon™ product development. The design thinking process employed by the Product Development team is best described using the empathize, define, prototype, test model. Because a mushroom bacon was novel to the market, it was important for Ecovative to get the product into the hands of customers quickly to inform the innovation process. To achieve this, Ecovative generated early prototype materials using their current production species of mushroom, which was safe to eat but was not familiar to the food industry. This would allow Ecovative to generate feedback from product testers on proof-of-concept-level prototypes, while the lab community set to task to grow pure mycelium products using culinary mushroom species, a substantial research goal that had previously never been accomplished. Ecovative took these prototype materials and cooked and packaged them in a variety of ways, then shipped the prototypes to innovators and influencers who were active within the plant-based meat market. The feedback generated from this process was insightful in crafting the product that Ecovative would be developing for the market.

One important finding that helped to shape Ecovative's design process was that the testers preferred to cook the bacon raw, both because of improved texture and because of the authenticity of the cooking experience. Most plant-based bacon products on the market are not cooked in the same fashion as pork bacon. Instead, they generally are purchased frozen and are either cooked in a pan with added oil or cooked in an oven. Ecovative found that the authenticity of the cooking experience was nearly as important as flavor, texture, and aroma, and therefore began developing a product that simulated as closely as possible the experience of purchasing bacon. The final product, therefore, was designed to be purchased refrigerated, placed with no added

314 *Case studies*

Stage	Aesthetics	Cooking Experience
Empathize	Plant-based food customers prefer food that is authentic to its ingredients, not a simulation of the original product	The cooking process is cathartic and important to the experience of the product
Define	**MyBacon™ should be authentically Mushroom based** MyBacon™ should celebrate that it is the world's first mushroom-based bacon, not cosmetically alter itself to look like the customer expects alternative bacon products to look like	**MyBacon™ should share the experience of cooking conventional bacon** MyBacon™ should be sold refrigerated, and should be cooked with no additional oil in a frying pan
Ideate	How should the appearance of MyBacon™ be enhanced? Adding food coloring to existing process step? What types of natural food colorants are available?	What methods can product developers use to supplement MyBacon™ with oil?
Prototype	Test colorants and application methods	Process testing and oil selection
Test	Distribute samples to gain customer insights	Distribute samples to gain customer insights

Exhibit 16.6 Design thinking at work to solve key product development questions

oil to a frying pan, and simply cooked to the desired "chewiness" just like pork bacon. From the perspective of the food product development process, this was the single most transformative finding that helped to shape the scope of Ecovative's product development and manufacturing system.

While initial prototypes were being tested by the Product Development group, the Pilot group began the process of developing scaled solutions for manufacturing food-safe mushroom bacon. After successfully cultivating a culinary mushroom species to produce slabs of mycelium (the first of its kind), the team began iterating to develop production methodologies that would maximize production efficiency and simplify the manufacturing process. To accomplish this, the team adopted a risk-tolerant mindset, giving Pilot team members the agency to test out ideas for process improvement in "production trials." This mindset gave team members the ability to take risks and "fail forward," a necessary step to the continuous improvement and development process. Team members were charged with developing "end run" ideas, which were not constrained by full experimental controls, but were used as initial justification for further investigation if they proved successful. This helped Ecovative to challenge its internal assumptions about what was necessary to produce state of the art material. Using these methods, Ecovative has been able to remove bottlenecks from the production process to achieve successful growth of pure mycelium products and give updated recommendations to engineering to inform the design of next generation growth chambers.

Wrap up: The TRIAL© framework

Ecovative's innovative culture and commitment to their environmental vision are the pillars that have guided the organization since its founding 2007. Using the TRIAL©

TRIAL Framework	

T - Technology & Tools	Patented Mycelium Technologies
	  - Mycocomposite
	  - Pure Mycelium Products
	New Manufacturing Systems
	Fundamental Research Platforms

R - Resources and Resilience	Recruitment of industry experts in new application spaces Target customer identification Organizational design around the development pipeline
I - Inquisitive & Imaginative Culture	Design Thinking in product development Identification of potential application spaces Capability expanding bench scale research
A - Achievement & Adaptability	Re-envisioning the business model Continuous Improvement
L - Leadership & Latitude	Commitment to sustainable mission and values Investment in employee agency Investment in personnel training

Exhibit 16.7 Application of the TRIAL© framework to business operations and organization at Ecovative Design [11]

framework, we can analyze how the company's decisions helped to foster innovation and bring new biological technologies to market as illustrated in Exhibit16.7.

Exhibit 16.8 illustrates how to apply the Enterprise Innovation Opportunities Model© to Ecovative as an innovation-driven organization [12] using the call outs 1 through 9.

(1) Ecovative was born from an entrepreneurial academic environment, where invention, innovation, and creativity were celebrated. After graduation, the founders utilized on-campus incubator spaces to grow the business's core technology from ideation to proof of concept.

(2) Ecovative's R&D department utilized Small Business Innovation Research grants to develop several technologies, which either led directly to commercial ventures or provided the fundamental science that led to commercializing the developed technology in a different market application.

(3) Ecovative developed and scaled new manufacturing methods for pure mycelium products using an aggressive scaling schedule and a continuous improvement methodology. Each of these pilot-scale facilities was used as a test bed to inform the design of the next 10–100 times increases in scale.

(4) Ecovative realigned the trajectory of the company by choosing projects within to add to the product development pipeline by meeting the following criteria: Must provide a high margin and be impactful at small scale relative to the competition; must align with the environmental mission of the company; and must be in a product application where mycelium adds value that other technologies have not been able to achieve.

(5) Ecovative hired food scientists and food production managers to bring key capabilities into strategic roles within the team. Similarly, the company invested heavily in personnel development to elevate their experienced and knowledgeable production team to support pilot-scale science and product development efforts, as well as engage in process development through a culture of continuous improvement.

316 *Case studies*

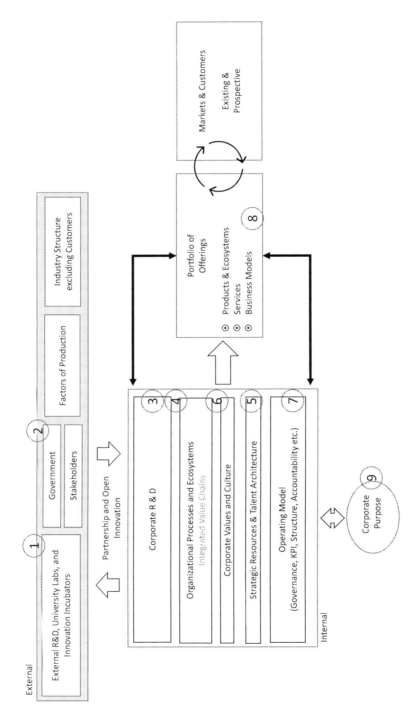

Exhibit 16.8 Applying the Enterprise Innovation Opportunities Model© to Ecovative as an innovation-driven organization [12]
Note: Please refer to Digital Learning Resources for TRIAL© framework worksheets.

Ecovative Design   317

(6) Ecovative adopted a mindset and operating principles that enabled agility and accepted measured risk to ensure rapid development. This was communicated using terminology such as "failing forward," giving employees the agency to test ideas and it resulted in challenging assumptions, which had previously artificially constrained the development process.

(7) Ecovative adopted "process ownership" programs to provide single-point accountability to the Operations team, increasing their agency and gaining valuable operations insights.

(8) Ecovative redesigned their business model to align with their core competencies more accurately in mycelium technology development and innovation. By externalizing the manufacturing process, Ecovative has been able to focus its efforts directly on moving innovative products through the development pipeline and preparing them to be onboarded by licensed manufacturing partners.

(9) Since its founding, Ecovative has remained true to its corporate purpose: To grow everyday materials that support and enhance spaceship Earth. The alignment of the company around this purpose helps to provide firm guideposts regardless of project or product application in the rapidly changing environment of technology development.

Case questions

(1) How should Ecovative balance their sustainable values with the practical needs of starting a new manufacturing business?

(2) What are the benefits of Ecovative's technology licensing business model? What are the risks?

(3) What role should partnerships with incumbent technology companies play as Ecovative moves into new application spaces? Should Ecovative seek to sell licenses to these large companies?

(4) How should Ecovative support fundamental research to inform future ventures when funding is so closely tied to short-term commercial success? Internal funding? Government research grants? Academic partnerships?

(5) What are the risks involved in Ecovative's rapid design iteration process? What are the benefits and drawbacks to continuous improvement systems?

(6) How should the company manage personnel advancement and succession planning in an industry such as applied mycology with limited academic programs to provide new entry level talent and where internally held knowledge is so important?

References

1. Oliver Campbell, 2016, "How One Dell Business Partner Has Grown Their Sustainable Idea Into Success," Dell Technologies, www.delltechnologies.com/en-us/blog/supporting-sustainability-innovators-how-one-dell-business-partner-has-grown-their-idea-into-success/

2. Chris Raymond, 2012, "Ecovative Design: Wiping Out Polystyrene with Fungus and Farm Waste," WIRED UK, www.wired.co.uk/article/we-grew-this-headline

3. https://mushroompackaging.com/our-process

4. https://mushroompackaging.com

318   *Case studies*

5. Senorpe Asem-Hiablie, et al., 2019, "A Life Cycle Assessment of the Environmental Impacts of a Beef System in the USA," Int J Life Cycle Assess, 24, pp. 441–455, https://doi.org/10.1007/s11367-018-1464-6

6. Alex Avery, and Dennis Avery, 2008, "Beef Production and Greenhouse Gas Emissions," Environmental Health Perspectives, 116(9).

7. Kieth Nunes, Mar 17, 2021, "Investments in Animal Protein Alternatives Surge," Food Business News, www.foodbusinessnews.net/articles/16029-investments-in-animal-protein-alternatives-surge

8. M. Shahbandeh, 2020, "U.S. Beef Sales Share by Cut Type, 2020," Statista, www.statista.com/statistics/191269/fresh-beef-category-share-in-2011/#:~:text=This%20statistic%20presents%20the%20category,the%20United%20States%20in%202019

9. https://ecovativedesign.com/ourfoundry

10. www.atlastfood.co/method

11. Vijay Pandiarajan, 2021, "TRIAL© Innovation Framework," WMBA 21Wint 2021 class notes, Ross School of Business, The University of Michigan.

12. Vijay Pandiarajan, 2021, "The TRIAL© Framework Enterprise Innovation Opportunities Model©," WMBA 21Wint 2021 class notes, Ross School of Business, The University of Michigan.

Glossary

Artificial Intelligence (AI) "... the science and engineering of making intelligent machines, especially intelligent computer programs. It is related to the similar task of using computers to understand human intelligence, but AI does not have to confine itself to methods that are biologically observable. At its simplest form, artificial intelligence is a field, which combines computer science and robust datasets, to enable problem-solving." https://www.ibm.com/cloud/learn/what-is-artificial-intelligence

Augmented Reality (AR) "... overlays digital content and information onto the physical world – as if they are actually there with you, in your own space. AR opens up new ways for your devices to be helpful throughout your day by letting you experience digital content in the same way you experience the world. It lets you search things visually, simply by pointing your camera at them. It can put answers right where your questions are by overlaying visual, immersive content on top of your real world." https://arvr.google.com/ar/

Big Data "... data that contains greater variety, arriving in increasing volumes and with more velocity. This is also known as the three Vs. Put simply, big data is larger, more complex data sets, especially from new data sources. These data sets are so voluminous that traditional data processing software just can't manage them. But these massive volumes of data can be used to address business problems you wouldn't have been able to tackle before." https://www.oracle.com/big-data/what-is-big-data/

Deep Learning "... a subset of machine learning, which is essentially a neural network with three or more layers. These neural networks attempt to simulate the behavior of the human brain – albeit far from matching its ability, allowing it to 'learn' from large amounts of data. While a neural network with a single layer can still make approximate predictions, additional hidden layers can help to optimize and refine for accuracy. Deep learning drives many artificial intelligence (AI) applications and services that improve automation, performing analytical and physical tasks without human intervention. Deep learning technology lies behind everyday products and services (such as digital assistants, voice-enabled TV remotes, and credit card fraud detection) as well as emerging technologies (such as self-driving cars)." https://www.ibm.com/cloud/learn/deep-learning

Machine Learning "... a branch of artificial intelligence (AI) and computer science which focuses on the use of data and algorithms to imitate the way that humans learn, gradually improving its accuracy." It uses statistical methods to train

320 *Glossary*

algorithms, which makes classifications or predictions, generating key insights for the given data set to make business decisions. https://www.ibm.com/cloud/learn/machine-learning

Mixed Reality (MR)   "… augmented reality's younger sibling. Where augmented reality is delivered through a handheld mobile device, i.e. a smartphone or a tablet, mixed reality is delivered through head mounted see-through glasses. The term was coined by Microsoft when they launched the Microsoft HoloLens in 2016. Apart from being head mounted, mixed reality also stands out from augmented reality through a more advanced understanding of the physical space and ability to place holograms in that space." https://virsabi.com/mixed-reality/

Neural Networks   "… also known as artificial neural networks (ANNs) or simulated neural networks (SNNs), are a subset of machine learning and are at the heart of deep learning algorithms. Their name and structure are inspired by the human brain, mimicking the way that biological neurons signal to one another. ANNs are comprised of a node layer, containing an input layer, one or more hidden layers, and an output layer. Each node, or artificial neuron, connects to another and has an associated weight and threshold. If the output of any individual node is above the specified threshold value, that node is activated, sending data to the next layer of the network. Otherwise, no data is passed along to the next layer of the network." https://www.ibm.com/cloud/learn/neural-networks

Quantum Computers   "… machines that use the properties of quantum physics to store data and perform computations. This can be extremely advantageous for certain tasks where they could vastly outperform even our best supercomputers. Classical computers, which include smartphones and laptops, encode information in binary 'bits' that can either be 0s or 1s. In a quantum computer, the basic unit of memory is a quantum bit or qubit." https://www.newscientist.com/question/what-is-a-quantum-computer/

Virtual Reality (VR)   "… the use of computer technology to create a simulated environment. Unlike traditional user interfaces, VR places the user inside an experience. Instead of viewing a screen in front of them, users are immersed and able to interact with 3D worlds. By simulating as many senses as possible, such as vision, hearing, touch, even smell, the computer is transformed into a gatekeeper to this artificial world. The only limits to near-real VR experiences are the availability of content and cheap computing power." https://www.marxentlabs.com/what-is-virtual-reality/

VR vs AR   We could think of AR as VR with one foot in the real world: AR simulates artificial objects in the real environment; VR creates an artificial environment to inhabit.

Index

Note: Page numbers in **bold** indicate tables; those in *italics* indicate figures.

3D and 4D printing 92
5G 88, 100; Ericsson 153, 285–286
9/11 116

Abilify MyCite 92
Abington Shoe Company 253
Abu Dhabi Investment Authority (ADIA)
  204
Accel 33
Accenture 14
achievement, TRIAL© framework 72–74
action, VASTEFA© leadership framework 77
adaptability: TRIAL© framework 72–74;
  VASTEFA© leadership framework 81–82
Adidas 253
Administrative Science Quarterly 5
Advanced Micro Devices (AMD) 98, 137
advertising *see* marketing
Aegerion Pharmaceuticals 91
Agarwal, Alok 204
agile product development 164
Airbnb 35; Apple partnership 236; business
  model innovation 6; customers 40; design
  thinking 151–153; investor community 32;
  support 78; World Wide Web 4
Airbus 94, 116, 117
air travel 115–117, *116*
Alcatel 136
Alibaba 118; cloud computing *44*;
  globalization 42; global logistics industry
  195; and governments 128; innovation
  leadership 45; Lyft investment 62; service
  industry 104
Allen, Bill 240
Allis Chalmers 93
Allscripts 105
Alphabet 234; corporate values 52; FedEx
  partnership 196–197; innovation
  leadership 45; Waymo 71
Amazon 118, 275–280; automated checkout
  51; cloud computing 242–243 (*see also*

Amazon Web Services); corporate values
  52; and FedEx 195–196, 199, 201;
  framework-based innovation approach 61;
  globalization 42; Go 23, 51, 107; grocery
  sector 23; health care 35; innovation
  leadership 45; leadership 66; lean
  enterprise 161; MXNet 90; net promoter
  score 137; ownership mindset 28–29;
  perennial innovation 63; pharmaceuticals
  sector 89; Prime 95; Rivian investment 97;
  service sector 104; third-party vendors 40;
  Web Services *see* Amazon Web Services;
  Whirlpool partnership 229; World Wide
  Web 4; Zappos acquisition 168
Amazon Web Services (AWS) 35, 276–278;
  competition 241; culture 277; disruptive
  innovation 14; dynamic capabilities 44;
  innovation strategy 24; pharmaceuticals
  sector 90; revenue *25*
Ambani, Mukesh 204–211
AMBER Alert Web Portal Consortium 127
Amdahl 21
Amgen 189–193
Ampère, André-Marie 4
Andreessen, Marc Lowell 151
Andreessen Horowitz 33, 62, 151
angles of attack 29–30, *29–30*
Ann Taylor 17
Ant Group 114
ANZ Taiwan 119
Aplos 307
Apollo 105
Apple: App Store 40, 232–237; automotive
  sector 35, 96, 134; business model
  innovation 62; competition 288, 290;
  consumer surplus 136; corporate culture
  19; cosmetic/survival innovation 9–10;
  credit card 114; design thinking 147, 149;
  digital tsunami 42; disruptive innovation
  14, 15; FaceID 141; history 232–234;
  innovation leadership 45; iPad 14, 15, 75,

232, 235, 236, 290; iPhone 9–10, 15, 20, 29, 32, 62, 75, 96, 136, 141, 232–234, 282, 288; iPod 75, 233; Mac computers 75, 232, 233, 235, 290; mergers and acquisitions 141; Microsoft investment 243; net promoter score 137; Objective-C 232–236, 238; operating system 32; partnership and open innovation 53; perennial innovation 63; resources and resilience 68; risk vs reward balance 137; semiconductors 98; Swift 233, 234–238; urgency, sense of 29; World Wide Web 4
Araripe, José Braz 95
Aras 94
Arhendts, Angela 156
Aristotle 73
ARPANet 278
Arqiva 109
artificial intelligence (AI): fintech 114, 115; flooding alerts 127; pharmaceuticals sector 89–90, 91; ride-hailing services 118; sustainability-focused innovation 174; *see also* machine learning
Ascena Retail Groups 17
aseptic packaging 10
AsiaSat 109
AstraZeneca: biosimilars 191; corporate R&D 51; COVID-19 vaccine 33, 91; tranSMART 91
AT&T: business model innovation 62; competition 135; disruptive innovation 15; internet protocol television 283; open innovation 70
athenahealth 105
Atomwise 90
attack, angles of 29–30, *29–30*
augmented reality (AR): cruise industry 109; education 112; Zara 263
automatic vehicle identification (AVI) 125–126
automotive sector 95–98; disruptive innovation 12–13; electronic module systems 19; government policies 33; semiconductors 99–100; sticky customers 21; urgency, sense of 31; *see also* autonomous vehicles; electric vehicles
autonomous vehicles 96, 97; FedEx 198; inquisitive and imaginative culture 71; taxis 118
auxiliary sales, as KPI 136
Avedro 31

Baby Boomers 176
Bachchan, Amitabh 206
Backhoe 93
Ballmer, Steve 240, 244
BankAmerica 156

banking sector 113–115
Bank of America 156–157
Barratts Shoes 17
Bayer, Eben 305, 306
Beats Electronics 141
Beddit 141
Belgium: industrial revolution 87
Bell, Robert 70
BellKor's Pragmatic Chaos 70
Benchmark 33
Benz, Karl 21
Benz Patent-Motorwagen 95
Berkshire Hathaway 249
Berners-Lee, Tim 4
Bershka 260
Bessemer Venture Partners 16
Beyond Meat 310
Bezos, Jeff 14, 66, 275–280
Bharat Sanchar Nigham 205
Bharti Airtel 205, 207
Biden administration 272
BigChaos 70
BigCommerce 42
big data 17; flooding alerts 127; personalized on-demand government services 122; pharmaceuticals sector 90–91; ride-hailing services 118; smart cities 127; sustainability-focused innovation 174; Zara 263
Bigfinite 90
Biogen 91
biologic drugs 92
Bionic 53
BioNTech 31, 54–55
biosimilars 189–193
Biosintez 297
Birkmeier, Dean 217, 219
Bitcoin 124
Bitzer, Marc 225
Blackberry 20, 75
BlackRock 97
Blaisdell, Betsy 255
Blank, Steve 161, 162, 163
Blecharczyk, Nathan 78
blockchain: fast food 68; FedEx 197–198, 199; fintech 114, 115; sustainability-focused innovation 175; voting 123–124
Blockchain in Transportation Alliance 198
Blockchain Research Institute 198
Bloomingdales 106
bluesign® system 179
Boeing 116, 117
Boot, Henry A. H. 11
Bose, Jagadis Chandra 98
Boston Scientific 220
Braskem 179–182
Braun, Karl 98

Index 323

Brayton, George 95
Brazil: citizen-government 126; pharmaceutical sector 295
Bristol-Myers Squibb 49, 89
British Home Stores 17
BromSite 297, 298
Brown, Tim 145
Bulldozer 93
Burberry 155–156
Burberry, Thomas 155
business models: automotive sector 96; Ecovative Design 308, 317; innovation 5, 6, 62; lean enterprise 163; Patagonia 268; Reliance Jio 208

Cadillac 95
Cambridge Enterprise 182
Camp, Garrett 62, 78
Canon 32
Canvas Network 111
Carbon Disclosure Project 264
Carere, Brie 198
Carlyle Group 92
Carnegie Mellon University 91
Carnival Corporation 108, 109
Carter, Rob 197
cash registry 106
Catalent 96
Caterpillar 63, 93
CATL 96
cavity magnetron 11
Celebrity Cruise 175
Celebrity Edge 109
Cequa 298
Chabbert, Martin 70
challenges embracing innovation 19–20, 34–35; market 21–23; organizational 23–31; stakeholders 31–34; triangular dilemma 20, *20*, 34–35
Chattem Chemicals 297
Chesbrough, Henry 53
Chesky, Brian 78, 151
chief innovation officers 49
child abductions 127
child labor 174, 177
China: electric vehicles 16; FedEx 199; fish value chain 42; healthcare 105; industrial revolution 87; service sector *104*, 104; Zhongguancun 33
Chouinard, Yvon 267
Christensen, Clayton 9, 11, 13
Chrysler 95; disruptive innovation 12–13, *13*; government policies 33
Circuit City Stores 56
Cisco 283
citizen–government redefined boundaries 126–127

ClassVR 112
climate change: automotive sector 33; Paris Agreement 180, 182; Patagonia 270, 272; sustainability-focused innovation 175, 180, 182; Zara 264
cloud computing: AWS *see* Amazon Web Services; disruptive innovation 14; Dropbox 167; dynamic capabilities 44; Ericsson 284; FedEx 197; heavy equipment sector 94; Microsoft *44*, 44, 90, 91, 94, 197, 240–243, 284; pharmaceuticals sector 90; worldwide market share *44*, 44
Coatue 62
Code Amber 127
Cognitive Class 111
collective genius framework 79, *80*
Colleran, Don 197
Collins, Jim 275
Colombia: blockchain-enabled voting 123–124
Colorifix 182–183
Commendo Research and Consulting 70
communication, VASTEFA© leadership framework 77
compartmentalization 25–26
competitive landscape, changes in 40–41
Confucius 110
construction equipment sector 93–94
consumers *see* customers
consumer surplus 31, 135–136, *135*
control, span of *28*, 28
Cook, Tim 233, 237–238
coopetition 40, 41
Corning 137
Corporate Business Services 198
corporate culture: Amazon 275–276, 277; Amgen 191; Apple 234; challenges 19, 26; defined 52; Ecovative Design 314, 315, 317; Ericsson 282; FedEx 199; inquisitive and imaginative 70–72; Microsoft 241–242; Patagonia 270–272; Procter & Gamble 249; Reliance Jio 210; Samsung 289–290, 292; as source of innovation 52–53; Sun Pharmaceutical Industries 299; Timberland 254, 256; Whirlpool 228, 230; Zara 261, 263–264
corporate research and development 49–51
corporate social responsibility *see* social responsibility
corporate values, as source of innovation 52
Cortex AI Studio 90
cosmetic/survival innovation 9–10, 17
Coursera 111
COVID-19 pandemic 44; air travel 116; banking sector 114; education 112; FedEx 195, 196, 199, 201; home working 67; Indian telecom industry 205; Patagonia

324 *Index*

272; Procter & Gamble 251; Reliance
Jio 204, 209, 210; social distancing 68;
Stryker 214–222; telemedicine 106;
Timberland 253; vaccine development 33,
54–55, 81, 91; Zara 264
Cradlepoint 285
Cruise 97
cruise industry 108–110
cryptocurrency 115
customers: Amazon 275–276; changes 40;
design thinking 146–149; Ecovative Design
307, 308; empathizing with 147–148,
157; Patagonia 267–270; problems,
understanding 148–149; product reviews
42; satisfaction 136–137; sticky 21;
Stryker 216, 217, 219; sustainability-
focused innovation 173–174, 176–178;
Timberland 253, 254, 257; Zara 261–262,
264
cybersecurity 114

Daimler 61
Daimler, Gottlieb 95
Dalhousie University 64
Daniel, John 215–216
Dark Sky 141
Darwin, Charles 81
data sharing 91
dedicated short-range communications
(DSRC) 125, 126
deed transfer 122
Defense Advanced Research Project Agency
(US) 32, 54
definitions of innovation 3
DEKA Development & Research 198
Deloitte 198
Democracy Earth Foundation 124
Denmark: smart cities 128
Department of Defense (US) 33, 54
Department of Energy (US) 61–62
Department of Health and Human Services
(US) 41
design thinking 145–146, 157; Airbnb
151–153; approach 147–151, *148*; Bank
of America Keep the Change Program
156–157; Burberry 155–156;
considerations 150, *150*; Ecovative
Design 313–314; Enterprise Innovation
Opportunities Model 151, *152*; Ericsson
153–155, *154*; lean enterprise 160,
164–165, *165*; Stryker 216–219, 221;
Thompson, James 5; why now? 146–147
DHL 67, 196
Didi 40, 117
Didi Chuxing 62
Diesel, Rudolf Christian Karl 95
Digg 167

digital cash 114
digitalized medication 92
digital tsunami 42–43, 88
disabled people, navigation assistance for
122–123
Disney: collective genius framework 79;
control, span of 28; corporate culture
72; Cruise Line 109; Disney+ 72; internet
protocol television 283; Movies Anywhere
108; Pixar 25, 72, 165; storyboards 151;
theme parks 107–108
disruptive innovation 11, 17; low-end 11–13,
12, *13*, 17; nascent market 13–15
diversity 173–174, 175–176, 183; Apple
237; challenges 24–25; Stryker 214, 215,
216
DoorDash 104
Doosan Infracore 93
Dorf, Bob 163
dot-com bubble 44
DoubleClick 22
Dowsing, H. J. 95
drones 197
Dropbox 167
Drucker, Peter 135, 163
Dubai: smart cities 127
Duke University 91
Dump Truck 93
DuPont 255
Duracell 249
Dusa Pharmaceuticals 297
dynamic capabilities 43–44; leadership 75

eBay: collective genius framework 79;
globalization 42; global logistics industry
195
Eberhard, Martin 61
eClinicalWorks 105
Eco Index 255
economic paradigm, new 39
economics of innovation *see* measuring
innovation
economies of scale: automotive sector 96;
corporate R&D 51
Ecovative Design 305–317
Edison, Thomas 69, 87
education sector 110–112
edX 111
efficiency of innovation *28*, 28
Eisenhardt, Kathleen 43
Eisenhower administration 93
Electric Illuminating Company 87
electric vehicles (EVs) 96–98; disruptive
innovation 13, 14; framework-based
innovation approach 61–62, 64–65;
measuring innovation 133–134; seismic
innovation 16; tax credit 183

Electrolux 225
electromagnetism 4
electronic medical records (EMR) 105–106
Emirates Airlines 117
employees: Amazon 276; challenges 24–25,
27–28, 34; control, span of 28; diversity
24–25; Ecovative Design 315, 317;
Ericsson 284; FedEx 198–199; incentives,
misaligned 27; micromanagement 27–28;
Microsoft 242; morale 136; Patagonia
267, 270–272; Procter & Gamble 249;
Reliance Jio 207–208; Samsung 289–290;
Stryker 214, 215, 216; Sun Pharmaceutical
Industries 296; Timberland 254; Whirlpool
225, 227, 228, 230; Zara 261–262, 263
endogenous factors impacting innovation
63–64, *64*; TRIAL© framework 65–66, *65*
Engine Alliance 117
Enron 56
Enterprise Innovation Opportunities Model©
49, *50*, 56; design thinking 151, *152*;
Ecovative Design 315–317
entrepreneurship 161
Environmental Protection Agency (EPA, US)
32, 173, 175
Epic Systems 105
Epogen 189, 190
Ericsson 153–155, *154*, 282–286
Ericsson, Lars Magnus 282
Estée Lauder 42
ethics: Reliance Jio 209; Samsung 290;
sustainability-focused innovation 174–175
Etsy 42
Euclid 93
European Union (EU): pharmaceutical sector
295; service sector 7; sustainability-focused
innovation 177
Eurostat 5–6
Eutelsat 109
Excavator 93
exogenous factors impacting innovation
63, *63*
experimentation, VASTEFA© leadership
framework 79–81

Facebook: action 77; Burberry 156;
corporate culture 19; design thinking
156; flooding alerts 127; lean enterprise
161; marketing 41, 206; Microsoft
investment 243; pharmaceuticals sector
89; Reliance Jio acquisition 204; resources
and resilience 68; retail sector 107;
sustainability-focused innovation 176;
Torch 90; user numbers 208; WhatsApp
and Instagram acquisitions 40–41; World
Wide Web 4
Fair Trade 270

Faraday, Michael 4, 98
Fashion for Good 182
Fashion Transparency Index 267
Federal Express (FedEx) 67, 137, 195–201
Federighi, Craig 235
feedback, VASTEFA© leadership framework
81
Ferdowsi, Arash 167
Fettig, Jeff M. 226
F. Hoffman-La Roche 294
Fiat Chrysler Automobiles (FCA) 12, *13*;
see also Chrysler
fintech 114–115
First Insight 176
Flatiron Health 89
Fleming, Alexander 89
FlipGrid 112
Flipkart 128
flooding alerts 127
Food and Drug Administration (FDA, US)
90, 92; Amgen 190; Stryker 219
Ford Motor Company 97; assembly lines
87; disruptive innovation 12–13, *13*;
government policies 33; innovation
shortcomings 63; service components 103;
sticky customers 21
Forever 21: 260
Formo, Joakim 153, 155
Fortis 105
Foxconn 96
framework-based innovation approach 61,
82; factors impacting innovation 63–64;
innovation in action 61–63; TRIAL©
framework 64–82; VASTEFA© leadership
framework 76–82
France: industrial revolution 87
Froelich, John 93
Fuji Film 32, 94

Gamble, James 247
Gap: collection renewals 261; financial loss
260; Higg Index 255
Gartner 183
Garvin, David A. 51
Gates, Bill 240
Gebbia, Joe 78
Gelco 195
Gellert, Ryan 270, 272
General Atlantic 204
General Electric (GE): aircraft engines 117;
competition 225; FastWorks program
169–170; leadership 74–75; lean enterprise
168–170
General Motors (GM) 97; disruptive
innovation 12–13, *13*; government policies
33; Lyft investment 62; SQL Server 94;
sticky customers 21

326 *Index*

Gen X: design thinking 146; sustainability-focused innovation 176
Gen Y/millennials: Burberry 156; customers 40; design thinking 146, 156; sustainability-focused innovation 176
Gen Z: customers 40; design thinking 146; sustainability-focused innovation 176–177, 183
geo-location 109
Germany: COVID-19 vaccine 54–55; industrial revolution 87; radar 10–11; service industry *104*; toll collection, automated 126
Gildan 255
Gillette 161
Github 235
GlaxoSmithKline (GSK): corporate R&D 49; Opiates 297
Global Eagle 109
global financial crisis (2007–2008) 44; General Electric 75; lean enterprise 161
Global Foundries 98
globalization: competitive landscape 40; vs localization 42
global positioning system (GPS) 126
global warming *see* climate change
Godin, Benoît 4–5
Goldman Sachs 114
Goldsmith, Stephen 121
Google: autonomous vehicles 71; cloud computing *44*, 44, 90, 241, 242–243; collective genius framework 79; control, span of 28; corporate culture 19, 71–72; design thinking 149; disruptive innovation 14; DoubleClick acquisition 22; Go 234; Google X 27, 28, 71–72, 82; lean enterprise 161; Makani energy kits 72; partnership and open innovation 53; perennial innovation 63; pharmaceuticals sector 89, 90; Pixel 3 phone 9; Reliance Jio investment 204; resources and resilience 68; revenue *22*, 22; risk vs reward balance 137; smartphone prices 136; TensorFlow 90; Tensor Processing Unit 90; urgency, sense of 29; Whirlpool partnership 229; World Wide Web 4; X 27, 28, 71–72, 82
government 121, 128; automated toll collection 124–126; blockchain-enabled voting 123–124; challenges 32–33; citizen–government redefined boundaries 126–127; digital thread and real-time alerts 127; local ecosystem 34; navigation assistance for the disabled 122–123; partnership with, as source of innovation 54; personalized on-demand service 121–122; smart cities 127–128; sustainability-focused innovation 183

gravitational wave detectors 99
Green, Logan 62
Green Dot 114
greenhouse gas emissions: Braskem 181; Patagonia 269; Samsung 291; sustainability-focused innovation 175, 181; *see also* climate change
grocery sector, supply chain 22–23
groupthink 276
growth trajectories 29–30, *29–30*
Grubhub 104

H&M: competition 260, 264; sustainability-focused innovation 175, 182–183
Haldor Topsoe 181
Harley-Davidson 63
Harry & David 104
Harvard University 91
Hasso Plattner Institute of Design at Stanford (d.school) 147, 148, 149, 150
HBO 283
HCL 79
healthcare sector 104–106; competitive landscape changes 41
Health Insurance Portability and Accountability Act (HIPAA, US, 1996) 41
heavy equipment sector 93–94
Hewlett-Packard 103
Higg Index 179, 255, 257
Hill, Linda 79
Hilton 6, 151
Hindustan Futuristic Communications 207
hiring *see* recruitment
historical perspectives of innovation 4–5
Hitachi 21, 93
Hogan, Kathleen 242
Holiday Inn 151
Holt, Benjamin Leroy 93
Home Depot 45
home working 67
Honda 97; disruptive innovation 12, *13*
hospitality sector 107–110
Houston, Drew 167

IBM: cloud computing *44*, 44; collective genius framework 79; competition 288; disruptive innovation 14; and Microsoft 240; partnership and open innovation 53; personal computers 75; pharmaceuticals sector 90; quantum computers 99; semiconductors 98, 99; sticky customers 21
Icahn, Carl 62
idea generation phase, design thinking 149, 155
IDEO 156
Iger, Bob 108

ILUMYA 297, 298
imaginative culture: vs innovation
   effectiveness *71*, 71; TRIAL© framework
   70–72
Impossible Foods 310
incentives: corporate culture 26; misaligned
   27; open innovation 70; risk vs reward
   balance 137–141; Zara 263
inclusiveness 173–174, 175–176, 183
Index Ventures 33
India: Bangalore 33; healthcare 105;
   industrial revolution 87; personalized
   on-demand government services 121, 122;
   service industry *104*, 104; smart cities 128;
   Sun Pharmaceutical Industries 294, 295,
   297, 298, 299; telecom industry 204–205;
   voting 123; Whirlpool 228–229
Inditex 260–265
Indonesia: flooding alerts 127; personalized
   on-demand government services 122
industrial revolutions 87–88; transportation
   115
Industry 4.0 88, 100; sustainability-focused
   innovation 174, 183
Industry Coalition 198
Infosys 14, 128
innovation strategy 49; challenges 23–24
inquisitive culture: vs innovation
   effectiveness *71*, 71; TRIAL© framework
   70–72
InSite Vision 297
INSITU-Boeing 94
Instacart 104
Instagram: Facebook's acquisition of 40;
   flooding alerts 127; marketing 41, 206;
   retail sector 107; sustainability-focused
   innovation 176
insurtech 115
integrated value chain, as source of
   innovation 51–52
Intel 90
intellectual property 40
IntelliCap® 92
Intelsat 109
internal innovation: innovation funnel 69;
   resources and resilience 69–70
internal rate of return (IRR) 138, 141
International Harvester 93
Internet of Things (IoT): Amazon 278;
   FedEx 198; heavy equipment sector 94;
   smart cities 127; sustainability-focused
   innovation 174
internet protocol television (IPTV)
   283–286
intraocular pressure monitoring 99
invention and innovation, differentiation
   between 3–4

inventory process innovation 6
investors: challenges 31–32; VASTEFA©
   leadership framework 76
iversity 111

Jager, Durk 248
Jahrer, Michael 70
Japan: automotive market 12, *13*; history of
   innovation 5; pharmaceutical sector 295;
   radar 11; service industry *104*, 104
Jassy, Andy 276, 278
JC Penney 63
JD.com 195
Jio Corporate 208
Jobs, Steve 232, 233; iPad 15; iPhone 32;
   leadership 75; Pixar 25, 165
John Deere 93
Johns Hopkins University 91
Johnson & Johnson: competition
   294; COVID-19 pandemic 91, 220;
   sustainability-focused innovation 175;
   tranSMART 91
Joint Enterprise Defense Infrastructure
   (JEDI) contract 242–243
Jones, Reginald H. 74
Jordan, Michael 78
Justice 17

Kadenze 111
Kalanick, Travis 62, 78
Kanjinti 192
Kano 243
Karow, Margret 192
Kawasaki Heavy Industries 94
Keap candles 307
Kellogg 310
Kelvinator 228
key performance indicators (KPIs),
   traditional 135–137
Khan, Shahrukh 206
Khan Academy 111
Khosla Ventures 16
Kodak 17; closed innovation 53; investor
   community 32
Kohl's 63
Komatsu 93
Korea Semiconductor 288
Koren, Yehuda 70
Kroger 22

Lafley, A. G. 248
Lane Bryant 17
latitude, TRIAL© framework 74–75
Lattner, Chris 234
L. Catterton 204
leadership: Amazon 275–280; Procter &
   Gamble 249; Reliance Jio 207, 209;

Samsung 288–290; Timberland 254; TRIAL© framework 74–82; VASTEFA© framework 76–82; Whirlpool 228, 230; Zara 264
Leadership in Energy and Environmental Design (LEED) certification 175
lean enterprise 159, 170; accelerated innovation 161–165; Dropbox 167; General Electric 168–170; innovation as mutually exclusive? 160–161; Pixar 165–167; Six Sigma 159–160, *160*; Thompson, James 5; Zappos 168
Lean Six Sigma 160
leap forward innovation 10–11, 17
Leather Working Group (LWG) 255, 257
Lee Byung-Chul 288
LEGO® : partnership and open innovation 53; perennial innovation 63
Lehman Brothers Holdings 56
Lemos, Fernando Lely 95
Lencioni, Patrick 52
Levitt, Theodore 103
LG: competition 225; electric vehicles 96, 97; smartphone prices 136
Li Auto 96
Licklider, Joseph 278
Liebherr Group 93
life expectancy 39, 89
life spans, product 41–42
Loader 93
local ecosystem, challenges 33–34
localization vs globalization 42
LOFT 17
Loli Beauty 307
Lonza Group 96
Lou & Grey 17
L.P 56
Lucas Film 25
Lucid 96
Lütke, Tobias 78
Lyft 117; automated checkout 51; business model innovation 62; customers 40; investor community 31; Swift 236

Ma, Brian 290
machine learning: fintech 114, 115; personalized on-demand government services 122; pharmaceuticals sector 90, 91; ride-hailing services 118; sustainability-focused innovation 174; *see also* artificial intelligence
Machine Learning for Pharmaceutical Discovery and Synthesis Consortium (MLPDS) 90
Macy's 106
Magento 42
Mahanagar Telephone Nigam 205

Mahindra Construction Equipment 93
mainframe computers, and sticky customers 21
Makani Power 72
Mandela, Nelson 77
Mango 261, 264
manufacturing sector 87–88, 100; automotive *see* automotive sector; heavy equipment 93–94; percentage of GDP 88; pharmaceuticals 89–92; semiconductor 98–100; sustainability-focused innovation 174
Maplin 17
Marcus 114
Mariani Group 179
marketing: Ecovative Design 311; Patagonia 269; product life spans 41; Reliance Jio 206; retail sector 107; Timberland 253; Zara 262
market innovation challenges 20; predictable M&A 21–22; stable supply chain 22–23; sticky customers 21
market opportunities, finding and prioritizing 163
Market Opportunity Navigator 163
market share, as KPI 136
Marks and Spencer 175
Marriott 35, 151
Martin, Jeffrey 43
Massachusetts Institute of Technology (MIT): Dropbox 167; Machine Learning for Pharmaceutical Discovery and Synthesis Consortium (MLPDS) 90; Radiation Laboratory 11; semiconductors 99
Massimo Dutti 260
Massive Open Online Courses (MOOCs) 111
Mastercard 175–176
Materiality Matrix 180
Maxaret, Dunlop 95
Maybach, Wilhelm 95
Maybank 118
McDonald's 68
MCI 56
McIntyre, Gavin 305, 306
McKinsey: COVID-19 pandemic 221; QuantumBlack acquisition 90; R&D survey 51; sustainability-focused innovation 174, 176, 183
measuring innovation 133–135, 141–142; organic vs M&A scenarios 138–141; risk vs reward 137–141; traditional KPIs 135–137
MediaKind 285
MediaRoom 283–285
Mendez, Wesley 229
MercadoLibre 114

Merck 89; biosimilars 191; competition 294
mergers and acquisitions (M&A): challenges
19, 21–22; Ericsson 284, 285; Microsoft
243–244; predictable 21–22; Procter
& Gamble 247; Stryker 215, 216; Sun
Pharmaceutical Industries 296–299;
valuing innovation 141; Whirlpool 228
Messenger 176
micromanagement 27–28
Microsoft: automotive sector 97; Azure
(cloud computing) *44*, 44, 90, 91, 94,
197, 240–243, 284; Cognitive Toolkit 90;
corporate values 52; disruptive innovation
14; Dynamics 107; FedEx partnership
197; history 240; innovation leadership
45; MediaRoom 283–285; Nadella era
240–245; .NET Framework 94; Nokia
acquisition 32; partnership and open
innovation 53; pharmaceuticals sector 89,
90; Reliance Jio investment 204; risk vs
reward balance 137; subscription model
95; Teams 112; World Wide Web 4
milestone plans 134
millennials *see* Gen Y/millennials
minimum viable products (MVP): Dropbox
167; General Electric 169; lean startups
161, 164; life spans 41; Pixar 165, 166;
Zappos 168
Ministry of Health (China) 105
models of innovation 9, *10*, 16–17;
cosmetic/survival innovation 9–10;
disruptive innovation 11–15; leap forward
innovation 10–11; seismic innovation
15–17
Moderna 54–55, 91
Monde Nissin 310
Moore's law 14, 15, 98
Morningstar Farms 310
Mosaic 151
Motorola: competition 288; Microsoft
MediaRoom 283; smartphone prices 136
MSC Cruises 109
Mubadala 204
Munro, Alfred Horner 95
Musk, Elon: action 77; experimentation 79;
feedback 81; Space X 33, 54, 77; support
78; Tesla 61, 66, 77, 78; vision 77
Mvasi 192

Nadella, Satya 240–245
Nadi X 113
Nalanda Academy 110
NASA 35; funding 32–33, 54, 56; vision 77
nascent market disruptive innovation
13–15
National Aeronautics and Space Agency *see*
NASA

National Institute of Environmental Health
Sciences (US) 173
National Institutes of Health (US) 32, 54
National Science Foundation (US) 32, 54
National Telecommunications Policy (1994,
India) 204
NationsBank 156
natural disasters: climate change 175; early
warning alerts 127
navigation assistance for disabled people
122–123
Neiman Marcus Group 17
Nepal: water pollution 182
Netflix: competition 72; internet protocol
television 283; lean enterprise 161;
open innovation 53, 70; partnership 53;
perennial innovation 63; subscription
model 95; World Wide Web 4
Netherlands: smart cities 128
net present value (NPV) 138–140, *140*,
141
net promoter score (NPS), as KPI 136–137,
136
Netscape 151
Neupogen 189, 190
Nevron 283
New United Motor Manufacturing
Incorporated 97
NeXT 232
NextGen Healthcare 105
Nike: consumer activism 177; digital tsunami
42; Higg Index 255; innovation leadership
45; marketing 253
Nikon 32
Nio 96
Nissan 12, *13*
Nokia: challenges 20; competition 75;
innovation shortcomings 63; investor
community 32; Microsoft's acquisition of
32; partnerships 285; smartphone prices
136; urgency, lack of sense of 29
Northvolt 97
Norway: smart cities 128
Norwegian Cruise Line 108
Novartis 89, 90, 297; competition 294;
Proteus investment 92; sustainability-
focused innovation 176
NVIDIA 89, 90, 98

Ocular Technologies 297
Odebrecht Group 179
Odomzo 297
Ohno, Taiichi 159
Omni United 257
One Equity Partners 285
open innovation 53–55; innovation funnel
69; resources and resilience 69–70

330 Index

operating model, as source of innovation 55–56
operational plans 134–135
OPPO 136
Oracle: cloud computing *44*; disruptive innovation 14; FedEx partnership 198; Proteus investment 92; retail sector 107; risk vs reward balance 138
organic scenarios, valuing innovation 138–140
organizational culture *see* corporate culture
organizational innovation challenges *20*; compartmentalization 25–26; control, span of 28; coordinated innovation strategy, lack of 23–24; diversity, lack of 24–25; incentive, misaligned 27; micromanagement 27–28; risk-averse non-experimental culture 26; urgency, lack of sense of 28–31
organizational processes and ecosystems, as source of innovation 51–52
Organization for Economic Co-operation and Development (OECD) 5–6
Orions Systems 243
Orr, Joseph 79
Ortega, Amancio 260, 264
Ortega, Marta 264
Orthopedic Frame Company 214
Osterwalder, Alexander 162
Other Half Processing 257
Otto, Nikolaus 95
Our Treaty 307
Overseas Development Institute 174
Owkin 89–90
ownership model vs utility/subscription model 40
Oysho 260

Pacific Gas & Electric Company 56
Padlet 112
Panasonic 96
Paradise Packaging 308
Paris Agreement on Climate Change 180, 182
partnerships: Apple 236; Ecovative Design 308; Ericsson 285; FedEx 196–197, 198; Microsoft 242; Patagonia 270; pharmaceuticals sector 89–90; Reliance Jio 204, 207–210; as source of innovation 53–55; Timberland 254, 256–257; Whirlpool 225, 228–229
Patagonia 175, 178–179, 267–273
patents: Amgen 189–190, 192; government funding 54; pharmaceutical sector 92, 294, 296, 299
PayPal 114

Paytm 128
Peloton 113
penicillin 89
Pentagram 79
personalized on-demand government services 121–122
PetaBencana.id. 127
Pfizer 89, 90, 96–97; collective genius framework 79; competition 294; corporate R&D 49; COVID-19 vaccine 33, 91; tranSMART 91; Vivli 91
Pharamlucence 297
pharmaceuticals sector 89–92
Philips 225
Pigneur, Yves 162
Pinterest 31, 107
Piotte, Martin 70
Pixar 108; adaptability 74; collective genius framework 79; control, span of 28; corporate culture 72; Disney's acquisition of 165; diversity 25; lean enterprise 165–167
Plato 110
Plebiscito Digital 124
Poland: navigation assistance for disabled people 123
Pola Pharma 297
population growth 39
Porter, Michael E.: diamond model 33; five forces competitive framework 40, 147; sustainability-focused innovation 173
Postmates 104
Poundworld 17
Pragmatic Theory 70
Pratt & Whitney 117
price, as KPI 135–136
Prices Cruises 109
Primera Impact 182
PrimeSense 141
process innovation 5–6
Procter, William 247
Procter & Gamble (P&G) 247–252; corporate culture 52–53; Gillette acquisition 161; GrowthWorks program 53; lean enterprise 161–162, 170; net promoter score 137; perennial innovation 63; resources and resilience 68; risk vs reward balance 137; sustainability-focused innovation 178
product innovation 5–6
property deed transfer 122
Proteus Digital Health 92
prototype phase, design thinking 149, 155
Pull&Bear 260
Pyke, Graham H. 173
Python 99

Index   331

Qiskit 99
Qualcomm 98
QuantumBlack 90
quantum computing 99
Quorn 310

radar 10–11
radio-frequency identification (RFID)
    scanners: inventory process innovation 6;
    retail sector 107; Zara 263
Rakuten 62, 195
Ranbaxy 297
Randall, John T. 11
Rawlinson, Peter 96
Raynor, Michael 9
recruitment: resources and resilience 69;
    Samsung 289; teams 78–79
Redback Networks 284
Red Bee Media 283, 284
Reddit 107
regional innovation challenges 24
regtech 115
REI 255
Reinhardt, Forest L. 173
Reliance Industries 204, 208
Reliance Jio 204–211
Reliance Retail 206
Rensselaer Polytechnic Institute 305
research and development (R&D): Amgen
    191–192; corporate 49–51; Ecovative
    Design 308–315; Procter & Gamble 249;
    Samsung 288; Stryker 216, 217; Sun
    Pharmaceutical Industries 294–296,
    298–300, 302; Whirlpool 225, 228
resources and resilience, TRIAL© framework
    68–70
retail sector 106–107
Revolutionary Armed Forces of Colombia
    (FARC) 124
rewards see incentives
ride-hailing services 117–118
Ries, Eric 162, 163, 164, 169
risk vs reward balance 137–141
Ritty, James 106
Rivian 97
robo-advisors 115
robots: autonomous vehicles 198;
    manufacturing sector 100; taxis 118
Roche Holding 89–90
Rock and Roll Hall of Fame 123
Rocket Lab 16
Rolls-Royce 117, 278
Royal Caribbean Cruises 108, 109

Safeway 22
SAGANA 182
Salesforce *44*m 95

Samsung 288–292; competition 225, 233;
    corporate culture 19; corporate values 52;
    design thinking 147; electric vehicles 96;
    framework-based innovation approach
    61; Galaxy 288, 290–291; innovation
    leadership 45; net promoter score
    137; NEXT 54; partnership and open
    innovation 54; resources and resilience
    68; semiconductors 98, 100; smartphone
    prices 136; urgency, lack of sense of 29
Sandia National Labs 94
Sanofi 294
Sany Heavy Industry 93
SAP 14, 107
Savory Institute 257
scaling: Dropbox 167; risk vs reward balance
    137–138; Zappos 168
Scannell, Timothy J. 215
Schaller, Bruce 117
Schaltegger, Stefan 177
Schumpeter, Joseph 4
SCMG Group 93
Sculley, John 232
Sears 17, 106
Secure Hash Algorithm (SHA)-256 124
seismic innovation 15–16, 17
self-driving vehicles see autonomous vehicles
SemGroup 56
semiconductor sector 98–100
Sensyne Health 90
Sequoia Capital 33
service sector 6–7, 103, 118–119; banking
    113–115; education 110–112; healthcare
    104–106; hospitality 107–110; percentage
    of GDP 103–104, *104*; retail 106–107;
    transportation 115–118; trends 103–104;
    wellness 112–113
Shanghvi, Dilip 294, 295, 299
Shazam 141
Shopify: globalization 42; global logistics
    industry 195; investor community 31;
    support 78
Shrine 307
Siemens 49
Silicon Valley: corporate culture 52–53;
    Ericsson 284; lean startups 161; local
    ecosystem 33
Silver Lake 204
Simon, Herbert 146
Sinclair, Rebecca 151
Singapore: Primary and Secondary Education
    System 119; smart cities 127
Singapore Airlines 119
single chip lidar 100
Six Sigma 159–160, *160*
SK Innovation 97
Sloan, Alfred 75

332 Index

smart cities 123, 127
smart contracts 115
smart pills 92
Smith, Fred 195, 196, 197, 198
Snapchat: marketing 41; retail sector 107;
  sustainability-focused innovation 176
Snyder, Nancy Tennant 226, 227–228
Soccorsi, Ella 183
social media: Burberry 156; competitive
  landscape changes 40–41; customer
  empowerment 42; design thinking 146,
  156; feedback 81; flooding alerts 127;
  marketing 41; new economic paradigm 39;
  Reliance Jio 206, 208; retail sector 107;
  sustainability-focused innovation 174;
  Zara 263
social responsibility: Patagonia 179,
  268–272; sustainability-focused innovation
  174, 179; Timberland 255, 257; Zara 264
solution ideation phase, design thinking 149,
  155
Sony: investor community 32; Walkman 75
sources of innovation 49, 56; corporate
  research and development 49–51;
  corporate values and culture 52–53;
  operating model 55–56; organizational
  processes and ecosystems 51–52;
  partnership and open innovation 53–55;
  strategic resources and talent
  architecture 55
Soviet Union: industrial revolution 87
Space X 35; achievement 73; government
  funding 33, 54, 56; vision 77
Spiliakos, Alexandra 173
Spotify: investor community 31, 32;
  subscription model 95
Sprint: internet protocol television 283;
  T-Mobile merger 285
SQL Server 94
Square 114
Sri Lanka: personalized on-demand
  government services 122
stakeholder innovation challenges 20, 31;
  employees 34; government 32–33;
  investor community 31–32; local
  ecosystem 33–34
Stanford University 33, 99, 216
Starbucks 118; control, span of 28; digital
  tsunami 42; net promoter score 137;
  ownership mindset 28–29; resources
  and resilience 68; sustainability-focused
  innovation 175, 178
startups: action 77; challenges 19–20, 26,
  28, 34; competitive landscape changes
  40; control, span of 28; corporate culture
  26; design thinking 146; employees 34;
  fintech 114; lean 161–170, *162*, *165*;

pharmaceutical sector 89; Reliance Jio
  209; support 78
Stepstone 232
Stradivarius 260
strategic plans 134
strategic resources, as source of innovation
  55
Stryker 214–222
Stryker, Homer 214, 221
Subramaniam, Raj 195, 197
subscription model *see* utility/subscription
  model
succession planning 76
Sun Pharmaceutical Industries 61, 294–302
supply chain: stable 22–23; sustainability-
  focused innovation 175
support, VASTEFA© leadership framework
  77–78
survival innovation *see* cosmetic/survival
  innovation
sustainability-focused innovation 173–176,
  183; Braskem 179–182; Colorifix
  182–183; Ecovative Design 305–310,
  314–317; Gen Z 176–177; Patagonia
  178–179, 267–272; Procter & Gamble
  178; Samsung 288, 291–292; secular
  growth driver 177–178; Timberland
  254–258; Zara 264
Sustainable Development Goals 180, **180**
Swarm 109
Swartz, Jeffrey 253, 254–255
Swartz, Nathan 253
Swersey, Burt 305
Swift, Jonathan 77
Swinmurn, Nick 168

tablet devices: Apple iPad 14, 15, 75, 232,
  235, 236, 290; disruptive innovation
  14, 15
tactical plans 134
Taiwan Semiconductor Manufacturing Co.
  (TSMC) 45
talent architecture, as source of
  innovation 55
Tandberg Television 284
Tapscott, Don 197
Target 198
Taro Pharmaceuticals 297, 298
Tarpenning, Marc 61
Tatung 283
Taylor, David 247
TCS 14
teams: collective genius framework 79, *80*;
  VASTEFA© leadership framework 78–79
Technicolor 284
technology: Amazon 276–278; business
  core shaped by 43; Ericsson 282–286;

pharmaceuticals sector 89, 90–91; Reliance Jio 206–207; Samsung 288–292; TRIAL© framework 66–68; Zara 263

Telecom Regulatory Authority of India (TRAI) Act (1997) 204

telemedicine 106

Telenor Satellite 109

Telesat 109

Tencent: cloud computing *44*; globalization 42; and governments 128; innovation leadership 45; Weibo 41

Tennessee State University 237

Tesla 21, 96, 97; action 77; feedback 81; framework-based innovation approach 61–62, 64–65; lithium-ion battery technology 64–65; Musk 61, 66, 77, 78; perennial innovation 63; risk vs reward balance 137; seismic innovation 16; support 78; urgency, sense of 31; World Wide Web 4

testing phase, design thinking 150–151

Tetra Pak 10

Texas Instruments 73

Thailand: personalized on-demand government services 122

theme parks 107–108

Thompson, James 5

Thread 257

Tie Rack 17

Tiger 195

TikTok: retail sector 107; sustainability-focused innovation 176

Timberland 61, 253–258

T-Mobile: operational plan 135; partnerships 153, 285

toll collection, automated 124–126, *125*

tools, TRIAL© framework 66–68

Töscher, Andreas 70

Tower Crane 93

Toyota 97; disruptive innovation 12, *13*; innovation leadership 45; lean enterprise 159; sustainability-focused innovation 175; Tesla investment 62

TPG Capital 204

training, VASTEFA© leadership framework 76

trajectories of innovation 29, *29–30*

Transcelerate 91

tranSMART 91

transportation sector 115–118

TRIAL© framework 61–66, *65*, *67*; achievement and adaptability 72–74; design thinking 146; Ecovative Design 314–315; inquisitive and imaginative culture 70–72; leadership and latitude 74–75; Reliance Jio 211; resources and resilience 68–70; service industry 119; Sun

Pharmaceutical Industries 300; technology and tools 66–68; VASTEFA© leadership framework 76–82

T. Rowe Price 97

Trump administration 33, 216

TSMC 98–99

Twitter: flooding alerts 127; marketing 206; retail sector 107; sustainability-focused innovation 176

Uber 117, 118, 196; Apple partnership 236; automated checkout 51; business model innovation 6, 62; customers 40; investor community 31, 32; Microsoft investment 243; support 78; World Wide Web 4

UberEats 104

Udacity 111

Udemy 111

United Kingdom: history of innovation 5; industrial revolution 87; M4 corridor 33; pharmaceuticals sector 92; radar 10–11; ride-hailing services 118; service industry *104*, 104; smart cities 128

United Nations: Braskem 180, 182; Sustainable Development Goals 180, **180**

United States: Affordable Care Act (2010) 190; air travel to and from 116, *116*; automotive market 12–13, *13*; child abductions 127; consumers 146; COVID-19 vaccine 33, 54–55, 214, 216–217; education costs 111; ethical sourcing 174; Federal-Aid Highway Act/National Interstate and Defense Highways Act (1956) 93; FedEx 195, 199; fish value chain 42; funding agencies 32–33, 54; Gen Z 176; greenhouse gas emissions 175; Health Insurance Portability and Accountability Act (1996) 41, 105; healthcare 105; heavy equipment sector 93, 94; history of innovation 5; industrial revolution 87; investor community 31; Joint Enterprise Defense Infrastructure contract 242–243; personalized on-demand government services 122; pharmaceuticals sector 92, 294–295, 297–299; Principles of War 81–82; retail sector 106; ride-hailing services 117–118; service sector 6–7, *104*, 104; Silicon Valley 33, 52–53, 161, 284; smart cities 128; toll collection, automated 125–126, *125*; voting 123

United States Patent and Trademark Office 54

United States Postal Service (USPS): and FedEx 195, 196; technology and tools 67

University of California (UC) Berkeley 33, 99

University of Michigan 91

334   *Index*

UPS: and FedEx 196; Flex delivery platform 196; risk vs reward balance 137; technology and tools 67
Upton, Lou 225
urbanization: automotive sector 95; grocery supply chain 23
urgency, sense of 28–31
URL Pharmaceuticals 297
Uterque 260
utility/subscription model: automotive sector 95–96; vs ownership model 40

validated learning 163–164
validation phase, design thinking 150–151
valuing innovation *see* measuring innovation
VASTEFA© leadership framework 75–76, 76; action 77; adaptability 81–82; Bezos, 279, 280; experiment 79–81; feedback 81; service sector 119; support 77–78; team 78–79; vision 77
Venmo 114
Verizon: business model innovation 62; competition 135; corporate culture 19; and Ericsson 153, 282; net promoter score 137; risk vs reward balance 137; Yahoo acquisition 22
Vesberg, Hans 283
VF Corporation 253–254, 256
Viber 107
VideoAnt 112
Vietnam: personalized on-demand government services 122
Vimeo 107
Viridor 178
virtual check-ins, cruise liners 109
virtual reality 112
virtual views, cruise liners 109
vision, VASTEFA© leadership framework 77
Vista 204
visually impaired people, navigation assistance for 122–123
Vivli 91
Vodafone: and Ericsson 153; Idea 205, 207
Volinsky, Chris 70
Volkswagen (VW) 97; collective genius framework 79; environmental law violations 183
Volta, Alessandro 98
Volvo 93
Votem 123
voting, blockchain-enabled 123–124

Walgreens 197, 198
Walmart: FedEx partnership 198; global logistics industry 195; innovation leadership 45

Washington Mutual 56
Watt, James 95
Waymo 71
wearable technology 109
WeChat: marketing 41; retail sector 107; sustainability-focused innovation 176
Welch, Jack 74–75
wellness sector 112–113
Wessel, Karl 95
WhatsApp: Facebook's acquisition of 40; retail sector 107; sustainability-focused innovation 176; user numbers 208
Whirlpool 225–230; innovation leadership 45; net promoter score 137; risk vs reward balance 137
Whitmer, Gretchen 216
Whitwam, David 226
Wing Aviation 196–197, 199
WingZ 117
WooCommerce 42
Wood, Chris 198
WorldCom 283
World Health Organization 173
World War II 10–11
World Wide Web (WWW): cloud computing 14; disruptive innovation 14; invention vs innovation 4
Wozniak, Steve 232

Xerox 53
Xiaomi 136
XPeng 96

Yahoo: complacency 22; open innovation 70; urgency, lack of sense of 29; Verizon's acquisition of 22
Yao, Dennis A. 54
Y Combinator 167
Yellow Cabs 6
yoga 113
YONSA 297
YouTube: Apple iPhone 232; education 112; marketing 41, 206; retail sector 107; sustainability-focused innovation 176

Zappos 168
Zara-Inditex 260–265
ZELPROS 297
Zimmer, John 62
Zimride 62
Zoom: education 112; investor community 31; service industry 104; wellness 113
Zoomlion 93
Zuckerberg, Mark 77

Printed in the United States
by Baker & Taylor Publisher Services